Red Star O-

Alongside the crescent, the star of the Soviets will be the great battle emblem of approximately 250 million Muslims of the Sahara, Arabia, Hindustan and the Indies.

— Tan Malaka, "De Islam en het Bolsjewisme"
(Islam and Bolshevism), *De Tribune*,
21 Sept. 1922

Red Star Over Malaya

Resistance and Social Conflict During and After the Japanese Occupation of Malaya, 1941–46

(Fourth Edition)

Cheah Boon Kheng

NUS PRESS
SINGAPORE

© Cheah Boon Kheng

Published by:

NUS Press
National University of Singapore
AS3-01-02, 3 Arts Link
Singapore 117569

Fax: (65) 6774-0652
E-mail: nusbooks@nus.edu.sg
Website: http://www.nus.edu.sg/nuspress

First Edition 1983
Second Edition 1987
Third Edition 2003
Fourth Edition 2012
Reprint 2014

ISBN 978-9971-69-508-8 (Paper)

National Library Board, Singapore Cataloguing-in-Publication Data

Cheah, Boon Kheng.
 Red star over Malaya: resistance and social conflict during and after the Japanese occupation of Malaya, 1941-46 / Cheah Boon Kheng. – 4th ed. – Singapore: NUS Press, 2012.
 p. cm.
 Includes bibliographical references and index.
 ISBN: 978-9971-69-508-8 (pbk.)

 1. Malaya – Ethnic relations. 2. Malaya – History – Japanese occupation, 1942–45. 3. Chinese – Malaysia – Malaya. 4. Communism – Malaysia – Malaya – History. 5. Malayan Communist Party. I. Title.

DS596.6
959.5103 — dc22   OCN715921756

Cover photographs courtesy of Arkib Negara Malaysia (Malaysian National Archives), Kuala Lumpur.

Printed by: Markono Print Media Pte Ltd

For

my son Lu Hsün, so that he will understand

CONTENTS

PART I: THE ROOTS OF THE CONFLICT

PART II: THE CONTEST FOR POSTWAR MALAYA, 1945–6

LIST OF TABLES

LIST OF FIGURES

LIST OF ILLUSTRATIONS (*between pp. 124 and 125*)

Members of the Malayan Communist Party secretariat staff taken outside its headquarters in Queen Street probably in 1945.

A gathering of the Singapore General Labour Union of All Nationalities taken probably in early 1946.

Japan as an ally. Lieutenant Yamaguchi to the rescue of the Malay hero Kamaruddin and his Sakai friends in Bekok, Keluang (Johor).

The hats suggest Chinese bandits pillaging and burning a Malay village in Johor.

Members of Force 136 (China) standing to a few minutes' silence at a memorial service outside the Singapore City Hall in Dec. 1945 in honour of their late commander Maj.-Gen. Lim Bo Seng.

Lt. Tsang Jan Man of Force 136 (China) who was air-dropped into Baling with Major Hislop in Apr. 1945.

Leaders of the Kuomintang (Malaya) with Lieutenant Tsang in Penang.

General Itagaki surrendering his sword to GOC Malaya, Lieutenant Messervy at a ceremony in Kuala Lumpur in early 1946.

Surrendering of swords by Japanese army officers, 1946.

The First Independent Regiment of the MPAJA receives a public welcome as it marches through a street in Chenderiang, Perak immediately after the Japanese surrender.

Admiral Mountbatten pinning a campaign ribbon on Liu Yau, supreme commander of the MPAJA, at the Singapore City Hall steps on 6 Jan. 1946.

Mountbatten congratulating the young Chin Peng before awarding him a campaign medal.

Sultan Suleiman Badrul Alamshah of Trengganu with Japanese officers, including Brig.-Gen. Ogihara and Malay court officials in front of Istana Kolam, Kuala Trengganu, 13 Dec. 1941 — about a week after the Japanese forces had landed at Kota Bharu.

The commander of the MPAJA Fourth Regiment (Johor), Chen Tien, speaking to his men at a disbandment parade in Dec. 1945.

A gathering of the Malay community at Batu Pahat in honour of Datuk Onn bin Jaafar, the District Officer and Kiyai Salleh.

The historic meeting at Taiping Airport on 12 or 13 Aug. 1945 — the only time Sukarno is said to have ever visited peninsular Malaya.

Politician as romantic hero. Datuk Onn bin Jaafar in traditional Malay warrior clothes or baju silat (for martial arts) with keris.

Kiyai Salleh as a young man.

Members of the Malayan Peoples Anti-British Army.

British Army officers taking the salute at the march past of a MPAJA regiment (top). The place is unidentified. Pictures at the centre and bottom show a gathering of the people and MPAJA troops at a meeting to celebrate the Japanese surrender in Klang, Selangor.

Disbanding of the MPAJA, December 1945. March past of its Fourth Regiment (South Johore) at Port Dickson, Negeri Sembilan.

Brigadier J.J. McCully of the British Army inspecting men of the MPAJA's Fourth Regiment (South Johore) at Port Dickson, Negri Sembilan.

A unit of the MPAJA assembled in the main street of one of the small towns of Malaya which the guerrilla army entered after the Japanese surrender.

The first patrol of the Fifth Independent Regiment (Perak) of the MPAJA. Place unidentified.

LIST OF APPENDICES

ABBREVIATIONS

AEBUS	Anti-Enemy Backing Up Society
AJA	Anti-Japanese Army
ALFSEA	Allied Land Forces, South East Asia
BMA	British Military Administration
CAB	Cabinet, London
CCAO	Chief Civil Affairs Officer
CCP	Chinese Communist Party
CEC	Central Executive Committee (MCP)
CIAM	Central Indian Association of Malaya
CO	Colonial Office, London
CPA	Chief Political Advisor
DCCAO	Deputy Chief Civil Affairs Officer
DO	District Officer
FMS	Federated Malay States
FO	Foreign Office, London
GLU	General Labour Union
IIL	Indian Independence League
INA	Indian National Army
ISUM	Intelligence Summary
JMBRAS	Journal of the Malayan Branch of the Royal Asiatic Society
JSEAS	Journal of Southeast Asian Studies
KMM	Kesatuan Melayu Muda
KMT	Kuomintang
KRIS	Kesatuan Raayat Istimewa
	Kesatuan Raayat Indonesia Semenanjung
	Kerajaan Raayat Indonesia Semenanjung
MCKK	Malay College, Kuala Kangsar
MCP	Malayan Communist Party
MMA	Malayan Military Administration (Japanese)
MNP	Malay Nationalist Party
MPAJA	Malayan People's Anti-Japanese Army
MPAJU	Malayan People's Anti-Japanese Union

MU	Malayan Union
OCA	Overseas Chinese Association
OCAJA	Overseas Chinese Anti-Japanese Army
PETA	Pembela Tanah Ayer (Defenders of the Fatherland)
PNI	Partai Nasionalis Indonesia
SACSEA	Supreme Allied Commander South East Asia (Mountbatten)
SCA	Secretariat of Chinese Affairs
SCAO	Senior Civil Affairs Officer
SEAC	South East Asia Command
SITC	Sultan Idris Teacher' College, Tanjong Malim
SSGLU	South Seas General Labour Union
SSCP	South Seas Communist Party
UFS	Unfederated Malay States
UMNO	United Malays National Organization
WIR	Weekly Intelligence Review
WIS	Weekly Intelligence Summary
WO	War Office, London

NOTE ON MALAY SPELLING AND CURRENCY

Throughout this book I have adopted the new Malay spelling, or *ejaan baru*. Johor is spelt in the Malay way without the letter *e* at the end of the word.

Unless otherwise specified, the currency referred to is the Malayan dollar, which was worth sterling 2s.4d. during the prewar period.

NOTE ON SPELLING OF CHINESE LANGUAGE SCRIPT

The Romanized spelling of the Chinese language characters in the text was originally done according to the Wade-Giles system. It has been retained in this edition.

PREFACE TO THE FOURTH EDITION

I would like to thank the publisher NUS Press for allowing me to revise and update *Red Star Over Malaya* for the fourth edition. Since the original work was completed more than 30 years ago, much new research material have become available on many aspects of the topic. Scholars now have greater access to official and private sources relating to the Malayan Communist Party and its wartime resistance movement since the party ended its armed struggle in 1989. In the last two decades published memoirs and stories of wartime experiences in the Japanese occupation have also helped to fill in the gaps and clarify important questions on the roles and policies of the Japanese military administration, Mountbatten's Force 136, the KMM and the MCP who were all key players involved in the major events described in the book. Of great value to researchers are the reminiscences of former Japanese Kempeitai officials, Colonel Oishi and Major Onishi, the MCP leader, Chin Peng, and the wartime Force 136 officer, John Davis, who now claims to be the British police case officer in charge of Lai Tek, the MCP chief whose activities as a double agent have been revealed more fully. In this edition I have incorporated a great deal of new information from the relevant historical sources; however, there is still scanty information on the wartime inter-racial conflicts. It remains a sensitive topic in Malaysia, and in Malaysian archives many files on the inter-racial incidents are still "restricted". Consequently, the topic has also attracted less academic research in recent years. Several new studies on the postwar BMA period, however, have appeared, based on recently opened records, and where relevant I have used them to bring readers up to date on the latest research. I would like to take this opportunity to thank Yeo Kim Wah, John Gullick, Simon Barraclough, and Anthony Stockwell who at different times reviewed the book, and provided detailed and very useful comments.

Cheah Boon Kheng
10 August 2011

FOREWORD TO THE THIRD EDITION

The theme of *Red Star Over Malaya* is not the Japanese occupation. Rather it is inter-racial conflicts between Malays and Chinese that occurred during the final stages of the occupation, and the social unrest and breakdown of law and order that occurred during a brief power vacuum at the end of the war. These conflicts came to a climax *during* and *after* the post-surrender two-week interregnum that lasted from 15 August to 3 September 1945. As the Japanese forces retreated into the big cities, the Chinese guerrillas of the communist-led resistance movement, the Malayan People's Anti-Japanese Army (MPAJA), came out of the jungle and took over some 70 per cent of the country's smaller towns and villages. The guerrillas' bloody reprisals against those accused of collaboration, especially Malay officials, policemen and village heads, created "a reign of terror". In several parts of the country Malays retaliated, and many Chinese died at the hands of bands of Malay religious zealots who had sworn to wage a *jihad* against their enemies.

The conflicts marked a crucial turning point in Malaya's nation-building history. The fighting ceased temporarily with the reestablishment of law and order by the British armed forces in September, but it later resumed and increased in intensity, continuing until March 1946. Then it came to an abrupt halt as the Malays turned their attention to opposing the British Government's constitutional plan for a Malayan Union that aimed to end Malay political supremacy and grant equal citizenship rights for the first time to qualified non-Malays in Malaya.

In the inter-racial conflicts, Malays were clearly the "victors". They had successfully resisted and defeated a wartime armed communist movement that was predominantly Chinese, and had tried to seize power in several parts of the country. It was not long before they also won their campaign against the Malayan Union, forcing the British Government to withdraw the plan. A Federation of Malaya that met many Malay demands succeeded the Malayan Union, but the rights of non-Malays remained a contentious issue. In the area of race relations the overall effects of the Japanese occupation were more negative than positive.

Red Star Over Malaya was also an attempt to write "autonomous" history. My intention was to find a historical space not dominated by the European or Japanese imperial power, in which the local people were the major actors. The aim was to achieve a neutral angle of vision by giving as many sides of the inter-racial conflicts as possible through an examination of the local actors who came into their own when Japanese authority collapsed. *Red Star* shows that the post-surrender interregnum was a time of failed opportunities for the radical Malay nationalists in the nationalist party, the Kesatuan Melayu Muda, and also for the Chinese communists and guerrillas. Both groups tried to stake out paths to power and national independence. Their failure is in sharp contrast to the success of the Indonesian nationalists under Sukarno, and the Vietnamese communists under Ho Chi Minh, who succeeded in seizing power at the end of the war. The Indonesian Revolution and the Vietnamese Revolution of 1945 were not the result of careful revolutionary planning, but spontaneous actions, due to a power vacuum after the Japanese surrender. In Malaya, instead of a revolution, there was chaos and inter-racial conflict. The Japanese became allies of the Malays and unwittingly made the occupation both an opportunity and an arena for communal confrontation. With their defeat, Japanese authority collapsed, and communal conflict turned into the first full-blown contest for postwar Malaya. The communists hesitated to make a real bid for power, and concentrated more on revenge, while the Malay radical nationalists were lost in confusion, and their major leaders ultimately fled to Indonesia.

The book presents a replay of epic violence and action at a given moment of history, when humanity was pressurized by events and the end of war unleashed uncontrollable social forces. It was a world turned upside down. Political terror, betrayal, racial strife and bloodshed abounded, and it is presented here from the viewpoints of the main actors. Given the sensitivity of the subject matter, I was glad that most reviewers of the first and second editions have commented on the high degree of objectivity achieved in documenting the inter-racial conflicts. It was most important to present a balanced account of the conflicts that could contribute to an understanding of the events that shaped Malaya's postwar politics and society. I hope this third edition will continue to be read with pleasure and profit by all interested in the subject of race relations.

Cheah Boon Kheng
Malaysia, July 2003

ACKNOWLEDGEMENTS

This work would not have been possible without the award of a research scholarship from the Australian National University from September 1975 to September 1978, for which I am most thankful. I wish also to express my appreciation to the University's Department of Pacific and Southeast Asian History for sponsoring my fieldwork from March 1976 to April 1977.

I am very grateful to Dr Anthony J.S. Reid and Dr David Marr for their wonderful assistance and support as supervisors of my doctoral thesis. Both were always accommodating and read successive drafts with infinite patience. Prof. Wang Gungwu, Director of the Research School of Pacific Studies, Australian National University, from 1976 to 1980, and later head of its Department of Far Eastern History, gave much encouragement and support during my research.

I have been greatly encouraged to revise and publish my thesis by the valuable comments and suggestions I have received from a number of people, including Prof. John Smail (Wisconsin University), Prof. K.J. Ratnam (Universiti Sains Malaysia), Michael Leigh (University of Sydney), and Anthony Short (Aberdeen University), all of whom read the thesis after it was completed. For their helpful criticism and comments on the drafts, I thank Alfred W. McCoy, Hank Nelson, and Mitsuo Nakamura, though I was not always able to take their good advice. My other academic colleagues — Khoo Kay Kim, Stephen Leong, Akira Oki, Robert Reece, Anton Lucas, Soeyatno, John Funston, and Louis Siegel — helped me in many ways, both personal and professional. Dr Siegel especially helped to locate several Chinese source materials regarding the MCP and "Overseas Chinese" associations in Singapore. To my A.N.U. colleague Wang Tai Peng I owe a special debt. His knowledge of "Overseas Chinese" history in Borneo and Malaya and his help in discussing and translating some difficult Chinese-language documents, pertaining to the MCP and the "Overseas Chinese", helped me gain valuable insights on the position of Chinese in Malaya during the Japanese occupation and in the postwar period.

I am also deeply appreciative towards my many informants and interviewees in Britain, Japan, Malaysia, and Australia, for their unfailing kindness and cooperation in providing me with whatever information they had. Since these persons are numerous and cannot all be named, I wish simply to give special thanks to Datuk (Dr) Awang Hassan, who was the Malaysian High Commissioner to Australia during 1976–8 when I was at the A.N.U., and to John Davis, the former chief of Force 136 in Malaya.

The libraries of the Australian National University, the Universities of Malaya and Singapore, the London School of Oriental and African Studies, Rhodes House, Oxford, the Institute of Southeast Asian Studies, Singapore, the National Library of Australia, and the National Library of Singapore gave me facilities and assistance which contributed significantly to the accomplishment of my research. Thanks are also due to the staff of the National Archives, Kuala Lumpur, and the Public Record Office, London, and to Soong Mun Wai and Encik Ibrahim of the University of Malaya Library for their interest and help.

The Visual Aids Section printed the photographs and Keith Mitchell of the Cartographic Laboratory, Research School of Pacific Studies, A.N.U., made the maps. Dr Voon Phin Keong of the Department of Geography, University of Malaya, and Soong Mun Wai provided me with information on the *mukim* of Batu Pahat and Muar, without which the maps for these areas could not have been done.

I would also like to take this opportunity to thank Mrs. Jean Marshall, wife of the late Mr. David Marshall, former chief minister of Singapore, for showing me a three-page letter written to her by John Davis (dated 17 March 1997) responding to points raised by former Force 136 member Tan Chong Tee, who went with Davis on his second entry to Malaya in July 1943, as given in Tan Chong Tee's book, *Force 136: Story of a World War II Resistance Fighter* (Singapore: Asiapac Books, 1995).[*]

---

[*] Chong Tee was captured by the Japanese and suffered one and a half years of imprisonment. He was bitter towards Davis and his fellow agents. Davis pointed out he was not Lim Bo Seng's deputy, and described his account as being full of "insinuations and innuendoes". Chong Tee, unlike Bo Seng, was not a "key man" in Force 136, said Davis, but he showed "great courage" in the work they did in the open "behind the enemy lines". Chong Tee was also not involved in the demobilization of the MPAJA (despite what he wrote on p. 310 of his book), as he was a KMT man, said Davis.

Chapter 2 was published in *Southeast Asia Under Japanese Occupation*, ed. Alfred W. McCoy (Monograph no. 22, Yale University Southeast Asia Studies, 1980); and Chapter 4 is a shortened version of an article entitled "The Japanese Occupation of Malaya, 1941–45: Ibrahim Yaacob and the Struggle for Indonesia Raya", published in *Indonesia*, vol. 28 (Oct. 1979), Cornell Modern Indonesia Project. Permission to use them here is gratefully acknowledged to Prof. James C. Scott and the Yale University Southeast Asia Studies Council and to Dr Audrey Kahin and the editorial board of *Indonesia*. Finally, I would like to thank my wife Ai Lin and son Lu Hsun for their understanding and forbearance during the difficult months of writing when it was not yet possible to see the light at the end of the long dark tunnel.

INTRODUCTION

My interest in the post-Japanese surrender interregnum in Malaya was first aroused while I was an undergraduate at the University of Malaya in 1969. Dr Anthony Reid taught a course on new approaches to the study of Indonesian history and introduced students to John Smail's stimulating work, *Bandung in the Early Revolution: A Study in the Social History of the Indonesian Revolution* (1964). Smail attempted to reconstruct the story of the Indonesian revolution based mainly on the oral accounts of Indonesians in Bandung. It inspired me to attempt a similar type of study in Malayan history. The only Malayan equivalent to his Bandung period, it seemed to me, was the post-surrender interregnum.

In May 1969, too, occurred the race riots in peninsular Malaysia (or West Malaysia), described by local and foreign newspapers of that time as the worst riots the country had ever experienced. The little knowledge I had then about inter-racial conflicts during the post-surrender interregnum of 1945 led me to believe that there were similarities with 1969. If so, why had the May 1969 riots occurred? Had people forgotten the lessons of 1945? In 1969 there was the similar phenomenon of the Malay martial and "invulnerability cults" in the countryside. In the urban centres, other racial groups had begun to put emphasis on the martial arts too — karate, judo, and the kung tow. The government did all it could to restrict discussion of the causes of the May 1969 riots in the mass media, on the principle that the less said about the episode the better for the country.

When I undertook postgraduate research on the post-surrender interregnum in 1975, I began to realize that my earlier expectations regarding the project were somewhat ambitious. I found I had one year to do fieldwork, which had to be divided between seven months in the archives in London and Tokyo and five months for working in the archives and conducting interviews in Malaysia. While I succeeded in collecting a great deal of relevant archival materials and research data, including private papers in London and Tokyo, I found that the five months left for research and interviews in Malaysia were insufficient to do the type of study brilliantly accomplished by Smail. He had spent two and a half years on fieldwork in Holland and Indonesia, and his study on Bandung was based primarily on interviews. Still, given the short time I had left in Malaysia, I selected two areas, one in Perak, the other in Batu Pahat (Johor), for fieldwork. Unfortunately, the political climate in peninsular Malaysia in late 1976 was not conducive to my field investigations.

This book is therefore a slightly revised version of my Ph.D. thesis submitted to the Australian National University in 1978. It focuses mainly on race relations and politics in wartime Malaya (that is, the name West Malaysia had before the federation of Malaysia was formed in 1963). When compared to the numbers of people killed and the areas affected during the post-Japanese surrender interregnum of 1945, the May 1969 race riots pale into insignificance. Yet, for some reason, many people in Malaya seemed to have shut their minds off to the 1945 period. Perhaps it was the magnitude of the killing and the terror of the times that shut people's minds off the subject. It was a time of much violence and suffering, when "the pistol and knife ruled". It was also notable for the "communist reign of terror". Only those in authority seemed to remember the 1945 incidents. The Sultan of Perak, in a speech in May 1975, reminded his subjects to support the Malaysian Government's anti-communist campaign "if you do not want a repetition of communist atrocities experienced immediately after the Japanese occupation".

While many studies of local history pertaining to the post-surrender interregnum in Malaya are beginning to appear, mostly done by Malay undergraduate students, there is as yet no study attempting a Malaya-wide spectrum. It was mainly to fill this gap that I decided to undertake research on the period. The theme is that of social and political conflict, a deadly serious contest for survival and advancement in which the main contestants were Malays and Chinese. The importance of this period has become more obvious than ever to me. Only by understanding what happened in that crucial period, I believe, can a Malaysian truly fathom Malaya's postwar politics and society. For instance, Malay political primacy today can only be comprehended in relation to the events of 1945. Secondly, Malay opposition to communism also stems mainly from that period, and is one of the reasons why the ongoing communist insurgency continued to fail. Finally, pan-ethnic cooperation and racial harmony, which are essential for the present and future peace and prosperity of Malaysia, can be strengthened not by Malaysians closing their minds about the past but by their learning from the lessons of the past. In studying what is clearly regarded as a sensitive topic in Malaysia today, I am mindful of the need to treat the topic objectively and not to pass moral judgements or to take sides. Like Smail, I too am aware that I have my own sympathies and aversions and hope I have been able to control my feelings in an academic study. If I have erred, it has probably been mostly in one direction. As a Malaysian of Chinese origin, I have found it easier to criticize Chinese than Malays. I hope, however, that I have been able to control even this tendency with the guidance I have received from my teachers and friends. If evidence of this still persists in the book, the fault must lie squarely on my shoulders.

There are ample sources for the study of the Japanese occupation and the post-surrender interregnum. In Britain, they are found mainly in the War Office records deposited at the Public Record Office in London. The volume of material in the South East Asia Command files alone (about 10,000 documents) is considerable. As a result, I spent several months reading through the files, and was rewarded by coming across several Force 136 papers on guerrilla activities in Malaya, which still remain classified in Force 136 files. There is also a splendid collection of private papers deposited at Rhodes House, Oxford, by former British civil servants in Malaya. The papers include those of former officials of the British Military Administration (BMA) such as H.R.H. Hone, W.L. Blythe, V.W. Purcell, and others. These British official and private records also contain numerous reports on inter-racial conflicts and communist activities during the Japanese occupation. However, there is still a paucity of documents of the Malayan Communist Party (MCP) for the Japanese occupation. This lacuna has been filled, to the degree that it is possible, by British and Japanese military intelligence reports. In Tokyo I was able to interview some members of the wartime Japanese administration, including Gen. Fujiwara Iwaichi and Professor Itagaki, and to collect materials from the Boeicho (Self-Defence Agency Archives). The help I was given by Dr Michiko Nakamura of Waseda University and Prof. Nagai Shinichi (then of the Institute of Developing Economies, Tokyo), was most valuable. I also interviewed Mr Shiro Mizusawa of the Equator Association, whose members were former administrators of Japanese-occupied territories during the war. Professor Itagaki took special interest in my research project and was responsible for arranging many vital interviews for me with other Japanese personalities — a favour for which I am most grateful.

In Malaysia the National Archives contains many important BMA (Malaya) records, which are now open to researchers. It also has collections of local newspapers, which carried MCP documents of the postwar period. I interviewed many local people of all races who had lived through the Japanese occupation. Although most of the interviews were done in Kuala Lumpur, Ipoh, Penang, and Singapore, the interviewees were able to recall experiences not necessarily confined to these areas.

Finally, some points deserve immediate mention. As of 1941, none of the three major races — Malays, Chinese, and Indians — had started to regard themselves as pan-ethnic "Malayans" with common duties and problems. This was the first problem, which had to be faced by them if the country was to advance towards nationhood and self-government. On the one hand, Malays cherished a definite loyalty towards their rulers, and this feeling conflicted with the development of any allegiance towards a larger unit than the state. On the other hand, non-Malays had to be weaned from their nostalgia for the homeland of their ancestors by making Malaya the real basis of an enduring loyalty. At the end of the war, it seems clear that none of the leaders of the major races in the country had thought seriously yet about resolving these problems; nor had the MCP. It was the British Government that introduced the Malayan Union plan, which, among other things, aimed at fostering a Malaya-oriented loyalty for non-Malays and an identity and nation-state larger than the Malay state for Malays.

The absence of a pan-ethnic "Malayan" nationalist movement in 1941 serves as the starting-point of this study. I then examine the political activities of various groups and the social conflict, which local peoples went through during the Japanese occupation and in the immediate postwar period of the British Military Administration. It was only after the bitter wartime and interregnum ordeal brought the conflict to a violent head that some understanding began to emerge of the long-term consequences of trying to share a nation and a future.

Fig. 1. Malaya during the Japanese Occupation, 1942–3

PART I

The Roots of Conflict

CHAPTER 1

Malaya's Plural Society in 1941

At present only in name is this a Malay country. The Malays are outnumbered by the Chinese who swarm in by the thousands every year and monopolise all the jobs, wealth and businesses of this country.

– Za'ba, *Al-Ikhwan*, 16 December 1926

In 1941 "Malaya" was a convenient British administrative and geographical term comprising three political units: (1) the Straits Settlements colony of Singapore, Malacca, and Penang; (2) the Federated Malay States (FMS) of Selangor, Perak, Pahang, and Negri Sembilan; and (3) the Unfederated Malay States (UMS) of Perlis, Kedah, Kelantan, and Terengganu.

Nineteenth-century British colonial policy had transformed Malaya from a collection of Malay states into a "plural" multicommunal society. Unrestricted immigration of Chinese and Indian labour (largely non-Muslim) for the tin mines and rubber estates had continued until 1921, but by then migrants already outnumbered the indigenous Muslim Malays. The 1921 census report showed that peninsular Malays and others of Malay-Indonesian stock numbered 1,623,014 (48.8 per cent of the total population), Chinese 1,171,740 (35.2 per cent), and Indians 471,514 (14.2 per cent). The British authorities generally regarded the Chinese and Indian immigrants as transients who for the most part, had little intention of making their permanent home in Malaya. Despite British colonial impressions to the contrary, the 1931 census report indicated about one-third of the Chinese and one-fourth of the Indians were local born and already showing a trend towards permanent settlement in the colony (see Table 1).

The Socio-Economic Setting

The preponderance of the Chinese and Indian communities in the economic life of the FMS was vividly illustrated by the fact that, according to the official estimates of 1934, Malays numbered only 643,003 out of a total FMS population of 1,777,421, Chinese came to 717,614, and Indians to 387,917. Of the four states in the FMS, Malays predominated only in underdeveloped Pahang where the total population of 186,465 contained 117,265 Malays. In the 1931 census, it had been established that in both the Straits Settlements and the FMS, the urban population was predominantly Chinese. The same was true of Johor (UMS). Even in Kedah (UMS) the largest single component of the urban population consisted of Chinese, though they just failed to equal in numbers the people of all other races combined. However, the towns of Kelantan and Terengganu (both UMS) were still essentially Malay. Indians were most numerous in the towns of the FMS, where they were very evenly distributed and formed just over one-fifth of the total urban population in each state. Race relations were good as far as they went. There had been no inter-racial friction, apart from Malay newspaper criticisms of Chinese and Indian immigration and of the growing economic disparities between Malays and non-Malays. Chinese criticisms against British protective measures on behalf of Malays, such as the Malay Reservations Enactment, were offset by major Chinese gains in the business and labour fields, while Indians were generally satisfied with gaining jobs in the public and private sectors and with the open atmosphere for business opportunities. However, Indian business enterprises were still small-scale, confined to money lending, shipping services such as stevedoring and ship chandling, textiles, and retail trade in towns and rural areas. But because Chinese numbers were far greater than Indians and Chinese business enterprises, more varied and challenging, the Chinese were seen by Malays as the greater threat to their economic and political future.

The Malay Sultans and their subjects were opposed to unrestricted immigration of Chinese and Indians, but since British policy

Table 1. Total Population of Malaya, 1921–47

	1921	1931	1947	*Percentages* 1921	1931	1947
Malays (and other		1,645,516	2,234,185		37.9	38.20
Malaysians)*	1,623,014	284,528	309,384	48.8	6.6	5.29
Chinese	1,171,740	1,704,452	2,614,667	35.2	39.2	44.70
Indians	471,514	621,847	599,616	14.2	14.3	10.25
Europeans	14,894	17,686	18,958	0.4	0.4	0.32
Eurasians	12,629	15,999	19,171	0.4	0.4	0.33
Other Communities	32,904	57,676	52,929	1.0	1.3	0.91
Total	3,262,695	4,374,704	5,848,910	100.0	100.0	100.0

Note: * The term "Malaysian" in the census reports means peoples of the indigenous races including Indonesian Malays and the aborigines.

Table 2. Number of Chinese and Indians Born in Malaya

	1921	1931	1947	*Percentages of the Total Chinese and Indian Populations* 1921	1931	1947
Chinese	258,189	533,205	1,633,332	22.0	31.2	62.5
Indians	58,676	131,474	298,674	12.4	21.1	49.8

Source: M.V. del Tufo, *Malaya: A Report on the 1947 Census of Population* (London, 1949), pp. 40, 84–5.

was nominally protective of and generally favourable to Malay interests, their discontent was stifled. British rule in the FMS left the traditional and regional elites with a certain degree of autonomy. In both the FMS and UMS, however, the British controlled the government, foreign affairs, and defence, while Malay customary law and the Islamic religion were in the hands of the Sultans. The British gave preference to Malays for employment in government service: only Malays were eligible to enter the elite Malayan Civil Service through which the British governed the country, and in 1913 a Malay Reservations Enactment was passed to prevent non-Malays from acquiring additional agricultural lands.* Only selected Malays, mostly of aristocratic background, were given higher education and groomed for high administrative posts in the civil service. Malay vernacular education was encouraged up to primary level, with emphasis on agriculture, handicraft, and educational fundamentals. Limited attention was paid to Malay agriculture, but British policy remained largely paternalistic and until 1941 was aimed at preserving the traditional Malay society behind walls of British protection.

Malayan economic development was restricted to the colony's two great industries, tin and rubber, supplemented only by the thriving entrepot trade of the Straits Settlements. Ownership of the rubber and tin industries was shared primarily between the British and the Chinese, with the former holding the major share. Towards the end of the last century, the British had broken into the Chinese monopoly of tin and the trend in the 1930s was increasingly towards greater degree of British control. Before the First World War, the British controlled only a quarter of the tin, but with the introduction of colossal machine dredges after the war, British production mounted sharply, until in 1929 it came for the first time to represent more than half of the total. By 1931 it had risen to 65 per cent.[1] In rubber there was a similar pattern. In the 1930s the largest rubber estates were in the hands of Europeans, those in the middle group in the hands of Chinese, and the smallest in the hands of Chinese, Malays, and Indians.

---

* It was a wave of land purchases during the first rubber boom, which aroused fears among the British Residents in the FMS that it would have a disastrous effect on the Malay peasantry if allowed to continue unchecked. A detailed discussion of their arguments and the measures that led to the introduction of the Malay Reservations Enactment of 1913 is found in Lim Teck Ghee, *Peasants and Their Agricultural Economy in Colonial Malaya, 1874–1941* (Kuala Lumpur, 1975), pp. 102–16. Apart from this policy, surveys and land policy in general were aimed at meeting the legal and administrative requirements of the modern sector and were not of much benefit to the peasant sector. See Gayl D. Ness, *Bureaucracy and Rural Development in Malaysia* (Berkeley, 1967), p. 33. The mining land policy, however, favoured large Western companies using machinery and labour-saving techniques of exploitation and led to a major shift in the control and ownership of tin mining lands from Chinese miners to Western companies. See Wong Lin Ken, *The Malayan Tin Industry to 1914* (Tucson, 1965), p. 22.

The major economic effect of British rule in Malaya was the growth of a dual economy. On the one hand there was the modern colonial sector dominated by three industries: trade, rubber, and tin. On the other there was the more traditional sector, most easily classified as the Malay peasant sector and concentrated in the UMS of the north and east. Smallholdings of rice, rubber, or coconut, characterized the latter. Up to 1941 there had been little modernization of peasant agriculture. Malaya was still a net importer of rice. Under the pressure of the expanding rubber industry, rice cultivation was given low priority. In 1935 only 300,000 tons or 40 per cent of the rice consumed in Malaya was produced inside the country, the bulk in the less developed UMS of the north. The remaining 60 per cent was imported from Siam, Burma, and elsewhere. The peasant sector has always been nearly self-sufficient in rice, while imports have been largely for the urban areas.[2]

Education

Maintenance of ethnic plurality was best seen in the schools, the most important social institution for the preservation of multiple cultural identities. There were four main and separate streams of education perpetuated through the efforts of the government, the Christian missions, and the independent Chinese school boards. While the missions devoted their efforts largely to giving education in the English medium (in which venture the government also had a part), the government more particularly sponsored Malay education. However, except for the Malay College, Kuala Kangsar (MCKK) which prepared high-ranking Malays for entry into the administrative government service, and two teachers' colleges (one for women in Malacca), there was no Malay secondary education to speak of, except those of a religious nature acquired in the Middle East. There were also Malay village schools, such as the *sekolah ugama* (religious schools where the Koran was taught), but the colonial government did not subsidize these schools.

Indian schools up to primary level were provided on the estates under a government regulation of 1912, most of them using Tamil as the medium of instruction. The Chinese, however, were left on their own. They built and financed their own schools up to the secondary level and introduced their own curricula in Mandarin (*Kuo Yu*, the Chinese national language). Most of the teachers were recruited from China. It was not until 1920, when the colonial authorities discovered that Chinese schools were involved in the politics of the Chinese nationalist movement, and were being used to inculcate Chinese patriotism and anti-British ideas, that legislation was introduced for the registration and control of Chinese schools and teachers. This move was strongly opposed by Chinese school-teachers. Agitation died down, however, when the legislation was accompanied by a scheme for grants-in-aid for Chinese schools. Although the government was able to control the teachers through an inspectorate and dissuade them from teaching overtly political subjects, it did not yet consider it necessary to revise the curricula or the textbooks used in the Chinese schools. The textbooks were about China exclusively; there was no mention in them of Malaya's history, geography, or the cultures of its mixed population.[3] The colonial regime was preoccupied with education in Malay and English. The emphasis on English, while meeting the demand of some Chinese and Indian parents for Western education, also served to provide the British business houses and the administrative service with clerks and office workers.

The only really national schools up to secondary level were the English schools, which instructed children of all ethnic groups and gave them a common curriculum. These schools were, however, heavily oriented towards English culture and history, especially the history of the British Empire.[4] More non-Malays than Malays attended English schools. One reason for the poor Malay attendance was that early English schools were run by Christian missionaries; the schools were also in urban centres far from the villages and were dependent on fees which most Malay peasants could ill afford. Only in the 1930s when the government began building secular English schools in the FMS for all races were Malay children urged to attend. Because of the large proportion of Chinese pupils in English schools in both the FMS and the Straits Settlements, Chinese began to push for the establishment of an English-medium university. In 1905 they succeeded in getting the government to establish the King Edward VII Medical College in Singapore, and hoped that this would be the nucleus of a university. In 1921 Raffles College, which taught sub-jects mainly in the humanities, was opened. Students who enrolled at both colleges were overwhelmingly Chinese and Indians. This led certain influential British administrators such as the Malay scholar and first principal of Raffles College, Richard Winstedt, to believe it was premature to establish a Malayan university, especially as Malays would find no place in it. Consequently, the government resisted

Chinese pressure to combine both colleges into a university, despite a Chinese undertaking to raise funds for the project. The University of Malaya was only established after the Second World War.[*]

While the FMS government's preferential "pro-Malay" policy enabled Malays to get into the lower and middle rungs of government service, there were fewer opportunities for non-Malays to join the civil service. Small numbers of Chinese were recruited into the government clerical service in the FMS, while Indians were recruited into the clerical sections of the Railways and Harbour Departments, which, like the rubber estates, used a greater pool of Indian labour. In 1934 the Straits Settlements Civil Service was formed which was open at the bottom to Chinese or to anyone else born in the Straits Colony.

Nationalism

Ethnic diversity, economic and cultural diversity, and diversity in the educational system were bound to produce a diversity of nationalist movements in Malaya. The origins of each movement will be discussed under each racial group.

The Malays

In the nineteenth century and early twentieth century, there had been a succession of Malay revolts against British rule, the last in 1928 in Terengganu. The British had crushed each revolt, reminding some Malays of the early defeat of the Melaka sultanate at the hands of the Portuguese in 1511. Despite what many British administrators have written, the Malays never welcomed British rule; it was always seen as interference in their political affairs.

Once the Malay rulers decided they had to come to terms with British power, they entered into treaties with the British, whereby the British undertook to "protect" their states, take over administration, and look after Malay welfare, defence, and foreign affairs,

---

[*] The unchanged position of Malays in tertiary education in post-war Malaya was indicated by the fact that Malays made up less than 10% of the total enrolment at the University of Malaya (that is, 90 out of 954 students) in 1953 (four years after the University was established). See Norton Ginsburg and Chester F. Roberts Jr., *Malaya* (Seattle, 1958), p. 235.

leaving only the Islamic religion and Malay custom in Malay hands. It was on the basis of these treaties that Malay leaders subsequently condemned the British for neglecting their interests and for allowing increased Chinese economic dominance in the FMS. Malay economic discontent led to a greater political consciousness among Malays and to the development of a Malay nationalist movement.

Foreign political influences also helped to fan nationalist feelings among the Malays. The reformist movement in Islam in the Middle East, during the first two decades of the twentieth century, had an impact on Malaya. Malay and Sumatran students who had studied either at Mecca or at Al-Azhar brought these ideas back. This led to the doctrinal debate between the *Kaum Muda* (the modernists) and *Kaum Tua* (the traditionalists), which extended to social and economic questions. The Kaum Tua, backed by the Malay aristocracy and the British, and represented in the orthodox religious institutions of the Majlis Ugama Negeri (State Religious Councils), succeeded in curbing the activities of the Kaum Muda, whom they regarded as subversive. Although the Islamic reformists did not aim at overthrowing the British regime, the British regarded them as a threat to the *status quo*. Reformists propagated new interpretations of Islamic teachings in order to equip Malays intellectually and socially for the modern world. They, however, tended to put the blame for Malay political weakness and economic backwardness on the ignorance of Malays themselves in following the commands of God.[5]

In the period between the two world wars, incipient Malay nationalism took on a secular form and lost its pan-Islamic flavour. Indonesian nationalist leaders, especially Sukarno and Hatta, had a great impact on a group of students at the Sultan Idris Teachers' College (SITC), which included Ibrahim Yaacob and Hassan Manan. These students were also influenced by Indonesian communist émigrés, such as Alimin, Musso, and Tan Malaka, who took temporary refuge in Malaya after abortive risings in 1926–7 to overthrow the Dutch regime in Indonesia. But Sukarno's influence on the SITC students was greater, and between 1928 and 1930 some of the students, including Ibrahim Yaacob, secretly enrolled as members of Sukarno's Partai Nasionalis Indonesia (PNI).[6] In 1938 this group (by now SITC graduates) teamed up with Malay graduates from agricultural and technical schools and the MCKK to found the first radical Malay party, Kesatuan Melayu Muda (KMM, or the Young Malay Union), whose aim was to achieve *kemerdekaan Melayu* (Malay independence) through *Melayu Raya* or *Indonesia Raya* (Greater Malaysia or Greater Indonesia), a political union of the Malay archipelago based on the Malay race.*

By 1941, except for the KMM *pemuda*, (youths, or young people), no group of Malays had begun to think seriously about the problems of achieving independence. What Ibrahim Yaacob and the KMM *pemuda* conceived as their ideal, Indonesia Raya, was that all people of Malay stock should come together and see themselves as One Race, speaking One Language, and belonging to One Nation, very similar to the Indonesian Youth Declaration of 1927. In other words, the KMM group wanted to create new and wider kinds of loyalties higher and above the level of the *puak* (ethnic group) and the *negeri* (principality or kingdom), which were the sources of ethnic and state parochialism fostered by the aristocratic state groups to perpetuate the latter's power and authority.

But these *pemuda* ideas had not been further developed by 1941. It should be noted that all the Malay States, except those in the FMS in a limited way, had not yet voluntarily come together to form a larger political entity and shed their separate provincialism. In 1941, the minds of the ruling class in the Malay States were not preoccupied with pan-Indonesia but with the question of state autonomy. Consequently, the appeal of the KMM's pan-Indonesia idea was confined to a minority of Malay-educated intellectuals who were largely influenced by Indonesian literature and political events. This fact, as well as the fact that pan-Indonesia would represent a higher stage of inter-regional Malay unity overriding the further obstacle of separate Malay geographical areas under different British and Dutch administrations, clearly suggests that the pan-Indonesia idea

---

* It is difficult to establish when and where the terms "Melayu Raya" or "Indonesia Raya", meaning an enlarged nation incorporating the Malay peninsula, the Borneo territories, Sumatra, Java, and the other Indonesian islands, first actually appeared. The idea of a closer union had already been raised in the 1920s. See William R. Roff, "Indonesian and Malay Students in Cairo in the 1920s", *Indonesia* 9 (Apr. 1970): 73–88. "Melayu Raya" is a term more commonly used by Malays, and "Indonesia Raya" by Indonesians. However, one does come across Indonesian-influenced Malays like Ibrahim Yaacob preferring the term "Indonesia Raya" or using both terms interchangeably. See I.K. Agastja, *Sedjarah dan Perdjuangan di Malaya*, p. 53, where he states, "Indonesia Raya itulah tudjuan Melayu Raya" (the aim of Melayu Raya is Indonesia Raya).

required much more thought, planning, and coordination of political action between the Malay peoples of British Malaya and the Netherlands East Indies before it could ever have any chance of success. It was only when both geographical areas came under Japanese occupation in 1942 that the idea had any chance of materializing.

Being of non-aristocratic background and influenced by Indonesian ideas, the KMM *pemuda* had also become strongly republican. However, they did not commit themselves to the removal of the Sultans or the traditional aristocracy on the grounds that the Malay *raayat* were not yet ready to get rid of these institutions, and therefore sought instead to accommodate them in their political schemes. Between 1938 and 1941, the KMM became greatly influenced by the policy of "non-cooperation" of Sukarno's PNI and adopted a similar policy. Ibrahim and other KMM leaders began a propaganda attack on British policies and on the "co-operators", the Malay bureaucrats and aristocratic groups, in various newspapers and publications. The KMM leaders also attacked the increasing foreign economic dominance of the country and of the colonial neglect of Malay welfare. By 1941, the KMM's anti-British agitation had been stepped up to the point where contacts were established between KMM leader Ibrahim Yaacob and Japanese agents with the idea of obtaining Japanese support for their objectives in return for KMM support for Japanese military plans to overrun British-ruled Malaya. As for the idea of union with Indonesia, it was hoped that this could be achieved too with Japanese support. This episode will be discussed in Chapter 4.

One other Malay movement of significance was the Persatuan Persatuan Negeri (State Associations), such as the Persatuan Melayu Selangor and Persatuan Melayu Pahang, led by the aristocrats. Some of those who formed the KMM had previously been members of these associations. They came to consider these associations "feudalistic", too absorbed with state rights, and with allegiance to the rulers and to the British administration. Leaders were English-educated lawyers and civil servants having connections with royalty, and organizations confined their memberships to Malays of a particular state.[7] State provincialism (*kenegerian*) was extremely strong. All Malays within a state owed their loyalty to the traditional state (*negeri*) ruler. A Malay tended to regard himself as an *orang Perak* (Perak man), an *orang Kelantan* (Kelantan man), or some other such state allegiance. The aristocracy of the various states encouraged this sentiment because they believed that if the *negeri* disappeared so too would their position and authority. The idea of a united Malay nation did not yet appeal to them. It was *kenegerian*, which dissuaded the ruling groups in the UMS from joining the British-sponsored FMS, formed in 1896. The ruling groups in the FMS did so only because of pressure, which British administrators brought to bear on them. *Kenegerian* meant that a united Malay nation was still a long way off.

The Chinese

Since the 1890s, most Chinese in Southeast Asia had regarded themselves as *Hua Ch'iao* (Overseas Chinese), owing allegiance to China.[8] Chinese born in the Straits Settlements were British subjects, and of these a large proportion were "Straits Chinese" who had lived in Malaya for centuries and assimilated a certain amount of Malay language and culture at the expense of Chinese language and dress (they were known as the *babas* and *nonyas*). Yet there were even some Straits Chinese leaders, such as Dr Lim Boon Keng, who became so aroused by the humiliation of China at the hands of Japan and the European imperialist powers that they took up Chinese patriotic activities.

In 1898 Overseas Chinese political consciousness had been awakened through the liberal reform movement of K'ang Yu-wei in China, who succeeded in influencing the Manchu Emperor to initiate the "Hundred Days' Reforms". Stimulated by China's humiliating defeat by Japan in Korea, the Reform movement was short-lived and K'ang Yu-wei fled the country when the Empress Dowager removed the Emperor and ushered in a period of conservative reaction. Kang came to Singapore in 1900 to raise funds to finance a revolt in Hankow, but the revolt proved abortive. After this Overseas Chinese participation in Chinese political activities increased, Kang continued to visit Malaya (he resided in Penang during 1900–1 and again during 1908–10) to publicize his liberal reforms, to build up support for his Royalist Party, and to found several Chinese schools which emphasized both Confucianist teachings and Western science.[9] He was able to win the support of Straits-born, English-educated Chinese like Dr Lim Boon Keng.

Another Chinese political leader, Sun Yat-sen, also fled China after failing in his attempts to raise a revolt in Canton. In 1900 Sun briefly visited Singapore, where he broke with the party of K'ang Yu-wei, whom he regarded as too conservative. The Overseas Chinese thus became more conscious than ever of the political struggle in China. During the first decade of the twentieth century, Sun organized several unsuccessful revolts, and when each uprising failed, the rebel leaders would take refuge in Penang or Singapore. However, the Wuchang Rising in 1911, also financed from Malaya, was successful. Sun, who was then in the United States, was not involved in the uprising. However, in 1912, when Sun's Kuomintang (KMT) was formed, branches of the party opened in Malaya.[10] In 1925, the Malayan Kuomintang was suppressed because its anti-British activities were considered subversive, and the British feared the Chinese government would regard Malaya as an *imperium in imperio*.[11]

Throughout 1910–30 Chinese education and politics in Malaya mirrored developments in China. However, it was not until 1924 that communist activities became noticeable in Malaya, five years after the formation of the Chinese Communist Party (CCP). This was because the Comintern (Communist International) did not give the directive to establish communist groups in Malaya until then. Within the same year, the task of recruiting communist cadres in Malaya was left to Indonesian communists like Tan Malaka and Alimin and a few CCP agents. In 1924 the KMT-CCP united front had been established, so that the first communist group in Malaya was formed in 1925 within the Malayan branch of the Kuomintang. This branch, in fact, became an overseas branch of the CCP. In 1927 the split in the united front also led to a split in the Malayan Kuomintang. After existing in various organizations, the communists finally formed the Malayan Communist Party (MCP) in 1930,[12] but a series of police raids disrupted its organization so that it did not really start operations until 1932 and up to 1941 the membership of the MCP was predominantly Chinese.[13]

Between 1930 and 1941, the activities of Chinese in Malaya continued to follow closely political events in China. The Japanese attack on China in 1937 aroused strong sympathies for China from the KMT and the MCP, and from other Chinese organizations in Malaya. Until the Japanese invasion of Malaya, the China National Salvation Movement, which both parties sponsored, organized boycotts of Japanese goods in Malaya and raised funds and other forms of relief for China. During the war in Malaya, it was the MCP, which took the lead in the anti-Japanese movement.

The Indians

The nationalist movement in India did not have an impact on Malaya until the years just prior to the war. Before 1937, Indian associations had existed locally throughout Malaya but had remained non-political. This was largely due to (1) the direct influence of the Indian Government Agent on Indian labourers in Malaya (which made the labourers feel that their welfare was being looked after), and (2) the lack of Indian-language newspapers in Malaya until the 1930s. It was only when Indian Congress Party leader Nehru visited Malaya in 1937 that the Central Indian Association of Malaya (CIAM) was formed. The CIAM was oriented towards India, especially Congress Party politics, and sought to represent and safeguard the interests of Indians in Malaya. The two chief political activities of the CIAM before the war were the evidence that it gave before the Shastri Commission investigating conditions of Indian labour in 1937 and its support of the Klang strikes in 1941. Although the CIAM consisted mainly of professional men who were not recruited from the local workers, they sought to identify themselves with the interests of the Indian workers.[14]

Conclusion

A plural society had emerged largely in the British interests of opening up Malaya. By allowing uncontrolled immigration of Chinese and Indians into the country, they were responsible for the situation in 1931 when the Malays were outnumbered in their own country. Legally, however, the British kept up the image of a "Malay Malaya" by following certain principles in their pre-war relations with the Malays. These principles (1) safeguarded the legal position of the Sultans, as laid down in the treaties, that is, sovereignty in each Malay state resting with the Sultans and not with the British Crown; (2) preserved Malay religion and culture in each state; (3) considered Malays as the indigenous people; and (4) accepted as a British responsibility the safeguarding of Malay welfare and the promotion of Malay advancement. Non-Malays did not yet seriously challenge this privileged status of Malays in 1941.

The Chinese were in by far the strongest economic position, "not only because they had amassed relatively large amounts of wealth, education, and experience but also because of their demonstrated capacity to adapt to changing circumstances and seize newly-offered opportunities".[15] Indians were in a nebulous second position, and the Malays appeared to be at the bottom of the economic ladder in British Malaya. However, by 1941, there were indications that such a situation was, in fact, storing up trouble for the future especially as the Malays, as the indigenous people, were already beginning to assert their political influence. Through their newspapers, they had clearly called for an end to alien immigration and demanded economic parity if not some improvement of their livelihood. They also viewed the Chinese (and to a lesser extent the Indians) as colonial parasites sucking away the wealth of their country hand in hand with British colonialism.

Given these differences, the low intensity of communal conflict in pre-war Malaya may seem surprising. But this is probably due to the fact that, with few exceptions, pre-war politics were "dispersed and fragmented" in the sense that the early political associations tended to be oriented towards issues arising beyond Malaya's borders. Their activities in Malaya were somewhat incidental to their primary concern. The politics of the Chinese and Indians were oriented towards those of their homeland, and even Malays such as the *Kaum Muda* (Islamic modernists) and the KMM radicals who were more concerned with developments in Malaya became politically motivated, as a result of reactions to events in Egypt, Turkey, and Indonesia. Consequently, as Gordon Means observed, the pre-war racial communities were "not inclined to view each other as political protagonists, since their political enemies were being defined outside the arena of domestic politics".[16]

Therefore, Malaya's plural society remained a fairly harmonious one until the outbreak of the Second World War. By keeping the three races isolated within distinct communities, allowing them to mingle only in the marketplace, British policy reduced the room for social conflict and social change. This policy required a delicate balancing and certainly could not have continued indefinitely without producing marked inter-racial tensions. As Gullick has rightly concluded, "The existence of three communities with conflicting interests and different viewpoints prevented the emergence of a united nationalist movement in the period up to 1942".[17] Clearly, no dialogue had yet emerged among local ethnic leaders to attempt to transcend racial, political, and economic differences; nor had any serious attempt been made at an accommodation of their diverse interests through a common campaign for Malayan national independence or the formation of a transcommunal "Malayan" identity.

There was also no evidence of any understanding yet of what a "Malayan nation" might mean or how the three races should regard each other as "Malayans".* The Japanese occupation was to demonstrate further the depth of these communal divisions, and to transform latent tensions into open and lasting conflicts.

---

* Oliver Stanley, wartime British Secretary of State for the Colonies, in a note to Admiral Louis Mountbatten, dated 21 Aug. 1944, had observed, "our pre-war experience offered hardly any sign of a conception amongst the three peoples that they were Malayans". See the quote cited in Mountbatten's letter, dated 11 May 1945, in WO 172/1763.

CHAPTER 2

The Social Impact of the Japanese Occupation of Malaya, 1942–5

The Japanese had turned Malaya upside down. The former social order was completely reversed. The "nobodies" of yesterday became the "big-shots" of the day.

– Chin Kee Onn, *Malaya Upside Down*, 1946

The change of regime and the violence of war brought about by the Japanese occupation of Malaya altered the pattern of race relations and raised the political stakes. To the local population, politics in the broad sense became a life and death struggle. Much of the interaction of Japanese policy and local responses, especially the changing Malay and Chinese perceptions of one another during the Japanese occupation, determined the direction of Malaya's post-war political development.

The Japanese Invasion: Initial Reaction in Malaya

The Japanese attack on Malaya began about four hours after their attack on the American naval base at Pearl Harbour — on 8 December 1941. One division of the Twenty-fifth Army (whose commander in chief was Lt.-Gen. Yamashita) landed at Kota Bharu, on the northeast coastal state of Kelantan. Another division opened the beachhead at Songkla in southeast Thailand, north of Kota Bharu, and immediately struck across towards its objective — Changlun in northern Kedah state. In a campaign lasting 68 days, the weight of the Japanese advance drove the British forces down the west coast of Malaya without meeting any effective check. On 12 December, Japanese troops entered Alor Star, the capital of Kedah; on 16 December, Penang; and on 28 December, Ipoh, the capital of Perak state. Kuala Lumpur, the capital of the Federated Malay States (FMS), fell on 11 January and Johor Bharu, the southernmost tip of the peninsula on 31 January. Singapore was finally captured on 15 February.[1] By the end of March, the whole of the Netherlands East Indies was also in Japanese hands.

Throughout 7 and 8 December, the British had begun rounding up the leaders and members of the Malay pro-Japanese organization, the Kesatuan Melayu Muda (KMM), after British intelligence had uncovered secret links between the KMM and Japanese military intelligence. Following the initial Japanese attack on 8 December, the British administration attempted to secure political support from the colony's communal leaders. On 10 December they put pressure on the four Sultans of the FMS —Selangor, Perak, Pahang, and Negri Sembilan — to urge publicly that their subjects remain loyal to the British and resist the invading Japanese forces.[2] Most important, the British initiated a belated rapprochement with their erstwhile local foe, the Chinese-dominated Malayan Communist Party (MCP). The two sides reached agreement ten days later on the training of communist guerrillas to fight behind enemy lines in the event of the Malayan Peninsula being overrun by the Japanese, a prospect that seemed imminent. On 23 December, to help the British obtain further local Chinese support, President Chiang Kai-shek in Nanking issued an appeal to all Chinese nationals in Malaya, especially members of his Kuomintang (KMT) party, to rally behind the British in resisting the Japanese. Apparently appreciating the value of cooperation now extended to the British authorities by both the MCP and the KMT, the Governor of Singapore, Sir Shenton Thomas, made a reciprocal gesture. He announced the lifting of the ban on the MCP, the KMT, and certain other Chinese associations.[3]

Both the MCP and the KMT joined with other Chinese anti-Japanese organizations and Chinese community leaders, including Tan Kah Kee, in setting up the "Overseas Chinese Mobilization Council". This body worked with J.D. Dalley of the Malayan Police, Special Branch, to recruit Chinese volunteers for Dalforce, an independent unit raised at the last minute and attached to the British army's Third Indian Corps. Dalforce was in the frontline of British positions on Singapore island and later put up a fierce fight against the advancing Japanese. It was reported to have inflicted heavy casualties on the invading troops, something that would be neither forgotten nor forgiven by the Japanese.[4]

While these events were unfolding in Singapore, the British defences on the mainland were rapidly crumbling as state after state was overrun by Japanese troops. It was during the British retreat down the peninsula that the first reports filtered through the ranks of the British army that Malays were actively collaborating with the invading forces as guides and interpreters. These reports were initially discounted by the British Command in view of the pronouncements of the four Sultans and the loyal service of two battalions of the Malay Regiment, which were fighting alongside the British troops and continued to do so right through the retreat to Singapore. The Malay collaborators were, in fact, members of the KMM movement, and had been working for Fujiwara Kikan, the Japanese military intelligence agency under Maj. Fujiwara Iwaichi based at Bangkok and in southern Thailand prior to the invasion.[5] This realization marked the beginning of British disenchantment with the Malays. Simultaneously, British attempts to persuade the Sultans to leave for Singapore, India, or Australia were rebuffed, and the British became concerned that these important symbols of authority might fall into the hands of the Japanese. But the Sultans refused to leave with the British, arguing that their duties required them to remain with their people. One spectacular instance of a Sultan's non-cooperation occurred when Tunku Abdul Rahman, later Malaysian Prime Minister, foiled the efforts of a British convoy taking his father, the Sultan of Kedah, to Penang, and removed the ruler to a place of safety.[6] Other Sultans, among them the Sultan of Selangor and the Raja of Perlis, were offered asylum in Singapore, but refused it; while the Sultan of Pahang left his palace and hid in the jungle until hostilities ended several weeks later.

As a result of the KMM's involvement in Japanese fifth column work, and the reaction of the Sultans, British distrust of Malays persisted right through the war to the time of their reoccupation of Malaya. During the closing stages of the war the British did, however, organize two Malay resistance groups. Until this rather late development, the British worked largely with the Chinese, supplying, training, and helping to organize Malayan Chinese communists in the MCP-controlled Malayan People's Anti-Japanese Army (MPAJA). These wartime developments were not without consequences, and

British distrust of the Malays was later to take the form of a post-war constitutional scheme to deprive the Malay rulers of their sovereignty.

Massacre of the Chinese

Although the British had surrendered on 15 February 1942 and the military campaign was virtually over, the Japanese Malayan Military Administration (MMA) was not formed until about two weeks later. The Japanese Twenty-fifth Army was preoccupied with the tasks of pacifying the population and establishing law and order. Looting and crime were widespread. The Japanese began to enforce order by means of summary executions: offenders were shot and beheaded on the spot, their heads displayed on pikes at prominent points in the city, particularly at marketplaces. The Kempeitai (Japanese military police), accompanied by local spies and informers, conducted house-to-house raids for stolen goods in selected areas. Anyone found hoarding goods for which he could not give a satisfactory explanation was hauled away to be shot. The campaign spread fear and panic among the local population, but was extremely effective in stopping looting and lawlessness.[7]

At the same time, the army began mopping up operations against "anti-Japanese elements", as resistance was reported in many parts of the country. The primary targets were British personnel who had avoided detention, Chinese Dalforce volunteers, civil servants and others who had worked for the British, members of the KMT and the MCP, members of Chinese secret societies (easily identified from the tattooed marks on their bodies), as well as other anti-Japanese organizations like the China Relief Fund Committee. Called "Operation Clean-up", or *sook ching* (meaning "purification by elimination"), the campaign first began in Singapore, now renamed *Syonan* (Brilliant South), and was then extended to the peninsula.[8]

The repressive campaign gathered momentum after the Twenty-fifth Army Headquarters issued a draconian decree on 17 February 1942. All male Chinese in Singapore aged between 18 and 50 years were ordered to concentrate at five assembly points at noon on 21 February, and were warned of severe punishment if they disobeyed. The campaign was planned by Lt.-Col. Tsuji and carried out by the Number 2 Field Kempeitai Group under the command of Col. Oiishi. It was Col. Tsuji who proposed the idea of the *sook ching* aimed at the "suppression of hostile Chinese" in retaliation for the tenacity of the Chinese volunteers in Dalforce. The Twenty-fifth

Army intended to move to Sumatra immediately after the capture of Singapore, but Col. Tsuji suggested that before they went the army should carry out a *sook ching* to eliminate all "Chinese anti-Japanese elements".[9] Another explanation for the *sook ching* was that the Twenty-fifth Army had come directly from the campaign in China, where it had encountered great resistance in fighting Chinese troops and guerrillas, and where the entire countryside was hostile to the Japanese occupying forces.[10]

As a result of the army's decree, five large "concentration camps" were established within the Singapore city area guarded by Japanese sentries. All Singapore Chinese were forced to assemble at these points. Japanese soldiers with Kempeitai armbands, accompanied by local informers, went around groups of Chinese and dragged away any whose name appeared on their wanted lists. The detainees waited their turn to be checked, classified, and given an identification stamp on their shirts, arms, or singlets. The waiting varied from a few hours to six days, during which time no food or drink was allowed into the centres. There were no toilets. Screening was done by making each Chinese walk past a row of hooded spies and informers — who were mostly pre-war Japanese agents, some captured communists, or Chinese secret society members who had agreed to give information to save their own lives. A nod from these "hooded terrors" signified recognition, and the victim was hauled away to a detention room.[11] By 3 March, a total of "70,699 anti-Japanese" Chinese had been detained, and it was reported that control of "anti-Japanese Chinese and anti-Axis persons on Syonan" was making good progress.[12] Among those arrested were leading bankers, merchants, and community and political leaders who included Dr Lim Boon Keng, the Singapore Chinese leader; Lim Chong Pang, the Singapore KMT head; and Wong Kim Geok (alias Lai Tek), the MCP's secretary-general.[13] Detainees were divided into several groups according to importance. Leadership groups were kept detained for use later as Japanese agents of social control, but the bulk of the detainees were transported by lorries to rural areas to be executed.*

---

* N.I. Low, in *When Singapore Was Syonan-to*, pp. 22–5, has an account by a Chinese survivor of a mass execution at Changi beach in Singapore. A batch of 400 Chinese had been brought in lorries from "concentration camps" in the city to the beach site, their hands tied behind their backs. At a given signal they were mowed down by machine gun fire.

By early March the *sook ching* campaign had been extended to the mainland. Initially, the same procedure of herding Chinese populations into "concentration camps" was followed in the main towns of Malaya. But as the Kempeitai troops moved further into the rural districts they became indiscriminate and tended to regard all Chinese as hostile. As a result, large-scale massacres of Chinese villages and settlements took place. For instance, on 18 March, at the Chinese village of E-Lang-Lang, not far from the town of Titi in Negri Sembilan state, about 20 to 30 soldiers under a Kempeitai commander, Iwahuzi, rounded up the villagers, said to be a few hundred, and killed them. The following are some accounts of survivors at E-Lang-Lang. All had seen relatives massacred:

> The prisoners were taken one by one to the spot where they were to die, and made to kneel down with a bandage over their eyes. The members of the third troop stepped out of the ranks one by one as his turn came to behead the helpless victims with a sword or stab him through the breast with a bayonet. All the corpses were burnt or buried in the wells or in holes, which the prisoners had dug earlier.

> The babies were thrown up into mid-air and as they came down, the soldiers pierced them with bayonet and sword.

> ... a group of innocent children stood at attention when the Japanese soldiers approached them. With hands raised to their foreheads, they screamed, "Tabek! Tabek!" [Malay word meaning Salute!] with great glee, only to be whisked away to be killed.[14]

The *sook ching* bloodbath, which continued throughout March, took a reported toll of 6,000 to 40,000 Chinese lives.* The *sook ching* struck terror in Chinese communities throughout Malaya and, in the words of former General Manaki, who served in Yamashita's army, it was the "biggest blot"† on the Japanese administration of

---

* Japanese figures of the total number of Chinese massacred tend to be less than Chinese figures. The figure of 6,000 is given in Mamoru Shinozaki, *Syonan: My Story*, p. 24, but Chinese figures vary between 30,000 and 40,000. See *Ta-chan-yu Nan Ch'iao (Ma-lai-ya chih pu)*, pp. 68, 69, 93, 97, 98, 99, 102–7.
† Manaki, now retired, made the statement during an interview in 1966. The harshness, which followed the purge of the Chinese community in Malaya, surpassed any measures taken against the Chinese in Indonesia. The Japanese policy towards the Chinese in Sumatra declared: "... As in Malaya, an attitude of strict

Malaya.[15] This single act inevitably alienated the bulk of the Chinese population from the Japanese administration. The army continued to treat the Chinese population with the greatest severity for the duration of the war, although it did not repeat such large-scale punitive massacres. The *sook ching* drove hundreds of Chinese youths and men into the jungles to join the communist-led resistance movement, the MPAJA.

A Gift of Atonement

On 2 March, while the *sook ching* was still under way, the Japanese army organized the MMA. Significantly, its first task was to deal with the Chinese problem. Prominent Chinese — Dr Lim Boon Keng, Lee Choon Seng (the acting chairman of the Singapore China Relief Fund), and the Shaw brothers (film magnates) — were rounded up and ordered to the Kempeitai headquarters. They were tortured, threatened with death unless they cooperated, and forced to form the Overseas Chinese Association (OCA), which was to raise M$50 million as a "gift" to the Administration to atone for the pre-war anti-Japanese activities of the Chinese in Malaya.[16] The communal leaders were divided into two groups — the Malayan-born or Straits Chinese, and the China-born Chinese. The former came under the wing of Mamoru Shinozaki, an officer in the Singapore Municipality, and the latter under Wee Twee Kim, a Taiwanese official.[*] Between March and June, the OCA leaders were coerced into raising the required sum from the Chinese population in Malaya, based on the adult individual's known sources of income. To ensure that no

---

surveillance should be adopted towards the Chinese, but goodwill of a slightly higher degree should be exerted towards the Chinese than towards those residing in Malaya". See Okuma Memorial Social Sciences Institute, *Japanese Military Administration in Indonesia* [*Indonesia no okeru Nihon Gunsei no Kenyu*] (Washington, 23 Mar. 1965), p. 152. It has an explanatory text for the policies relating to Indonesia and Malaya, and is extremely valuable for understanding the documents in Harry Benda *et al.* eds., *Japanese Military Administration in Indonesia: Selected Documents* (New Haven, 1965).

[*] Wee Twee Kim was a storekeeper in Singapore before the war. During the Japanese occupation a considerable number of Taiwanese and Koreans were employed as Kempeitai informers. Y.S. Tan, "History of the Formation of the Overseas Chinese", pp. 2–3.

one cheated in paying his share, the MMA provided the OCA with property reports from the Land Office, Registrar of Companies, and Income Tax Office. Although the MMA had not yet banned pre-war British currency, the OCA found it difficult to raise the expected sum, owing to the disruption and hardship caused by the war. By 20 June the OCA had only raised $28 million from the Chinese population in Malaya, despite repeated extensions of the deadline by the MMA. Finally, Takase Toru, the self-styled "expert" on "Overseas Chinese affairs" in the MMA, devised a compromise. The Chinese could raise a loan to make up the remaining deficit of $22 million from the Yokohama Specie Bank to be paid up within a year at 6 per cent interest. On 25 June the $50 million "gift" was presented to General Yamashita, who accepted it as an act of atonement of the Chinese for their pre-war anti-Japanese attitude.[17]

Pattern of Administration

The clock was put forward one and a half years in line with Tokyo time. The Christian calendar was discarded and the year 1942 followed the Japanese calendar and became 2602.[18] Throughout their administration, the Japanese regarded Malaya both as a military stronghold and as a colony within the empire. There was close co-ordination of both personnel and policy in Malaya and Japan. Plans for the political control of Malaya, the exploitation and distribution of its raw materials, and the use of local shipping were formulated as part of the larger Japanese plans for the Southern Regions.

An integration of policies for Malaya with those of the empire was indicated in late 1942 when Tokyo ordered that, although the army was supreme in the actual administration of Malaya, it had to consult with civilian agencies in Japan in choosing suitable technical personnel to immigrate to Malaya to work under the Military administration.[19]

Malaya and Sumatra were consolidated into one political unit on 28 March when the whole of Sumatra was placed under the control of the Twenty-fifth Army based in Singapore. A single military command was imposed on the two territories because they were considered the nucleus for the Japanese management of the southern areas. This administrative integration was carried through despite the different pre-war economic and political systems of the two territories (Sumatra had been under Dutch rule, Malaya under British). Apparently because of these differences, they were separated in April 1943.* In line with this latter decision, the headquarters of the Twenty-fifth Army moved to Bukit Tinggi in Sumatra, while the Twenty-ninth Army took charge of Malaya and established its headquarters at Taiping in Perak state.[20] It was also decided to place the mainland Malay state of Johor under the direct control of the headquarters of Seventh Army, in Singapore under Gen. Seishiro Itagaki — command delineations which remained in force from mid-1943 until the surrender in August 1945.[21]

Malaya itself was partitioned in October 1943 when the four northern Malay sultanates of Kelantan, Terengganu, Kedah, and Perlis were ceded to Thailand. The transfer was done ostensibly to honour Thailand's friendship and its support for the Japanese military campaign in Malaya, but the real aim was to reduce the area of command in northern Malaya in order to free more Japanese troops for the Burma campaign. Malaya was reduced in area and also lost a significant source of food, as the four states were all major rice-growing areas.

For the four northern states, the cession to Thailand was of extreme importance. The Thais set up a military regime in each state. Over them was a "Chief Administrator" who had the rank of a Thai army major general whose task was to oversee a junior administrator in each state. The administrator in Kedah was a police major; in Kelantan he was a first lieutenant. Japanese liaison officers were appointed to the four states, and the Emperor of Japan conferred a minor Japanese Order of Merit on the Sultans in recognition of their service to the Japanese military administration.

In December 1943 the Thai authorities announced plans to turn over the administration of the four states to their respective Sultans, in direct variance from the Japanese practice in the rest of the peninsula. The Thais declared, "Following the abolition of the Military Administration, a State Government will be established with the Sultan at its head while the present [Thai] military administrators will remain as advisers."[22] The Thais also declared their intention to establish similar municipal governments in each of the capitals subsequent to the organization of the state governments. The proposed state administration resembled that formerly employed by the British,

---

* The fact that Sumatra was a separate island nullified to a considerable extent the gain to peninsular Malaya of its added territory and population. There was probably no greater contact between the respective populations during the 1942–3 period than there had been when the two were separate British and Dutch territories.

whereby a British adviser assisted the Sultan, the sovereign of the state, in his duties. The adviser did most of the actual governing, but the Sultan was not without authority and prestige, and a greater proportion of natives held responsible positions than in the FMS.

The transfer of sovereignty was carried out smoothly on the whole. But there remained two major sources of tension: (1) Thai-Japanese disagreement over a financial settlement, and (2) special legislation which was adverse to Malay interests, for example, the banning of polygamy* and the imposition of a surtax for those between the ages of 20 and 45 unable to read and write the Thai language by the end of the year.[23] The second problem became more serious just before the war ended and led to the emergence of an anti-Thai movement among the Malays in Kedah and Kelantan. This movement continued until 1947 and was ended only through British intervention.†

The transfer of these four states marked the beginning of Malay disillusionment with the Japanese military administration, and placed the Malays numerically behind the Chinese in Malaya for the first time in their history. In 1931, although the total population of Chinese and Indians in Malaya, including Singapore, outnumbered the Malays, the latter still formed the largest single ethnic group in the country. Now, deprived of its four northern states, Malaya, including Singapore, had more ethnic Chinese residents than it had Malays; and the Japanese MMA consequently began to give more consideration towards Chinese communal interests. Table 3, showing estimates of population statistics for 1936 and 1945, indicate the impact of the loss of territory in 1943 on Malaya's racial balance.[24]

Japanese and British Systems of Administration: Continuity and Change

In contrast with the pre-war British practice of having a dual form of government, that of direct and indirect rule, the Japanese governed

---

* Islam permits a Muslim to have up to four wives.
† The present support given by Malaysian Malays to the Muslim irredentist movement in Pattani, southern Thailand, is believed to be a continuation of the wartime struggle. Tunku Abdul Rahman, however, found the Thai administration in Kedah tolerable. Among the Thai military officers sent to Kedah were friends from his Bangkok and Cambridge days. He used their influence to get himself appointed "Superintendent of Education, Kedah". See Harry Miller, *Prince and Premier*, p. 68.

Table 3. A. Total Population of Malaya, Including Singapore, in 1936 (estimates)

Malays	2,095,217	44.6%
Chinese	1,821,750	38.8%
Indians and others	779,299	16.6%

B. Total Population of Malaya, Including Singapore, but Excluding the Four Northern States Ceded to Thailand in 1943 (1945 Estimates)

Malays	1,210,718	34.3%
Chinese	1,699,594	47.7%
Indians and others	651,948	18.0%

Source: Memorandum entitled "Marai dokuritsu mondai" [On the problems of the independence of Malaya], Political Affairs Section, Ministry of Foreign Affairs, Tokyo, 20 Feb. 1945, in the Wason Collection, Cornell University.

Malaya as a single integrated colony under one supreme government headed by the MMA in Singapore.* In so doing, the Japanese reduced the status of the Malay Sultans to that of minor officials, heads of their state's Islamic affairs bureau, in contrast to their position under the British when they enjoyed the prestige of being, at least nominally, heads of their own states. With the exception of Singapore, which became a Special Municipality with a Mayor, all Malay states — plus Malacca, Penang, and Province Wellesley — were converted into provinces administered by Japanese governors. The Sultans also lost part of their authority over matters concerning the Islamic religion until 1943/4,† while in pre-war days these responsibilities had been left entirely in their hands. Initially the

---

* The post-war British Military Administration (BMA) continued to use the Japanese-type integrated government for the whole of Malaya, with central authority based in Singapore, from September 1945 until 1 April 1946 when the Malayan Union civil government took over.

† The Majlis Ugama Islam, or State Religious Councils, were abolished, and not reintroduced until 1943. The Chief *Kathi*'s Consultative Committees also disappeared. In Perak the Sultan bitterly resented the loss of his prerogative to appoint *Kathi* and Assistant *Kathi* to the Japanese Governor. See Yoji Akashi, "Japanese Military Administration in Malaya: Its Formation and Evolution in Reference to Sultans, the Islamic Religion and the Muslim Malays, 1941–1945", *Asian Studies* 7, 1 (Apr. 1969): 103–4.

stipends of the Sultans were cut, sometimes by two-thirds of the pre-war amount, depending on the degree of cooperation extended by each Sultan.[25] The government post of *Mentri Besar* (Chief Minister), held by a titled aristocrat, or a member of the royal family in certain states such as Johor and Kelantan, was also initially allowed to lapse.

With these significant exceptions, the Japanese administration in Malaya resembled the British administrative system it superseded. In the early months of occupation, the Japanese made few changes in pre-war staff but later pursued a policy, which favoured Malay appointees over Chinese and Indians.[26] The most important changes occurred at the higher levels, where the Japanese replaced British civil servants, while the provincial and local government staffs remained much as they were before the war. In both the FMS and the UMS, which had Malay administrations before the war, "trustworthy" Malay officials continued to occupy high administrative positions, now under Japanese supervision. In the smaller Straits Settlements, where a larger number of non-Malays had been employed in the British civil service, pre-war officials of all races continued to hold office in 1942 and 1943, but Malay officials increased in numbers and rose more rapidly through the service. One of the main instruments of the "pro-Malay" policy was the *Koa Kunrenjo* (leadership training schools), which were established at Singapore, Malacca, and Penang. Seventy per cent of the trainees were Malays, and graduates were given high appointments.[27]

Japanese military officers occupied a few top positions such as governors, while Japanese civilians, among them former residents of Malaya and technical experts or representatives of large Japanese companies, were chosen as heads of departments, mayors, governors, and appointees for important staff positions. For this second group a rich source was the Malayan Association (made up of former residents of Malaya), which was formed in Japan soon after conquest of the peninsula.* About 500 of its members were persuaded to return to Malaya, many of them to accept positions under the MMA. The

---

* Before the war there were only 5,000 Japanese in all of Malaya, 4,000 of them in Singapore. Their principal interests were mining, exports of iron ore and bauxite, banking, fishing, and shop keeping. OSS, "Japanese Administration in Malaya", p. 8. See also Yuen Choy Leng, "Japanese Rubber and Iron Investments in Malaya, 1900–1941", *Journal of Southeast Asian Studies* 5, 1 (Mar. 1974): 18–36.

recruitment of this large number of civilians was reported to have been due to the lack of trained military staff for government service. Owing to insufficient data, it is not possible to state whether the number of Japanese administrators in Malaya exceeded the pre-war number of British administrators.

The Provincial Government (*Seicho*)

The Mayor of Singapore and each of the governors of the ten provinces were responsible to the *Somubucho* (director general) of the MMA, and each of their administrations had divisions, which corresponded in general to those at MMA headquarters. The ten Japanese governors included bureaucrats of the powerful Ministry of Interior or retired generals on the reserve list.[28] As chief executives they replaced the Sultans as heads of state and thus combined most of the duties of both the former British advisers and the Sultans. In 1943, for example, when the State Regional Advisory Councils were set up, they served as chairmen and the Sultans as vice chairmen.

There was, however, little coordination between individual governors and the local garrison headquarters, and governors received directives from army area commanders. Military operations, such as those against guerrillas, were carried out independently of the governor who was only informed if the military thought it necessary. Of all the governors, only the Governor of Perak, T. Kubota, appeared to have adapted himself well to the local situation and established good relations with the Malay aristocracy, most particularly with the State Sultan Abdul Aziz. On the occasion of the Muslim festival, Hari Raya Haji, on 19 December 1942, he joined in the celebrations by wearing royal Malay robes presented to him by the *Raja Muda* (Crown Prince).[29] All courts ceased to function by reason of the occupation, but a Military Court of Justice of the Nippon Army was established on 7 April 1942 by a decree of the commander of the Nippon Army. On 27 May 1942 the civil courts (as distinct from military courts) were reopened and allowed to follow the former colonial laws insofar as they did not interfere with the military administration. Many prominent lawyers were appointed as new judges and magistrates.[30]

It was at the local government level that the Japanese promoted a large number of Malays to the post of district officer (DO), formerly held mainly by British officers. In Selangor five of the six DOs were promoted from pre-war posts of assistant DO, magistrate, or

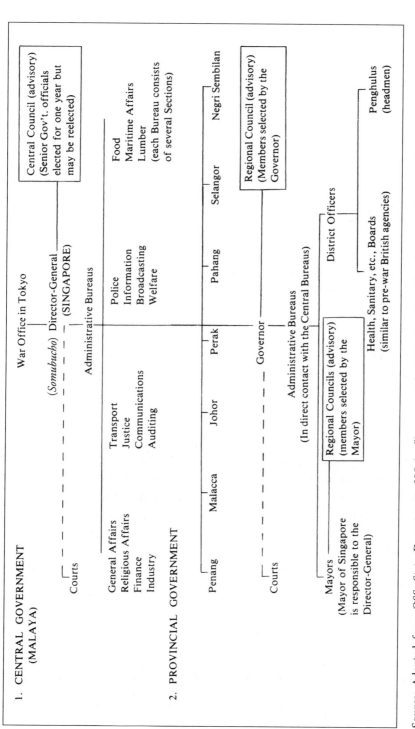

Source: Adapted from OSS, State Department, U.S.A., "Japanese Administration in Malaya," marked "Restricted", 8 June 1944, in *BMA/ADM9/1*.

Fig. 2. Japanese Military Administration in Malaya (1944)

land officer. The Japanese came to rely on the DOs and their subordinates, the *penghulu* (district headman) and the *ketua kampung* (headman), far more than the British had done in order to requisition rice, labour, and volunteers for the Japanese war effort.

In her important study of the wartime period, Halinah Bamadhaj has suggested that the steady increase in the number of Japanese top government officials, the proliferation of control organizations, and the appointment of the *Shidokan*, or Improvement Officers, who supervised the DOs closely and accompanied them whenever and wherever they went on field visits, made the impotence of Malay officials apparent to all.[31] She claims, however, that the DOs were not hated particularly by the Malays, unlike the *mata-mata padi* (rice policemen) who supervised the rice requisition, or the Malay informers of the Kempeitai.[32]

However, we should not forget the constant clash of interests between the DO, the *penghulu*, and the *ketua kampung* on the one hand and the Malay, Chinese, and Indian population on the other. While it was the DO who received the orders of his *Seicho* (provincial government) for army rice quotas of non-Malay labour, this did not always work for, as she shows, when there were not enough non-Malays around, the DOs had to fall back on Malay recruits.[33] Such recruitment was most unwelcome, as it was commonly feared that the labourers might never return again alive to their villages. In such a situation administrative impotence was not likely to be appreciated, but rather despised as a betrayal of trust and respect held by the villagers for the DO. Consequently, caught in this sharp conflict of interests, the DO frequently came out the loser — either with his own community or with the Indians and Chinese.[34] He and his subordinates, the *penghulu* and *ketua kampung*, were natural targets of reprisals by the MPAJA guerrillas, who in many localities included members of the three races, although the Chinese usually dominated.* In fact, the MPAJA and its grassroots support organization, the Malayan People's Anti-Japanese Union (MPAJU), operated

---

* One of the DOs killed by the MPAJA was the DO Kluang, Esa bin Abdullah. He was abducted and executed during the transitional period following the Japanese surrender in August 1945. One reason given by the MPAJA for his death was his conscription of a large number of Malays and non-Malays as labourers (Interview with Dr Awang Hassan, 1978). The DO Batu Pahat, Ismail bin Datuk Abdullah, was killed by the MPAJA in June 1945. See Anwar Abdullah, *Dato Onn* (Petaling Jaya, 1971), p. 95.

an efficient intelligence network in the villages and small towns, and usually picked their targets for elimination with accuracy. Information given by Malay informants and stories found in Malay novels reveal clearly that the local government officials from the DO downwards were unpopular with both Malays and non-Malays.[35] The reasons why these divisions at the lower level of Malay society did not flare up into violent intra-Malay class conflicts will be discussed when we come to the question of inter-racial conflicts.

Japanese Militarization Policy

The Japanese governed Malaya by tight military measures. Great emphasis was placed on the use of local manpower in internal security control and local defence units. As an adjunct to the state and military police forces, the Japanese established *Jikeidan* (Self Defence Corps) with their companion *tonarigumi* (Neighbourhood Associations) throughout the country. In the early months of occupation, the Japanese found that crime and violence had increased in the less settled parts of the country. As the problem of maintaining peace and order became acute and existing measures were found inadequate, the Japanese instituted the Jikeidan system, under which a certain number of households were made collectively responsible for any untoward happenings. The chief function of the Jikeidan was to register all families in a neighbourhood and report on all strangers and suspicious events. In September 1943 Singapore was reported to have 80,000 members divided into 55 sections, with a leader for each section. As of 18 March 1944, Jikeidan organizations were reported from Perak, Penang, Malacca, and Selangor, and the system is presumed to have existed throughout Malaya.[36]

However, it was largely with police and volunteer forces that the Japanese carried out large-scale mobilization and militarization of young men, mostly Malays, who became a new elite, a military elite, exposed to intense training and exhortation to patriotic sacrifice.

The civil police force was divided into two sections: regular police and the Jikeidan. Except for a few changes, the Japanese maintained the British colonial police organization. Shortly after the fall of Singapore, all pre-war police personnel were ordered to report to their respective offices for work. Officers of the pre-war Special Branch were assigned to deal with political affairs, especially anti-Japanese activities, and became known as the *Tokko ka* (political police). Its agents and informers were everywhere — in coffee shops, amusement parks, hotels, and gambling farms. Provinces were divided into the same number of police districts as before the war, and police district officers had vast powers. Malays and non-Malays served as police district officers, or *Sho Cho*, until the end of 1943, when Japanese replaced them. The *Sho Cho* was empowered to issue orders to shoot or behead anyone suspected of anti-Japanese activities, and even the DO, the local civilian administrator, was subordinate to him.[37] Out of necessity, the Japanese used the experienced staff of the former British police force, which consisted of Malays, Chinese, Sikhs, and Punjabis recruited from India, but later the Special Police, a paramilitary organization, was formed specially to carry out operations against the communist guerrillas. It consisted of young recruits from the pre-war police force who were willing to swear loyalty to the Japanese Emperor.[38] The Japanese also laid emphasis on training Malay officers at a Malay Police Officers' Training School established in Singapore. By February 1944, six classes, each averaging over 300 recruits, had graduated.

The volunteer units such as the Heiho (Auxiliary servicemen), Giyu Gun (Volunteer Army), and Giyu Tai (Volunteer Corps) were not meant to be sent outside Malaya for combat, but to relieve Japanese forces, which could then be used against the Allies. Members of these units were frequently used by the Japanese to raid guerrilla bases and to cut off guerrilla food lines.

Recruitment for the Heiho began first in June 1943 and was open to all races, but Malays eventually formed the majority. The recruits were given military training like Japanese soldiers. In Perak the Heiho recruits began their day's training with a six-mile run, and learnt how to handle anti-aircraft guns, artillery, and machinery. The Heiho were attached to the Japanese forces to assist in labour service and were not required to carry arms, as they were not considered regulars like the Giyu Gun. Most Heiho were employed in the transport sections of the army, or as guides in Japanese raids on guerrilla hideouts. The popularity of the Heihos was demonstrated by the creation of a Malay Women's Auxiliary Corps in late 1944.[39]

Unlike the Heiho and the Giyu Tai, the Giyu Gun was organized and trained like the Japanese Army, with a central training camp and barracks at their headquarters in Johor Bharu. Despite an intense publicity campaign, recruitment again came mainly from Malays, a response encouraged by the appointment of a Malay political leader, Ibrahim Yaacob, as army commander. After completing a six-month training course, he was appointed Lieutenant-Colonel, believed to be one of the highest ranks ever given to a non-Japanese. In March 1944 the Japanese tried to attract educated men to enlist by offering officer ranks to doctors, lawyers, and teachers, but the appeal had limited success.

Financial incentives were few and candidates were expected to be ideologically motivated. Salaries were quite low — soldiers' pay varied from $30 to $40 and officers' from $130 to $300 — and the only material incentives were free food and clothing. Candidates were, therefore, required to have the following qualities: (1) they had to have a burning desire to serve their country; (2) they had to be brave and physically fit; (3) they had to be of good conduct and possess a sense of responsibility; and (4) they had to be single.[40]

The first intake began in December 1943, and by April 1944 there were said to be 2,000 men in the Giyu Gun. The first graduation ceremony on February 1944 in Singapore ended when Captain Zainal, on behalf of the officer candidates, who were almost all Malays, pledged "to serve in the front line and to obey the Nippon forces".[41] The recruits had been trained in artillery and armed combat and were taught to admire strength, courage, bravado, and *Nippon Seishin* (Japanese spirit). Five guiding principles were given to recruits to memorize:

1. We, the Malai Giyu Gun are to be loyal to the Empire of Nippon above all.
2. We, the Malai Giyu Gun are to assimilate and to display the spirit of Nippon soldiers.
3. We, the Malai Giyu Gun are to undergo training after the model of Nippon soldiers.
4. We, the Malai Giyu Gun are to complete the defence of the peninsula with the Imperial Forces as the nucleus.
5. We, the Malai Giyu Gun are to contribute to the attainment of the prosperity of Malai [Malaya] and the reconstruction of *Dai Toa* [Greater East Asia].[42]

Although training was meant to equip the Giyu Gun to assist the Japanese Army in defending Malaya in the event of an Allied invasion, the only combat members saw was against communist guerrillas in east Johor. Ibrahim Yaacob had hopes that the Giyu Gun would be the nucleus of a Malay National Army to fight against the British for the cause of Malay independence, but he failed to deploy the Giyu Gun for this purpose before the Japanese surrender.

Economic Conditions

Pre-war Malaya exported a surplus of raw materials and imported most of its food and consumer products. The Japanese occupation, however, cut off the principal markets for Malaya's raw materials, created a shipping shortage, which drastically reduced essential imports, and consequently inflated prices.[43] The operations of the large-scale rubber and tin industries, on which Malaya's pre-war economy had been entirely dependent, were drastically curtailed. Despite efforts of major Japanese corporations to revive production, they failed to produce even half the pre-war amount of tin and rubber. The price of both rubber and tin fell below a minimal margin of profit, and many labourers in these industries became impoverished. As shortages caused food prices to soar, the local population turned to the cultivation of foodstuffs as their only hope of survival. Fortunately land was plentiful, but their efforts in this direction were only partially successful. The loss of life caused by malnutrition was considerable.

As the economic situation worsened, two basic tasks confronted the MMA: to develop and export essential raw materials to Japan; and to produce and distribute consumer goods and foodstuffs within Malaya. Initially, the administration closed all banks and blocked their balances. Branches of leading Japanese banks were established in order to extend Japanese financial power, and currency was issued directly by the military authorities, but later owing to the local population's reluctance to transact business with them, Chinese and Indian banks were allowed to resume operations.[44] To curb inflation, the Japanese initiated several schemes. Gambling farms were opened and regular lotteries held with tickets sold throughout the country at one dollar each.[45] Banks offered prizes and attractive interest rates in order to encourage savings. The Japanese also regulated business and industry in Malaya by a licensing system which led to large-scale corruption by Japanese and local officials. As economic conditions worsened, stricter control of many aspects of business was instituted in addition to the licensing system. Prices were fixed for about 800 types of goods, including such necessities as clothing, drugs, petroleum, tyres, and tubes. Rationing and other restrictions were imposed on sales of most consumer goods (rice, sugar, salt, flour, matches, soap, etc.), and led to a pervasive "black market" where one could get anything at a price. "Japan's failure to keep Malayan currency under control was a consequence of the faltering economy", says one source, and the collapse of its export industries threw large numbers of people out of work.[46]

Adding to these hardships, Japanese big business exploited Malaya. Japanese companies, big and small, took over most of the property, which had belonged to British, American, and Dutch interests, now enemy aliens. Among local inhabitants the Chinese were the principal sufferers. Chinese suspected of loyalty to the Chungking government had their properties ruthlessly confiscated, but most of the small producers, retail dealers, and suppliers were allowed to continue in these roles for Japanese firms.[47] Mitsui and Mitsubishi monopolized several principal industries, driving the Chinese out of business. The rice monopoly, for example, went to Mitsubishi, and the sugar and salt monopolies to Mitsui.[48] These and other companies formed *kumiai* (syndicates) and, with the help of military units acting as brokers or dealers, monopolized the market in certain commodities. The *kumiai*, described by one Malayan Chinese writer as government-protected divisions of the "black market", were in fact mainly responsible for creating shortages of goods:

> Every *kumiai* was nothing but a monopoly to fleece the public. As soon as a *kumiai* for any particular commodity was formed, that commodity soon disappeared from the markets and became difficult to get.[49]

In spite of widespread unemployment in Malaya, the Japanese found it necessary, on 20 December 1943, to form a Labour Service Corps, which impressed workers throughout the country. An apparent cause for the labour shortage was fear that workers would be sent to Thailand or Burma where conditions were bad.[50] The Japanese had many urgent defence projects, and the obvious method of acquiring sufficient manpower was a labour draft. From every 250 inhabitants, 20 aged between 15 and 45 were selected to serve in the Labour Corps. A leader was appointed for each unit of the Corps under the direct control of the Auxiliary Police. Lists of names were submitted by the *penghulu* in the rural areas, while those in the towns were handled by community control organizations such as the Overseas Chinese Association (OCA), the Malay Welfare Association, and the Arab Welfare Association. As an additional step to secure sufficient labour, the authorities of the Singapore Special Municipality decided on 1 January 1944 to register all workers on the island, expected to number about 140,000 in the various fields of industry, commerce, and agriculture. The Japanese even went further and imported labour from Java in spite of the acute food problem in Malaya, and introduced a "Grow-More-Food" programme to make Malaya self-sufficient. The MMA imported Japanese agricultural experts and techniques, introduced new paddy strains (such as Taiwan rice), opened up new lands, and released restricted Malay lands to non-Malays.[51] Much of the land developed at Endau in northeast Johor and Bahau in Negri Sembilan had been restricted by pre-war Malay Land Reservations Enactments to prevent immigrants from acquiring more Malay lands. The Japanese, however, ignored this legislation and established farming settlements for groups of Chinese, Indians, and Eurasians in many of the provinces. Chinese who took part in this project came mainly from Singapore and received land allotments from the Japanese-sponsored OCA.[*] Other colonies were established in Perak, Selangor, Malacca, and Province Wellesley. The Japanese provided loan equipment and seeds, and helped to build schools, houses, and roads. A similar project for Malays was started in Geylang, Singapore, called Malay Farm, and another at Pulau Bintan, one of the Riau islands.

These Japanese-sponsored agricultural settlements coincided with migration of a substantial portion of the urban population, mostly Chinese, to rural areas to grow food, and were key factors in the genesis of the "Chinese squatter problem" in post-war Malaya. The clustering of Chinese squatters outside the urban areas was a marked feature of the Japanese occupation, and they became an important source of food, supplies, and intelligence for the communist-led resistance movement.[†]

---

[*] Mamoru Shinozaki, an official in the Singapore Special Municipality, was involved in the establishment of the Endau and Bahau settlements. See Shinozaki, *Syonan: My Story*, pp. 79–92.

[†] During the Malayan Emergency when the communist insurrection was at its height, the British authorities forcibly evacuated and resettled Chinese squatters from the jungle fringes of many states. The communist guerrillas had used their settlements as bases. See Victor Purcell, *Malaya: Communist or Free?* (London, 1954), p. 73, and Kernial Singh Sandhu, "The Saga of the Squatter in Malaya", *Journal of Southeast Asian History* 5 (1964): 143–77.

Cultural and Military Values

From the very beginning of its regime, the MMA set out to Nipponize the local population of Malaya through the mass media and the educational system. Propaganda about Japan's advocacy of *Hakko Ichiu* (universal brotherhood), promotion of the Greater East Asia Co-Prosperity Sphere, and the declaration of the liberation of Asia from Anglo-American political and cultural influence were constantly reiterated by the military-controlled mass media, as were the slogans "Asia for the Asians" and "Japan is the light of Asia".[52] The "superior culture" of Japan was espoused as a model for progress for Malaya as well as other areas of Japanese-occupied Southeast Asia.

In the schools Emperor worship and Japanese language, music, religion, and history were stressed, and the *Nippon Seishin* (Japanese spirit) extolled. The English language was banned as a medium of instruction. In April 1942 only Malay and Tamil schools were re-opened and only Japanese, Malay, and Tamil languages were allowed. Chinese schools were permitted to reopen in October, but were prohibited from using Mandarin as a medium of instruction — a discriminatory policy designed to punish the Chinese for pre-war anti-Japanese activities in which Chinese schools had played a major role. In July 1943 the Japanese relented and allowed the Chinese language to be taught for three hours a week, but a year later the ban was re-imposed and only Japanese was allowed.[53] Courses in the Japanese language were also obligatory in technical, medical, marine, and normal schools.

Outside the schools classes were conducted in all government and commercial offices to promote the study of *Nippon go*, the Japanese language. Proficiency in Japanese was the means to obtain quick promotion and salary increases. "Nippon go Weeks" were proclaimed in the major cities, occasions characterized by contests in essay writing, public speaking, and debating. The Japanese failed, however, to overcome the use of English as a common medium of communication, especially in newspapers and in the civil service where English language correspondence and announcements were still tolerated.[54] Supplementing Japanese language instruction, the authorities encouraged teaching of Nippon salutations and Nippon manners, customs, and songs, and banned Anglo-American films and music. This intensive Nipponization during the three and a half years of Japanese rule produced a generation imbued to some degree with Japanese cultural values.[55]

The Japanese army was another agent of Japanese values and behaviour, especially *bushido* (warrior code). Thousands of local people recruited into defence and police units were given Japanese-style military training by Japanese instructors eager to instil in them the spirit of the samurai warrior. Even women and schoolgirls were encouraged to take part in mass drills, parades, and gymnastics emphasizing physical vigour and spartan discipline.* The wartime situation and frequent Japanese use of violence created a climate of brutality, which affected both the civil population and the resistance forces. People adopted drastic measures to settle old scores, and communist guerrillas meted out the same cruel treatment as the Japanese to Kempeitai informers and collaborators whom they caught.[56]

The MMA tolerated different religions, although attempts were made to indoctrinate the local population with Shintoism. A large number of Shinto shrines were constructed in Malaya, and local people were urged to worship at them. Despite this policy, the MMA did not hesitate to mobilize Muslim, Christian, and Buddhist religious leaders in support of its programmes. Much attention was also paid to various religious festivals. The Japanese granted holidays to mark these occasions and frequently participated in the celebrations as well.[57]

Race Relations and Social Change

Race relations in Malaya before the war had been peaceful. Despite the British "pro-Malay" policy and the segregation of the various races, inter-racial conflicts had not broken out. Japanese policy towards the Chinese was different, and its racialist inclination manifested itself in the massacre of thousands of Chinese immediately after the conquest of Singapore. As a corollary to this, the Japanese continued the pre-war British "pro-Malay" policy, thereby helping to create social and political conditions, which brought Malays and Chinese into conflict. The Chinese were discriminated against in the government service, in schools, and in business; while Malays dominated the bureaucracy and served in larger numbers in the

---

* In allowing the INA to establish a women's regiment, and in recruiting Malay women into the Auxiliary Corps in 1944, the Japanese made a small contribution towards the political awakening of women in Malaya.

police force and in the various volunteer local defence units. This discrimination aroused resentment among most Chinese towards the Malays. The Japanese reliance on Malay support was natural, given their fear and distrust of the Chinese population as potential enemies. The Chinese reciprocated with non-cooperation and resistance. Although the Japanese attempted to make amends with the Chinese from late 1943 onwards — by integrating them with other races in advisory councils, business, education, and government, they failed to overcome Chinese hostility, which continued until the end of the war.

There is, however, little evidence to show that the Japanese deliberately promoted racial animosity between Malays and Chinese as a matter of policy. It was the overall social tensions, which their policies created, and the local interpretations of these policies by Malay and Chinese communities, which led to bitter inter-racial conflicts. Compared to the Chinese, Indians suffered far less discrimination from the Japanese, and in fact enjoyed special treatment largely because of Japanese plans for the invasion of India.

The Malays

Although Japanese rule produced greater social divisions within Malay society than under British rule, these divisions did not manifest themselves in violent intra-ethnic conflict when the Japanese occupation ended, as happened in Sumatra and Java. During the early phase of Japanese occupation, the Sultan was deemed not a ruler but merely a religious leader. This policy, however, made no difference to his subjects, who continued to pay obeisance to him as both their head of state and head of their Islamic religion. In January 1943 the MMA allowed the Sultans to use the honorific title of Sultan, but still confined their authority to religion.[58] In 1944 the Sultans were given back a great deal of their pre-war allowances and powers, but not their status as sovereign rulers. In the state councils set up in 1944 the Sultans became vice chairmen and advisers to the Japanese governors, the chairmen, a reversal of the roles, which existed before the war when the Sultan was chairman and the British Resident the adviser.[59]

There were divisions within several ruling royal houses — especially those of Selangor, Terengganu, Kelantan, Perlis, and Kedah — where Japanese appointees succeeded to the throne. However, the rivalry between the pro-Japanese and pro-British factions was kept very much in the background.[60] The traditional Malay elite, especially the English-educated members of the pre-war government service, continued to maintain their traditional relationships with the rulers and the *raayat* (Malay subjects). Dealings between this administrative elite and the Japanese governors were limited, as the governors tended to maintain their titular office with some reserve. Corresponding to the MMA central government *somubucho*, administrative matters at the provincial level were in the hands of the provincial Somubucho, a role regarded by the Malay administrators as similar to that of the pre-war British adviser. Provincial Somubucho and other Japanese officials who acted as administrative superiors seemed to have extracted more work from the Malay elite than the British had to meet both administrative and military demands.

Not much information is available on the relationship between the Malay bureaucratic elites and the Sultans, but if the scanty evidence on the relationship between the Malay elite and Sultan Ibrahim of Johor is any indication, it was not cordial. Sultan Ibrahim had been accustomed to exerting some authority in his state before the war, and was considered the most independent and outspoken ruler in the country. But the Japanese administration made it difficult for him to have any say in the running of the government, since the Malay elite apparently chose to carry out the orders of the Japanese rather than those of Sultan Ibrahim. The Malay elite, more than the *raayat*, was aware that the Sultan had lost most of his pre-war powers and could no longer protect them as in pre-war days. The Malay elite feared the Japanese and, moreover, the Japanese, by promoting many Malay civil servants to top positions, gave them an incentive to become pliant and cooperative. After the war, Sultan Ibrahim refused to forgive the Johor Mentri Besar, Ungku Aziz, and other top Malay civil servants for what he considered their "traitorous" behaviour towards him.[*]

---

[*] This was the main reason he subsequently gave for signing the treaty with Sir Harold MacMichael, the British Government's plenipotentiary, on 18 October 1945, by which he transferred his jurisdiction in the state to the British Crown. See the Maxwell Papers, National Archives Malaysia, 1, 4. In his memorandum to MacMichael, dated 18 Oct. 1945, Sultan Ibrahim also said: "It is regrettable that the reliability of the Malays at present has completely changed. They are

Socially and economically, the British-trained bureaucratic elite fared extremely well throughout the occupation in comparison with other elite groups. They were generally trusted, well paid, and well treated, and the Japanese came to rely heavily on their services and advice. Because of their comfortable position, the elite appeared to have realized that they were being forced to tread a dangerous path between the "onerous duties" of the Japanese and the hatred of the masses. Many apparently attempted to get closer to the people by joining in community work projects. They grew food and did other manual work after office hours in their own backyards or farms, instead of keeping their hands clean as in pre-war days. There can be little doubt that the experience, which this elite gained during the Japanese occupation, strengthened their political self-confidence and enabled them to assert themselves forcefully when the British returned.

Islamic groups had always played an important social and political role among the Malays, but, unlike their policy in Java, the Japanese did not have a special policy to utilize them. The Japanese did not seek to establish control over any Islamic sect or movement; nor did they try to use the *alim ulama*, the religious scholars and teachers, for nationalist purposes. There does not appear to have been a coherent Japanese policy towards Islam in Malaya, although they subtly interfered in Islamic affairs by appointing Japanese officers in the administrative service to oversee the Islamic religious affairs departments, and in several states like Johor used the mosques for propaganda purposes by getting the *kathi* to support Japan in

---

no longer reliable. This is due to the 3 1/2 years under the Japanese rule and influence which has spoilt them, making them more unreliable, leaving only a few who can be trusted. They have become double-faced in order to please the Japanese. This came as a great surprise to me as I never expected them to do so. On the entry of the Japanese into Johor many of the Malays from the lower to the higher classes were only too ready to follow the whims of the Japanese, and only a very few kept away from so doing, It was shameful to witness all this but what could be done?"
See his memorandum in CO 273/675/50823/7/3, Pt II. Although this memorandum implies that he had been more "patriotic" than the Malay civil servants, it would seem that his anger at the civil servants was based on some deeper conflict, which he did not care to reveal to MacMichael.

their sermons on Friday prayers.* Probably because mosques were being politicized, a study of social and religious life in Johor shows that there was a high incidence of absenteeism at Friday prayers in several districts in that state, especially in Batu Pahat, Muar and Pontian since the beginning of the war. Absenteeism was particularly high in the months of April and May 1945, aggravated partly by the then prevailing tension in ethnic relations in those districts (to be discussed in Chapter 8).[61] A major social impact of the occupation on Malay-Muslims in Johor was in the breakdown in traditional relationships, in a high divorce rate, an increase in the freedom of women, who went out to work in large numbers unlike in pre-war times when they were confined to their homes. Malay-Muslim women even joined women's auxiliary groups of the army and volunteer corps, and took part in public displays of military drills. The Japanese endeavoured to control the religious and political authority of the Sultans, who were also the spiritual heads of the Malays. The curtailment of the Sultan's religious authority, in fact, might have been welcomed by Islamic reformists, such as the Kaum Muda (modernist) group, and other non-conformist groups such as the Sufis whose activities were suppressed under British rule by the Sultan's Majlis Ugama (Religious Council), the bastion of orthodox religious authority.

During the initial months of their administration, the Japanese first relied on a pro-Japanese non-aristocratic nationalist group, the Kesatuan Melayu Muda (KMM), led by Ibrahim Yaacob, as a source of intelligence and manpower. But the political dominance of the KMM was short-lived. It was banned only five months after the Japanese conquest, in line with Tokyo's policy that indigenous nationalist movements should not be encouraged prematurely. The Japanese used the KMM cadres as political agents and advisers, but relied on the British-trained Malay elite to help them run the administration. Only in early 1945, when Japanese plans to grant

---

* This is apparent despite the convening of the Malaya-Sumatra Islamic Conference in Singapore on 5–6 April 1943. The purpose of that meeting was merely to win the confidence of the Muslim Malays in both territories, through the support of their leaders, "to inject the Japanese view of the world into the people's minds and to unite all religious groups". See Akashi, "Japanese Military Administration", pp. 100–1. The conference was too concerned with discussing and adopting resolutions pledging Muslim support for Japan in the war.

independence to Indonesia were advanced, was the KMM revived in the hope that Malaya might be brought within an independent Indonesia in the form of Indonesia Raya (or Greater Indonesia), the aspiration of the KMM leaders. KMM members gave themselves a new name, KRIS (Kesatuan Rakyat Istimewa, or the Union of Special People), but before KRIS could be launched the Japanese surrendered.

Social tensions did exist between the KMM non-aristocratic elite and the traditional Malay elite. When the KMM was banned, its leaders became politically isolated, though they remained a part of the privileged elite of "collaborators". Thereafter, social divisions developed between the traditional Malay elite and the lower levels of Malay society. As mentioned earlier in the discussion of the role of the district officer (DO), the conflict of interests between the DO, the *penghulu*, and the *ketua kampung*, on the one hand, and the *raayat* (masses) on the other, were accentuated by the increasing demands of the Japanese authorities. When the DOs received pressure from the top, they passed it along to those below them. It was ordinary folk, both Malays and non-Malays, who felt the full brunt of Japanese policy.

One might have expected such pressures to produce severe intra-communal social conflicts among ethnic Malays. In a multi-ethnic environment such as Malaya, however, the full development of Malay intra-ethnic conflicts was checked by the presence of an alien group, the Chinese-dominated MPAJA. Although both Malays and non-Malays felt the full weight of oppression from the Japanese administration and the Malay DOs, it was the armed Chinese guerrillas in the MPAJA who pulled the trigger and took credit for execution of "wicked" Malay DOs, *penghulu*, and *ketua kampung*.

Given the overall segregation of Malays and Chinese between pro-Japanese collaborators and resistance guerrillas, inter-ethnic clashes were virtually inevitable. In each area where MPAJA units exacted taxes, supplies, men, or information from already depressed villages, they were in direct competition with the Malay officials of the Japanese regime. Most Malays saw the larger conflict as one between the Japanese and the MPAJA/Chinese, with Malay villagers caught in the middle, like the proverbial mouse deer between two fighting elephants. The MPAJA pursued collaborators of both Malay and non-Malay origin, but a numerical majority of the victims were Malays, particularly those serving in the Police Force and in the volunteer defence units. Increasing Chinese anger towards Malays exacerbated the situation. MPAJA killings and mutilations committed on murdered Malay "collaborators" ran counter to many Islamic precepts concerning treatment of the dead.

Finally, it seems probable that the MPAJA's "interference" in Malay social conflicts — between the DOs and their subordinates, on the one hand, and the *raayat*, on the other — was resented by the Malay upper elite and sparked a strong intra-class unity. The DOs, the *penghulu*, and the *ketua kampung*, as well as the traditional Malay administrative elite and the Sultans, became "one" in opposing the Chinese led by the MPAJA. As collaborators, the elite all feared the MPAJA's harsh retribution;[62] and in traditional Malay politics, based on patron-client relations, the *raayat* listened to the views of their "patrons". In any case, the Chinese in the MPAJA clarified the issue for the *raayat*. Their general distrust of Malays, their refusal to give Malays an equal role in the movement, and their failure to ensure that reprisals against Malay officials were carried out only by Malays were all construed as examples of Chinese chauvinism and Chinese political attempts aimed at dominating the Malays and their country. Given the general climate of hostility, it only required some minor misunderstandings at the local level to spark off an inter-racial conflict between Malays and Chinese.

The Chinese

The leaders of the pre-war Chinese communities in Malaya consisted mainly of officials of clan or guild associations (whether merchants, petty traders, or artisans), representatives of English-educated professionals in the state legislative councils, and various voluntary organizations. These could be further divided into the China-born and Chinese-educated business group, and the Straits-born and English-educated business and professional components. The businessmen or *towkays* held high social status and influence within the Chinese communities, as they were men of wealth, while English-educated groups were influential politically in Chinese mediations with the British administration. Both groups of Chinese leaders were involved in the anti-Japanese movement that emerged after the Japanese army invaded northern China in 1937. When the Japanese attack on Malaya began, it was these groups who threw their weight behind the British war effort and mobilized the Chinese community to fight the common enemy of the fatherland.

When the fall of Singapore was imminent, several Chinese leaders sought refuge in India, Thailand, and Indonesia since their anti-Japanese record made them fear for their lives. While most of those who remained behind in Malaya were arrested and tortured, a few escaped the massacre of Chinese carried out after the fall of Singapore. The pardon extended to these leaders must be regarded as a carefully considered Japanese strategy of social control since all surviving Chinese leaders later emerged as heads of the Japanese-sponsored Overseas Chinese Association (OCA) in Singapore and of similar associations in the mainland states. The Chinese in the resistance movement, while standing for unity of all classes of Chinese against the Japanese, tended to regard the OCAs as "arch collaborators" and enemies. Although the aim of these associations was clearly to marshal Chinese support and cooperation behind the Japanese regime, the OCAs also acted as a "shield" for the protection of pre-war Chinese leaders and their supporters. The OCAs never became political organizations like the Indian Independence League; nor did the MMA make any attempt to link the OCAs with the pro-Japanese government of Wang Ching-wei in Nanking. The Japanese made a minimal overture in this direction in 1944 when financial remittances to families in Chinese territory under the control of his government were authorized. Throughout the war, the political orientation of the Chinese in Malaya towards China, especially to the more popular government of Chiang Kai-shek in Chungking, was growing stronger as many Chinese hoped for deliverance from the Japanese regime by Chiang's army.

In contrast to the *towkays* in the OCAs, a large number of young Chinese refused to cooperate with the Japanese, joined the resistance movement, and came to regard the older leaders in the OCAs as "traitors" and "collaborators". The average age of youths who joined the MPAJA was 19, but most matured politically because of the war. Gradually, as the resistance movement gained strength within the Chinese community, the *towkays* who had become identified as spokesmen and apologists of the Japanese administration lost the prestige they enjoyed before the war. Though it was known that many of the OCA leaders were initially coerced into joining the OCAs, their continued cooperation with the Japanese eventually cost them their credibility. And, as they became more closely identified with Japanese repressive measures, many OCA leaders were eliminated by the MPAJA.[63] Only in a few exceptional cases was there any cooperation between the MPAJA and the OCA at the local level. The MPAJA reasons for killing OCA officials cannot readily be traced to their pre-war political affiliation with the KMT or their status as "capitalists" but was done largely because they were "collaborators" and thus one of the targets of the anti-Japanese struggle. With the exception of the KMT guerrillas along the Thai-Malay border whom they regarded as "bandits", the MCP/MPAJA tended to avoid both political rivalry and the pursuit of class struggle among the Chinese, preferring instead to encourage Chinese of all classes to unify in the face of a common Japanese oppression.

During the occupation, regional or dialect divisions among the Chinese appear to have abated considerably since all groups viewed the Japanese as a common threat. The raising of the M$50 million "gift" was an example of close cooperation and a successful attempt at mediation of regional and dialect differences. The collection committee of each state OCA comprised representatives of the eight major regional groups in Malaya — including Hokkien, Cantonese, Hakka, Hylam, and Teochiu. And to ensure that individual members of the different groups did not avoid their financial responsibilities, Hylam examined the properties of Teochiu, those of the Hylam by Hokkien, and so on.[64] In late 1944 when the Japanese attempted to improve relations with the Malayan Chinese in order to obtain their cooperation on economic problems confronting the administration, the Teochiu rice traders in Singapore and Penang played an important role in keeping open the rice supply from Thailand to Malaya. Initially this was done through smuggling and racketeering, in which Japanese officials were suitably bribed. Later the services of these Teochiu traders were officially mobilized within the *Epposho* (reading clubs), an agency through which the Chinese residents could voice their grievances and cooperate voluntarily with the Japanese authorities. Chinese of all regional and dialect groups now became indispensable for supplying rice, vegetables, and other goods to both the general public and the military. The vital nature of these contacts was exemplified by the Teochius in Penang and Singapore who had links with Teochiu rice traders in Thailand, and used them to operate a junk traffic in rice which brought in more than 3,000 tons of rice a month, at a time when Japanese overland and seaborne traffic was largely paralysed. The trade in Thai rice helped the Teochiu *pang* (group) rise to a leading position in post-war Malaya.[65]

The Indians

At the beginning and towards the end of the Japanese occupation, the Indians suffered the same hardships caused by the occupation and the war as did the other races. Thousands of Indian estate labourers were initially reduced to poverty, but soon a central Indian organization, the Indian Independence League (IIL), appeared on the scene to help reduce their distress. Since the Japanese planned to invade India, the IIL was the only political organization allowed to exist after June 1942 when the Malay KMM was banned. It established branches throughout Malaya, and these branches quickly organized medical and food relief for Indians wherever possible.[66]

Not until the Provisional Government of Free India was established under Subhas Chandra Bose on 21 October 1943 were Indians in Malaya given any exemption from labour recruitment. Until then the IIL was ineffective in preventing the impressments of thousands of Tamil estate labourers to various Japanese work sites, including the construction of the notorious Thai-Burmese "death" railway.[67] After Bose took over the IIL, and established the Provisional Government, he exercised enough political influence to ameliorate the plight of the Indian population. Indians were allowed to serve the Indian National Army (INA) and other allied services of the Provisional Government, and about 20,000 men were recruited into the INA from the ex-British Indian Army prisoners-of-war and 30,000 from among the Tamil public. Bose, a charismatic personality and persuasive orator, aroused strong national sentiments among the Indians and encouraged them to serve his cause to liberate India from British rule. Indians of all walks of life, both Hindus and Muslims, continued to join the IIL/INA and contribute large amounts of their savings and jewellery. Under pressure from the Japanese to support the Indian independence movement, subcommunal groups like the Ceylonese, Indian Muslims and others who were initially reluctant to participate in the IIL, were forced to sink their differences to identify themselves with its cause and the movement.[68] Bose also succeeded in forming a women's unit in the INA, the Rani of Jhansi Regiment, under the command of a woman doctor in Singapore.* This was a small but important contribution

---

* She was Capt. Laxmi Swaminathan. The Rhani of Jhansi Regiment was named after the heroine of the 1857 Indian Mutiny who led her troops against the British. Joyce Lebra, *Jungle Alliance*, p. 121.

to the political awakening of Indian women, who took special pride in being trained to fight for Indian freedom. The leadership of most of the IIL and its branches throughout Malaya came from the pre-war Central Indian Association for Malaya (CIAM), and consequently there was continuity of Indian leadership in the IIL.

When the seat of the Provisional Government was transferred from Singapore to Rangoon in 1944 the Indians lost their protection from the worst abuses of Japanese administration. Despite the special treatment still given them, the local IIL branches were unable to prevent the Japanese authorities from resuming compulsory recruitment of Indian labour. After the disastrous campaign at Imphal in June 1944, in which INA and Japanese forces were defeated in their battles with the British Army, the hopes of IIL began to falter and the liberation of the Indian motherland seemed an unlikely prospect. Nevertheless, the Indians in Malaya had been accorded special treatment and many Indians had taken advantage of the security and protection, which the IIL gave them. Only a small minority of Indians, including former Indian Army officers and soldiers and some of the English-educated professional classes, stayed aloof from the IIL.[69]

Although most Indians were not involved in inter-racial conflicts with Chinese or Malays, the Sikhs, who served in the regular police force, earned considerable animosity from both Malays and Chinese. Sikh policemen were regarded as efficiently ruthless and loyal to the Japanese authorities, and were among the MPAJA guerrillas' prime targets.[70] On the whole, however, Indian collaboration with the Japanese aroused little hostility among Malays and Chinese, as their involvement in the INA was viewed sympathetically as a just cause for the liberation of their motherland from British rule. Hence, many anti-British INA members were recruited later as leaders of MCP-led labour unions after the war.

The Question of Independence for Malaya

Although the Japanese Army administered Malaya as a colony throughout the war, Tokyo did consider the question of granting independence to Malaya. In February 1945 a study group in the Political Affairs Bureau of the Ministry of Foreign Affairs examined the possibilities of granting political independence to Malaya, and in a working paper suggested three possibilities: (1) to incorporate the four sultanates of Kelantan, Terengganu, Kedah, and Perlis into Thailand, and the rest into China; (2) to grant autonomy through the creation of a political administration with the cooperation of the Chinese, the main race in Malaya, and the Malays (for instance, like Sino-Malay Mixed Administration); and (3) to make Malaya a state of a federated Indonesia.[71]

The incorporation of the four northern sultanates into Thailand had already occurred in October 1943. The idea of integrating the remaining states of Malaya into China was based on a change in the colony's demographic balance following transfer of the four northern states to Thailand. The Chinese population thereafter constituted 47 per cent, the Malays 34 per cent, and the Indians and others 18 per cent. Based on these estimated figures, the study group concluded that the "main race" in Malaya was the Chinese:

> Therefore, in granting independence to Malaya it is impossible to ignore the Chinese on population grounds alone, even without taking into consideration their economic activities.... These days, the present Malayan Military Government is starting to show signs of changing the policy enforced in the early stages of military administration and which had been claimed to stand for principles emphasizing the position of Malays, because it has become impossible to ignore the power of Overseas Chinese merchants in various areas such as commerce, industry, and labour.[72]

However, in reconsidering the question the group concluded in another document that it was not feasible to grant independence to Malaya owing to the low level of political sophistication and the conditions of the indigenous people (that is, the Malays).[73]

The idea of granting independence to Malaya and other occupied territories in Southeast Asia had been secondary to the Japanese aim of using these areas to supply resources vital to the war effort. Tokyo began to consider the idea only when Japan suffered major reverses at the Battle of Midway in June 1942 and later when the American navy inflicted heavier losses on the Japanese naval fleet. After defeats at Guadalcanal and at Buna in Papua in January 1943, Japanese strategy became largely defensive[74] and the military began to justify the continuing hardship to the Japanese people as sacrifices in the cause of "the liberation of Asian peoples".[75] There was also hope that, if and when Southeast Asia became a battleground, its inhabitants would fight with the Japanese rather than the Allies. This could only be the case if some major political concession such as independence was granted.

Once these considerations began to influence Tokyo the question arose: which of the occupied countries of Southeast Asia was ready for independence? One criterion for determining this was the pre-war record of the nationalist movements in each of the occupied territories. Certain "lobbies" within the Japanese armed forces and the government, each having some pre-war contacts with and commitment to certain nationalist groups, now began to assert themselves. In January 1943, moved by such pressures and their need for the frontline cooperation of the ruling oligarchy in the Philippines and the pro-Japanese groups in Burma, Tokyo promised to grant early independence to both these countries. Indochina was still under the Vichy French administration, but contacts with pro-Japanese groups were stepped up as part of Japanese political maneuvers to establish an independent Indochina within the Greater East Asia Co-Prosperity Sphere.

The IIL was also encouraged through the formation of the Indian National Army aimed at liberating India from British rule. But in the Netherlands East Indies and in Malaya no moves were made in early 1943 to promote a movement towards independence. Soon, forced by the deteriorating military situation to act on its promises, Tokyo granted independence to Burma on 1 August and the Philippines on 14 October 1943. Nine days later, Tokyo extended recognition to the Provisional Government of Free India, an act being prompted by the military imperative of launching a counter-offensive in Burma. In November the heads of these governments, as well as those of Thailand and of the pro-Japanese government in Nanking, attended a Greater East Asia Conference in Tokyo.

In contrast to its policy elsewhere, Japan planned to delay independence in Malaya and Indonesia. The 31 May 1943 policy, labelled "Major Principles of Political Guidance in Greater East Asia", stated:

> Efforts will be made for developing Malaya, Sumatra, Java, Borneo, and Celebes as the sources of supply for important resources and for winning their political support. The native populations shall be granted political participation according to their standards; however, the military administration will be continued for the time being.[76]

However, on 16 June 1943 Premier Tojo announced in the Imperial Diet that the local populations of Malaya and the former Netherlands East Indies would be allowed a certain amount of "political participation" during the latter part of the year, "in conformity with the desire of the natives and in accordance with their various cultural levels". These measures would first be enacted in Java "as promptly as possible in view of its [Java's] cultural level and in response to the confidence of the people".[77]

As the Allied forces mounted full-scale offensives in 1944, there were further shifts in policy in the direction of granting full independence to the whole of the former Netherlands East Indies. In February 1945 the question of granting independence to Malaya was raised as part of this continuing discussion. Two considerations now seemed to assume great importance. First, the greater the geographical isolation of an occupied territory from Japan, the greater the need to accelerate the movement towards independence. Second, there was the hope that Southeast Asian countries would fight on the Japanese side against the Allies once some major political concessions were granted.

For Malaya there was still no hint of Japanese plans to grant independence, and the only positive sign was the formation of certain advisory bodies during 1943/4 in which local participation was encouraged. State and city councils were established from August 1943 to January 1944, but even these were similar to the former pre-war British executive councils for the Straits Settlements Colony and the Malay states.[78] Although the functions of these bodies were nominal and advisory, they had the potential for development into a system of self-government. The abrupt Japanese surrender forestalled this possibility, however, unless some local organization was able to pick up where the Japanese had left off.

Except for the idea of including Malaya within an enlarged independent Indonesian state, or Indonesia Raya, none of the other ideas within the Foreign Affairs Ministry document of 20 February 1945 had any known supporters within the MMA. Support for Indonesia Raya within certain sections of the MMA indicates that there were greater sympathies within the administration for the Malays than for the Chinese. The plan involved revival of the KMM group under Ibrahim Yaacob, and the dispatch of an eight-man Malay delegation comprising KMM officials and Sultans (or their representatives) to attend the Indonesian independence ceremony in Jakarta. These initiatives can be traced to the efforts of Professor Itagaki

Yoichi, of the research department of the MMA, in charge of Malay affairs. He convinced the Somubucho that the Malays should be prepared for self-government on the grounds that Japan had now decided to grant Indonesia independence. Whether Itagaki or the Somubucho was aware of the Foreign Affairs Ministry plan is not known, but it would seem likely that the Somubucho had some inkling of it. It is not clear how this plan was to be reconciled with the creation of advisory councils in 1943/4, in which representation had been given to Chinese, Indians, and other non-Malay groups. Probably it was thought that these councils could continue to function within Indonesia Raya, while the autonomous government of Malaya would be placed in Malay hands. In any event, these plans were cut short by news of the Japanese surrender.

Conclusion

Under the Japanese, Malaya's administration underwent several important changes. For the first time in the country's history an integrated government was imposed for the whole of Malaya, with a central authority based in Singapore — a marked contrast to the pre-war dual system of direct rule (Straits Settlements) and indirect rule (Malay States). The Japanese demoted the Sultans by removing their nominal status as rulers, which the British had allowed, thus turning them into minor officials. Like the British, the Japanese pursued a "pro-Malay" policy of appointing more Malays than Chinese and Indians in government service. But they went further than the British in encouraging Malays to rise to higher positions than had been allowed in the pre-war era. These Japanese policies, together with its initial support for the KMM and the cause of Indonesia Raya, were responsible for a resurgence of Malay nationalism during the war and in the post-war period.

Japanese policies to "Nipponize" the local population had limited success because the exposure to Japanese cultural, economic and military values lasted only three and a half years, and most of the impact was eroded in the post-war period. However, military values imparted during training to members of the Heiho, Giyu Gun, and Giyu Tai probably had a more lasting impact. Many former trainees organized themselves in 1946 into a militant youth organization, Angkatan Pemuda Insaf (API, or Youth for Justice Corps), and agitated for Malay independence within Indonesia.

Japanese support provided a belated fillip to the KMM/KRIS cause of Indonesia Raya. Although the KRIS disintegrated as a political organization as soon as the British returned to Malaya, its impact on Malay politics was considerable and it gave early post-war Malay politics a radical pro-Indonesian hue. Initial British attempts at suppression of this pro-Indonesia movement failed and it continued until 1948.

The Japanese occupation enabled the predominantly Chinese MCP to increase its political influence in Malaya during the war and in the post-war period. As the only political organization prepared for an active anti-Japanese insurgency, it attracted widespread support among the Chinese who suffered greatly from the brutality of the Japanese. The MCP succeeded therefore in creating a strong politico-military resistance movement, the MPAJU/MPAJA, in the midst of the Chinese community. There was, however, less support for the MCP from Malays and Indians because Malay and Indian cooperation with the Japanese was clearly greater than that of the Chinese. Nonetheless, because of its large guerrilla army, the MCP emerged a major political force in post-war Malaya.

The Japanese occupation helped to bring about certain changes in the structure of Chinese society in Malaya. Traditional Chinese leaders either had fled the country or were forced to cooperate with the Japanese if they remained. Consequently, the pre-war elites were discredited and frequently despised. Their place tended to be filled by Chinese communists who were mostly of a younger generation. On the whole, the Japanese occupation and the war experience strengthened Chinese nationalism and their sense of ethnic identity.

The major effect of the Japanese occupation on the Indians was to increase their sense of nationalism and make them more conscious of the need to liberate India from British rule. But like most Chinese in Malaya, the Indians' major problem in post-war Malaya would be to divert their political orientation away from their homeland towards their immediate interests in Malaya.

The greatest overall change produced by the Japanese administration was in the area of race relations. Although the Japanese did not deliberately foster racial conflict between Malays and Chinese, their policies had this effect. Repressive measures against the Chinese led to the formation of a Chinese-dominated resistance movement; their "pro-Malay" policy created an undercurrent of resentment and distrust among Chinese towards Malays. Malay cooperation made them appear a chosen instrument of the Japanese. The muted antagonisms over economic and political disparities between Malays and Chinese in pre-war Malaya were released as Japanese wartime conditions and policies brought both groups into collision in the competition for limited economic resources and political favours. In this competition, Malays secured a better political leverage as they had Japanese support; Chinese, on the other hand, having incurred Japanese hostility, had to fall back on their own efforts. The Japanese relied on Chinese business skills to operate the retail trade and the black markets, but this was a small gain when the economic hardships were so severe. It was the encroachments of Chinese as settlers and farmers in traditional Malay reservation lands and in rural areas, which posed a direct challenge to the pre-war special position of Malays, even though such a resettlement policy was encouraged by the Japanese to alleviate the food shortage.

In the political and economic struggle between Malays and Chinese (the minority Indians were not seen as a threat by either group), the MPAJA appeared to Malays as a Chinese-dominated organization, not only competing with the Japanese administration for taxes, foodstuffs, and manpower but increasingly as a defender of the Chinese population and of Chinese interests, despite its proclaimed support for multi-racialism. Malays viewed it as a weapon of terror and intimidation resorted to by local Chinese to avenge themselves against any abuses of authority or excesses of Japanese officials and their subordinate Malay staff. Finally, the largely Malay units of the Heiho, Giyu Gun, and Giyu Tai were, in fact, as racially divisive as the Chinese MPAJA, and their deployment by the Japanese in operations against the predominantly Chinese resistance movement contributed further to widening the racial cleavage in Malaya. As Willard Elsbree later observed, had there been equal proportions of Chinese and Malays in the resistance as well as in collaboration, "the bitterness which came in the wake of the occupation would not have had such a pronounced racial tinge".[79]

CHAPTER 3

The MCP and the Anti-Japanese Movement

The guerrilla tactics of the MPAJA were inherited from the accumulated experience of the anti-Japanese guerrilla war in China, but adapted to the Malayan locality.

– Hai Shang Qu, *Ma-lai-ya-jen-min k'ang jih chun*
(The Malayan People's Anti-Japanese Army), 1945

The Japanese occupation caused the demise of several pre-war political parties in Malaya, especially the Kuomintang, the Central Indian Association of Malaya (CIAM),[*] and the aristocratic-led Malay State Associations (Persatuan-Persatuan Negeri Melayu). Only two organizations survived; one, the pro-Japanese Kesatuan Melayu Muda (KMM) lasted briefly for six months before the Japanese dissolved it. There will be a fuller discussion of its wartime role later, as the Japanese authorities initially encouraged it to be active politically and later presented it with an opportunity to secure independence. The other organization, the resilient anti-Japanese Malayan

---

[*] The only political organization, which the Japanese permitted to operate in Malaya, was the Indian Independence League (IIL), but the IIL was formed in Bangkok before 1941 and moved to Malaya with the Japanese invasion forces. Although many former CIAM officials and members joined the IIL under an IIL-Japanese pact to fight for the liberation of India in the INA, the CIAM itself was not revived. For details of the IIL, see Joyce Lebra, *Jungle Alliance: Japan and the Indian National Army* (Singapore, 1977).

Communist Party (MCP), survived underground throughout the occupation during which it raised and directed a strong resistance force in the country — the Malayan People's Anti-Japanese Army (MPAJA). Because of this force, the MCP emerged as a formidable social and political movement at the end of the war. A brief outline of the origins, programmes, and strategies of both the MCP and the MPAJA, as well as those of the other groups in the resistance, will throw light on their respective strengths and weaknesses, as well as the local balance of power, which existed at the end of the war.

Brief Background of the MCP

The Chinese Communist Party's close relationship with communist activities in Malaya in the beginning turned the MCP into a mainly Chinese organization instead of a multi-racial one (see Chapter 1). While the CCP cadres failed to direct the orientation of Chinese members away from China towards Malaya, the local Chinese themselves lacked a local identity and hence were prone to look to the CCP or the Kuomintang or anyone else who had a "homeland" focus.[1] In the 1930s, despite the Comintern's takeover of communist activities in Malaya, the MCP still faced problems in extending its mass organizations to Malays and Indians. Chinese MCP labour leaders were frequently arrested and banished to China for clandestine trade union activities. An ineffective Chinese leadership of poor intellectual calibre could not overcome language and other communal problems and the low level of political consciousness among Malay peasants and Indian workers. Consequently, the MCP's hoped-for class unity of all races in Malaya failed to emerge.[2]

In 1936 the MCP underwent an internal crisis and changed its policies. A weakened party attempted to direct all races into "anti-Japanese Fascist" and "anti-British Imperialist" struggles, while encouraging Malays, Chinese, and Indians to pursue their own separate racial or national independence struggles. Such diversity of objectives was aimed merely at securing short-term psychological or propaganda advantages. Their adoption was accompanied by an admission that "our mass organisations and politics have not reached the stage strong enough to overthrow British imperialism".[3] The anti-Japanese China National Salvation Movement, which the MCP dominated, took precedence over its other struggles, from 1937 to the Japanese invasion of Malaya in 1941. The party placed greater importance on external than on local conditions for determining its struggles. While this strategy was based on a correct assessment of the immediate Japanese threat to Malaya, it secured only the support of local Chinese whose patriotic feelings were aroused by the Japanese occupation of northern China in 1937.[4] Internally, the party secretly advocated the strategic slogan of "Establish the Malayan Democratic Republic".[5] This decision was to enable the MCP to maintain flexibility of action in case the British accepted its offer of mutual cooperation in local defence in the event of a Japanese invasion. The offer was first made in July 1941, a month after Germany had attacked the Soviet Union. Britain was now aiding both the Soviet Union and China. The MCP offer had been conditional on the British accepting its minimum demand — that they should grant "democratic rights" to the people, and the party, in turn, would suspend its "anti-British Imperialism" policy and rally its forces behind the defence of Malaya.[6] But the overture met with a British rebuff. Nonetheless, the secret strategy of "Establish the Malayan Democratic Republic" meant that the MCP was ready to take advantage of the opportunity to expel the British from Malaya as soon as practicable. If Japan should invade Malaya, the communists would continue to support an anti-Japanese front, but only as a means of extending communist influence.

Because of its anti-Japanese policy, the MCP was well placed to exploit the situation to its advantage when the Japanese attacked Malaya on 8 December 1941. The MCP immediately repeated its offer of aid to the British. After Japanese troops made a rapid advance in Malaya, secret contacts were established between MCP officials and the British police, during which they discussed terms including the release of communist detainees. The underground MCP came out publicly in a statement to support British defence measures, and its supporters vied with those of the Kuomintang to exhort Malayan Chinese to renew their pledges of assistance to the British. In this campaign Tan Kah Kee, the pro-left Singapore Chinese leader, took the lead.[7] Communists joined with other Chinese groups to call on the government to raise a Chinese militia to assist in the defence of Singapore. As British military reverses were reported, including the sinking of the British warships *Prince of Wales* and *Repulse*, the British government and the War Office in London gave approval to accept the MCP offer.[8] On 15 December some leftist political prisoners were released from detention. The following day the Chinese section of the Police Special Branch, Singapore, put out "feelers" for the formation of a united organization to mobilize Chinese activities to deal with the effects of bombing and to profit from the lesson of Penang island in the northern part of the peninsula, where bombing casualties had been high.[9]

On 18 December, when the MCP had still not heard from the British authorities, the Central Executive Committee held a meeting in Singapore and decided to "go ahead and rely on the people's efforts alone" in mobilizing a local defence force.[10] That very day, the British contacted the MCP and accepted its offer. A secret "cloak-and-dagger" meeting was held in Singapore between two British officers and two MCP representatives, one of whom was Lai Tek, the party's secretary-general, who had long been secretly a British agent without the party's knowledge. One of the British officers was Freddy Spencer Chapman who represented the "Oriental Mission" of London-based Special Operations Executive (SOE). The other was a Chinese-speaking police Special Branch officer whose identity has been confirmed recently as John Davis, Lai Tek's case officer.[11] Davis was involved in negotiating the arrangements because of his familiarity with the case history of Lai Tek. It was agreed that the MCP would raise, and the British train, resistance groups to be left behind enemy lines in the event of the whole of Malaya being overrun by the Japanese. The MCP agreed that the trained MCP recruits would be used as the British Military Command saw fit.* The recruits were to undergo training in sabotage and guerrilla warfare at 101 Special Training School (STS) in Singapore, run by the Malayan wing of the SOE.

On 19 December the MCP inaugurated its own "Malayan Overseas Chinese Anti-Japanese Mobilization Society", which became a broad front comprising groups like the KMT, the Chinese Chamber of Commerce, and other Chinese organizations, as well as the MCP, to raise Chinese volunteers for an independent force, later known as Dalforce, whose head was the British Special Branch officer, Lieutenant-Colonel J.D. Dalley.[12] A week later, a meeting of this society was held at the Singapore Special Branch headquarters. The participants agreed to set aside their party and clique differences

---

* F. Spencer Chapman, in *The Jungle Is Neutral* (London, 1949), gives details of this agreement. "This conference," recalled Chapman, "took place in a small upstairs room in a back street of Singapore, and, to complete the air of conspiracy, both Chinese wore dark glasses."

and picked Tan Kah Kee to be leader of the newly formed "Mobilization Council".[13]

On 21 December the training of MCP recruits at 101 STS began. Individual courses lasted ten days and a total of seven classes, consisting of 165 enthusiastic party members selected by the MCP, rushed through the training programme. The graduates became the nucleus of the MPAJA.

The original British plan was for each MCP "stay-behind" party to be led by a British officer to ensure that British instructions and policy were carried out. However, owing to the rapid advance of the Japanese, this was not possible and the first class of MCP graduates of 101 STS was hurriedly sent out to Selangor in early January to work on its own. The second class went to Negeri Sembilan and the third to north Johor. The fourth and final classes infiltrated through Japanese lines into south Johor on 30 January 1942. Each group eventually established liaison with the State Committee of the MCP in the area where it operated. From March onwards the groups were recognized by the MCP's CEC as the First, Second, Third, and Fourth Independent Regiments of the MPAJA respectively.[14]

In Singapore, the communists formed the largest group of volunteers in Dalforce, which included Kuomintang members and independents. It was the tenacity with which Dalforce volunteers fought Japanese troops in the defence of Singapore that led the Japanese to carry out a purge of the island's Chinese population immediately upon capturing Singapore on 15 February 1942. In the search for communists and other anti-Japanese elements, the Japanese captured several MCP officials, including Lai Tek, and forced them to become spies and informers.* The rest were put to death.

The MPAJA Organization

Since much has been written already about the MPAJA's history and organization,[15] hence only a brief outline of its development is given here. During the first year and a half of its existence, the MPAJA fared badly, lacking food, capable leadership, and sufficient training and experience in guerrilla warfare. Japanese terrorism prevented people of all races from helping the guerrillas. One-third of the guerrilla force was said to have died during this period. The second

---

* Lai Tek's role as a Kempeitai agent is discussed on pp. 83–101.

period, from mid-1943 to mid-1944, saw the MPAJA improve its organization, food supplies, communications system, and military training; consequently, it was said to have increased four times in size. The third period, from mid-1944 until the end of the war, was one of consolidation and growth and the establishment of close MPAJA-Allied cooperation. The MPAJA henceforth received supplies of arms, medicines, and money from the headquarters of South East Asia Command (SEAC) under Admiral Mountbatten based in Colombo.[16]

Up to November 1942, the MPAJA comprised only the first four Independent Regiments made up of 101 STS graduates and other recruits located in Selangor, Negeri Sembilan, and in north and south Johor. Later the MPAJA established four more regiments owing to an increase in the number of recruits and extended its activities to other parts of the country. The additional regiments and the dates when they were formed are as follows: the Fifth Independent Regiment (Perak) was established on 1 December 1942; the Sixth Independent Regiment (West Pahang), 13 August 1943; the Seventh Independent Regiment (East Pahang, which also covered Terengganu and Kelantan), 1 September 1944; and the Eighth Independent Regiment (Kedah) in early August 1945.[17] The Fifth Independent Regiment was formed from a "traitor killing" unit set up in mid-1942. The Sixth Regiment was originally a training and propaganda unit, which sponsored the People's Academy said to have been set up by Lai Tek. The commander of the People's Academy, Ch'en Kuang, was reputed to have been a graduate of Mao's Eighth Route Army guerrilla school (*K'ang-ta*) in Yenan. He was reported to have patterned his training system on that used by communist armies in China. Former members of the Communist Eighth Route and New Fourth Armies brought some of the texts used from China.*

---

* F. Spencer Chapman (*The Jungle Is Neutral*) is the key source of the influence of the Eighth Route Army on the Sixth Independent Regiment in Pahang. He cites a number of instances where the tradition of the Eighth Route Army was scrupulously followed: such as 15 minutes' no-talking rule during mealtime, singing as a vehicle of propaganda, and girl recruits. Chapman also gives details of Eighth Route Army personnel in the camp, particularly about a patrol leader, Ah Loy. Based on his Yenan experiences, Ah Loy led a rescue party, which attempted to break down the door of a district gaol where MPAJA guerrillas were kept. But the attempt was a disaster. The Japanese put all their guerrilla prisoners to death. Chapman, *The Jungle Is Neutral*, pp. 153, 163–74.

After it was formed in June or July 1942, the Central Military Committee of the MCP acted as supreme command of the MPAJA. Liu Yau was chairman of the Central Military Committee.[18] Initially each state had a Military Affairs Committee whose members were elected from various state area units of the MPAJA. In addition, each MPAJA regiment had a "Political Commissar". At the end of 1942, the "Political Commissar" system was abolished and replaced by a three-man Central Military Committee whose other members besides Liu Yau were Lai Tek and Chin Peng.[19] The abolition of the "Political Commissar" system is believed to have been caused by the loss of most of the "Political Commissars" in a Japanese ambush of a Central Executive Committee meeting at the Batu Caves in Selangor on 1 September 1942. Henceforth the three-man Central Military Committee directed the MPAJA not only for the rest of the Japanese occupation but until the MPAJA was demobilized by the British in December 1945. Although the committee was in strategic command, individual local commanders were given freedom to conduct operations in their areas as they saw fit. Owing to frequent betrayals by traitors in the MPAJA and in the MCP, liaison between regiments was forbidden; every communication between regiments had to pass through "Central". Even a patrol leader could not visit another camp in his group without permission from group head-quarters. Communication was carried out not by wireless transmission but by means of couriers who had to move slowly through the jungle from one area to another, sometimes over long distances.[20]

The total strength of the MPAJA at the time of the Japanese surrender was reported to be between 3,000 and 4,000, but at the time of demobilization it was said to be between 6,000 and 7,000.[21] The increase at the time of demobilization was due to the inclusion of a sizeable force of MPAJA guerrillas in many areas who, for one reason or another, had not come into contact with Force 136 officers during the war. Appearance of these additional guerrillas raised British suspicions that they had been part of an MCP "secret army". British intelligence subsequently concluded that such a "secret army" had been formed as the result of an MCP directive issued after April 1945, when the MPAJA was being equipped with new weapons by SEAC to implement the agreement reached between Lai Tek and Force 136.[22] The directive ordered the formation of secret as well as open units of the MPAJA. Secret units were to consist of long-tested members and most of the important MCP leaders. They were to remain incognito and to stay in the jungle. To arm itself, the secret force was given the job of collecting and confiscating as many arms as possible. The force was to be used not only against the Japanese but also in an armed struggle against the British "if a People's Republic was not set up after the war to the liking of the MCP".[23] The "open" units, however, were formed from those units, which had come into contact with Force 136 and were armed with British weapons to assist in the Allied landing.

Such a "secret army" existed, but whether it was the idea of Lai Tek or Liu Yau, chairman of the MCP's Central Military Committee, is not known. When the terms of demobilization were worked out between Lai Tek and Force 136 in September–October 1945, Lai Tek agreed to call in all MPAJA guerrillas who had not been in liaison with Force 136 during the war. The British, however, believed that only a part of this "secret army" laid down their arms during the demobilization, the other having hidden their weapons in the jungle. In fact, British troops afterwards reportedly uncovered many secret MPAJA training camps and caches of arms in one or two states of which Force 136 officers had no previous knowledge. Although Lai Tek was to deny the existence of this "secret army" during police interrogations in 1946,[24] British intelligence believed that it existed and that it was reactivated when the MCP launched its armed struggle against the British in June 1948. Chin Peng in his auto-biography, *My Side of History*, however, confirms the existence of the "secret army": "All in all, our secret army units were able to stash away some 5,000 individual weapon pieces in jungle caches of which no more than 10 per cent were acquired through Force 136 air supplies."[25]

Each "open" MPAJA regiment comprised five or six patrols, and the average regimental strength was between 400 and 500 members. The headquarters of the Fifth Independent Regiment (Perak), to which Col. J.P. Hannah of Force 136 was attached in March 1945, was reported to have consisted of 23 men distributed as follows:

Commander	Itu (Liao Wei-chung)
Second-in-command	Wong Lup
Secretary	Lau Mah alias Ah Chung alias Chin Wei Seong
Quartermaster	Chin Tse
4 couriers	
1 bodyguard section (15 men)[26]	

The Fifth Regiment became the most important MPAJA regiment under the able joint leadership of Chin Peng, the Perak State Secretary, Itu, and Lau Mah. It was the regiment, which established the first contacts with the principal Force 136 officers such as Colonel Davis and Maj. Richard Broome.

There was no class distinction in the MPAJA. The common form of address was "comrade". Even the chairman of the Central Military Committee was addressed as comrade, but discipline was tight. Though the MCP organized the MPAJA, many of its members were not communists. The link between the MCP and the MPAJA was political education.

An MPAJA camp usually emphasized military practice and drilling, political education, cooking, propaganda, collection of food supplies, and cultural affairs. Mandarin, the Chinese national language, was the *lingua franca* of the MPAJA and was used in all correspondence and official statements. Concessions to the Malay, Tamil, and English languages were made in some of the propaganda newssheets published by the MPAJA's propaganda bureau.

British reports revealed that the guerrillas carried out a number of military engagements with Japanese troops and sabotage operations against Japanese installations.[27] The MPAJA's own account claims its guerrillas undertook 340 individual operations against the Japanese during the occupation, of which 230 were considered "major" efforts — "major" meaning the involvement of an entire regiment.[28] There is no report of any operation involving two or more regiments. For the entire occupation period, the MPAJA claimed to have eliminated 5,500 Japanese troops (it is not clear whether this includes local police and volunteers) and about 2,500 "traitors", while the MPAJA itself lost only 1,000 men.[29] On the other hand, Japanese records indicated they lost 600 killed or wounded, and the local police 2,000, while inflicting 2,900 casualties on the MPAJA.[30] The Japanese figures appear more conservative, although they are probably only approximate.*

It should be noted further that the Japanese and guerrilla casualty figures from the time of the Japanese surrender to 31 August

---

* A senior Force 136 officer regarded the Japanese casualty figures as fairly accurate. However, he noted that the Japanese figures of guerrilla casualties did not include "many thousands of men, women and children living beneath the hills who were brutally massacred in reprisals". *Weekly Intelligence Review* 25, Indian Division, 12 Dec. 1945, in MU Secret 335/46.

1945 (a period of two weeks) almost equaled each other — 506 (Japanese and local police) to 550 (guerrillas). But the number of Japanese casualties was high, for such a short period, in contrast to the period from February 1944 to 14 August 1945, when only 523 Japanese and local police casualties were reported. Two reasons may be given for both the increase in guerrilla actions and in the high Japanese casualty figures. Until March/April 1945, the guerrillas were too badly armed to carry out any major operations. Later, equipped with new weapons supplied by the SEAC, the guerrillas found the surrender an opportunity to settle accounts with the Japanese.

The MPAJA and the People

Its Central Military Committee regarded good relationships between the MPAJA and the people as extremely important. Initially, the MPAJA attempted to live near the Chinese squatter areas, which had formed outside most towns near the jungle fringes. However, as the Japanese method of retaliation against the guerrillas was to burn down most of these villages, the MPAJA patrols were forced to retreat to the jungle slopes of the Main Range. Many Chinese farmers followed them and cleared large fields where they planted vegetables, sweet potatoes, and tapioca to feed themselves and the guerrillas. In Perak and Pahang the Senoi (aborigine) territory of Cameron Highlands and the Jalong Valley were considered "friendly" territories.[31]

At first the guerrillas were careful in their relations with the local population — extending whatever cooperation and assistance the people needed, always paying for foodstuffs and never using coercion. But as the war dragged on and Japanese reprisals became more harsh and unrelenting, the guerrillas became more indiscriminate. They would attack not only Japanese and their informers but also any hostile or uncooperative local people. Whenever MPAJA guerrillas knew that a particular village or town was collaborating with the Japanese they would raid the village, assault the population, and exact taxes and foodstuffs. Many Malay villages were targets for such measures because they were hostile to the MPAJA.[*] Japanese-

---

[*] Chapman, *The Jungle Is Neutral*, pp. 137–8, narrates several incidents in which Malays guided Japanese troops to areas to attack the British officers and MPAJA guerrillas. Instances of conflict between Malays and MPAJA guerrillas are also

sponsored settlements, such as those of Endau and Bahau, were also attacked and the officials of the "collaborative" Overseas Chinese Association abducted or killed.[32]

The MPAJA's main link with the local population in the areas where it operated was the Malayan People's Anti-Japanese Union (MPAJU). The MPAJU fed the guerrillas, raised funds, collected clothes, fighting materials, food, and gathered intelligence. It also arranged guides to take MPAJA patrols through unknown territory and formed corps of couriers. The MPAJU pursued an "open" policy of recruiting people of all races, classes, religions, and political creeds who were opposed to the Japanese regime. It therefore absorbed Chinese (who constituted the majority of its supporters) but also aborigines, Malays, Indians, and others.[*] It welcomed within its ranks businessmen, KMT members, Chinese secret society members, and even government officials. The MPAJU operated a fairly efficient spy network and did not hesitate to put out feelers for some understanding and cooperation with Malay, Chinese, and Indian government officials and policemen, as well as local defence volunteer units. Such efforts, however, met with only limited success. Fear of the Japanese administration's terror tactics made those in government service keep away from the MPAJU.[†] Only a few administrators might occasionally cooperate with the MPAJU.

Generally, Malay policemen and Malay government staff, such as district officers and village chiefs, kept aloof from both the MPAJA and the MPAJU. In Chapter 2, it was shown that the Japanese treated

---

cited in John Cross, *Red Jungle* (London: [publisher?], 1957), pp. 73–7, 82, 119, 132. Cross was a member of one of the original British "stay-behind" parties who remained in south Johor. In one incident, the *penghulu* of a village near Layang Layang in Johor informed the Japanese of the guerrillas' presence, and soon after a raiding party came to the village. The MPAJA patrol leader waylaid two Malays spying on the camp. One escaped, the other (a woman) was killed.

[*] Besides the Chinese squatters, good relations are said to have been established between the aborigines and the Chinese guerrillas. See Anthony Short, *The Communist Insurrection in Malaya, 1948–1960* (London, 1975), pp. 441, 447.

[†] Refusal to cooperate on the part of an individual found within an MPAJA camp area meant certain death. This was what happened to an Indian medical dresser who wandered into the area of headquarters, Seventh Independent Regiment, in Pahang. He refused to cooperate with communists, even when he was told that unless he did so he would be executed. See Thatcher and Cross, *Pai Naa*, pp. 166–7.

Malays more favourably than Chinese in the first two years of their rule; hence Malays found little cause to dislike the Japanese or to support the MPAJA or MPAJU, which they considered a Chinese resistance movement. However, by the end of 1943, there was a change of attitude among Malays as the Japanese began to neglect Malay interests and to create more economic hardships affecting Malays. Relations between the MPAJU and MPAJA and the Malay population became more cordial. On the other hand, relations between the MPAJU/MPAJA and local government officials, such as the District Officer and the *penghulu* and *ketua kampung* deteriorated, mainly because the latter were used to requisition labour for Japanese government and military projects, as well as to collect rice and other commodities in their areas for the Japanese army. These officials became the targets of MPAJA killings. In some Malay areas such MPAJA killings, exactions, and lack of tact combined with local misunderstandings sparked off inter-racial clashes between Malays and Chinese.*

The MCP and the MPAJU/MPAJA

The reasons for the lack of tact or circumspection shown by the MPAJU/MPAJA towards some sections of the Malay population may be attributed to the MCP, the controlling authority for both organizations. It had party representatives in every unit of the MPAJA, but not in every area of the MPAJU. The MPAJU was loosely established at a village, town, or district on the basis of anti-Japanese feelings. Each area section would have its own committee, including a president and a secretary. Members of the MPAJU may not be communists but they would include a cross-section of the people. But once they had been recruited they maintained contacts with the MCP and the MPAJA through intermediaries in their area. MCP cadres might, however, try to proselytize MPAJU members and officials to recruit them into the party.

Unlike the MPAJU, the MPAJA received political education from the party. The content of political courses given to MPAJA guerrillas related to theories of communism, discussions of international affairs, explanations of MCP policies, and "self-criticism" sessions. However, since the MCP's CEC had not spelt out the

---

* The inter-racial clashes will be discussed further in Chapter 7.

nature of the "Malayan revolution" fully, nor how the main goal of its anti-Japanese programme, a "Malayan Democratic Republic", was to be achieved, political discussions at the MPAJA level were rather rudimentary.[33]

More important, the MCP was either unaware of, or indifferent to, some very sensitive human and racial issues, which were developing within the MPAJU and MPAJA. First, the membership of the MPAJU/MPAJA was overwhelmingly Chinese — about 95 per cent. Although both organizations subsequently acquired a few Malay and Indian members (the MPAJU more than the MPAJA), their Chinese character was never lost. Leaders were mostly Chinese, speaking and writing mainly Chinese. Very few of them could speak any Malay. MCP and MPAJA statements were mainly in Chinese. Three-fifths of all MPAJA broadsheets were in Chinese, and only one-seventh in Malay.[34]

Neither the MCP nor the MPAJU/MPAJA meant to foster racial antagonism or a policy of discrimination between Chinese, Indians, and Malays. In fact, their policies were aimed at trying to rally people of these three major races in Malaya to their banner and to their cause of establishing a "Malayan Democratic Republic". The MPAJA advocated multi-racial unity, symbolized by the three yellow stars on its red flag. Yet things did not work out as they intended. The MPAJU/MPAJA fared much better in establishing cordial relationships with the local Chinese population than with Malays and Indians; and the closer their relations with Chinese groups the more difficult became the job of winning over the others.

Japanese policies may be said to have created certain problems for the Chinese-led resistance movement. While the Japanese did not foment racial discord, their propaganda frequently identified Chinese resistance elements as "communists" and "troublemakers". The MCP failed to counter such propaganda effectively and to demonstrate that besides Chinese it had other races within the MPAJU/MPAJA. There was no evidence to show that MCP policies took account of Malay sensitivities and fear of communism, or made any attempts to understand Malay customs and the Islamic religion.

Such considerations only became evident in the MCP leadership after the lessons of the Malay-Chinese clashes in 1945. Only after the war did the MCP's CEC adopt in September 1946 a working plan which took cognizance of the party's "inadequate leadership" of the Malays and which called for a "Malayanization" of the party and development of a "Malay national movement". This working plan embodied the following aims: (1) to investigate the conditions, interests, racial characteristics, customs, and religion of the Malay race; (2) to intensify the Party's propaganda campaign among the Malays for the purpose of making them fully understand the Party's outline, and winning them over to the Party; (3) to overcome all difficulties in training Working Committee members and personnel for work among the Malays; (4) to train systematically those Chinese who were well versed in Malay affairs, and who may have to adopt their religion and nationality [apparently this means race], if necessary, for organizing the Malay people; (5) to establish a Central Racial Committee for discussing the various racial problems and the work connected therewith; (6) to get the members of the Party more interested in work among the Malay people; and (7) to submit regular reports to Central regarding the Malays.[35]

The working plan on "Malayanization" of the party also recommended discussion and study among members to show that the party was charged with the "duty of emancipating Malaya from the imperialists". Party members were told to become "Malayan citizens". While interest in China's politics was to be allowed, Chinese members should "pay more attention to the party's own needs and activities in Malaya".[36] The MCP's orientation before 1946 had thus been Chinese rather than Malayan in character. It only began to think in truly Malayan terms after the war.

Lacking a "Malayanization" policy either before or during the war, the MCP allowed Chinese members within the party and within the MPAJU/MPAJA to have a free play of their "chauvinistic" feelings. It should be noted that in its 1940 programme the MCP had made a distinction between the "Malayan Chinese" (*Ma Hua*, or Malaya-oriented Chinese), and the "Overseas Chinese" (*Hua Ch'iao*, or China-oriented Chinese). It had implied that the former had the correct "Malayan" orientation to join the MCP's anti-imperialist struggle, whereas the "Overseas Chinese" were mainly interested in China. But this distinction between the two groups was a nascent one, and the idea does not appear to have been developed further. Although the MCP may be credited with being the first organization to put its finger on this distinction in 1940, it did not become important to members of the Chinese community until the post-war period. In October 1945 the issue of which group of Chinese was entitled to the British government's offer of Malayan Union citizenship became controversial. The British government specified that those Chinese born in Malaya, or who had resided there at least

15 years, were eligible for Malayan Union citizenship. This forced further discussion among the Chinese as to what it meant to be *Ma Hua* and *Hua Ch'iao*. Both geographical/political orientation and nationality became important considerations from 1946.

An inherent weakness of the MCP during the war was that a significant portion of its leaders and members were "Overseas Chinese", or CCP elements.[37] The Japanese occupation also increased ethnic Chinese unity. The Japanese regarded all Chinese in Malaya as "Overseas Chinese" owing allegiance to either the Chiang Kai-shek government or that of Wang Ching-wei. Partly because of Japanese oppression of the Chinese in Malaya, the MCP might have thought it unwise to re-emphasize its earlier distinction between the two groups. However, if the MCP's "ideological line" was firm and well known, it was possible for the "Overseas Chinese" to reorientate themselves towards a Malayan national liberation struggle.

The evidence also suggests that there was a certain reluctance to accept Malays as full partners or comrades-in-arms with Chinese in the anti-Japanese movement. Mutual distrust between Malays and Chinese began in the first year of Japanese rule. Numerous British accounts have shown how frequently Malay villagers betrayed the MPAJA camps to the Japanese. Therefore, the attitude of the MCP and the MPAJU/MPAJA leaders was that Malays were "unreliable", if not "downright treacherous". In this connection, Chinese accounts always used the derogatory term *chou kou* ("running dogs") to refer to Malays as informers and lackeys of the Japanese.[38] In every reported Japanese raid on MPAJA hideouts, Malay guides and informers (and, in some instances, Malay and Indian guides) were involved and they would participate in the execution or torture of Chinese victims. They would also be allowed to cart away whatever booty they could collect from the raids.*

As indicated earlier, several British Force 136 officers have re-called the presence of armed Malays in Japanese raiding parties on MPAJA camps, and reported that Malay villagers often reacted with fear and hostility towards both the British officers and the guerrillas.

---

* Some time in 1943, Japanese troops accompanied by Malays, raided the Chinese settlement at Lenggong (Perak) and burnt down 20 to 30 houses in a hunt for guerrillas. The Malays removed the settlers' rice harvests. Twenty Chinese were taken to the local police station where they were interrogated and Malay police-men allegedly beat some to death. Li Tieh Min *et al.*, *Ta-chan yu Nan Ch'iao*, pp. 28–9.

Chapman has described the instances when MPAJA patrols had to move camp every time Malays either out hunting deer or gathering fruits discovered the presence of the Chinese guerrillas. Such discovery always meant the arrival of Japanese troops, and the guerrillas would be forced to move deeper into the jungle.[39] While neither Chapman nor other Force 136 personnel recorded any instance of MPAJA retaliation on the Malays for such treachery, it would not be surprising if it occurred without their knowledge, either locally or at greater distance. A Chinese informant described it as "the pot boiling over". This was what probably happened in southwest Johor in May 1945, which led to Malays attacking the MPAJA and Chinese retaliating (see Chapter 8).

Nonetheless, this should not obscure the fact that the MCP and the MPAJU/MPAJA did accept a small number of Malays within their ranks.[40] But these Malays probably had to overcome Chinese political distrust of Malays. In early 1945, a few instances were reported of Malays, especially Malay policemen, going over to the MPAJA with their arms.[41] In one instance, in Pahang, the MPAJA treatment of these policemen was shabby. Instead of incorporating them into the guerrilla forces, the MPAJA leaders took their arms away, gave them to Chinese guerrillas, and sent the Malays to work on farms.[*]

The inter-racial situation was worsened by the fact that Malays formed the bulk of the police force as well as the volunteer forces used by the Japanese in anti-guerrilla operations. The lines of battle were thus neatly drawn along racial lines. Apparently, some attempts were made to establish an understanding and cooperation between the MCP/MPAJA and the Malay Giyu Gun (Volunteer Army). Lt.-Col. Ibrahim Yaacob, commander of the Malay Giyu Gun, claims that contacts in 1944 eventually led both sides to agree to cooperate to fight both the Japanese and the British for the purpose of achieving

---

[*] Nona Baker narrates the incident in 1945 in which a group of Malay policemen at Cherating, Pahang, after reading an MPAJA leaflet in Jawi agreed to desert to the guerrillas on a given night. True to their promise, the Malays set fire to the police station and decamped, complete with rifles, but the MPAJA commander treated them shabbily. She comments: "They [the Malays] very much resented what they considered to be their degradation, and when I saw one of them at the plantation they complained bitterly about their treatment, and considered that they had been robbed, instead of rewarded for their gallantry." See Thatcher and Cross, *Pai Naa*, pp. 165–6.

Malayan independence.* Ibrahim promised to bring his volunteer army over to the MPAJA's side at a later date to be agreed upon, and in the meantime would try to ensure that his army avoid any further military engagements with the MPAJA guerrillas.[42] The agreement was put to the test in July 1944 when the Japanese moved the volunteer army for operations in the Ipoh area where the MPAJA's Fifth Independent Regiment was known to be active. Because no skirmishes occurred between the Malay volunteers and the MPAJA in the area, the Japanese became suspicious. The army was recalled to its headquarters in Singapore, its components broken up and attached to various Japanese units. Ibrahim became general adviser to the army in October and then was made a colonel, but his power was taken away.[43]

If Ibrahim's story is true, there is contrary evidence that the understanding between the two sides was ineffective. Probably some time after the understanding, a serious military engagement occurred between the two forces in the Kota Tinggi area of Johor, in which 25 MPAJA guerrillas were killed. Shortly after, in the Mersing area (also in Johor), the Malay Giyu Gun clashed again with the MPAJA. In both operations, the Malay volunteers were under Japanese command.[44] Two Malay volunteers who took part in both operations said they discovered subsequently from one of their senior officers that there had been an agreement with the MCP/MPAJA, but apparently it had been difficult for Lt.-Col. Ibrahim to observe it strictly in defiance of instructions of the Japanese commanders. If the Japanese had found out about their secret understanding, they said, Ibrahim would have lost his life and the Malay Giyu Gun would have been disbanded. They also revealed that the shift to Ipoh, reported by Ibrahim, in fact led to the collapse of the "understanding". The MCP/MPAJA contacts in Ipoh were reported to have asked the Malay Giyu Gun for information on its future movements and the disposition of certain Japanese forces, but the Malay Giyu Gun

---

* The contacts were said to have been established through Sutan Djenain, an Indonesian communist resident in Malaya, on behalf of the KMM. Liaison was maintained with Tan Mai Sang, said to be a commander of an MPAJA unit in Johor, who in turn was in touch with MCP secretary-general Lai Tek, and "the Singapore branch headquarters of the MPAJA" (though no such branch is known to have existed) through "Lo Thiam Po and his friends" (the man's identity is not known). See Ibrahim Yaacob, *Sekitar Malaya Merdeka* [Concerning Malayan independence] (Jakarta: Kesatuan Malaya Merdeka, 1957), p. 32.

officers were afraid to give the information in case the Japanese found out.[45] These incidents may have helped to increase the MCP/MPAJA's distrust of Malays.

When the Japanese surrender was announced in the midst of the inter-racial clashes in Johor, Chin Peng in his autobiography, reveals that contacts between the MCP/MPAJA and a 280-strong unit of the Malay Giyu Gun did take place in Muar (Johor state), on 21 August 1945. The initiative had come first from the Japanese, and then from the Giyu Gun, both asking for cooperation, to fight the returning British but the MCP rejected both offers:

> The Malays made their position quite clear. If we were willing to go ahead and continue the fight against the British they were willing to join us. It was this issue that had spurred the heated debate within the Party's North Johore Committee [whether to accept Japanese cooperation]. Perhaps fortuitously, perhaps not, Lai Tek's directive [not to fight the British] settled matters and the anticipated union of Chinese, Malay and Japanese forces against Britain came to naught. The Giyu Gun force had then to dissolve. A number of its leaders, knowing full well that the British would haul them before war crimes courts, decided to flee to the Dutch East Indies — Indonesia.[46]

By the closing stages of the war, it may be said that the MPAJA had disguised its distrust of Malays by advocating the theme of multiracial unity, but without actually putting much faith in real mutual cooperation with Malays. Its attitude and the attitude of most Chinese might be paraphrased as, "We can be victorious in our resistance struggle without the support of the Malays. We have done without them so far, we can continue to do so without them." As far as is known, the MCP did not issue any statement before or during the war on language or ethnic policy or on ethnic representation in any future communist government.[*]

---

[*] Lt.-Col. Ibrahim Yaacob, commander of the Malay Giyu Gun, however, has described the objective of the MCP/MPAJA programme as "the establishment of a Malayan Democratic Government under a leadership comprising seven Malays, five Chinese, three Indians, and one representative of other races". See his *Sekitar Malaya Merdeka*, p. 32. Ibrahim cites no MCP source. It can only be surmised that an MCP supporter had given this as one possible way in which the MCP would form a government. But no such details have been spelt out in MCP statements.

The MPAJA and Force 136

On 24 May 1943 the first Force 136 reconnaissance party, consisting of Col. John Davis and five Chinese agents, arrived in a submarine off the Perak coast and landed in Malaya. This operation was code-named Gustavus I. Other groups were introduced in the same manner, in operations Gustavus II, III, and IV, the last taking place on 12 September 1943.[47] Besides Davis, the other officers were Capt. Richard Broome and Maj. Lim Bo Seng, a Malayan KMT member and agent of the Chinese government in Chungking. Their subordinate staff was all KMT Chinese trained in wireless operations and intelligence work. Force 136 was attempting to set up its own intelligence service by using KMT agents. This is evident because only after the KMT agents had been established in cover jobs in Ipoh was contact made on 30 September with Chin Peng, representative of the Perak MPAJA headquarters.[48]

On 1 January 1944 Lai Tek and Chin Peng, both representing the MCP, MPAJU, and MPAJA, arrived at the Force 136 camp and held talks with the three Force 136 officers, who had now been joined by Maj. F.S. Chapman, a member of one of the original "stay-behind" teams left in Malaya after the fall of Singapore and who was co-opted into the Force 136 team. The three Force 136 officers described themselves as representatives of Admiral Mountbatten, the British Supreme Allied Commander for Southeast Asia. It was agreed that in return for arms, money, training, and supplies the MPAJA would cooperate with and accept the British Army's orders during the war with Japan and in the period of military occupation thereafter. The British also agreed to finance the MPAJA with 150 taels of gold (about £3,000 sterling a month) and instructed that all arms would have to be handed back after the Japanese defeat.[49] The policy of SEAC, which controlled Force 136, was to arm the guerrillas, place them under the control of British officers, and prepare them for the time of an Allied invasion. Political matters were excluded from the agreement. Both sides agreed that no question of post-war policy would be discussed.

News of the agreement, however, did not reach SEAC until a year later. This was due to the loss of wireless sets and the inability of the Force 136 officers to keep several rendezvous dates with British submarines.[50] It was not until 1 February 1945 that the terms of the agreement were transmitted to SEAC, and on 26 February another Force 136 party was parachuted in to join Davis. On 17 March a second meeting was held with two MCP representatives, at which the terms of the agreement were reaffirmed.

Once the MCP had committed itself to place the MPAJA under SEAC, SEAC decided to ensure that the MCP did not repudiate the agreement. This meant that SEAC had to retain some control of the MPAJA guerrillas through Force 136 officers — a difficult but not impossible task — while keeping its part of the bargain to supply funds, arms, and stores to the MPAJA. From February 1945, the Force 136 officers kept SEAC informed on the MPAJA's activities.[51] An over-generous Force 136 estimate in May 1945 gave the MPAJA strength as not less than 10,000 and that they were organized into eight semi-independent groups, of which only five had contact with Force 136. SEAC therefore decided to send in more Force 136 staff and devised four additional means of contact and control: (1) a British liaison team under Davis would be attached to Central MPAJA Headquarters in Perak; (2) Group Liaison Officers (GLOs), each a lieutenant-colonel, would be attached to each regimental headquarters of the MPAJA (except Pahang which had no contact with Force 136 at all and it was decided, for strategic reasons, to leave it alone); (3) each GLO would have five Patrol Liaison Officers (PLOs), with a major's rank, under him attached to each of the five MPAJA patrols; (4) 13 Gurkha support groups (each of 19 men) would be infiltrated to support MPAJA and other guerrilla forces in strategic areas.*

But the MCP was not unaware of British motives. SEAC was told that MPAJA Central Headquarters in Perak was unwilling to have any British officer in their camp. Central was determined to preserve the secrecy of its whereabouts and the composition of its staff. It also wanted to guard against any possible British retaliation in the event of an outbreak of hostilities with the British after the war. However, Central did agree to allow Force 136 staff into the other MPAJA camps and appointed a CEC member of the MCP to stay with Davis and his group. He was Chin Peng, who had organized the meeting, which led to the SEAC-MCP agreement. Davis was agreeable to the arrangement because he had been able to work well with Chin Peng. Force 136 officers did not command the

---

* In the end, only six Gurkha support groups were parachuted into Malaya before the Japanese surrender.

MPAJA patrols, but it was agreed they should have "tactical command" during operations. Their influence over the MPAJA was strong
in military matters but weak in political matters. By 13 August 1945,
there were at least 80 Force 136 senior and subordinate officers
liaising with the MPAJA and other resistance movements and communicating with SEAC headquarters in Ceylon through about 40
wireless telecommunications sets.[52]

Opposing Resistance Movements

Until shortly before Mountbatten's troops landed in Malaya, all the
guerrilla groups, including the MPAJA, wore no Allied uniforms and
not all carried weapons. The only readily available source of new
arms during the latter part of the Japanese occupation was Force 136
and it only supplied 2,000 weapons.[*] If they required more arms,
the resistance movements had to raid the police stations or Japanese
military installations.

The Japanese saw the MPAJA and the KMT movements as one
and the same army, the Chinese Resistance Forces, and regarded
them all as "communist bandits".[53] Because the guerrillas operated
locally, it is doubtful if there was much confusion among the local
population as to their political affiliations. At the end of the war,
when the Force 136-"controlled" guerrillas were supplied with Allied
green uniforms, the MPAJA and KMT resistance forces distinguished
themselves from one another by the number of stars worn on their
five-cornered service caps. Chungking KMT agents and the KMT
"Overseas Chinese Anti-Japanese Army" (OCAJA) in Perak and
Kelantan wore "one-blue star" caps; the OCAJA was called the One-
Star Army, or Bintang Satu, in Malay. Some KMT guerrillas were

---

[*] A Force 136 memorandum by Lt.-Col. D.G. Gill-Davies, dated 13 Sept. 1945,
Singapore, says that only "2,000 arms" were supplied to the MPAJA up to 13
August 1945 when all arms sorties were cancelled. The earlier target had been
"3,500 armed MPAJA guerrillas", but the Japanese surrender made further arming
unnecessary. See the memorandum in BMA PSD/39. However, O'Ballance,
56, mentions "3,500 arms" as having been parachuted to the MPAJA, while
Clutterbuck, 40, gives the figure of "4,765 arms" as having been supplied to the
MPAJA. Apparently, neither O'Ballance's nor Clutterbuck's figure is accurate.
Though they have not indicated their sources, O'Ballance's figure seems to be
based on the original Force 136 target, while Clutterbuck's figure appears to
be based on the number of weapons handed in by the guerrillas at the time of
demobilization.

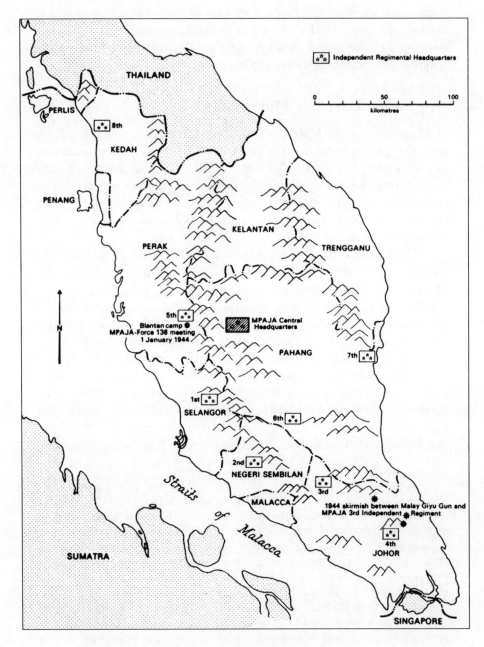

Fig. 3. Locations of the Eight Regiments of the MPAJA

known to wear two stars on their caps, but what these two stars represented is not clear. The MPAJA was known as the Three-Star Army, or Bintang Tiga, the three stars signifying the three major races in Malaya — the Malays, Chinese, and Indians. A Japanese report gave what seemed to be a bewildering picture to the Japanese, but actually revealed a diversity of factions among the guerrillas.[54] Their observations show that, first, there was a mushrooming of armed guerrilla units under the title of "AJA" (Anti-Japanese Armies); second, that the MPAJA troops were identified with "the Chinese Resistance Army"; and third, that there were clashes among the "Chinese Resistance Army" as well as between the various AJAs and the MPAJA.

In a few cases the resistance forces were bound by the common cause of fighting the Japanese and their collaborators; in most cases, they did not cease to make clear their differences by fighting one another. Rivalry between the MPAJA and KMT troops was one instance of opposing guerrilla groups. Chin Kee Onn made out the various guerrilla groups as follows:

> the "Malayan Communists" (more often referred to as "hill people") were composed of four parties: (1) Communists proper, who believed in the ideology of Communism; (2) Kuomintang members who were just anti-Japanese; (3) outraged farmers and townsfolk, who desired nothing but revenge; and (4) bandits who enlisted to see what could be got out of the adventure.[55]

Giving the best overview of the diversity of the guerrilla forces during the Japanese occupation, pro-KMT writers N.I. Low and H.M. Cheng observed that "many thousands of guerrillas remained outside the ranks of Force 136; in other words, that the resistance movement was a large circle which included in it a much smaller circle — Force 136 — and that the two were not exactly coincident".[56]

The KMT Guerrillas

Three armed groups of KMT guerrillas, totalling about 400, operated loosely in north Malaya under the name of the Overseas Chinese Anti-Japanese Army (OCAJA). Their leader was Lee Fong Sam, a reputed gunman who operated on either side of the Malay-Thai border. The respective strengths and locations of the groups were reported to be as follows: (1) about 100 armed men encamped in the jungle on the Thai-Kelantan border; (2) another group of 100 armed men on the Thai-Perak border; and (3) 200 scattered guerrillas along the line of the east coast railway between Krai and Merapoh in Kelantan.[57]

British military intelligence in 1945 thought that these guerrillas had assumed a connection with the KMT more as a fiery cross than for ideological reasons. But in 1948 after raids for documents were conducted on various Chinese premises in Lenggong (Perak), British police established that the guerrilla bands had either been formed by the KMT party in Malaya or by the KMT government in China. The guerrillas were mainly Kwongsais (from Kwangsi province in China), who wished to resist the Japanese invader and who were organized into several guerrilla bands under the leadership of Lee Fong Sam and his assistants who swore allegiance to Chungking. They were referred to as KMT guerrillas by Force 136, which had contacts with the two groups at the Thai-Kelantan and Thai-Perak borders, and which hoped to influence them and to prevent any premature flare-up with Japanese forces in Thai territory before the Allied landing. Force 136 armed none of the three groups of KMT, though they did receive supplies.[58]

Hostility developed between MPAJA groups and these KMT guerrillas. The former regarded the KMT guerrillas as bandits who resorted to looting, extortion, and intimidation of the local population; and the KMT guerrillas considered the MPAJA as communists to whom they were politically opposed. The KMT groups in upper Perak under Lee's assistants, Hong Chee and Tai Man, clashed several times with MPAJA guerrillas who had attacked their camps near Grik and Lenggong. Force 136 officers initially tended to side with whichever group they were in contact with. But higher echelons finally intervened and stopped the fighting.[59] Similarly, in Kelantan MPAJA and KMT groups fought each other in the Krai-Merapoh area. Both sides suffered heavy casualties. Malay villagers were often executed or had their houses burnt down when suspected by one side of helping the other. Force 136 finally forced Lee Fong Sam to withdraw his men from the affected area, and MPAJA guerrillas based in the Merapoh area were withdrawn to Perak. The MPAJA group withdrew only when Force 136 threatened to cut off arms and supplies if it refused. However, the trouble did not stop. Whenever armed MPAJA and KMT guerrillas were in the same area, fighting broke out.

Like the MPAJA groups, the OCAJA groups were equally distrustful of Malays. In early 1943 the OCAJA sacked and burnt Kampong Temengor in upper Perak not far from their Lenggong base. One Malay account, which clearly identifies it as the "One-Star Army", describes the incident as a massacre in which about 80 Malay villagers, including women, children, and the aged, were reported killed. Ten Malays were taken prisoner, seven of whom were subsequently released and put to work on the OCAJA farms at Sungai Kepayang.[60] No reason for the attack is given, but it was probably in retaliation for the *kampung* supporting a Japanese raid on a Chinese settlement in Lenggong (see footnote on p. 71).

The Malay Guerrillas

The total armed Malay guerrilla strength never exceeded 500. The first British Force 136 party to contact the Malays was dropped by parachute into north Perak in December 1944 and was led by Lt.-Col. (then Major) Dobree. He found the Malays in that area only too enthusiastic to take up arms against the Japanese and had to discourage many from joining him. He started arming and training small sections and gave them the name Askar Melayu Setia (AMS) or the Loyal Malay Army. In Pahang, Maj. J.D. Richardson was able to contact a Malay district officer, Yeop Mahidin, who secretly set up the Tentera Wataniah (Fatherland Patriotic Army) for raising and training Malays with their own officers with the borrowed authority of "Sir Abu Bakar, Sultan of Pahang".[61] It was to be the great regret of the British that their scheme to recruit and organize a resistance force among the Malays was started belatedly at the closing stages of the war. It appears that initially the British were rather reluctant to encourage their development. As Aziz and Silcock have observed, the history of post-war Malaya would have been very different had the British created more Malay guerrilla forces than Chinese guerrilla forces to fight the Japanese.[62] However, many Malays were on the side of the British during the war. Among those who worked with SEAC were Mohamed Suffian bin Hashim (Malaysia's ex-Lord President) and Tan Sri General Ibrahim bin Ismail (former Chief of the Armed Forces Staff in Malaysia). Chapman[63] reported that there was a plan to organize a Malay resistance force, although he thought that the Malays with their freedom of movement in the country were more valuable "for collecting information than actual fighting, especially as their security was not very good".* Despite the British distrust of the Malays, Force 136 officers obtained good support from the two resistance forces, which they belatedly raised and trained. According to O'Ballance, the MPAJA took the field against the units of the Askar Melayu Setia in north Perak and Kedah, while it clashed with those of the KMT guerrillas near the Siamese border, and succeeded in breaking them up. In west Johor there were also clashes between the MPAJA and armed groups of Malays. However, the Malay account of Askar Melayu Setia mentions no such clashes with the MPAJA.[64] There was little or no liaison between the MPAJA and the Malay guerrillas.

The Ho Pi Tui (Reserves), Chinese Secret Societies, and Personal Resistance

One way for recruiting manpower for the MPAJU was to raise volunteer units known as the Ho Pi Tui (Reserves) in every village, town, and district. These volunteers were mostly Chinese, with a sprinkling of Indians and Malays. They did not leave their local areas until they were called up by the MPAJA. Not all the Ho Pi Tui came under the command of party members. Some were left under the command of respected village elders, secret society chiefs, and trusted KMT officials who were to use the volunteers as a "self-defence" force to safeguard their homes and villages. Instead, many of these Ho Pi Tui, owing to lack of stringent supervision by the Party, degenerated into gangs of robbers and bandits, given to rape, looting, and terrorism.†

---

* The reason was that the British were generally doubtful about the loyalty of the Malays whom they believed to be favourably disposed towards the Japanese. About 150 Malay members of KMM and their leader Ibrahim Yaacob were rounded up and imprisoned by the British just before the fall of Singapore on charges of working with the Japanese. Moreover, it should be remembered that all the Sultans refused to listen to British requests to retreat to India or Australia. See Chapter 2.

† R. Balan, a former MPAJA leader of Indian origin, is the source of information on the Ho Pi Tui. Interview, Kuala Lumpur, 2 Apr. 1973. Chinese-speaking Balan joined the MPAJA in the jungle in 1942 and while there, worked in the propaganda section of the MCP, editing the Tamil newssheets. The MCP leadership displayed a great deal of trust and confidence in him and before long had accepted him into the party as a member. After the war, Balan became the party's key activist in the estate labour unions. He was elected into the MCP's central committee in 1947, after he had attended the Empire Conference of Communist Parties in London with two other MCP representatives (Wu Tien Wang and

There were two other types of resistance groups. One type consisted of small roving bandit gangs of all races, which operated during the occupation. They were armed with weapons picked up during the war or bought from others who had done so. They would include the Chinese criminal gangs or secret societies known variously as Samseng Tong, or Hong Mun, specializing in "protection" rackets. Some of these gangs were converted by the MPAJA and joined the Ho Pi Tui. However, most continued to exist on their own, claiming to be "Anti-Japanese forces", MPAJA or KMT in whatever manner suited their best interests at the time.[65] In Perak the most notorious bandit gang was the Kwangsai group led by Hong Chee, who was a member of the KMT resistance force, the OCAJA. These bandit gangs gave both the MPAJA and the KMT a very bad name.

The other type of secret society was one formed by individuals or groups for the purposes of self-protection, or to carry out their own forms of resistance against the Japanese. One was that of the Sikh, Gurchan Singh, a former policeman who operated under the name "Singa" ("Lion" in Malay). He and three friends operated an independent resistance group, which succeeded in carrying out intelligence work and sabotage of Japanese communications and installations in various parts of the country. Another was the Eurasian woman Sybil Karthigasu who, with her doctor-husband, treated wounded guerrillas, was arrested, and endured Japanese torture.[66]

The MCP between 1942 and 1945: Lai Tek as Kempeitai Agent

Lai Tek's arrest by the Japanese Kempeitai and his work as their agent was to cause great harm to the MCP's organization. An attempt will be made to piece together his wartime dealings with the Japanese, a little-known aspect of events in this period. But first it should be disclosed that this was not the first time he had worked with the

---

Rashid Maidin). While involved in an estate labour strike in June 1948, Balan was arrested and detained. He remained in detention throughout the period of the Emergency until his release in 1961 (13 years). In 1955, while still in detention, Balan was elected vice-president of the MCP's central committee. At the time of our interview he was 60 years old and in poor health. Anthony Short describes Balan as one of the most skilful and successful communist union organizers, who, when he was arrested, was within six hours of taking to the jungle. Short, *The Communist Insurrection in Malaya*, pp. 60, 66, 92.

police. Lai Tek's long and chequered career as a secret agent began, according to Malaysian government sources, long before the war when he served first as an agent of the Russians (Comintern) and then the French. In 1934 or 1935 a British officer recruited him in Hong Kong to work for the Singapore Special Branch.[67] A Chinese-speaking Vietnamese, Lai Tek, had infiltrated the Indochinese Communist Party (ICP), while working as an informant of the Surete (French Intelligence). But his cover was "blown" and he was passed on to the British. He arrived in Singapore with a "dazzling reputation": He was said to have been a representative of the Third International; had studied communism in Russia and France; had assisted the ICP in its early struggles; and had served on the Shanghai Town Committee of the China Communist Party.[68] He spoke French as well as English.[69] His entry into the MCP's top hierarchy was facilitated by the party's crisis of 1936.

According to a war-time Japanese military source, Lai Tek was introduced to the party as a trouble-shooter and Comintern liaison chief in Hong Kong who had been ordered to visit Malaya to deal with the MCP's crisis.[70] He impressed everyone in the party with his alleged Comintern credentials and his organizational ability. He was said to have resolved the party crisis during an intensive six-month "offensive against the opportunists". Wu Tien Wang records that Lai Tek directed the major portion of the purge, restoring the "ideological unity within the party" and wiping out the "last remnants of incorrect inclinations". After this, Lai Tek emerged "the beloved leader of the party".[71] His appearance coincided with a series of demonstrations and strikes, which the MCP organized throughout the country to exploit labour grievances.[72] The most spectacular strike was at the Batu Arang coalmines in March 1937, during which communist-led workers established a short-lived "Soviet" government. Lai Tek was said to have played a prominent role in the formation of strike committees. His claim to leadership would subsequently rest on this performance. At the MCP's Sixth Enlarged Plenum in April 1938 he was elected secretary-general, a post he held for ten years before party leaders unmasked him in 1947.[*]

---

[*] Lai Tek is said to have remained in hiding in Singapore until August 1947 when he went to Hong Kong. From here he went to Thailand and an intercepted MCP message subsequently reported that he had been eliminated. His death, however, has never been officially confirmed. Short, *The Communist Insurrection in Malaya*, p. 41n.

The Kempeitai in Singapore arrested Lai Tek in early March 1942. He was then known as Wong Kim Gyock (or Giok), one of his many aliases. There are several versions of how he was arrested. According to a Japanese source he was "easily found by the Kempeitai because he was sending wireless transmission".[73] A British Special Branch source, however, claims that Lai Tek was pointed out to the Japanese by former Chinese detectives of the Singapore Special Branch. The conclusion was that it was difficult for him not to betray the MCP as he was really an "imperialist" agent and, to save his own life, he cooperated with the Japanese Kempeitai throughout the occupation.[74]

Maj. R.J. Isaacs, formerly of SEAC headquarters, who got the story out of Maj. Sartoru Onishi of the Kempeitai, gave another account of his arrest.[75] It was reported that on 26 March 1942 Sgt. Mitsuo Nakayama, with the assistance of a Malay and a Chinese, arrested a person known as Wong Show Tong. He was taken to Kempeitai headquarters where he admitted that he was an executive member of the MCP. The information he gave impressed Major Onishi and orders were given that he should be treated well, given good food, cigarettes, and special accommodation. In a matter of weeks "Wong Show Tong" and Onishi were on very good terms. One day, to Onishi's surprise, "Wong Show Tong" confessed that he was in fact Wong Kim Gyock, the secretary of the MCP, that there was no such thing as a central committee and that he in fact was in a position to order and direct the whole of the communist activities on Singapore island and on the mainland of Malaya.[76]

Through interpreter Lee Yem Kong, a former photographer in Johor, Onishi and "Wong Kim Gyock" struck a bargain. They agreed that Lai Tek would give the names of the MCP's top executives and gather them in one place where the Japanese could liquidate them. In return, Lai Tek's life would be spared and he could earn a considerable sum of money. Towards the end of April he walked out of Kempeitai headquarters "a free man with a bundle of dollars in his pocket".[77] Contact was thereafter to be established at a certain cafe in Orchard Road, or Lai Tek would call on his bicycle at the home of Lee Yem Kong, who acted as interpreter for Warrant Officer Shimomura, the man present to receive all information. As one Japanese writer recalled the agreement:

> So he agreed and accepted the *Kempeitai's* offer. And he promised to work for the *Kempeitai* by supplying them with information. He told the *Kempeitai* they must keep everything top secret so

he could continue to maintain contacts with all quarters; if they [the Party] knew he had been arrested by the *Kempeitai* then all communications will be cut, then he will have no more information. He proposed to the *Kempeitai* that they should only appoint two of their staff to have contacts with him ....[78]

Consequently, the arrest of Lai Tek and his employment as an agent was a well-kept secret within the Kempeitai itself. Only four people in the Kempeitai were said to have known of Lai Tek's capture — Col. Oiishi, the head of the Kempeitai; Maj. Sartoru Onishi, his second-in-command; and two junior individuals, Warrant Officer Shimomura and Sgt. Yamaguchi, detailed to keep in close touch with Lai Tek and to collect information which he passed to them.[79] Lai Tek had been taken into custody with his whole family. Apparently the Kempeitai kept a hold on some family members to ensure his compliance or threatened to betray his collaborating activities to the MCP if he failed to perform properly. His wife had a shop in Singapore but he himself was said to be constantly changing his address.[80]

In making the bargain with Onishi, Lai Tek was mainly motivated by personal gain. If his pre-war pattern of cooperation with the British authorities were any guide, Lai Tek would demonstrate once again that he had no scruples about sacrificing party members and officials to serve his personal interests. He had been intelligent enough not to reveal all that he knew, or all that the British authorities wanted to know about the Communist Party. This was evident by the fact that the MCP continued to be a main source of unrest between 1936 and 1941, when Lai Tek was known to be working as a police informant. Lai Tek was shrewd enough to realize that if he disclosed everything to the government it would destroy the party organization completely, end what had been a perennial source of trouble to the government, and lead the police to dispense with his services as an informant. To Lai Tek the MCP, the British, and the Japanese were merely different means for serving his own ends. In his dealings with the Kempeitai Lai Tek was to show again that he would scrupulously fulfill his part of the bargain — and give away little else.

MCP officials in Singapore, in fact, knew about the arrest of Lai Tek. In the wake of the Japanese *sook chings*, the story which circulated within the party then was that Lai Tek had been seen being picked up by the Japanese some time in March while he was riding on his red bicycle. He was suspected as a KMT cadre, and when the Japanese found out that he was innocent, he was released.* The communists apparently did not want to believe that the arrest was the end of their secretary-general! At that time members of the Singapore Town Committee congratulated themselves on their luck

---

* This was revealed by Ng Yeh Lu, a former Singapore Town Committee member of the MCP who was captured by the Japanese in April 1942, in his statement "How MCP Central's Secretary General Lai Tek slaughtered KMT, MCP and Allied Forces cadres. To all people who love and protect the MCP and wish to uphold justice" (Ma-kung chung-yang tsung-shu-chi Lai T'e ju-ho sha-hai kuo-kung liangtang chi lien-chun kan-pu kei yi-ch'ieh ai-hu Ma'kung yuan-hi ch-t'ai kung-tao-ti jen-men), in *Kuo ji shi pao* (International Times), Singapore, July/Aug. 1968, pp. 20–8. Ng Yeh Lu was the pseudonym of Wee Mong Chen, who would later serve as Singapore's ambassador to Japan from 1973 to 1980. See Chin Peng, *My Side of History*, p.119. For more biographical details of Ng Yeh Lu, see also C.F. Yong, *The Origins of Malayan Communism*, pp. 186–8. His denunciation of Lai Tek is believed to have appeared first in a Penang Chinese newspaper (name unknown) in September 1945, but the story was regarded by the MCP as incredible and initially dismissed as the fabrication of a former Kempeitai agent. Yeh Lu had, in fact, worked as a translator for the Kempeitai and he was released in 1943 after a year's detention. It was while working for the Kempeitai that he discovered that it had been his highly respected party leader Lai Tek who had betrayed him and other MCP officials. Yeh Lu claims in his statement that his own conscience was clear, as he did not betray any MCP member during his work for the Kempeitai. He was moved to write the statement to reveal the "truth" to the party to help it get rid of the "poisonous" Lai Tek who was still in office and enjoying still greater influence after the war. The statement was published by *Kuo ju shi pao* for purposes of historical record, as the editor claims in his preface that Yeh Lu had given the statement to him in 1945 at the end of the war. Yeh Lu had also contacted the British police officer, A.E.G. Blades (who later became Commissioner of Police in Singapore), in an attempt to get the British to detain Lai Tek. Blades, however, advised Yeh Lu to leave the matter in police hands. Soon after this meeting, the editor said, instead of punishing Lai Tek for his betrayal of Lim Bo Seng and other Allied personnel, the British continued to use Lai Tek to control the MCP. See the editor's preface, "Wo sou chi dao de Lai T'e yu Yeh Lu" [What I know about Lai Tek and Yeh Lu], *Kuo ji shi pao*. The newspaper's editor, Chuang Hui-tsuan, was a former KMT member and a close friend of the late Lim Bo Seng. Anthony Short in his *The Communist Insurrection in Malaya*, pp. 38–9, refers to Yeh Lu's denunciation, although he does not mention Yeh Lu's name or the name of the Penang newspaper, which published it. In a personal communication, dated 23 May 1978, Short confirms that the former Malaysian Commissioner of Police, the late Sir Claude Fenner, had told him that it was Ng Yeh Lu who had written the Penang article exposing Lai Tek. See also Harry Miller, *Menace in Malaya* (London, 1954), p. 62.

because of his release. The personality cult surrounding Lai Tek had been built up during the last days before Singapore fell into Japanese hands. Banners had been hoisted outside the Singapore MCP head-quarters proclaiming, "Support our able leader Lai T'e" and "Lai T'e the most loyal disciple of Stalin". MCP cadres strongly believed that if only Lai Tek could survive the future of the MCP would be bright.[81] Such faith blinded party officials to any possibility that he could betray them and made them loyal to him. Ironically, most of the officials in the Singapore Town Committee who rejoiced at Lai Tek's release were shortly to be betrayed by him to the Japanese by being killed or imprisoned. Ng Yeh Lu, one of the imprisoned Singapore Town Committee, was to reflect with some insight at the end of the war:

> When we think back we begin to understand what happened in March 1942. Then we realise that whenever the Japanese arrested a person, there was little possibility of releasing that person, whether he was innocent or not. That is the evidence that Lai Tek had already collaborated with the Japanese at that time.[82]

When communists imprisoned in Singapore discovered Lai Tek's connections with the Kempeitai, at least two known attempts were made to pass the information to the party outside. Each time, how-ever, Lai Tek succeeded in neutralizing their actions. After July 1943, a Singapore Central Committee member named Li Ying Kang made the discovery and managed to pass a message to party comrades outside the prison. Curiously, the word got back to Lai Tek who then deviously contrived his release. When Li re-established con-tacts with the party, his story was disbelieved and his integrity was questioned. He failed to get a pardon from the party and was buried alive in Jurong (Singapore). In April 1944 another released com-munist, Ah Ling, of the Singapore Town Committee, attempted to pass a message to party officials, but he was executed in Johor Bharu, apparently as a traitor to the party.[83] In most cases Lai Tek and the Kempeitai ingeniously used released communists as scapegoats, so that the party would suspect these former detainees as having betrayed the party.

Japanese sources confirm that Lai Tek was responsible for the arrest or elimination of the MCP's entire pre-war Central Executive Committee throughout Malaya and the break-up of the whole com-munist network in Singapore by April 1943.[84] The betrayals began in May when he revealed the identities of the Singapore Town Committee members who were subsequently arrested or killed in Japanese raids on their homes or meeting places. This was followed by further arrests in July in Johor when he exposed the Johor State Committee. He then moved to Negeri Sembilan, Malacca, and Selangor, passing on details to the Kempeitai each time he made contact with the MCP committees.[85]

The MCP's Central Executive Committee, before their elimination, succeeded in convening a meeting on 30 May 1942. Apparently Lai Tek attended the meeting, which carried out an "analysis of the present political situation". The committee's conclusion was that the anti-Japanese struggle was for the national liberation of Malaya, and should thus be extended to prevent the Americans or the British from returning to rule Malaya. The anti-Japanese struggle had to be coordinated with favourable international conditions, especially the victory of Soviet Russia. More importantly, the committee stressed that the party should rely on its own strength and on the strength of the Malayan people to coordinate its counter-offensive with those of the Allied powers. "The future of Malaya should be decided by the people themselves and by the strength of the party", the committee declared.[86] This decision meant the party would launch an all-out struggle against both the Japanese and the British, and take advantage of any opportunity to seize power.

However, in August 1942 Lai Tek began a plot to liquidate the CEC. Through the Selangor State Committee leader, So Chun, he arranged to attend a full meeting of the CEC, state party officials, and group leaders of the MPAJA at the Batu Caves, about ten miles from Kuala Lumpur. The meeting was to review the party's political and military struggle. Lai Tek relayed information on the meeting to Onishi, who took personal charge of the initial investigation. The Batu Caves is a popular holiday picnic area. Taking advantage of this fact, one or two Sundays before the fateful day some Japanese soldiers were seen frolicking and picnicking in the area with cabaret girls. Outwardly they seemed just ordinary soldiers, but in fact they were Kempeitai officers in disguise. They were surveying the area and collecting information for Onishi.[87]

Lai Tek had called the party meeting in a small village near the caves. On the last day of August, a large number of Japanese troops moved into position.[88] At daybreak of 1 September, as the group leaders, CEC members, and their bodyguards were resting in the village, the Japanese attacked. The battle was reported to be fierce, but when it ended 29 party officials, including four MPAJA "Political Commissars" and their bodyguards were dead, 15 were arrested, and only a handful managed to escape.[89] Chapman narrates how a girl guerrilla was the heroine of the clash: "While the men made their escape a girl gave them covering fire with a Tommy gun until she herself was shot."[90] Japanese casualties were one NCO killed and three soldiers injured. Machine guns, automatic rifles, and grenades were recovered and several printing presses seized.[91]

Those who escaped immediately went into conference to review the situation, to count their dead, and to wonder who had betrayed them. One thing gladdened their hearts. Lai Tek, the secretary general, had not arrived and was therefore safe. Lai Tek, in fact, "was sitting peacefully and contentedly in his own home in Singapore".[92] Subsequently, the Japanese Kempeitai threw a reception to celebrate the event. As Isaacs related the occasion:

> … the *Kempeitai* in Kuala Lumpur were toasting Major Onishi who supplied the information obtained in Singapore. If you had been in Major Onishi's private rooms, you would have been astonished for Onishi was toasting none other than the leader of the MCP, Lai Tek himself.[93]

Some time after 1944, Major Onishi wrote briefly in the Kempeitai magazine an account of how to make use of counter-spies. "It is an interesting but dirty story — distrust, double-cross, selling your friends, covering up yourself", recalls a Japanese writer.[94]

When he met party officials later, Lai Tek consoled them. He said that the party's losses meant that everyone would have to work harder. He told them the car, which he was using to come up from Singapore, had broken down.* The MCP set down 1 September as the date on which they would commemorate each year the "martyrs" who had lost their lives at the Batu Caves. After this incident communist activities in the urban centres of Malaya were temporarily at a standstill. There is a theory that Lai Tek's reason for betraying the CEC and State group leaders to the Kempeitai was to purge the party of those who were getting too strong and were liable to wrest

---

* Isaacs' report, *Malay Mail*, 31 Aug. 1953, claims that Lai Tek was in Singapore when the incident at the Batu Caves occurred. However, Anthony Short, in *The Communist Insurrection in Malaya*, p. 20, says that Lai Tek was then known to be in Kuala Lumpur, not far from the Batu Caves.

control from him. However, in view of the bargain, which Lai Tek had struck with Maj. Onishi, this theory is purely speculative.[95]

In October some of the remaining CEC members arrived in Singapore to revive the Singapore Town Committee. They set up a secret organization known as the Self-Defence Corps, which published a periodical called *Self-Defence Monthly* and tried to recruit new members, to reorganize the Singapore Committee's branches, and to raise morale. But on 19 December, after a tip-off from Lai Tek, the Kempeitai raided the meeting place and eliminated these officers. After this raid the Kempeitai was alerted for further MCP action, as this December 1942 report shows:

> The MCP is suffering from the numerous arrests and scarcity of food. Their economic difficulties are increasing all the time. It may not be easy for them to re-establish the MCP again. However, as has been seen in the past, remaining communists will reorganise the party. We should not relax and allow them to do so.
>
> According to the information we have received, the measures the communists are likely to take are: (a) to strengthen unity among the party and armed units; (b) to intensify political and military training of members; and (c) to obtain money from people and sympathizers, based on their cultural propaganda.... We must take the initiative to eliminate the MCP vigorously at this time it is declining.[96]

In February 1943 Lai Tek reportedly convened a meeting of the "rump" CEC, which, comprised three remaining members including Lai Tek. It adopted a nine-point programme, the first objective of which was to expel the "Japanese Fascists" from Malaya and to establish a "Malayan Democratic Republic".[97] The other aims of the programme included an elected "national government", the establishment of democracy, improvement of the people's livelihood, free education in all languages, and absorption of the Anti-Japanese Army into a national army. The party would combine with Soviet Russia and China to support "the struggles for independence of the oppressed nations in the Far East", as well as join with the Japanese people "to fight against Fascism".[98]

By April 1943 none of the Central Committee members who were elected into office during the sixth and seventh expanded conferences of the CEC was left except Lai Tek.[99] From January to April 1943 the Kempeitai continued to carry out raids and arrests in Singapore to disrupt attempts made to reorganize the Singapore

Town Committee. Either the communists were not reading the danger signs clearly or they were provoked by Lai Tek to show themselves. In January 1943, seven Singapore Town Committee members were arrested. A few days later, five more were picked up. MCP officials tried to revive activities again in April, and this time 11 MCP members were arrested. In each of these incidents Lai Tek was said to have informed the Kempeitai, providing the number of persons involved, their names, the time and place of the meeting. After this raid communist activities in Singapore were reported to have ceased completely.[100]

The Kempeitai's successful operations began to raise suspicions about traitors within the party and led to several purges. The Fifth Independent Regiment of the MPAJA in Perak formed mobile "killer squads" to hunt down suspected party traitors and police informers. In August 1943 their Ipoh killer squad succeeded in killing 24 informers and detectives. Onishi recalls that these counter-intelligence operations were so successful that he told Lai Tek to lie low for a while.[101]

Despite these MPAJA efforts, Lai Tek's contacts with the Kempeitai were not discovered. His position in the MCP remained unchallenged. In fact, after April 1943, there was neither a proper central committee nor politburo. Lai Tek now ran the party single-handed. He made all the decisions himself and consulted only those whom he trusted. He kept his movements secret, and maintained contacts only with certain key elements in the MCP and MPAJA network. He did not seem to care very much for the MPAJU. His contacts regularly reported area activities to him. The fact that he kept the MPAJA organization intact and operational and a number of the party's state and district committee officials loyal to him alive suggests that he had his own plans for the communist movement. Onishi indicates that only when the British interrogated him at the end of the war did he come to know that Lai Tek had held back a great deal of information from him. Onishi gave this interpretation of Lai Tek's conduct:

> ... he [Lai Tek] was far-sighted. He realized that Japan would not win the war; therefore he did nothing to damage the real war effort as he was looking forward to his future as dictator of the Malayan Communist Party.[102]

This was an *ex post facto* conclusion, which Onishi made under British interrogation. It was probably meant as a warning to the

British of the danger, which Lai Tek might pose to them. That Lai Tek increased his powers and consolidated his position during the occupation was incidental to his primary and unswerving aim of serving his self-interest.

Lai Tek's system of contacts in mainland Malaya was incredibly open. He travelled with ease, by car on the main roads, and yet this is not known to have aroused party suspicions. Not content with receiving regular reports from MCP couriers at his Singapore base, Lai Tek visited Perak, Selangor, and north Johor once a month to keep in touch with the more important state leaders. District committee and MPAJA commanders of other states would send messages or representatives to meet him at secret places. He used a Morris 8 H.P. Saloon, bearing the number S4678, property of the Singapore Kempeitai, on his trips. Occasionally his Vietnamese mistress accompanied him. The first place visited was usually Kuala Lumpur, where Lai Tek would stay either at the Coliseum Hotel in Batu Road, or at a Chinese hotel in Jalan Sultan.[103]*

The contact point in Kuala Lumpur was a Chinese sundry goods shop at the corner of Klang Road. It was here that Lai Tek would be informed by his men of the meeting place and would be provided with a guide. The normal venue for meetings with communist leaders was a mill, 12 miles out on the Ipoh Road. Yeung Kuo, the Selangor state secretary, and other communist leaders would then report to him of the situation in other districts.[104]

Perak would be the next place of call, and near Bidor Lai Tek would meet Chin Peng, the Perak state secretary, of whom Lai Tek was extremely fond. Then aged 24, Chin Peng was known as Lai Tek's little boy, and was slowly being groomed by Lai Tek as his second-in-command.[105] In 1943 Lai Tek appointed him a member of the Central Standing Committee, a member of the Military High Command and a representative of the MPAJA to liaise with Force 136 officers. Despite his close association with Lai Tek, Chin Peng appears not to have known of Lai Tek's contacts with the Kempeitai. It was Chin Peng who subsequently played a leading part in the investigations, which unmasked his role as British agent.[106]

---

* In April 1945, Davis, Broome, Chapman, and Col. J.P. Hannah, who had parachuted into Davis' camp, met Lai Tek at a mill nearby. As usual he told the group a story of how he got there in a Japanese car by bribing the driver. Statement of J.P. Hannah to Yap Hong Kuan, p. 67.

Lai Tek's monthly trips to the mainland, during which he discussed party affairs with important communist leaders, lasted two or three days and were carried out with the full knowledge of the Kempeitai. Lai Tek had a special arrangement with the south Johor district committees, which organized secret contacts to deliver to him written messages by the independent regiments of the MPAJA. Couriers, usually women, would carry these messages to Singapore. They travelled mainly by rail, as it was found that the Kempeitai did not carefully watch the stations. On arrival at Singapore, the couriers would disembark at Bukit Timah. At the contact point they would request a personal meeting with Lai Tek, and hand him the messages. There were occasions when Lai Tek met couriers personally at Bukit Timah station. Messages were all written in code. Very small pieces of paper, 10 centimetres square, were used for reports, so the characters had to be written very small.[107]

As a result of his cultivation of a faithful party leadership, a cult of personality grew around Lai Tek. His aliases were legion, but everyone in the party knew he was their secretary-general. Not only party members but also supporters had heard of his superhuman qualities. Circulating around him were numerous anecdotes and fables. An Englishman who stayed with a MPAJA regiment in south Johor recalled how one Chinese MCP member rhapsodized about the great wisdom of Lao Wu (another of Lai Tek's aliases) with the following anecdote: During a bicycle journey from Kuala Lumpur to Singapore (more than 200 miles) Lao Wu saw a poor crippled worker. He gave him the bicycle and finished his journey on foot.[108]*

Lai Tek left the MPAJA very much alone, under its own High Command. The reason for this is probably that it was a British creation. It was likely to prove of value to him if the fortunes of war changed in favour of the British and the Allied powers, as it eventually did. However, Lai Tek initially appears to have been somewhat doubtful about the British ability to mount a successful counter-offensive against the Japanese. There are indications to show that between July and October 1943, when the three Force 136 officers —

---

* Chapman also mentions Lai Tek's legendary abilities, one of which was to pass through Japanese positions easily. Stories were told in his camp of the MCP secretary-general being credited with innumerable attributes — "being able to pilot an aeroplane, drive a tank, speak many languages, and hoodwink the Japanese in any way he liked" — *The Jungle Is Neutral*, p. 58.

Davis, Broome, and Lim Bo Seng — had landed on the Perak coast, Lai Tek passed information he had obtained from MCP agents to Onishi. He gave details of their landing sites, and Onishi deployed a large Singapore Kempeitai field force to Perak to comb the area.[109] But the three Force 136 officers had vanished into the jungle, and their KMT agents had been safely set up in cover jobs in Ipoh. The Kempeitai raids, however, recovered all the supplies, wireless sets, and arms that the Force 136 officers had hidden on the beach.

With further information from Lai Tek, more raids were carried out on the Perak coast, and a rendezvous with a British submarine by the Force 136 officers was disrupted. Onishi claims that owing to the information Lai Tek gave, arrangements were also made with the Japanese navy and air force, which succeeded in sinking the submarine.[110] Despite the damning Kempeitai evidence, which has turned up against Lai Tek, Davis and Broome have taken an extremely charitable view of Lai Tek's role as a Japanese informer. They maintain that Lai Tek did not betray any British officer to the Japanese, and the death of Maj. Paddy Martin, the Force 136 officer who landed in Kota Tinggi in east Johor in March 1945, was not due to Lai Tek at all. Broome says:

> We [Davis and he] did not know that Lai Tek was a Japanese informer. The thought may have crossed our minds, but if so we rejected it. I feel fairly safe in saying, also, that he did not betray any British officer. I have no direct information about Major Martin, but Davis does not think it was a betrayal. In fact I think with regard to our mission Lai Tek worked perfectly genuinely, in spite of all that has been revealed.[111]

It would seem that Davis and Broome set much store by the agreement, which they subsequently concluded with Lai Tek. Either on 31 December 1943 or 1 January 1944 at Blantan, a camp in the Perak jungle, Lai Tek (under the alias Chang Hong) and Chin Peng met Major Chapman and the three Force 136 officers — Davis, Broome, and Lim Bo Seng — for talks on MPAJA assistance for the Allied cause. Details of the agreement have been discussed above. None of the British officers knew the true identity of "Chang Hong" until after the war. Chapman reported that at this meeting Chang Hong, whom Chapman called "the Plen" (short for plenipotentiary) was "most meticulous in getting a clear-cut decision on every decision, discussing each point in detail, and it was equally clear that he meant to stand by everything in detail". However, Chapman also noticed that there was a "certain air of cautiousness and even cynicism".[112] The "cautiousness and cynicism" apparently referred to Lai Tek's behaviour, and might explain his doubts about the Allied potential for a counter-offensive. He was carefully weighing his options, and the agreement meant that he had decided to play a double game. In his postwar report to the MCP's central committee in January 1946, Lai Tek said that the CEC had sent "Chang Hong" (meaning himself) in September 1943 to conclude a military pact with the Allies "for the sake of liberating Malaya from Japanese fascist rule".[113]

The true identity of Lim Bo Seng was apparently not known to Lai Tek, as Lim used the alias Tan Choon Lim. In March 1944 when Lim moved down to Ipoh to contact his KMT agents, he and his agents were all rounded up.[114] Thus, the KMT intelligence network collapsed, leaving Davis, Broome, and Chapman helpless and dependent on the MPAJA. Lai Tek could have proceeded to betray the three men and the whole Force 136 in Malaya subsequently, but he refrained from doing so. It was in this latter respect that Davis and Broome may be right in stating that Lai Tek did not betray them — when he certainly could have done so.

Subsequently, Chin Peng reported to Davis that the Central Executive Committee of the MCP had ratified the agreement. This apparently comprised Lai Tek, Chin Peng, and a few other faithful state committee officials carefully handpicked by Lai Tek. On 15 April 1945 a second meeting was held between the MCP representatives, "Chang Hong" (Lai Tek), and Chin Peng, and Davis, Broome, and Chapman. Maj. Lim Bo Seng's absence must have been noted, but there is no record of it having been raised by anyone at this meeting, which was concerned with ratifying the points reached in the earlier agreement. Apparently because he had now read clear signs that the Allies were going to win the war, Lai Tek appeared more accommodating than a year before. John Davis, on recollection, believes that Lai Tek then knew that his life would later depend on the British, even though the British did not know then that he was working with the Japanese.[115] The extent of concessions, which Lai Tek is believed to have made to the British at this second meeting on behalf of the MCP, may be gauged from Chapman's succinct account:

> ... at this conference the atmosphere from the beginning was
> one of complete understanding and cordiality: there was no bar-
> gaining whatsoever. It seemed clear that the Plen had come from

his headquarters with instructions to "get on with the war" and there was not a point of disagreement throughout. He was perfectly frank about the powers and limitations of the guerrillas, and whenever we hesitated to ask him to do things, he not only consented but usually broke in to go further than we asked. No written agreements were made or were necessary, as the conference was largely devoted to methods of carrying out the agreement previously made. The principle arrived at was the tactical decentralization of the guerrillas, increase of powers for all their officers, and encouragement of individual initiative.

After spending most of the night encoding and sending reports of the conference to Colombo, we returned to Burun [base camp] with the feeling that all the guerrillas would now be told that it was their duty to cooperate to the full with British officers, and that the days of shilly-shallying and secretiveness were over.[116]

In May 1945 Germany unconditionally surrendered to the Allied powers. If Lai Tek was reading the signs he knew that this meant that the whole military might of the Allies would now be shifted to defeating Japan. Lai Tek might have calculated that it would be a matter of time before the war was over. If he wanted the MPAJA to seize power, he had to make elaborate preparations. According to one writer, the idea of opposing the British had in fact been canvassed in the closing stages of the war among sections of the MPAJA. In Johor particularly, suggestions had been made that all Force 136 officers attached to MPAJA units should be killed and the forces of reoccupation be presented with a takeover of power as a *fait accompli*.[117] However, nothing came of this suggestion, apparently because Lai Tek vetoed it. Although the MCP had a 1943 programme, which advocated a Malayan Democratic Republic as its primary goal after the "Japanese Fascists" had been expelled, it appears that it was not Lai Tek who was interested in seizure of power. Members of the pre-war CEC had worked out the idea of a republic before the Kempeitai eliminated them.[118] However, since these policies had geared the communist cadres to a militant struggle for national liberation, there was a likelihood of dissension and conflict if the party failed to continue with a revolutionary line. The issue came to a head when the party learnt about the Japanese surrender, announced on 15 August 1945.

At a meeting of the Central Executive Committee of the MCP, Liu Yau, chairman of the party's Military Affairs Committee, was reported to have suggested that the party carry out a *coup d'etat*, so as to present the British with a *fait accompli* before their return. But Lai Tek who advised against such a move overruled him.[119] His attitude is said to have been influenced by his fear that Chiang Kai-shek's troops might be sent temporarily to occupy Malaya or part of it. Lai Tek wavered under the pressure of his colleagues, and even when he saw that the Chinese nationalist troops would not after all be moving into Malaya he still opposed the idea, having realized what the British military opposition to such a move might be.[120] From this account, it is clear that Lai Tek had decided to cooperate with the British again. While the others in the CEC were keen on the *coup d'etat*, only Lai Tek was against it. As he held the powers within the party, his voice was decisive.

Lai Tek was also said to have turned down a last-minute request of Ibrahim Yaacob's Malay Giyu Gun to the MCP/MPAJA to join their forces, oppose the return of the British and fight for Malayan independence. On 18 August 1945 Ibrahim dispatched a 280-strong unit of the Giyu Gun based in Singapore to Malaya to place themselves at the command of MPAJA headquarters, but the next day the force was stopped at Muar by the MPAJA. Two days later the Giyu Gun force was told to disband, as the MCP/MPAJA had decided not to resist the returning British because the Allied Radio in New Delhi had broadcast a statement of the British government's intention to establish a democratic government in Malaya. Ibrahim has bitterly criticized Lai Tek for rejecting this opportunity to continue the armed struggle, saying: "Those responsible for allowing the British to return are the MCP/MPAJA leader Lai Tek and his comrades".[121]

The minutes of this crucial meeting of the MCP's CEC are not available, and one can only conjecture what other arguments Lai Tek must have presented to win the CEC over to his views. Regarded as an experienced communist with a CCP and Comintern background, Lai Tek might have convinced the CEC that a moderate policy was, in fact, in the party's own best interests and a correct reading of the Comintern line of the "Popular Front". He advocated cooperation with the British. As the Soviet Union was an ally of Britain, America, and China, this was still acceptable. As a wartime ally of the British, the MCP could benefit from post-war constitutional measures, which the British might be expected to introduce in Malaya on their return. Considering the MCP's excellent relationship with SEAC, this was still a credible position. Furthermore, cooperation meant British intentions could be tested, and if they were willing to bring about self-government and allow the MCP to operate unhindered, developments would then help the party to move in the direction of achieving power. The CEC's decision to abandon revolution was collective. But Lai Tek, as a pre-war British agent, had certainly encouraged such mild strategies more in line to suit British expectations. C.B. McLane suggests that advice given to the MCP by the Chinese and British communist parties in the post-war period tended to support Lai Tek's moderate policies,[122] although they played no part in influencing the August decision.

As a result of the CEC's decision, on 27 August 1945 (five days after the Japanese administration in Malaya had confirmed news of the surrender), the party announced publicly its intention to cooperate with the British government but to demand reforms, civil liberties, and improvement of the people's standard of living. The lengthy manifesto of the CEC issued by the party's Selangor State Committee gave an analysis of the "favourable" international situation and internal conditions, which the end of the war had brought about.[123]

With the defeat of Japan, the party said its armed struggle had come to an end. Britain was returning to rule Malaya, and cooperation seemed most advantageous to the interests of the party. The party's manifesto contained an eight-point programme, which the CEC had adopted:

1. Support the Allies of the Soviet Union, China, Britain and America, and the new International Peace Organization [that is, the United Nations].
2. Establish a democratic government with an elected National Assembly and an elected State Assembly based on an electorate drawn from all races in each State and the Anti-Japanese Army.
3. Abolish Fascism, Japanese political structure, and laws.
4. Allow freedom of speech, publications, societies, and public meetings. Assure the legal position of all parties and organizations.
5. Reform the educational system and introduce democratic education in the respective national languages. Expand national culture.
6. Improve the living conditions of the people. Develop industry, agriculture, and commerce; relieve the unemployed and refugees; increase wages universally and practice the eight-hour work system.

7.   Stabilize prices, and punish traitors, corrupt officials, hoarders, and profiteers.
8.   Ensure good treatment of the Anti-Japanese Army and provide compensation for the families of those who died for the Allied cause.[124]

In justifying this programme, the party said that the end of the war had resulted in a favourable international and local situation for the Malayan people. "New Democratic"* movements had sprung up everywhere.[125] The United Nations had approved the principles of democracy, self-government, and human rights. The "capabilities and intelligence" of the party's leadership in the anti-Japanese struggle had won the people's support. The spirit of resistance and the unity of the people had also increased, as a result of the three years of war and struggle. The party's manifesto continued:

> Today Malaya is located in a new situation and in a new generation.... The problem of Malaya has become a part of the international problem. All advanced countries of the world and their peoples will certainly help us.... As a result, the National Liberation of Malaya has obtained more beneficial terms, and is certain to be successful and victorious in the end. The future prospect of Malaya is unlimitedly bright.[126]

The manifesto had painted an extremely optimistic future to support the leadership's policy for playing a constitutional role. But its goal of the Malayan Democratic Republic embodied in the party's 1943 programme now became a long-term goal, while "preliminary steps" embodied in the eight-point programme were adopted first. This was explained as follows:

> We had suggested before, "Establish Malaya into a Democratic Republic". Today we are not deviating from this programme, because it is the object of our struggle. We have been consistent for 20 years, because we want Malaya to be established into a Democratic Republic. But in order to cope with the demands of the present situation, we again suggest the present eight principles. These eight principles are to realise the preliminary steps of the

---

* The term "New Democratic" refers to Mao's "New Democracy" indicating that the MCP had begun to adopt the CCP's policy. Much was to be heard of "New Democracy" in the MCP's post-war propaganda.

Democratic Republic, because they are part of the requirements of the Democratic Republic.[127]

The whole party was asked to consolidate its gains and apply the United Front strategy in party work under the in-coming British administration. However, the moderation and restraint of the MCP leadership was entirely contrary to the rising anti-British mood in the party and the enthusiasm of the guerrillas for revolutionary action (as will be shown in Chapter 6).

The 27 August 1945 policy was later repudiated and bitterly criticized by the new leadership under Chin Peng who replaced Lai Tek in 1947. This criticism has been repeated ever since in the party's anniversary review of its history:

> ... at the crucial point when the Japanese Fascists surrendered, our Party adopted the Right capitulationist line, i.e., the revisionist line advanced by the enemy agent, Lai T'e, gave up the armed struggle, watered down the programme for a Democratic Republic and National Liberation into a programme for self-government, thus betraying the Party of the fruits of victory.[128]

Lai Tek's role as a Kempeitai agent certainly accentuated the problems of the MCP. The weaknesses in party policies and the destruction of the party organization, which he engineered, ensured that the MCP was unlikely to be in a position to take advantage of opportunities which came its way in the vacuum following the Japanese surrender.

CHAPTER 4

The Malay Independence Movement

Comrades, Japan's victory is not our victory.

– Ibrahim Yaacob, 17 Feb. 1942[*]

In the struggle for Malaya, the revolutionary pro-Japanese political organization, the Kesatuan Melayu Muda (KMM), or Young Malay Union, whose activities before 1941 have been discussed in Chapter 1, clearly emerged as a rival to the Malayan Communist Party (MCP). Both organizations had their own programmes to achieve power and national independence, but their aims and interests were clearly opposed to one another's. The MCP stood for a multi-racial communist republic, and advocated equality and justice for all races, while the KMM was for "Malaya Merdeka" (Independent Malaya), which was to be joined to an independent Indonesia in a political union to be called Melayu Raya or Indonesia Raya (Greater Malaysia or Greater Indonesia).[1] In such a merger Malays would be in the majority over the combined total strength of Chinese, Indians, and

---

[*] Mustapha Hussein, the former vice-chairman of the KMM, in a personal communication to me, dated 4 March 1984, claims that it was he, not Ibrahim Yaacob, who actually made this statement. He further alleges that Ibrahim Yaacob had "misappropriated" the statement in order to "whitewash his erroneous pro-Japanese policies during the war". Ibrahim attributes the above statement to himself in the book entitled, *Sedjarah dan Perjuangan di Malaya*, p. 96, which he wrote under his adopted Indonesian name of Iskander Kamel Agastya.

other races in Malaya as well as politically dominant in government. However, to insure themselves against the risks of Japanese collaboration and defeat the KMM nationalists tactically established secret and close links with the pro-Allies MCP/MPAJA. While the latter did not spurn these contacts, there was mutual suspicion and distrust between the two organizations. In fact, the KMM nationalists feared that the MCP/MPAJA would attempt to take over the country, in the event of Japan's defeat. Likewise, the MCP/MPAJA distrusted the KMM in view of their collaboration with the Japanese, though, under its interim "united front" strategy to defeat "Japanese Fascism" and "British imperialism", it was prepared to work and cooperate with the KMM.

In this chapter we shall see how the KMM attempted to "go its own way" to achieve power and national independence with Japanese support, conscious all the while that, in the wings, lurked the MCP/MPAJA. In any assessment of the KMM's war-time role, its single major contribution was no doubt the resurgence of Malay nationalism. It was during the build-up of international tensions over Southeast Asia in 1940 and 1941, caused by the competition for economic and military interests in the area between Japan and the Western powers, that the KMM nationalists who were anxious to topple British colonialism, were drawn into Japanese espionage activities in support of Tokyo's plans to invade and occupy Malaya. The KMM support of the Japanese was allegedly given conditionally — in return for Japanese money and promises that Malay independence would be considered, that Malay sovereignty, religion, and customs would be upheld, and that Malay women and property would be respected. The KMM also requested Japanese support for the establishment of an independent Malaya, which was to be federated within "Indonesia Raya".[2] Japanese accounts, however, deny that any political promises had been committed, but reveal that a sum of M$18,000 was paid to the KMM leader, Ibrahim Yaacob, to purchase the newspaper *Warta Malaya* from Syed Hussain Alsagoff, an Arab. The terms the Japanese attached to the transaction were that the paper should be made into a subtle propaganda organ for the Japanese, that Ibrahim act as a propagandist for the Japanese "New Order in Malaya", and that he should help Japan in the coming war against Britain and cooperate with the Japanese after they had taken Malaya.[3]

The KMM operated openly as a legal political organization which made little attempt to conceal its hostility towards British policies, but secretly it was allied to a Japanese-sponsored fifth column organization called *Kame* (Japanese for "tortoise"), inspired and directed clandestinely by the Japanese Consulate-General in Singapore. The KMM's involvement in *Kame* was eventually uncovered by British police, who on 4 December 1941 began a series of arrests and detentions of about 110 KMM members and officials in various parts of the country. These arrests continued throughout the Japanese invasion in December and were concluded only at the end of the month. Ibrahim Yaacob and his colleague, Ishak Haji Muhammad, the editor-in-chief of *Warta Malaya*, were picked up on 7 December, the eve of the attack. But they did not have to wait long for their release.

As the invading Japanese troops moved down the peninsula, KMM members and officials who had evaded arrest came forward to render assistance as guides and interpreters.[4] However, despite their demonstrated acts of support and cooperation, the KMM nationalists failed to secure the national independence they had expected from the Japanese. In January 1942, after Japanese forces had entered Kuala Lumpur, a conflict of aims emerged when Mustapha Hussein asked the Japanese commanders to back a proclamation of Malay independence, citing Japan's promise to liberate Malaya from British rule. But the request was turned down. As an example of the distrust with which the KMM leadership in general regarded Japanese intentions, a freed Ibrahim Yaacob claimed he told a KMM gathering on 17 February after his release: "Comrades, Japan's victory is not our victory. Our struggle has still a long way to go ...."[5]

Although the KMM made an immediate impact on Malay society, it only enjoyed a brief period of glory, from February to June 1942, when it was ordered to dissolve. This change of policy was caused by Japanese fears that a premature flare-up of Malay nationalism might be dangerous to Japan's immediate interests. Probably as a sop to assuage the KMM nationalists' disappointment, the Japanese military administration began to treat the KMM members well and to adopt a perceptible "pro-Malay" policy. Consequently, Malay enthusiasm and cooperation for the Japanese administration was ensured. This, in turn, led to an overall upliftment of Malay morale, confidence, and political consciousness.

Despite the banning of their organization in June 1942, Ibrahim and his colleagues stood out as the most progressive and outspoken spokesmen of the Malays. Ibrahim's opinion and advice continued to be consulted by the Japanese and his voice was heard over the radio, but the struggle to remain at the top as a close ally of the Japanese was an uneasy one. Although other pre-war Malay political associations and groups, including those headed by the aristocrats, had disappeared in the wake of the British defeat, their elements — especially the English-educated bureaucrats and the traditional aristocracy — persisted in opposing the KMM nationalists. This was largely due to the competition between them for Japanese favour and influence as well as to a renewed conflict of interests, dating back to pre-war days. These rival groups rejoiced at the KMM's dissolution, but politically they were unable to supplant the KMM leaders as close and trusted aides of the Japanese, largely because the latter had clearly demonstrated their loyalty and support to the Japanese in the crucial stages of the war. The other groups had been branded as "co-operators" of the pre-war British regime.

The KMM and Malay Society

Between February and June 1942, the KMM's standing in Malay society rose, largely because the Japanese relied on local KMM members and officials in the rural areas for information and man-power. As a result, the organization became extremely influential. During the first two months of the occupation its membership was reported to have leapt spectacularly to about 10,000.

KMM members emerged as the new privileged political elite, whose prestige superseded that of the Malay aristocracy and the British-trained Malay bureaucratic elite. With easy access to Japanese officers, political influence, information, special food rations, and allowances, they could extend protection and help to the ordinary Malays and so became their new patrons.* Consequently, the Malay aristocracy and the Malay bureaucrats resented the KMM elite, a feeling that was increased by the fact that in many areas the KMM members were responsible for the arrest and interrogation of "unco-operative" Malay aristocrats and civil servants. Some indication of

---

* In addition to giving protection, they were able to fulfil most requests from the Malay people for licences to move goods and buy or sell rice, and for letters of safe conduct. See Halinah Bamadhaj, "The Impact of the Japanese Occupation of Malaya on Malay Society and Politics, 1941–1945" (M.A. thesis, University of Auckland, 1975), pp. 76–86.

the resentment against the KMM can be found in these recollections of a member of the Malay bureaucratic elite:

> The KMM officials swaggered about in the villages and in the government offices, throwing their weight around as if they were the government. No doubt the Malay population appreciated what they had done during the transitional period of Japanese take-over. They saved Malay lives and helped to protect Malay women and property.
>
> But they were ill qualified to take over the administration. Most were clerks, primary school teachers, and held junior positions in government service. The senior civil servants initially had to take orders from them, because the Japanese Army officers relied on them for advice and they were also the eyes and ears of the Japanese. They were extremely arrogant; but later when the Japanese realized they could not rely on them to run the government they turned to the pre-war British-trained civil servants.[*]

Open conflict between these different elite strata, however, did not materialize, partly because, in the interest of achieving Malay unity under KMM leadership, Ibrahim encouraged the KMM to accommodate elements of the Malay aristocracy and bureaucratic elite within their ranks, and enough members of the traditional elites quickly adjusted themselves to the new situation. Many aristocrats joined the KMM, including Raja Shariman in Perak, Datuk Hamzah bin Abdullah in Selangor, Tengku Mohammad bin Tengku Besar in Negeri Sembilan, Tengku Mohammad bin Sultan Ahmad in Pahang, Datuk Onn bin Jaafar in Johor, and others.[6] Several were even allowed to assume leading positions in KMM rural branches. The brevity of the KMM's reign also meant that real social divisions

---

[*] Datuk (Dr) Awang Hassan, Malaysian High Commissioner to Australia. Interview, Canberra, June 1978. During the Japanese occupation, Datuk Awang was a medical officer at Kluang (Johor). A similar attitude survives in Kampung Jawa, the home village of KMM leader Onan Haji Siraj. Onan is remembered there as an extremely influential and high-handed village administrator and "informer" during the Japanese occupation. One Malay account described him as "berjewa borjuis dan berfaham fascist pula" (a bourgeois and also a fascist). See A. Talib bin Hj. Ahmad, *Riwayat Kinta* [The Story of Kinta] (Kuala Lumpur, 1959), pp. 95–6, 105–6. The writer was secretary of the conservative Persatuan Pemuda Melayu Perak (Perak Malay Youth Association), which was loyal to the local aristocracy, and a rival of the KMM.

did not have a chance to develop in the competition for rewards and political influence in Malay society.

In fact, after the KMM's dissolution in June, the aristocratic groups quickly reasserted themselves and exacted revenge on the KMM. Ibrahim bitterly recalls the actions of these aristocrats as betrayals:

> Throughout the Japanese occupation none of the numerous pre-war Malay associations [a reference to the aristocrat-led Malay State Associations known as the Persatuan-Persatuan Negeri] dared to rise to defend the rights of the Malays either openly or in secret. The leading *raja* and *datuk* [titled aristocrats] were only interested in safeguarding their own security. Initially they took refuge within the KMM and became members of the KMM leadership in the districts. But when the KMM was dissolved, some of them betrayed several KMM district members, causing the latter to be detained and tortured by the Japanese.[7]

During its years of suppression Ibrahim was unable to keep the movement intact underground or to maintain close touch with party elements and branches, which slowly disintegrated. KMM members, lacking leadership or an organization to give them political cohesion, became preoccupied with their own survival.

Japanese accounts indicate that the KMM's dissolution in June 1942 was part of a Japanese military policy aimed at discouraging political activities by any local group.[8] It was feared that if the KMM was encouraged, then Chinese, Eurasians, and other groups might ask for similar privileges. Only the Indian Independence League (IIL) was backed because it was an India-oriented organization and was part of Japanese military designs for the invasion of India. There is little evidence to support the general assumption that the KMM's fortunes were affected by Major Fujiwara's posting to Burma in March 1942,[9] for he, in fact, had done little for the KMM. Fujiwara himself says, "I did not encourage the KMM, because of the multi-ethnic nature of Malayan society. I did not want to upset the status quo. But I saw to it that Ibrahim and some KMM members got jobs as rewards for their cooperation."[10] Ibrahim's dream of achieving Indonesia Raya with Japanese support, therefore, suffered a setback, checking the KMM's initial growth as a mass movement. By the end of 1942, the movement collapsed totally. Lacking either a legal political organization or an efficient underground movement, the disillusioned Ibrahim nevertheless clung to Japanese patronage to realize his political aims.

Ibrahim in Office

Perhaps as a move to mollify Ibrahim for the abolition of the KMM, Captain Ogawa, secretary to General Watanabe, the Somubucho Malai Gunsei Kanbu,[11] invited him, along with other community leaders, to accompany the Director-General on an upcountry tour from which they returned at the end of July.[12] About a week later, Ogawa invited Ibrahim and four other KMM members to dinner, during which he expressed sympathy with Ibrahim's complaints about Japanese treatment of the KMM. He suggested that Ibrahim accept a government post as adviser on Malay affairs to the Singapore-Malaya administration in Singapore. An advisory board consisting of five to six Malays would be appointed which Ibrahim could select and head, although its secretary would be a Japanese (a Mr Hosai, a civilian with the rank of colonel). Ibrahim recalls that as a result of discussions within the KMM's "inner council", consisting of Ibrahim and a few trusted executive colleagues, it was finally agreed that he should accept the appointment.[13]*

As adviser on Malay affairs to Director-General Watanabe, Ibrahim came very much into the limelight, making radio broadcasts and public speeches calling on Malays to cooperate with the Japanese administration and hinting that they would achieve their nationalist goals in the near future. He saw to it that such KMM officials as Ishak Haji Muhammad, Abdullah Kamel, Taharuddin Ahmad, and Muhammad Zallehudin were satisfactorily employed on the *Berita Malai* and other Malay publications issuing from the Propaganda Department.

Some KMM officials, however, such as Mustapha Hussein, Ahmad Boestamam, Idris Hakim, Abdul Kadir Adabi, and M.N. Othman did not participate, as they had already left Singapore before May 1942, dissatisfied with Ibrahim's leadership and the refusal of the Japanese to meet the KMM's demands on Malay independence. Ahmad Boestamam and Idris Hakim both returned to Ipoh where they worked in the local Propaganda Department, and M.N. Othman returned to his job with the Malayan Railways in Kuala Lumpur.

Mustapha's withdrawal as vice-president of the KMM had been precipitated by an incident in which he was kicked and slapped by

---

* Ibrahim claims he was forced to accept the appointment because the Japanese advice was "filled with threats".

a Japanese soldier because he got in the latter's way when trying to fix his bicycle on the road.[14] Convinced by this that the Japanese were not only unreliable but also barbaric, Mustapha wished to have nothing more to do with them. He had also found his KMM position untenable because of his differences with Ibrahim and his clique. Ibrahim had criticized Mustapha's conduct during the Japanese campaign when he had asked the Japanese to proclaim Malayan independence. "The demand of independence was premature and could have cost you your head," Ibrahim is alleged to have rebuked Mustapha.

The other three KMM executive committee members were similarly dissatisfied with what they described as Ibrahim's "autocratic" leadership, "arrogant" behaviour, and formation of "cliques".[15] Besides an "inner circle" of KMM officials, Ibrahim was said to have his own group of trusted confidants, including his brother-in-law Onan Haji Siraj. His "inner circle" had included by turn Mustapha, Hassan Manan (KMM secretary-general), Abdul Karim Rashid, Ishak Haji Muhammad, Mohd. Isa Mahmud, and M.N. Othman (all KMM executive committee members), and he was also known to have an "outer circle" and an "ordinary circle". KMM executive committee members Ahmad Boestamam and Idris Hakim belonged to the "outer circle" and were usually sealed off from policy making.[16] The public sinecures, which Ibrahim finally secured in the latter part of 1942 and in 1943/4, went only to him and the "inner circle".

In June 1943, when Japanese Premier Tojo, after a visit to Singapore and Thailand, announced in the Imperial Diet the coming independence of Burma and the Philippines, he also promised that the administration of the "Indonesian peoples" would move forward, and that political participation would be granted to the natives in Malaya, Sumatra, Java, Borneo, and Sulawesi.[17] This speech was received with great enthusiasm by the Malay press. On 28 July, Ibrahim led an eight-man delegation from Singapore and the Malay states on a three-month tour of Japan. All the delegates were members of his Malay Advisory Board, but they included aristocrats whom Ibrahim had recruited to gain their support.[18*] Another group from Sumatra joined the delegation, and during the tour their activities were widely reported by Domei news agency.[19]

---

* These were Nik Ahmad Kamil (Kelantan), Raja Sulaiman Ahmad (Selangor), Datuk Bandar Seremban (Negeri Sembilan), and Tengku Ibrahim (Terengganu).

Ibrahim and the Giyu Gun

While Ibrahim's delegation was in Japan, Domei announced that the Japanese had adopted measures "to rouse Indonesians, including Malays, from the stupor into which they had fallen during the Dutch and British regimes". In Java they had initiated "the first steps in provincial autonomy" in line with Tojo's statement. They hoped that this would "inspire the people in Malaya to work in even closer cooperation with the authorities in the hope that when the time is ripe they too will be accorded similar privileges". Domei also remarked that Japan had brought "a new gospel of coexistence and co-prosperity" to the Malays and that the "right has been restored to Malaya to determine its own future".[20] These statements were made on 10 August 1943. On 20 August, however, Japan signed away the four northern Malay states of Perlis, Kedah, Kelantan, and Terengganu to Thailand. The formal transfer of these states was made on 18 October, and Ibrahim returned to Malaya in time to witness it.[21]

Ibrahim's dismay over the transfer was apparently only alleviated when the Japanese told him that he had been chosen to help establish the Giyu Gun (Volunteer Army) and Giyu Tai (Volunteer Corps). The former was to be a fighting force used only for the defence of Malaya, and the latter was to be employed for defence of the coastline and the preservation of public order. These units would supplement the Heiho (Auxiliary Servicemen) created by the Japanese in June to assist their forces in labour services. Ibrahim was instructed to organize Malay *pemuda* (youths) into both the Giyu Gun and the Giyu Tai, and was himself to undergo six months' military training in order to take command of the Giyu Gun.* Although the Japanese originally envisaged the Giyu Gun as a multiracial army, it ended up mainly as a Malay force. Ibrahim, who had previously asked the Japanese to establish a Malay army, was quite willing to take up the appointment in the hope that he could convert the Giyu Gun into a real national military force.

The formation of the Giyu Gun and Giyu Tai in Malaya coincided with that of similar groups in Sumatra and Java. The Japanese aim was to persuade the local people to assume a role in defence

---

* Occasionally Ibrahim refers to the Giyu Gun as PETA, which stands for Pembela Tanah Air (Defenders of the Motherland) and was the same name of the volunteer army in Java. See Ibrahim Yaacob, *Sekitar Malaya Merdeka*, pp. 32–4.

against Allied attacks. They were now prepared to put more reliance on and trust in the local people, mainly because of Japan's uncertain position in the war and the greater deployment of Japanese troops on the battlefronts in Burma and the Pacific.

The KMM journalists on *Berita Malai* and other Malay publications mounted a big publicity campaign, including the staging of *sandiwara* (dramatic shows), for the Giyu Gun, using Ibrahim's appointment as its commander to arouse the interest of young Malays. On Japanese urging, Ishak Haji Muhammad, who was now chief editor of *Berita Malai*,* made speeches and broadcasts exhorting Malay youths to join the Giyu Gun and Giyu Tai. The monthly magazine *Fajar Asia* (Dawn of Asia) also made strong appeals to Malay youths to enlist:

> The Giyu Gun is a genuine Army, which will consist only of Malays. The recruits must be those who genuinely wish to defend their motherland. The second unit has already been formed and only awaits the arrival of more dedicated youths who are prepared to carry out their responsibilities to the motherland. Malay pemuda must seize this excellent opportunity to show the world that within their breasts flows the blood of Hang Tuah [the Malay warrior] who once reminded us: "The Malays shall not vanish in this world." Mr Ibrahim Yaacob who has been appointed commander of the Malay Giyu Gun says he wishes to see every male Malay enlist as a soldier and establish the Army.[22]

Other writers in the magazine made similar appeals to Malay youths to "rise to the defence of their motherland". Earlier, in arguing that the Malays should prevent the British from landing again on Malaya, the journal declared: "The Malay *keris* [dagger] demands blood, after centuries of being locked within its sheath by the oppression of Western colonialism."[23]

In their speeches Ishak and the KMM leaders portrayed the Giyu Gun as serving the cause of Malay independence, but in fact KMM leaders did not select all the Giyu Gun recruits. They were also recruited, instructed, and trained by Japanese officers, and

---

* In early November 1943 Ishak visited Tokyo to attend the Dai Toa (Greater East Asia) Journalists' Conference. In his absence the chief editor of *Berita Malai*, Rahim Kajai, died, and on his return Ishak took over the post. Interview with Ishak.

Ibrahim has been blamed for an arrangement whereby KMM leaders were denied the right to "indoctrinate" the Giyu Gun.*

While Ibrahim was busy with the Giyu Gun, the Japanese administration announced the formation of *sangi kai* [regional councils] for Singapore and the other states to allow local participation in political administration. Only in Singapore were KMM members included in these councils; in the other states titled aristocrats and senior civil servants represented Malays. In Singapore, on Ibrahim's nomination, Onan Haji Siraj and Daud bin Mohd. Shah of the KMM, were appointed. An important shift in policy was that more seats were given to Malayan Chinese on the regional councils, reversing the Japanese administration's discriminatory and repressive policy towards the Chinese. This followed the recall of the hard-liner Watanabe in March 1943[24] and the transfer of the four northern Malay states to Thailand, which resulted in the remainder of Malaya becoming overwhelmingly non-Malay in composition.[25] Clearly this increase in Chinese political representation had been achieved at the expense of Malay interests, and Ibrahim's response was to strengthen the Giyu Gun.

Recruiting proper for the Giyu Gun began on 9 December 1943, and in a 1944 New Year's Day message Ibrahim made a personal appeal to Malay youths to enlist in the army:

> I am living in a camp somewhere in Syonan [Singapore] under-going rigorous training as a founding officer of the Giyu Gun. The

---

* This criticism appears indirectly in A. Samad Ismail's semi-autobiographical novel, *Patah Sayap Terbang Jua*, where the character Hashim represents Ishak, and Shamsuddin, Ibrahim Yaacob. The author describes how during the establishment of the Giyu Gun, an Indonesian revolutionary, Mas Parjo, arrived secretly in Singapore to assist the KMM. He criticizes Ibrahim's mishandling of the recruitment exercise: "I said to him [Ibrahim], Bung [brotherl, get ready now. Without preparations how can you struggle? Bung, you must organize the idealist youths. You must educate them with our nationalism. With the aspirations of Indonesia Raya. With the anti-Japanese spirit...." and again, "How do we fight the British and the Americans if our soldiers [i.e., the Giyu Gun] are not educated as nationalists? This was what I told Bung. Don't let the Japanese pick the men for the Giyu Gun. Bung, you must pick them yourself." A. Samad Ismail, *Patah Sayap Terbang Jua* [A broken wing can fly too] (Kuala Lumpur, 1968), pp. 148–9. During the Japanese occupation, the 20-year-old Samad worked as a journalist on the *Berita Malai*. Later, he credited his political maturing in this period to Ishak. Interview, Kuala Lumpur, June 1973.

Giyu Gun and the Giyu Tai will form the Giyu Hei or the Malai
Protection Army, which, I believe, will symbolise the desire of
every able-bodied Malai* youth to serve his country.

Never in my life and during my difficult career as a leader
of the Malai people have I felt more gratified at the prospect of
being able to serve more actively as a soldier to defend my beloved
Malai, and to help complete the construction of New Malai.

My training here, though rigorous, is strengthening my spirit
and my faith, and will help to qualify me better to serve my
people....[26]

Before June 1944 Ibrahim completed his training and was given the
rank of lieutenant colonel. About 2,000 Malay youths were recruited
into a single unit at a central training camp and barracks at Johor
Bharu. In July the Giyu Gun was sent on an anti-guerrilla operation.
Despite an understanding between Ibrahim and the MCP/MPAJA
prior to the operation, their forces clashed in the jungles off Kota
Tinggi, with the result that 25 guerrillas were killed.[27] In another
operation in Ipoh, when not a single engagement occurred between
the Giyu Gun and the MPAJA, Japanese suspicions were aroused.
The Giyu Gun unit was suddenly withdrawn to Singapore, its officers
and men dispersed among different Japanese army units, and from
then on Japanese distrust and tight control rendered the Giyu Gun
impotent. Although Ibrahim was made an adviser and promoted to
the rank of colonel,† he had little power.[28]

As a military officer, Ibrahim's movements were now restricted,
but he still tried to keep in touch with KMM officials in Singapore.
By this time, as the result of a tiff with Onan Haji Siraj, Ishak Haji
Muhammad had given up his job as editor of *Berita Malai*. He left
for Bintan Island, south of Singapore, in 1944, ostensibly to help
the "grow more food" campaign there. Ibrahim recalled him to
Singapore,‡ but he soon went back to his *kampung* in Pahang, where

---

* "Malai" in Japanese means either "Malay" or "Malaya".
† It should be noted that Ibrahim's rank of colonel was one of the highest ever
accorded to a non-Japanese officer.
‡ Ishak disliked Onan for his arrogance and said that Ibrahim gave his brother-
in-law "too much face". When Ishak was in Bintan, Ibrahim repeatedly called him
to return, but to no avail until he sent a close friend, Pacik Ahmad. Interview,
Jan. 1977. For Pacik Ahmad's account, see Appendix D, Abdul Malek, "Kesatuan
Melayu Muda", pp. 363–7.

he remained until the Japanese surrender. Ishak's disillusionment, which was aggravated by the KMM's failure to make any political headway, is well captured in Samad Ismail's novel. The character Hashim (i.e., Ishak) says:

> People like us are no longer of any value. We are nationalists. So long as we remain so, we will be neglected. If we try to be active, we are obstructed. If we oppose, we lose our heads. Shamsuddin [i.e., Ibrahim] knows. He wanted an Army. The Japanese said, why not? But Shamsuddin has no authority. His Army is not a political Army. It's an Army instilled with the Bushido spirit to serve only the Japanese. Now he regrets. He tries to reorganize his front. I said, who will now believe you any more? Every plan of ours has failed. Every effort of ours is half completed. We don't have enough people. The old comrades are scattered. It's not easy to select new people. We can't choose people who are pro-British. We can't choose people who are full of sympathy for the Japanese, either. We must only choose people who are pro-us....[29]

The KRIS and Indonesian Independence

Ibrahim's patience was finally rewarded when Japan's position in the war deteriorated further. The political advancement promised by Tojo was taken a stage further by his successor, Koiso. On 9 September 1944, Koiso promised to prepare the territories of the former Netherlands East Indies for independence, with Java to be given priority.[30] In the early months of 1945, the KMM group, inspired by developments in Java where Sukarno and other nationalists were permitted to take on a greater political role, soon revived their pan-Indonesian aspirations. Malay newspapers and magazines began to give support to the idea of Indonesia Raya.[31] The opportunity for which Ibrahim had been waiting finally came.

When the Japanese accelerated their plans for Indonesian independence in May 1945, two Japanese civilian officers in the Malayan Military Administration sympathetic to the KMM decided to support the Indonesia Raya idea. They informed the group of the Japanese plans for Indonesian independence. These officers were Itagaki Yoichi, of Hitotsubashi University, a specialist in Malay affairs, and his superior, Professor Akamatsu, head of the Malayan Military Administration's Research Bureau.[32] Itagaki was among the officers who attended the meeting of Japanese administrators from Java, Sumatra, Sulawesi, and Malaya held in Singapore on 2–3 May 1945, to discuss preparations for Indonesian independence. According to Itagaki, while the meeting was underway he decided to take the initiative and, with permission from the Chief of Staff in Singapore, he personally instructed Ibrahim to convene an urgent meeting of his group.[33]

The meeting held at Ibrahim's house in Tanjong Katong, Singapore, on 4 or 5 May 1945, was attended by about seven or eight KMM members, including Onan Haji Siraj. Itagaki began:

> What I have to say tonight is unofficial, but I think the independence of Malaya is coming. To be ready for this, you should all start making preparations. Today I have secured the permission of the Chief of Staff, so that Ibrahim can function as leader of the Malay nationalist movement. I hope you will all think seriously about the idea.[34]

Ibrahim replied:

> Independence of Malaya has been our desire for a long time, but it has been totally suppressed by the Japanese administration. Of course, we believe the words of Professor. However, we cannot reply immediately. We cannot start anything without Mustapha Hussein, the vice-chairman of KMM. If there is no agreement from Mustapha, there is no hope of success. To mobilize 800 comrades, his support is indispensable. To make matters worse, he has been insisting that he would not cooperate with the Japanese since the incident in which he was kicked and slapped.[35]

Itagaki expressed regret for the incident and promised to accompany Ibrahim to Taiping, where Mustapha lived, to persuade him to rejoin the movement. The KMM group withdrew briefly for a private discussion. When they returned, Ibrahim announced that they had picked on the name KRIS or Kekuatan Rakyat Istimewa (literally Special Strength of the People) for their movement.[36] Ibrahim subsequently referred to KRIS as "Kesatuan Rakyat Indonesia Semenanjung" (Union of Peninsular Indonesians).[37] A third interpretation of KRIS is believed to be "Kerajaan Ra'ayat Indonesia Semenanjung" (Government of Peninsular Indonesians).[38]

After this meeting, Itagaki and Ibrahim left for Taiping where Ibrahim contacted Mustapha. The latter, however, refused to join KRIS, as he did not believe Itagaki's assurances that Japan would grant independence to Malaya. Both Itagaki and Professor Akamatsu met Mustapha to try to convince him, and they then arranged for the whole group to meet with General Umezu, the new Somubucho Malai Gunsei Kanbu. At Itagaki's request, Umezu, who shared the two professors' sympathies for the nationalist movement, agreed to do what he could to persuade Mustapha.

At their meeting, Umezu made an immediate impact on Mustapha when he said: "I wish to speak honestly with you all today. Our policy towards the Malay nationalist movement all this while has been wrong. We realize this too late. We must change our policy. We should now do our best to respond to your nationalistic desires. Although the war is still on, we must do our best to implement this policy."[39] Itagaki, who was interpreting, recalls that he noticed a sudden transformation in Mustapha's demeanour. He was smiling. Later Mustapha told Itagaki he had been impressed by Umezu's sincerity, especially his admission of the Japanese mistake. This, he claimed, few Japanese would ever do. When the group returned to Itagaki's residence they became exuberant and began dancing and singing. Tears welled up in Mustapha's eyes.[40]

Between May and July Ibrahim tried to form KRIS branches throughout Malaya. He attempted to use former KMM branches as nuclei, but found that their officials were now scattered and disorganized, and he spent much time looking for them and recruiting new members. However, he did succeed in setting up several branches of about ten members each. In July, to make sure that Malaya was included in the Indonesian programme for independence, Ibrahim sent three representatives to meet Sukarno. They conveyed a message from him and the Malay *pemuda* requesting that Malaya be included in the forthcoming Indonesian nation.[41]

In Jakarta the 62-member "Badan Penjelidik Usaha Persiapan Kemerdekaan Indonesia" (Indonesian Independence Preparatory and Research Body) had been inaugurated on 28 May 1945 with Japanese approval. In mid-July it discussed the boundaries of the future Indonesian state and whether these should include: (1) just the former Netherlands East Indies, (2) the former Netherlands East Indies *plus* Malaya, New Guinea, North Borneo, and Portuguese Timor, or (3) the former Indies *minus* New Guinea. Muhammad Yamin advocated Indonesia Raya, the second alternative. In supporting him Sukarno revealed that three young *pemuda* from Singapore had arrived in Jakarta with a request for Malaya's inclusion within Indonesia. Sukarno also reported that a well-known Malay leader, "Lt. Colonel Abdullah Ibrahim" (that is, Ibrahim Yaacob), had made a similar request.[42] Although he recognized the political risks involved in including Malaya within Indonesia, Sukarno said that the interests of Indonesia's defence and sovereignty required territories on both sides of the Straits of Malacca to be in Indonesian hands. Put to a vote, the second alternative was approved by 39 votes, with 19 going to the first proposal and 6 to the third. Mohammad Hatta, who was in favour of the first proposal, said he did not object to Malaya's inclusion if it was so inclined.[43]

On 29 July, a second meeting of Japanese regional administrators in Singapore discussed the necessity of accelerating the programme of Indonesian independence. Itagaki recounts that after this meeting he was convinced that no more time should be lost by the KRIS organizers, as Indonesian independence was imminent. He suggested to Ibrahim that an All-Malaya Pemuda Conference be convened on 17 and 18 August at the Station Hotel in Kuala Lumpur to inaugurate KRIS. The meeting would declare KRIS support for Indonesian independence, express the Malay people's wish for union with the Indonesian people, and approve a delegation to attend the official independence ceremony.[44]

Ibrahim made intense preparations for the Pemuda Conference throughout the first two weeks of August, dispatching agents to every state to invite KRIS branches and interested Malay bodies to send delegates to the conference. At the same time, reportedly, he was planning to set up an interim government in Malaya to coincide with the declaration of Indonesian independence. Included in its cabinet were the Sultans of Perak, Pahang, and Johor as well as the aristocrats Datuk Onn bin Jaafar, Datuk Abdul Rahman (Johor), Datuk Hussein Mohd. Taib (Pahang), and Raja Kamarulzaman Raja Mansor (Perak).[45]* It was also decided that an eight-man delegation would be sent to attend the Indonesian independence ceremony, consisting of four Sultans and four KRIS officials (Ibrahim, Dr Burhanuddin, Onan Haji Siraj, and Hassan Manan). Ibrahim consulted Sultan Abdul Aziz of Perak, who agreed to be a member.[46]

In the midst of these preparations Ibrahim and Itagaki went to Taiping to discuss their plans with officers of the Twenty-ninth Army, including General Umezu, the Somubucho, who reportedly

---

* It is believed that the sultans agreed to the formation of KRIS, but when the question of forming a government to be called "Kerajaan Ra'ayat Indonesia Semenanjung" (Government of Peninsular Indonesians) was broached, the sultans balked. See Arena Wati, *Cherpen Zaman Jepun*, p. 26n.

gave his full approval to the KRIS programme. A key Malay source claims that the idea of forming an interim government was casually raised with Umezu, while more detailed plans on cabinet members were kept secret.[47] (Neither Ibrahim nor Itagaki mentions the proposed formation of a cabinet or an interim government in their writings.)

On 8 August an Indonesian delegation headed by Sukarno and Hatta stopped briefly in Singapore on their way to Saigon for talks on Indonesian independence with Field-Marshal Terauchi, the Supreme Commander of Japanese forces in Southeast Asia. Hearing of the visit, KMM supporters raised the red-white flag of Indonesia atop the Cathay cinema building in Singapore, and KMM officials, including Onan Haji Siraj, Hassan Manan, and Pacik Ahmad, went to the airport to meet the Indonesian leaders. After the Indonesian delegation had left, Hassan Manan and Pacik Ahmad travelled to Taiping to report to Ibrahim, leaving Onan Haji Siraj in Singapore.

Returning after their talks with Terauchi, the Indonesian delegation on 12 or 13 August stopped in Taiping* — apparently to meet Ibrahim. Ibrahim, Itagaki, and the KMM officials who had arrived from Singapore went with General Umezu to welcome the party. Sukarno's delegation and Ibrahim lunched with Umezu at his residence and then returned to the airport where the Indonesians held discussions with Ibrahim and the KMM *pemuda* from which Itagaki was excluded.[48] According to Ibrahim's account, he reported to Sukarno and Hatta that the Malays desired to achieve independence for Malaya (excluding Singapore) within Indonesia Raya. He proposed, too, that "Malayan independence" be proclaimed at the end of August (either at the same time as or after the Indonesian

---

* This itinerary of Sukarno's delegation is based on Ibrahim Yaacob, *Sekitar Malaya Merdeka*, p. 29, and Agastya, *Sedjarah*, pp. 136–7. Gen. A.H. Nasution, the Indonesian Army historian, however, in his *Sekitar Perang Kemerdekaan Indonesia* [Concerning the war of Indonesian independence) (Bandung, 1977), vol. I, p. 273, claims that on 13 August 1945 Sukarno's delegation stopped in Taiping on their way to Saigon, and on their way back to Jakarta stopped in Singapore where they met Ibrahim again. This seems unlikely as the delegation was back in Jakarta on the 14th. Strangely, Mohammad Hatta omits any mention of the Taiping meeting in his *Sekitar Proklamasi 17 Agustus 1945* [Concerning the proclamation of 17 August 1945] (Jakarta, 1970), pp. 24–5. The two key sources for the Taiping meeting are Ibrahim and Itagaki, who provided a group photograph, which includes Sukarno and Ibrahim as evidence.

proclamation), and that an eight-man delegation including himself and Sultan Abdul Aziz of Perak would attend the independence ceremony in Jakarta. Sukarno, with Hatta next to him, was apparently overcome by Ibrahim's enthusiasm. He shook Ibrahim's hand and said: "Let us create one motherland for those of Indonesian ethnic stock." Ibrahim replied: "We Malays will faithfully create the motherland by uniting Malaya with an independent Indonesia. We Malays are determined to be Indonesians." The aircraft carrying the Indonesians then made a brief stop at Singapore for the second time, and at another meeting with Onan Haji Siraj both sides repeated their hopes and expectations regarding Indonesia.[49]

There are conflicting versions of Hatta's reaction to Ibrahim's proposal to include Malaya within the Indonesian state. Itagaki says, "Ibrahim later told me Sukarno showed an appreciation of his proposal, but it was Hatta who welcomed it wholeheartedly. This was an idea, which Hatta had always advocated."[50] On the other hand, another source claims that two representatives of the Sultan of Johor, Maj. Datuk Haji Muhammad Said and Musa bin Yusof (Pak Lomak), who were also present at the Taiping meeting, recalled that Hatta and another member of the Indonesian delegation (not identified, possibly Dr Radjiman Wediodiningrat) rejected the Indonesia Raya union idea.[51] The latter account seems more probable, as it conforms with Hatta's vote at the BPKI meeting in mid-July. In contrast to his glowing admiration for Sukarno, Ibrahim has nowhere shown any affection for Hatta. (Probably reflecting the lack of importance Hatta attached to the KRIS union idea, he has not referred to the proposal in his own memoirs of the period.)

Meanwhile, the Station Hotel in Kuala Lumpur had become a hive of activity with *pemuda* representatives arriving from various parts of the country. Apparently in anticipation of plans to include Malaya within Indonesia Raya, delegates also arrived from Patani (southern Thailand) and the Riau islands, south of Singapore. Datuk Onn Jaafar came from Johor while the lawyer Sardon Haji Jubir and A. Samad Ismail arrived from Singapore. Sardon recalls that most of the *pemuda* had difficulty in getting through to Kuala Lumpur because of MPAJA roadblocks. The train carrying Sardon, who was travelling with Tengku Hussein, president of the Singapore Malay Welfare Association, and two Japanese, was stopped outside Kuala Lumpur by the MPAJA, but it managed to get through. A. Samad Ismail claims that MPAJA guerrillas derailed his train so that he only arrived for the conference on 17 August.[52]

On 15 August news of the Japanese surrender became known, and Itagaki informed Ibrahim of it when they were travelling by car to Kuala Lumpur. Itagaki recalls,

> He [Ibrahim] was not surprised, because he had some hint of it from his KMM colleagues. I told him, "Japan can no longer help your movement or you or your people's aspirations. What do you intend to do now?" He said, "Please ask the Somubucho in Singapore to provide me with a plane. I want to escape to Java." I told Ibrahim, "If you want to be the future leader of Malaya, you should never run away from the motherland. You must hide yourself in some place in the country."
>
> "Some social disturbances will occur. Try and conceal yourself, meanwhile. The British arrested Jawaharlal Nehru and Gandhi, but they were never killed. The British do not kill political prisoners." He uttered no sound, but merely looked out the window. Finally he said, "When we reach Kuala Lumpur, I will discuss with my friends and I will then inform you of my final plans."[53]

On reaching Kuala Lumpur, Ibrahim convened an emergency meeting of the KRIS committee on either 15 or 16 August instead of on the scheduled 17 August.[54] At that meeting the delegates focused on three major issues: the first was whether to push through Malayan independence within Indonesia Raya; second, how to prevent Chinese MPAJA domination of the country and safeguard Malay rights within the administration; and third, how to resolve the stigma of collaboration which hung over the KRIS delegates. Dr Burhanuddin called on the Malay *pemuda* to resist the British landings,[55] which, though expected on 20 August, did not actually begin until 2 September. Rumours that the landings were imminent added a note of special urgency to the meeting. Apparently at Ibrahim's suggestion, the meeting decided that he and two other KRIS officials should leave immediately for Singapore where the Malay Giyu Gun was based, to arrange for units to move to the mainland and start the armed struggle against the British. Ibrahim and his colleagues would then leave for Jakarta to attend the Indonesian independence ceremony, and Dr Burhanuddin would take over as KRIS chairman in Ibrahim's absence.[56]

The most important of the twelve resolutions reportedly adopted at the meeting was that the establishment of the government of Malaya Demokratik Rakyat (Democratic People's Malaya) should be proclaimed over the radio stations at Penang and Kuala Lumpur.

The new cabinet would be led by Sultan Abu Bakar of Pahang, who would also be the head of state, and it would include Sultan Abdul Aziz of Perak, Sultan Musa Uddin of Selangor, Datuk Onn bin Jaafar of Johor, Ibrahim Yaacob, Mustapha Hussein, Hassan Manan, Dr Burhanuddin AI-Helmy, A. Karim Rashid, and Ishak Haji Muhammad.[57] Many names were included without their owners' prior agreement, and the meeting appointed two delegates to approach the nominees. Once this had been obtained Ibrahim was to be informed in Singapore. The meeting finally decided to instruct KMM *pemuda* throughout the country to destroy quickly all oil installations, airfields, bridges, and telecommunications lines to prevent these from falling into British hands, and some *pemuda* groups were also ordered to raid Japanese arms depots to seize weapons for the impending armed struggle against the British. When the meeting closed Ibrahim left for Singapore.[58]*

On the night of 17 August KRIS supporters held a reception at a house in Kampung Bharu, a Malay district of Kuala Lumpur, attended by about 20 people, including Itagaki and his colleagues, Yamada Hideo and Professor Ono Seizaburo. Itagaki told the gathering that the birth of the KRIS movement was intended to be a prelude to Malayan independence within Indonesia Raya, "But I am sorry that that scheme has been totally disrupted by the Japanese surrender.... Malayan independence is now your problem. You are on your own."[59] Dr Burhanuddin, the acting KRIS chairman, made an impassioned speech, which was well received, declaring that KRIS would carry on the struggle to achieve Malaya's independence through Indonesia Raya. Datuk Onn bin Jaafar, however, struck a note of discord when he urged the Malays to think carefully before talking of Malay independence. "We must improve our economic standards first," he said. "We must make use of Malay lands, build up agriculture and establish cooperatives. We must endeavour to achieve economic independence first."[60]†

---

* Itagaki said that with great difficulty he had secured a seat for Ibrahim on the night train to Singapore. Itagaki, interview. Hassan Manan, however, claims that Ibrahim left by car for Singapore on 16 August, after attending the emergency KRIS meeting. Hassan Manan to Zubaidah, 30 April 1970. The second version seems unlikely, because of MPAJA roadblocks throughout the country.

† Datuk Onn, a scion of the royal house of Johor, was born in Johor in 1895 and educated at Aldebury Lodge School, Suffolk (U.K.) and at the MCKK. He was subsequently appointed district officer of Batu Pahat by the Japanese in 1945. He was

When news arrived that the Indonesians had already proclaimed their independence without informing KRIS, the initial reaction of the KMM *pemuda* was surprise. Uncertainty also set in and inhibited initiative. The KMM had drawn up elaborate plans to take over Japanese military installations and public buildings, but now only small groups of *pemuda* moved independently to carry them out. Most of the young Malays were too shocked and confused to act, and efforts to oppose the British without Japanese or other support soon began to collapse. Some *pemuda* representatives returning by train to Singapore came under attack from the MPAJA guerrillas, and their train was derailed. When they eventually completed their journey, most of the KRIS delegates dispersed to their hometowns to await the return of the British, when many, like A. Samad Ismail, were arrested.

In Singapore, Ibrahim was instructed by Japanese army headquarters to disband the Malay Giyu Gun. Realizing that Japanese support for his Indonesia Raya idea had now collapsed, he reportedly made contact with Chinese in the MCP, proposing that the Giyu Gun join with the communist MPAJA to fight both the Japanese and the British. Ibrahim claims that both the MCP and the KMM had earlier agreed to this in principle.[61] According to his account, on 19 August, without waiting to hear from the MCP, he sent a 280-man regiment of the Malay Giyu Gun under Maj. A. Manaf, Capt. Zakaria, and Lt. Mohd. Said to Kuala Lumpur to place themselves under MPAJA headquarters. However, the Malay troops were stopped at Muar (Johor) by the MPAJA, and on 22 August the officers were forced to disband their forces because the MCP had rejected Ibrahim's offer and adopted a policy of cooperation towards the British. The MPAJA had decided not to resist the returning

---

a well-known journalist and politician before the war, who had frequent public quarrels with Sultan Ibrahim of Johor. He had known Ibrahim Yaacob well when the latter owned the *Warta Malaya* in 1941, and was one of the first Malay aristocrats to join the KMM during its short rise in 1942. During the Japanese occupation, his son Datuk Hussein Onn, the former Malaysian Prime Minister was a captain in the British army in India. Apparently, the shrewd Datuk Onn calculated that with the Japanese surrender, chances for the success of the KRIS plan were slim. Shortly after the British return, he emerged into public prominence as the founder–president of the United Malays National Organization (UMNO), now the major component in the ruling coalition in Malaysia.

British because of the Allied radio broadcast of the British government's intention to establish a democratic government in Malaya on their reoccupation of the territory.[62] In other words, the MCP had already decided to set aside revolution in Malaya. This decision did not mean that the MCP had rejected cooperation with the KMM. In fact, under its broad united front strategy, it gave support to the KMM in its struggle for Indonesia Raya in post-war Malaya, despite the fact that the KMM's aims were clearly in opposition to the MCP's own goal of a communist republic in Malaya. Ibrahim later paid tribute to the MCP and MPAJA for shielding many KMM and Giyu Gun members from arrest by the British army.[63]

The disbanded 280-man Giyu Gun regiment joined other Malays in the inter-racial clashes with the Chinese, which erupted in the Muar and Batu Pahat (Johor) areas, and some Giyu Gun soldiers were able to acquire more arms from their Japanese superiors, who apparently were only too happy to see the Malays fighting the Chinese-dominated MPAJA in these clashes.[64]

Ibrahim was unaware of these developments, for on 19 August he left for Jakarta aboard a Japanese aircraft, accompanied by his wife, his brother-in-law, Onan Haji Siraj, and Hassan Manan. His departure added to the confusion of the *pemuda* and meant that he abandoned leadership of the Malay independence movement at a time when he was critically needed. His hasty exit is still the subject of heated controversy among his KMM colleagues, with some even accusing Ibrahim of cowardice, while others argue, as did Ibrahim, that by going to Indonesia he was continuing the struggle for Indonesia Raya.[65] When he arrived in Jakarta, Sukarno told him: "The union idea including Malaya is not convenient, as we would have to fight both the British and Dutch at the same time." He was also advised that he and his colleagues should join in the struggle in Java to achieve the aspirations of Indonesia Raya.[66*]

Dr Burhanuddin, whom Ibrahim had had appointed his second-in-command in Malaya, lacked Ibrahim's charisma in the eyes of the *pemuda*. Nor had Ibrahim left him clear and specific instructions. As a result, although the KMM *pemuda*, like their Indonesian

---

* Nasution, *Sekitar Perang Kemerdekaan Indonesia*, p. 275, reveals that Ibrahim Yaacob was left in the care of Winoto Danuasmoro, Sukarno's close friend, in Sukabumi. Nagai states that Ibrahim became active in the Indonesian independence struggle and later joined Tan Malaka's Persatuan Perdjuangan.

counterparts, were poised for militant action, their uncertainty and confusion led to chaos. At least six groups were hastily organized in different parts of the country, such as Ipoh, Taiping, Kota Tinggi, and Singapore. They attacked Japanese arms depots, seizing weapons for the resistance struggle they had been told to expect against the British. With the collapse of the KMM plan for armed struggle, however, they smuggled the arms to the Indonesian islands of Karimun and Batam. The Giyu Gun leader Major Manaf escaped to east Sumatra to join the Indonesian armed struggle, dying in battle against the Dutch at Tanjung Batu, Pulau Karimun.[67]

Malay disillusionment with the KMM was a setback to the movement's hopes to lead the independence struggle. Nasution claims that except for the areas of Muar and Batu Pahat, where the Malay population welcomed elements of the disbanded Giyu Gun, Giyu Tai, and Heiho units in the fighting against the MPAJA and the Chinese, most of the Malay *pemuda* were "stoned and abused" as they returned to their villages. They in turn focused their anger on their sponsors, who were well known as "anak-anak Fujiwara" (Fujiwara's children) — Ibrahim, Onan Haji Siraj, and other KMM leaders. They began to curse their sponsors as *penjual romusha* (sellers of *romusha*), and tried to hunt them down.[68†] The taint of collaboration with the Japanese, however, involved all strata of Malay society, including the rulers, and could not be erased. In addition, the political threat posed by the Chinese and the MPAJA guerrillas soon impelled the Malays to close ranks.

---

* Nasution comments ironically that in Indonesia, by contrast, the sponsors of the romusha on Java became national leaders and "heroes" of the independence struggle. "Romusha" means "forced labour".

Members of the Malayan Communist Party secretariat staff taken outside its headquarters in Queen Street probably in 1945.

A gathering of the Singapore General Labour Union of All Nationalities taken probably in early 1946. Note the MPAJA flag (three stars) and the MCP flag above the portraits of Stalin, Marx and Lenin.

Japan as an ally. Lieutenant Yamaguchi to the rescue of the Malay hero Kamaruddin and his Sakai friends in Bekok, Keluang (Johor). Illustration from Muhammad Hj. Kidin's novel, *Kerana si Kuntum*, Penang, 1961.

The hats suggest Chinese bandits pillaging and burning a Malay village in Johor. Illustration from Muhammad Hj. Kidin's novel, *Kerana si Kuntum*, Penang, 1961.

Members of Force 136 (China) standing to a few minutes' silence at a memorial service outside the Singapore City Hall in Dec. 1945 in honour of their late commander Maj.-Gen. Lim Bo Seng (Photograph courtesy of Tsang Jan Man).

Lt. Tsang Jan Man of Force 136 (China) who was air-dropped into Baling with Major Hislop in Apr. 1945 (Photograph courtesy of Tsang Jan Man).

Leaders of the Kuomintang (Malaya) with Lieutenant Tsang in Penang. Taken in Dec. 1945 (Photograph courtesy of Tsang Jan Man).

General Itagaki surrendering his sword to GOC Malaya, Lieutenant Messervy at a ceremony in Kuala Lumpur in early 1946 (Arkib Negara Malaysia [Malaysian National Archives], Kuala Lumpur).

Surrendering of swords by Japanese army officers, 1946 (Arkib Negara Malaysia [Malaysian National Archives], Kuala Lumpur).

The First Independent Regiment of the MPAJA receives a public welcome as it marches through a street in Chenderiang, Perak immediately after the Japanese surrender. Note that the slogans in the triumphal arches are all in Chinese. The bottom picture shows the First Regiment under an arch bearing the Chinese characters which mean "The People's Autonomous Council Welcomes the MPAJA. Whole Heaven is Rejoicing".

Source: Li Tieh Min *et al.*, *Ta-chan yu Nan-ch'iao (Ma-lai-ya chih pu)* (The World War and the Overseas Chinese in Nanyang — The Malaya Section), Singapore 1947 (New Year's Day), issued by the Singapore New Nanyang Publications Company on behalf of the General Association of Nanyang Overseas Chinese.

Admiral Mountbatten pinning a campaign ribbon on Liu Yau, supreme commander of the MPAJA, at the Singapore City Hall steps on 6 Jan. 1946 (Imperial War Museum, London).

Mountbatten congratulating the young Chin Peng before awarding him a campaign medal (Imperial War Museum, London).

Sultan Suleiman Badrul Alamshah of Trengganu (centre) with Japanese officers, including Brig.-Gen. Ogihara (right) and Malay court officials in front of Istana Kolam, Kuala Trengganu, 13 Dec. 1941 — about a week after the Japanese forces had landed at Kota Bharu (Photograph courtesy of Datuk Mohamed Haji Salleh).

The commander of the MPAJA Fourth Regiment (Johor), Chen Tien, speaking to his men at a disbandment parade in Dec. 1945 (Arkib Negara Malaysia [Malaysian National Archives], Kuala Lumpur).

A gathering of the Malay community at Batu Pahat in honour of Datuk Onn bin Jaafar, the District Officer (seated centre) and Kiyai Salleh (seated to his left with a garland of flowers). Beside the flag of Islam (crescent and star) is believed to be the flag of UMNO.

The historic meeting at Taiping Airport on 12 or 13 Aug. 1945 — the only time Sukarno is said to have ever visited peninsular Malaya. Left to right: Prof. Akamatsu Kaname, Dr Hatta, Radjiman Wediodiningrat, Sukarno, Ibrahim Yaacob and Prof. Itagaki. The individual at the rear is believed to be Pacik Ahmad (Photograph courtesy of Professor Itagaki).

Politician as romantic hero. Datuk Onn bin Jaafar in traditional Malay warrior clothes or baju silat (for martial arts) with keris.

Kiyai Salleh as a young man.

Members of the Malayan Peoples Anti-British Army. Standing L to R: Itu, _____, Choo Yong Pun, Liew Yan [possibly Yau], Ah Yong, Teng Fook Loong, sitting L to R: Lau Mah, Pai Tze Moke, Chin Tien, Wong Ching, Ong Chin Wah (Photograph courtesy of US National Archives [RG59 846E.00/3-2849]).

British Army officers taking the salute at the march past of a MPAJA regiment (top). The place is not identified. Pictures at the centre and bottom show a gathering of the people and MPAJA troops at a meeting to celebrate the Japanese surrender in Klang, Selangor.

Source: Li Tieh Min *et al.*, *Ta-chan yu Nan-ch'iao* (*Ma-lai-ya chih pu*).

(Top) Disbanding of the MPAJA, December 1945. March past of its Fourth Regiment (South Johore) at Port Dickson, Negeri Sembilan.

(Bottom) Brigadier J.J. McCully of the British Army inspecting men of the MPAJA's Fourth Regiment (South Johore) at Port Dickson, Negri Sembilan.

Source: Arkib Negara Malaysia (Malaysian National Archives), Kuala Lumpur.

(Top) A unit of the MPAJA assembled in the main street of one of the small towns of Malaya which the guerrilla army entered after the Japanese surrender.

(Bottom) The first patrol of the Fifth Independent Regiment (Perak) of the MPAJA. Place unidentified.

Source: Li Tieh Min *et al.*, *Ta-chan yu Nan-ch'iao* (*Ma-lai-ya chih pu*).

PART II

The Contest for Postwar Malaya, 1945–6

CHAPTER 5

The Post-Surrender Interregnum: Breakdown of Law and Order

....An instigator of the sabotage of the Police will be severely punished. Anyone who hoists the Red Flag or one who instigates the masses by unfounded rumours will also be punished....

– Japanese Armed Forces Proclamation,
Singapore, 3 Sept. 1945

After the Japanese surrender on 15 August 1945 there was a brief period in which law and order collapsed, rumour dominated fact, and diverse groups in Malaya were faced with critical decisions.

One of the most important rumours was that the British army would land on 20 August to reoccupy Malaya. As it turned out, it was not until 3 September, or 19 days after the Japanese surrender that the first British reoccupation force landed at Penang. As we have seen earlier, however, the rumour of immediate British arrival was a key factor inhibiting the Malay KRIS group in Kuala Lumpur from actually forming a provisional government and declaring national independence. The rumour probably had the effect of causing KRIS leader Ibrahim Yaacob to flee to Jakarta — one of the reasons why the Malay independence movement disintegrated.[1]

Many rumours had some grain of truth, but it was only a matter of hours before they were embellished or distorted in transmission and became sources of mass confusion. The initial rumour of Japan's surrender thus reached people in such strange terms that it was impossible to know what was happening. It was said, among other things, that units of Chiang Kai-shek's army were to come to Malaya for temporary occupation duty. Others simply wanted to believe that the end of the war had arrived.

The immediate Japanese response was to discount all peace rumours and to threaten rumourmongers with dire punishment. Without referring to the atomic bombs or the surrender at all, the *Syonan Shimbun* of 15 August in effect ordered everyone to keep quiet and await official instructions:

> No one has any sympathy for those who deliberately repeat idle rumours and get themselves into trouble over it. But for the sake of the good citizens, it is desirable that all foolish rumours should be stifled and those who are given to gossip warned of the serious harm which indulgence in what might seem harmless gossip might lead to. The insensible type of gossiper has had enough time and warning. If they persist in their foolish ways, they must be taught a severe lesson.[2]

While some people in Malaya took rumours of Japan's surrender seriously and acted immediately, others thought there was reason to be cautious. One person recalled his disbelief and hesitancy in the following terms:

> The newspapers came out with a report of the bombing of Hiroshima with a bomb of a hitherto unknown type. The damage was negligible, however, they said. Two days later came an admission of thousands of casualties. But in the interval there had been an unprecedented crop of rumours to which we lent greedy ears. The effects had been cataclysmic, we were informed. Japan's will-to-war had been pulverised. She was suing for peace. The news seemed too good to be true. A cold fear gripped our hearts. Could it be that the rumours emanated from the *Kempeitai* [Japanese military police) and were disseminated by their underlings to tempt disaffection to rear its head…. No, we were not going to throw caution to the winds.[3]

It was about the time of the surrender too that the rumour of the impending arrival in Malaya of the Chinese Nationalist Army of Chiang Kai-shek started. There was no basis for this rumour other than the association of Chiang's name with the Potsdam Declaration of the Allied leaders. However, it elated and encouraged the most chauvinistic speculation by the Chinese population. On the other hand, the Malay population was most unhappy and fearful of the consequences of such an arrival, as they feared that Malaya would then come completely under the heel of the Chinese. A Malay informant who lived in Singapore at that time, recalled:

> We Malays thought that the Chinese troops would land on the island first because of the large Chinese population there. In fact, some of my Chinese friends expected this to happen. Many Chinese suddenly became quite chauvinistic and arrogant. We were quite worried and did not know whether it was true.[4]

A Malayan Chinese informant who had heard the rumour thought that it was the KMT elements in the Communist-dominated MPAJA who had spread the rumour:

> Thinking people discounted the rumour. Only the very gullible hawkers and others in the market place thought that that was quite possible. It is my view that such rumours were circulated by KMT elements in the MPAJA to bolster up the morale of the Chinese throughout the country. Some British supporters were getting frustrated and disappointed with the British for their belated return. The rumours were a psychological ploy to play up Chinese admiration of Chiang Kai-shek as one of the heroes of World War Two. In those days, the heroes were: Churchill, Stalin and Chiang Kai-shek.[5]

Even the MCP, whose MPAJA guerrilla units had British liaison officers from Force 136 equipped with short-wave radio sets, were reported to have been influenced by these rumours. Although the British officers had informed them that it would be the British army that would reoccupy Malaya, the MCP leaders had their doubts. It is possible that fear of the arrival of the KMT Chinese army in Malaya played a part in influencing the decision of the MCP's central committee not to attempt a *coup d'etat*.[6] An example of the persistence of this rumour was the display of Chinese posters and slogans on triumphal arches by some groups of Chinese in certain areas to welcome the Chinese army and the other Allied forces.

In Malacca, Nakazawa Kin'ichiro, editor of a Japanese news agency, noted that on the night of 15 August when he took a walk in Malacca Park, citizens appeared to know that the war had ended.

> A few days earlier the Allied radio had reported that the Japanese had accepted the terms of the Potsdam Declaration. The blackout

was lifted after this. There was a change in the night scene. The streets became brighter. There was a multitude of people in the park. It was a moonlit evening. The attitude of the people towards the Japanese appeared not to have changed. Japanese songs were still being sung.[7]

Several days later, smoke was seen coming from the chimneys of State government buildings in Malacca. Japanese civilian and military officers were burning all their secret and confidential documents. The state government had also ordered government stores and Japanese firms to release stocks of food to the citizens, and there was a stampede among the local people to get at the goods. Malaccan shops suddenly became stocked with foodstuffs and goods, and prices fell rapidly. The goods were sold to absorb the military scrip, which the Japanese burnt in order to lessen Japan's ultimate liability for war indemnities. The governor ordered the people and the military to conduct themselves with prudence and not indulge in lawless activities.[8]

Rumours of Japan's possible surrender had circulated as early as the evening of 10 August, and were confirmed on 15 August by those who had listened to Allied radio broadcasts reporting the Japanese Emperor's speech. Official news of this event, however, appears to have spread rather slowly in the country, owing to Gen. Itagaki Seishiro, commander of the Seventh Area Army who, on 15 August, announced from his headquarters in Singapore that his forces would resist the British.[9] Itagaki's defiant attitude created only apprehension rather than relief among the local people. A day after his speech, Itagaki is believed to have been summoned to Dalat to meet Field-Marshal Terauchi, Supreme Commander of Japanese forces in Southeast Asia. Itagaki flew back to Singapore about 19 August,[10] and on 20 August all Malayan newspapers carried the Emperor's 15 August speech. It was then clear that Itagaki had bowed to the imperial order and would offer no resistance to the Allied forces.

On 21 August there was a conference of all the area commanders under Itagaki. At this meeting, held at his headquarters at Raffles College in Bukit Timah Road, Itagaki declared:

Now that the Emperor has accepted the Potsdam Declaration, we must lay down our arms. Obeying the Emperor's order, we shall not fight. We must keep peace and order and we shall not make any trouble.[11]

Some of Itagaki's staff officers were distraught when they heard his speech, and were reported to have taken their own lives. Though most of Itagaki's staff agreed to comply with his order, a few officers favoured the idea of going to Sumatra, especially to Aceh where the Japanese army was believed to stand in good favour with the local people. Among those who deserted to Aceh were Maj. Ishijima, head of the intelligence section Ibaragi Kikan, and his subordinates, Captain Adachi and Captain Kondo. Itagaki was furious when he heard of this and signalled immediately to the army commander in Sumatra to round up Ishijima and his fellow fugitives.[12] Other Japanese officers and soldiers were reported to have fled with their arms and ammunition to the neighbouring islands of Singapore. Some were later caught and brought back to Singapore by Itagaki's troops.[13] On 23 August, after meeting with the imperial envoy who had arrived in Singapore, Itagaki made a strong appeal to his troops:

> We were ready to fight to the last man prior to the receipt of the Imperial Command, which is absolute and irrevocable. Now, and without hesitation, we shall obey the wishes of the War Council.[14]

In this connection, Japanese preparations for "fading into the landscape" in anticipation of the Allied invasion of Malaya (i.e., prior to the Japanese surrender) are of some interest.

Chin Peng in his autobiography revealed that within hours of Emperor Hirohito's surrender broadcast on 16 August, Japanese military commanders in Negeri Sembilan, Perak and Kedah began sending out feelers to the MCP seeking negotiations and looking for an alliance with the party and the guerrilla army to carry the party's fight to the returning British forces. The proposal led to a heated debate within the party's state committee members, with an overwhelming majority keen to accept the Japanese offer, but the offer was rejected by Lai Tek, who was apparently considering his personal survival after the war and his intention to renew his old contacts with the British police intelligence agency.[15] Chin Peng also disclosed the shocking news that some 100 Japanese soldiers who had come over to the party's side in Kuala Kangsar had to be put to death at Lai Tek's orders, while smaller groups were secretly rescued, hidden and recruited in the jungle, without Lai Tek's knowledge.

There were reports suggesting that in Johor the Japanese were trying to make friends with Chinese communist guerrillas. Captain

Adachi of Ibaragi-Kikan was reported to have attempted to contact the MCP leadership in Batu Pahat on 13 August to propose some sort of deal "to fight as Asians against the returning British imperialists". He was hoping to be captured by the MPAJA and brought to MCP leaders, but these efforts were cut short by the surrender and by a very sharp order from Singapore to desist.[16] Many Japanese soldiers did, in fact, retire to the hills to join the communists, apparently under the impression that all communists were automatically anti-British. Some were later captured or killed by British troops, but a small number did successfully achieve this mission.[17] The MCP's guerrilla force at the Malaysian–Thai border included two Japanese World War Two holdouts who survived until the end of the MCP's insurrection in 1989, and eventually were repatriated to Japan.[18]

It was probably to prevent extremist actions by individual hotheads that a certain measure of disarmament was reportedly carried out among Japanese troops in Malaya as early as 22 August.[19] However, as far as relations with their various satellites were concerned, Japanese attitudes varied. The Malay Giyu Gun (Volunteer Army), Giyu Tai, and Heiho were disbanded on 18 August. This was probably a measure of self-protection to ensure that whatever arms held by these units did not fall into the hands of anti-Japanese elements.[20] Towards the Indian National Army the attitude was somewhat different. Where Japanese forces had withdrawn, INA troops that remained behind had orders not to fight but to ensure their own protection. On one occasion when a Chinese guerrilla party attacked an INA camp, the Japanese were reported to have placed two tanks at the disposal of the INA commander. The question of INA surrender was left to their own commanders. Probably some time before 26 August, an order was put out by the rear headquarters of the INA, addressed to all units and formations in Singapore and Malaya, commanding cessation of hostilities and preparations for handing over all INA arms and military stores to the British authorities.[21]

General Breakdown of Authority

Following Itagaki's obedience to the imperial order and his willingness to accept the orders of Admiral Mountbatten through Marshal Terauchi in Saigon, Japanese troop movements throughout Malaya followed a two-phase plan: first, the halting of any strategic moves in progress; second, the progressive concentration of units in certain specified areas. With regard to the first, the Thirty-seventh Division, strung out from Thailand in an apparent move to strengthen defences in Malaya, was ordered to split, one regiment in the latter country, the remainder of the unit in the Bangkok area.[22] The concentration of outlying troops into certain areas led to the build-up of detachments and units at communication centres at Ipoh, Taiping, Kuala Lumpur, and Kluang. The Japanese reaction to local disturbances was to protect themselves and maintain law and order until the arrival of Allied forces. In the larger towns such as Singapore, Taiping, Ipoh, and Kuala Lumpur, Japanese military control remained firm. Sentries were posted at major buildings and military installations. This was done too in other areas where there were sufficient Japanese troops. However, when the Japanese withdrew their outlying detachments from the smaller towns, the anti-Japanese resistance guerrillas began moving in and taking over, and many local disturbances broke out.[23]

Japanese commanders persisted with these withdrawals, initially to remove their troops from public sight, to avoid provocation and reduce vulnerability. They continued to withdraw in compliance with Allied directives, even though they knew that in the countryside this meant the breakdown of law and order. The guerrillas moved into the small towns and other pockets in force and began dealing out summary justice to the police, to *Kempeitai* collaborators, and to profiteers. Girls who had been the mistresses of Japanese were among those who suffered. Many of those arrested by the guerrillas were marched or dragged through the streets and given a "people's court" trial.[24]

The Japanese troop withdrawals could be said to have led to the breakdown of the rural district administration in Malaya. The district officers, *penghulu*, and *ketua kampung* were no longer able to get Japanese support and protection. Nor were the local police of much help, as the police stations had become the first targets of attack of the guerrillas. Consequently, many DOs and Malay headmen were captured and executed. Among those killed was the DO of Kluang, Esa bin Abdullah.[25] The Chinese guerrillas — the only armed force — initially went unchallenged and exercised their new power to the hilt.

Guerrillas meted out reprisals to police officers, detectives, and informers of the Kempeitai. Even the ordinary *matamata* (policeman) were vulnerable to anyone seeking revenge for the slightest insult or injury suffered during the heyday of Japanese power. It was when the reprisals extended to the Malay policemen and to the Malay *kampung* that Malay-Chinese inter-communal violence erupted.[26] Only in a few instances did Japanese troops go to the rescue of their former local agents of authority and repression. During these weeks the police force became utterly demoralized and a large portion of the men went into hiding and singly tried to survive until the British army arrived. One informant, a Malay ex-police sergeant who served the Japanese, still shuddered visibly when he recounted to me memories of those days:

> "It was a world gone mad, a world turned upside down. Suddenly, people seemed to remember every little wrong I did, even when I did not do them. There was a lot of anger and hatred about. This resulted in people being abducted, beaten, and murdered. Initially, before the violence became racial, even some of our Malay kinsmen believed that the police force was the *tali barut* (lackey) of the Japanese and had discredited themselves. But they came to our help later when they could not bear some of the things done to the Malay policemen, such as their bodies being mutilated and their eyes gouged out.... These actions, which the people seeking revenge did, were no different from the Japanese troops against whom they railed. They had degenerated to the same level of barbarism...."[27]

Consequently, inter-racial clashes (which will be discussed more fully later) broke out on 15 August (the day of the Japanese surrender) in Perak and Johor. Malays in Sungai Manik (Perak), near Teluk Anson, clashed with the MPAJA and local Chinese settlers after the MPAJA attempted to take over Sungai Manik and other neighbouring towns. Fighting raged until the arrival of British troops in September. So forceful was the Malay counter-attack that by September the Sungai Manik basin was cleared of both the MPAJA and all local Chinese. They were forced to seek refuge in Teluk Anson, a larger and predominantly Chinese town which became an MPAJA stronghold. In Batu Pahat (Johor), fighting between Malays and Chinese, which had raged intermittently since May, resumed in intensity on or about 21 August after the MPAJA swept into town.

The disintegration of law and order in the major towns of the peninsula states is conveyed, too, by several Japanese reports. In Taiping, Perak, a Japanese officer attached to the Twenty-ninth Army Propaganda Unit, Shigeru Saito, reported that soon after news of the surrender was known train services to Taiping grounded to a halt. Resistance forces cut the north-south peninsula railway lines at various points, and this had caused one train to be derailed. Saito and his unit were ordered to move to Kuala Lumpur, but on the way encountered a guerrilla roadblock. A skirmish followed in which both the Japanese and the guerrillas suffered casualties. Before he left Taiping, Saito had noted that Japanese authority was being defied in many places. Looting and plundering had started. Many Japanese collaborators had left town to avoid capture and execution by the guerrillas and other armed groups moving in.[28]

In Malacca, news agency head Nakazawa observed that public peace and order in the state worsened from about 20 August, as the manoeuvres of the MCP's guerrillas became more overt. But whether in fear or in deference to the Japanese, no one, especially the Chinese shopkeepers concentrated in the city centre, yet displayed the MCP flag, the Chinese national flag, or the Union Jack. However, many MCP members had infiltrated Malacca town. Civil servants and influential Chinese merchants, who had collaborated with the Japanese army, went into hiding. The president of the Malacca Chinese Merchants' Association, Ch'en Ssu-an, and the vice-president, Lo Chin-shui, slipped out of town unnoticed by MPAJA supporters. Many of the local policemen at the city police station went over to the communists, carrying their weapons with them. Every evening, large numbers of MCP members would occupy the parks in the city, agitating and spreading propaganda, and many appeared at the local recreational clubs. However, no injury was inflicted on any Japanese person.[29]

It was near the Malacca state borders that the disturbances developed. The main trunk road between Singapore and Malacca was under threat of communist and irregular guerrilla bands, and travel between these two centres was impossible. Around Batu Pahat and Muar Japanese vehicles were attacked. Nakazawa learnt that communist guerrillas were in complete control of the countryside and were attacking Japanese storehouses and arms depots in every region in search of weapons, ammunition, food, and vehicles. His speculation was that they were trying to arm themselves before the British return.[30]

Some areas were more unsettled than others. Particularly bad were the four Malay states taken over by Thailand in 1942 — Perlis, Kedah, Kelantan, and Terengganu. Previously KMT guerrillas had dominated the area, and with the infiltration of MPAJA guerrilla bands after the surrender, disturbances occurred.[31] The degree of Thai control in the area did not appear great. The MPAJA was reported to have occupied the state capital of Kuala Terengganu, killing collaborators. One local source said it then moved towards Kota Bharu, capital of Kelantan state, but it was too late as the town was already in the hands of the KMT guerrillas. In the northwest states of Perlis and Kedah, several MPAJA guerrilla takeovers also took place. The island of Penang remained quiet, however. In Kuala Lipis, capital of Pahang State, the MPAJA leader was reportedly responsible for spreading anti-British propaganda, banditry, and intimidation of the local population. Elsewhere in Pahang the situation was reported normal. In Sungai Patani, Kedah, Perak and Selangor, Japanese troops were reported to be disposing arms to local civilians, and they were also sold either to bandits or to MPAJA and KMT guerrilla units. Inter-racial clashes between Malays and Chinese were reported to have broken out in Malacca and Johor, particularly at Kluang, Mersing, and Batu Pahat.[32]

Not only Japanese authority was being defied, but also Force 136 influence in MPAJA camps was growing ineffective. The 80 British officers who had parachuted into the country by 13 August were not in direct command of any MPAJA patrols. They had to defer to local MPAJA commanders who reacted to the situation very much as they saw fit. In some areas close cooperation between Force 136 and MPAJA was achieved, but in other areas, particularly Kedah and north Johor, MPAJA commanders appeared hostile.[33] British officers discovered that so long as the guerrilla forces with which they had liaison were confined to jungle camps their control tended to weaken as guerrillas continually slipped out of their camps to take over towns. But as soon as the guerrillas were allowed openly to enter and take over areas the officers were able to reassert some influence.[34] SEAC headquarters had instructed Force 136 officers to ensure that guerrillas avoid engagements with the Japanese, as they feared that any premature flare-up might upset the landing plans of the reoccupation forces. This instruction had been difficult to observe, however. The guerrillas made repeated attacks on individual Japanese troops and sentries, police stations, and small garrisons to seize weapons. In areas taken over by guerrillas not in contact with British officers the scale of these attacks was higher.[35] After the towns had come under their control, guerrillas marched along the main streets under triumphal arches erected in their honour by supporters. The Chinese population especially came out in large numbers to greet them. What happened after the guerrilla takeovers will be discussed in the next chapter.

The intensity of guerrilla attacks on the Japanese forces suggests that they found the Japanese surrender an opportune moment to settle accounts. At any rate, some MPAJA attempts to take over areas did meet with resistance from Japanese garrisons. A belated Force 136 assessment in November tried to play down the significance of the skirmishes:

> At the time of the Japanese surrender there were something over three thousand guerrillas in contact with British liaison officers of Force 136. They had received orders to remain in their camps pending a clarification of the situation. Later, they were allowed to take over areas evacuated by the Japanese, but not to enter areas still under Japanese occupation. Only in North Johor and in Kedah — where liaison contacts were bad — was there any marked disobedience of these instructions. At this time there were also many guerrillas throughout the country who were not in contact with Force 136. These men were not well armed to attack the Japanese even if they wished to do so; but they did take over most of the minor police stations in the country. The Japanese themselves withdrew the arms from all except the most outlying posts, and so in no case could entries into police stations be classed as attacks — as the police did not remain to be attacked.[36]

Force 136, of course, wanted to create the impression of a situation under control. Japanese reports, however, presented a more realistic picture. Between the date of surrender and 31 August the guerrillas were reported to have "suddenly burst forth furiously" against both the Japanese army and the local police. They carried out a total of 212 attacks, of which 42 were against the Japanese army, 66 against the police, 38 against cars, 11 against railways, 9 against factories and stores, and 46 were "miscellaneous".[37] On 27 or 28 August an attack mounted by guerrillas of the Fifth Regiment, MPAJA, at Songkai, near Slim River (Perak), resulted in 34 Japanese and 3 guerrillas being killed. The incident was said to have been provoked by an excess of zeal on the part of a guerrilla road-check.[38] Col. J.P. Hannah, the senior Force 136 officer attached to this regiment, appears to have been unable to stop the guerrillas from carrying out their action.[39] In fact, the high Japanese losses so infuriated the Japanese local commanders that they carried out a reprisal on 31 August on the Fourth Regiment, MPAJA, patrol stationed at Serendah (Selangor) police post, in which one guerrilla was killed.

The fighting was stopped after the Force 136 officers, Col. John Davis and Col. Douglas Broadhurst, contacted both the Japanese and MPAJA sides for a parley. During the negotiations the Japanese refused to recognize the MPAJA guerrillas as part of the British force and, in fact, invited the British officers to their side to assist in maintaining law and order.[40] None of the British officers accepted the invitation.

The extent of the breakdown in Force 136 authority in the countryside is best exemplified by a Japanese appeal broadcast from Singapore on 25 August urging Force 136 officers to cooperate wholeheartedly with the Japanese forces in maintaining peace and order prior to the arrival of the Allied forces. The broadcast said such cooperation had become necessary owing to increasing violence and guerrilla clashes with Japanese troops. The Japanese gave the impression that the guerrilla attacks on them had been instigated by Force 136 officers. Because of this the Japanese Command said it had instructed its forces throughout Malaya to cease military operations completely as from zero hour of 25 August. The broadcast went on:

> ... The wishes of the Headquarters to assemble the forces in order to negotiate with the British command in a peaceful manner, will be extremely difficult to carry out in the face of subversive conduct on the part of armed elements, believed to be under the command of agents of the British Army.
>
> Recently such activities as destroying railway lines, attacking trains, clashing with military or police forces and seizing arms and food supplies by force, have increased to such an extent that they can hardly be expected to cease immediately.
>
> ... The Japanese Armed Forces have no intention of clashing with forces under the command of the British Army agents, and are prepared to surrender Malai, as well as Syonan, in a peaceful, orderly manner. They are only endeavouring to maintain peace and order until the arrival of Allied forces, and therefore request the British Army agents to cooperate in carrying out these wishes.[41]

Despite the unilateral Japanese decision to cease military operations against the guerrillas, the latter continued to launch attacks against the Japanese forces. Force 136 officers were unable to enforce a ceasefire order on the guerrillas.

The delay in the arrival of British troops in Malaya was also responsible for prolonging the chaos in the countryside. British Force 136 officers and their Gurkha support of 20 men each which had been airdropped into some guerrilla camps about two months before the surrender, quickly showed up in several towns as advance parties of the British army. While the welcome they received everywhere from the local population was said to be warm and enthusiastic, they were not numerous enough to deter lawless elements or to enforce order on their own. Consequently, they had still to rely on the MPAJA and other guerrilla forces to carry out police duties, as the Japanese-appointed police force had broken down completely.

Singapore and Penang

In Singapore, newspaper reports indicated that after the news of the surrender had been officially confirmed on 20 August, violence and other lawless behaviour in the city soon increased. This is surprising when it is realized that Singapore had one of the biggest garrisons of Japanese troops.[*]

Mamoru Shinozaki, head of the Welfare Department in the Syonan Tokubetsu Shi (Singapore Municipality), recalled that some people hoisted the Chinese national flag over their homes, which were then torn down by Japanese soldiers. He saw that a nasty situation could develop and decided to make a public announcement of the end of the war at the Majestic theatre in New Bridge Road (this was a day or two before the news was officially released by the Japanese military authorities). How he thereby endangered himself is told in his recollection:

> "There is no need now to evacuate to Bahau or Endau [settlements on the Malayan peninsula]," I told the audience. "The war

---

[*] The total strength of Hqs 7th Area Army amounted to 77,245 troops including 27,192 at the Singapore Garrison. The headquarters was in direct control not only of Singapore Island but also of the mainland state of Johor, the garrison of the Riau and Lingga archipelagos south of Singapore, and the Annambas and Tambelan islands between Malaya and Borneo. The mainland of Malaya, excluding Johor but including the neck of Siam to the Kra Isthmus and the Andaman and Nicobar islands, were under the command of Hqs 29th Army at Taiping (Perak). The total strength of the 29th Army was 45,980. See the statistics in Hqs 14th Army (SUM No. 50 based on information up to October 1945, in SMA PSD/29).

is over. The Emperor has accepted the Allied proposals. Peace has come at last. But, as you can see, there are many Japanese still armed and still willing to fight. This could lead to a dangerous situation. I therefore ask you to be peaceful and calm. Do not aggravate a dangerous situation. Do nothing rash.

"Wait patiently until the Allied forces arrive. Do not, meanwhile, put up flags." I left the Theatre and was driven direct to the railway station to stop the evacuation train from leaving.

That night, pistol shots could be heard. Several officers had decided to kill themselves rather than face surrender. Hand grenades were used for mass suicides. The next day I was summoned to Army headquarters and severely reprimanded for announcing the end of the war without authority. Certain young officers threatened to kill me. I hid in the *Poh Leong Kok* (home for the rehabilitation of women) in Pearl's Hill. Two days later, Major-General Kamata, the General Officer commanding Defence Headquarters, addressed his officers and men. He restored discipline.[42]

In the second week of the interregnum, the Japanese army first withdrew its troops from the city centre to Jurong, about 20 miles away, and then moved them across the Johor causeway to Kluang where they remained until disbandment. This meant that the security of Singapore was left to a small police force and a few Kempeitai officers, with disastrous consequences for public order.

As soon as they learnt that the Japanese troops were withdrawing from the Singapore city centre, the MPAJA guerrillas from the mainland of Johor state crossed over to Singapore. When a political vacuum had clearly emerged in the city centre a few days before the arrival of British troops they showed themselves and established their headquarters at the Japanese Club (the present Selegie Complex). Thus began what Shinozaki described as "a second period of terror and confusion for Singapore" (the first being the Japanese occupation on 15 February 1942). Those local collaborators able to do so fled to Hong Kong. Some gave themselves up to the police, feeling safer in prison than outside.[43]

As in Singapore, so in every other state on the mainland peninsula, officials of the Overseas Chinese Association (OCA) fled into hiding immediately on news of the surrender. Because they had been identified as instruments of Japanese policies and had allegedly failed to ameliorate Chinese sufferings, OCA leaders were prime targets for retaliation. On 23 August it was announced that the

Syonan OCA had dissolved itself. The guerrillas succeeded in capturing the Taiwanese adviser to the OCA, Wee Twee Kim, who had played a major role as the Japanese "hatchet man" in extracting the $50 million "gift" from the Chinese in March 1942. Shinozaki records how Wee and other collaborators met their deaths:

> Those were the days — no more than a few days, fortunately — of the Whispering Terror. Whispers could bring about death. Tan Boon Wu was stabbed in the heart because of a whisper. His body was left hanging on a tree. Wee Twee Kim, the Taiwanese, was another summarily executed....[44]

The *Syonan Shimbun* of 22 August reported widespread elation and celebrations of the end of the war (the word "surrender" was not used at all by the Japanese-controlled newspapers). Blackouts ended and the streets of the city once more became brightly lit after nearly four years of war. No restrictions were placed on the public's expression of joy and relief, but some concern was expressed lest the public enthusiasm impeded the maintenance of order. The Japanese authorities emphasized that it was their responsibility to prevent any looting or lawlessness in order to keep the city intact. The newspaper, in its editorial, "Be calm, be exemplary", urged every responsible citizen to consider himself "a policeman":

> ...not necessarily vested with the powers of policemen in the accepted sense, but feel by duty bound as a good citizen to tactfully discourage acts of hooliganism and immediately communicate with the regular police or auxiliary police should any acts come to their notice which are likely to disturb public peace and safety....[45]

The newspaper seemed unconscious of the ironical implications of the word "policemen", because with Japanese authority crumbling no one but "anti-Japanese elements" would now become "policemen" to try to take the law into their own hands.

On 25 August the Japanese authorities appealed for further public restraint. The *Syonan Shimbun* said it had been specially requested to draw the attention of the public to the need for strict discipline pending the changeover. It stressed that the Japanese government was still in full control of the city and would continue to be in full control until an official announcement was made. The authority of the military administration would be fully exercised against those who attempted to commit any acts of disrespect for law and authority. It described objectionable actions as acts of hooliganism, the displaying of flags of countries "other than Nippon and allied Dai Toa (East Asia) nations", and acts liable to "excite national emotions and cause inter-racial friction". The public was urged especially "to show consideration for the feelings of Nippon nationals".[46] The use of short-wave radios was still prohibited. The Japanese army headquarters also warned that since all buildings and establishments being used by the Japanese were scheduled to fall under the jurisdiction of the Allied powers, severe punishment would be meted out to anyone attempting to loot or damage such property.[47]

On 1 September the British fleet carrying the occupation forces was reported to have anchored off Penang and to have held surrender talks with Japanese commanders there. Between that date and 5 September, when British troops arrived in Singapore, authority collapsed completely in the city centre. Proclamations were issued one after another in an attempt to stop the violence. By this time the communist guerrillas had infiltrated into Singapore in larger numbers and made their presence felt. Raids on army depots, attacks on individual Japanese, and killings of collaborators had taken place. The rooftops and windows of buildings and shophouses began displaying the Communist Party's red flag as well as some Allied flags including those of China and the Soviet Union. It now became exceedingly difficult for the Japanese authorities to try to stem the tide of defiance being manifested everywhere. A proclamation of 3 September declared:[48]

PROCLAMATION TO ALL CITIZENS

It is highly regrettable that some citizens, who are under the impression that the landing of the Allied Forces would be effected today or tomorrow, have acted ruthlessly and lawlessly by taking advantage of the interim period believing that they will not be punished by any authority....

DATE OF NEGOTIATION UNKNOWN:
LANDING ONLY AFTER NEGOTIATION COMPLETED

... As a result of a thorough understanding on the part of the Allied Forces, the Japanese Armed Forces are to bear the responsibility of maintaining peace and order, therefore sabotage and all other acts violating peace and order will be punished severely by the Japanese Armed Forces. The Police Forces must carry on their duty as before because they will be transferred intact to the Allied Forces to maintain peace and order just as they did before.

An instigator of the sabotage of the Police will be severely punished. Anyone who hoists the Red Flag or one who instigates the masses by unfounded rumours will also be punished....

Stop all unnecessary violence and shedding of blood. Do not commit any evil act but calm yourself.

Japanese Armed Forces

In its last issue on the eve of the British arrival, the *Syonan Shimbun* proclaimed a prohibition against any public assembly. This was apparently to ensure that there would be some semblance of order at the time of the changeover.

PROCLAMATION

All the under mentioned actions are hereby prohibited:

1. Gatherings of over 500 persons
2. Demonstrations or activities of a similar nature
3. Other activities likely to bring about disorder

Japanese Armed Forces
4 Sept. 1945[49]

In Penang, the breakdown of order had already started a few days before 3 September when the British troops landed on the island. As in Singapore, communist guerrillas and other armed groups of Chinese crossed over from the mainland to the island. The Communist Party made its headquarters at a Chinese restaurant in the city centre, while guerrillas roamed about the island exercising power and meting out rough justice to police personnel and to those they suspected of being informers, traitors, and profiteers. While some people had reason to fear the communists and the chaos, others who had been outraged by the Japanese administration and who had suffered hardship and personal loss rejoiced at these moments of retribution. One who saw the retribution as "judgement day" was a Chinese journalist of an English-language newspaper:

Many people were abducted or taken from their homes because they had been informers and henchmen of the hated *Kempeitai*. They were never seen again. The communists carried out most of these summary executions. They had a very good spy network and as far as the Chinese population on this island was concerned, they were regarded as heroes, dedicated and fearless fighters against the Japanese and their lackeys. While I don't support communism, I believe that some of the people who were killed deserved their fate, especially the evildoers and the informers. Someone who found out that he was listening to a short-wave radio informed upon my brother. He was executed, but he was not a communist. The informer later died at the hands of the communists because he had betrayed my brother and others to the *Kempeitai*.[50]

A few hours after the British fleet arrived off Penang on 2 September, Vice-Admiral Walker accepted the surrender of the Japanese commanders on the island aboard his flagship, *H.M.S. Nelson*. The next day 480 marines landed at 0800 hours to begin the takeover. There were no incidents. Strategic points on the island were occupied and Japanese forces were evacuated first to a concentration centre at Glugor and later to the mainland. The Officer-in-Charge at Penang was Capt. T.J.N. Hilken, who found his principal difficulty was guarding from widespread looting the many food dumps left scattered over the island by the Japanese. Several riots occurred in the struggle over food dumps in Indian localities between Hindus and Indian Muslims. The rioting went on day and night, for several days, before British troops established control and distributed food rations.[51]

The non-recognition of Japanese currency, which Hilken immediately announced and made effective, caused a great deal of hardship to the people of Penang. As he thought further food riots would break out he immediately sought and obtained SEAC headquarters permission temporarily to retain some purchasing value for Japanese currency. The suggested rate was 100 Japanese dollars to one British dollar, until sufficient new British currency was in circulation.[52] In this respect Penang became an exception to the general BMA policy for demonetization of Japanese currency. As tension decreased in Penang, shops reopened and labour returned to work. However, there were some disturbances caused by 200 communist guerrillas from the mainland, who had taken over the Ayer Hitam district on the island. A conference of senior naval and civil affairs officers on 9 September was interrupted by information that the communists would attack Bayan Lepas airfield that night. Following this alarm, 75 marines were posted at the aerodrome, but nothing happened. After this scare it was decided that armed and uniformed Chinese guerrillas would be banned from crossing over from the mainland to Penang. Apart from these disturbances the British military occupation proceeded smoothly.[53]

Soon after the British fleet's arrival in Penang, two naval officers, Lt. Russell Spurr and Sub-Lt. Frank Worth, commandeered a car and set off on a 500-mile trip down the peninsula to Singapore. Their eyewitness account, published in the *Straits Times* of 8 September, is interesting for the information they revealed of the situation on the mainland. The local population gave them a warm and enthusiastic welcome wherever they stopped, and they got the support of the Chinese resistance forces and also the whole-hearted cooperation of the Japanese Army. They saw evidence of the damage and trouble the guerrillas had caused the Japanese army. Bridges had been blown up, and roads cut. Between Taiping and Ipoh the Japanese insisted on providing them with an armed escort as "communist guerrillas" were said to have made the road unsafe. Further argument was useless. They could not tell the Japanese of their arrangement with the Chinese resistance army at Taiping. At Ipoh an armoured car was considered necessary for their escort because in their safety "lay the honour of the Japanese Army". The police posts now let them pass without question. Just before Segamat the armoured car broke down, and they had to proceed on their own. Previously, whenever a great crowd collected around their car, Japanese troops had appeared and the crowd had melted away. But now no Japanese troops appeared to disperse the crowds. In the last stretch of the road from Segamat to Singapore, the officers saw further evidence of the work of the guerrillas. Bridges had been set on fire by the resistance army, and had to be crossed very carefully.[54]

Near Johor Bharu the roads became choked with sullen, evacuating Japanese troops. Lines of trucks were parked at the roadsides, most of them broken down, frantic drivers tinkering with the engines. Baggage and equipment was piled high in every truck, some carrying beds and furniture, and one with a small car on the back. The Japanese were piled as high as their baggage, hanging on by every available means. A small crowd cheered the two British officers, saw the Japanese, and changed their mind. Japanese troops lined the road and scowled at their Union Jack. Military police blocked the entrance to the Johor causeway, which was choked with traffic. Empty lorries were preparing to return to Singapore, and more laden trucks were pouring out of the city. A staff car containing high-ranking Japanese officers cleared the way for them, and they forged through past the saluting sentries into Singapore.[55]

On 4 September, the British cruisers *Sussex* and *Cleopatra* steamed into Singapore waters, after destroyers and minesweepers had cleared a path through the heavily mined Straits of Malacca. Gen. Itagaki, the Seventh Area Army commander responsible for Malaya, Sumatra, and Java, led a delegation aboard the *Sussex* to discuss surrender arrangements for Japanese forces in Singapore.[56] Itagaki was alleged to have broken down at the signing ceremony at the end of three hours of discussions with Lt.-Gen. Christison and Adm. Holland.[57] Early on 5 September a large convoy of troopships sailed into Singapore. The occupying force landed on the island immediately thereafter. Later in the day the first civil affairs units went ashore to start setting up the military administration. The Chief Civil Affairs Officer (CCAO), Maj.-Gen. Hone, and the Deputy CCAO (Singapore), Brig. P.A.B. McKerron, accompanied this party. The proclamation by the Supreme Allied Commander, Admiral Mountbatten, establishing military administration, had already been posted at the railway station and at other public centres a few hours earlier.[58]

On 8 September a civil affairs detachment passed through Singapore and reached Johor Bharu. Then, on 9 September, the main landings were made on the Morib beaches between Port Swettenham and Port Dickson, as originally planned for Operation Zipper. On the 10th, seven Civil Affairs detachments and other units went ashore. The Deputy CCAO (Malaya), Brig. H.C. Willan, reached Kuala Lumpur on 12 September and set up his headquarters. For the other regions, three to five weeks elapsed before British forces or civil affairs units arrived to establish the military administration.[59]

On 12 September in Singapore Admiral Mountbatten accepted the formal document of surrender signed by General Itagaki as personal representative of Field-Marshal Terauchi, who was too ill to travel from Saigon to attend the ceremony.[60] On their way to the ceremony at the Singapore City Hall, Itagaki and six other Japanese area commanders were hissed and jeered at by a large Chinese crowd that had gathered at the public field opposite the building. Shouts of "*Baka daro!* (you fool!)" rent the air. The crowd had been waiting for this moment for more than an hour and the cry of "*Baka daro!*" became more intense than before. Many among the crowd broke through the barricade of British troops, threw stones at the car, which brought the Japanese, and pushed forward towards the Japanese, who were protected by the British troops. "It grieved me greatly", recalled Gen. Shibata Taichiro, one of the commanders with Itagaki, "to think the Chinese felt such intense hatred towards the Japanese Army."[61]

The surrender ceremony formally brought the Japanese regime to an end. However, for the British the task of reoccupying the country was not yet completed. Large areas of the outlying districts were still in guerrilla hands. For instance, in the remote northeast state of Terengganu, Force 136 officer Lt.-Col. D. Headley, who had been in the jungle with the guerrilla forces for two or three months before the surrender, established himself as the SCAO, Terengganu, early in September. The state of affairs in the countryside is best illustrated by an account of the situation that met Headley in Terengganu:

> Headley was warmly welcomed by the inhabitants and on his journey from Dungun to Kuala Terengganu, the capital, he was accompanied by the State judge, Tengku Paduka Diraja. On reaching the capital he found that it was in a mess. The top Japanese officials had fled to Siam by way of Telemong and, since the surrender, power had lain with the MPAJA. They had taken the law into their own hands, tried and killed suspected Japanese collaborators, and even went to the extent of ransacking the local police station, and seizing available rifles and ammunition. The Commissioner of Police Tengku Segera was a powerless and frightened man. Obviously the first task of Headley was to establish law and order. Assisted by the ageing Mentri Besar, Dato Jaya Perkasa, Headley registered members of the MPAJA paid them salaries and supplied them with new rifles and ammunition. This registration later facilitated their demobilisation and the return of these arms. Meanwhile, with the arrival of Indian troops, the morale of the people was raised and law and order restored....[62]

CHAPTER 6

The MPAJA Guerrillas Takeover

Under our administration, all murders ceased and all robbers disappeared and people happily settled down.

> – Ma-Iai-ya jen min k'ang-jih chun chan-chi
> (The War Diary of the MPAJA), 1946

Banners are waving, drums are beating,

We celebrate a victory;

Heroes of battle step from the ranks,

And smiling,

Stand to receive our thanks, to receive our joyful thanks.

'Glory to our heroes!' Comrades cry;

Ovations rise to the sky, to the sky.

> – MPAJA song, *Victory Celebration**

---

* From Mona Brand and Lesley Richardson, *Two Plays about Malaya* (London, 1954), Appendix III, p. 143. The MPAJA song is one of four authentic Malayan guerrilla songs translated from the Chinese and appended to Lesley Richardson's play, *For Our Mother Malaya!* The play is sympathetic to the MPAJA and tries to show what motives influenced the guerrillas to suffer endless reprisals rather than relinquish their struggle against the British in 1948.

Owing to the delayed arrival of the British occupation forces, Force 136 officers in the field were daily reporting signs of unrest in the MPAJA ranks.[1] The Japanese had begun withdrawing their garrisons from outlying towns and districts on 22 or 23 August. In remote areas the Japanese had left much earlier, thereby leaving a vacuum in these areas. There were some in the MPAJA who were obviously glad that the Japanese were defeated, but who no longer wished for the return of the British. Their aim was an independent republic for all Malayan peoples based on the MCP's programme. These factions attempted to usurp authority in areas vacated by the Japanese. There are no indications, however, that they had received the blessing of the MPAJA headquarters. On the other hand, there were also no indications of any rebuke forthcoming from the MPAJA head-quarters. Local communist publications had been publishing criti-cisms of the British administration. There had been advances to the Japanese to sell their arms; and there were indications that Force 136 officers had difficulty in controlling guerrilla groups not in con-tact with them.[2]

By 23 August the British occupation forces were still not in sight. The small advance parties of Force 136 officers and support staff, totalling not more than 350 men, were scattered in different parts of the country and posed no real challenge to the MPAJA guerrillas. It was reported that the MPAJA was about 7,000 strong at this time.[3] Most of the British officers in MPAJA camps could have been detained. There was a suggestion from the MCP ranks in Johor to the central committee that all Force 136 officers attached to MPAJA units should be killed, and that the forces of reoccupation be presented with a *fait accompli* takeover of power.[4] The MCP leaders, who also failed to endorse the guerrilla takeovers by declaring inde-pendence and establishing a national government, took neither of these ideas up. Instead, the policy statement of 27 August called on party cadres and guerrillas to cooperate with the returning British and to adopt a constitutional line of struggle. With hindsight, Chin Peng admits in his autobiography that Lai Tek's policy was nothing more than a move to appease the incoming British, that it was against a militant stance by the party, and that it "represented nothing less than a 180-degree turn" of the party's programme of continuing armed struggle against the British and achieving national independence, but despite this change of policy, he went along with Lai Tek's arguments on the grounds the guerrilla army was numerically weak and the party was only strong among the Chinese, and not among the Malays.[5]

With this policy, Lai Tek sought to dampen the anti-British mood now rising within the party's ranks. Its branches and satellites were asked to endorse the central committee's decision. One by one they did so. The Selangor State Committee's endorsement of 27 August came first. On 1 September, the Fourth Independent Regiment (in charge of South Johor) and the South Johor MPAJU came out jointly in support of the party's eight-point programme "drawn up for the present situation".[6] They adopted the following slogans: (1) "Uphold the democratic league of China, the Soviet Union, Britain, and America"; (2) "Welcome Great Britain to administer Malaya"; and (3) "All races unite to establish a democratic Malaya". In their joint statement in Chinese, the two organizations said:

> ... We trust that a righteous and just policy will be executed by the British Military Administration in future in order to bestow on us happiness and freedom. As Great Britain is a righteous nation we believe we shall be granted proper rights and given the opportunity to offer our cooperation to the British Government. Simultaneously, we expect all races and political parties to join with us in the task of establishing a New Malaya under the democratic flag ....[7]

While the expectations expressed in the above statement may seem unduly optimistic, it is a fact that many communists after the surrender came to believe that some post-war British rewards to the MCP and the MPAJA for their wartime cooperation were inevitable. A strong belief lingered among groups of MCP members that some sort of bargain had been struck with the MPAJA command, or offers made, which meant that the British would allow them to play a political role in post-war Malaya.[8] It appears that subtle British propaganda spread by broadcasting stations was largely responsible for this (to be discussed shortly). On the other hand, there were also communists who distrusted British motives, who considered that while they had to go along with the party leadership's decision to abandon the armed struggle, a "cooperative" policy towards the British could only be tactical, in line with their own strategic assessment that "British colonialism" was still the party's enemy, and that before long the interests of both sides would again clash.

On 11 August, when Japanese surrender was imminent, a SEAC message was sent to Force 136 officers to inform the guerrillas that victory was near, and that allied forces would soon reach them. The guerrillas were congratulated on the part they had played. They were instructed to avoid military engagements with the Japanese and not to enter any towns or districts where Japanese were present. In areas where there were no Japanese they could, in conjunction with Force 136 officers, enter and take over responsibility for ensuring law and order until Allied forces arrived.[9] The Force 136 officers were also told in the same message:

> It will be some days before regular Allied Forces arrive. In the interval it is essential to avoid clashes between AJUF [the Anti-Japanese Union and Forces — the SEAC name for the MPAJA] and Japanese and *to prevent AJUF seizing power*.[10]

However, on 16 August, Force 136 officers were told that the guerrilla forces should not come out of their camps until it was known beyond doubt that the Japanese would obey the surrender orders.[11] It is not known whether these various orders were passed on immediately to Chin Peng to be relayed to MPAJA headquarters. In any case, between 15 and 17 August, MPAJA guerrillas were continually slipping away from their camps to the towns and populated areas. Force 136 officers found their control weakening.

Only when guerrilla forces were allowed formally to enter such areas were British officers able to accompany them and revive their authority.[12] This indicates that MPAJA headquarters did not act on SEAC's "standstill" order, although the Force 136 mission claimed that it was being obeyed.[13]

In fact, on or about 22 August the MPAJA central headquarters ordered its eight regiments "to take over all small and big towns in the country".[14] The regiments were also instructed to coordinate their efforts with MPAJA branches in each state to establish People's Committees and to assume responsibility for security, rescue of refugees, and restoration of communications. The MPAJA/MPAJU branches in each state were ordered to convene jointly a State People's Representatives Congress. The aim behind the exercise, the MPAJA's official history says, was "to put the initial chaotic situation in order".[15] The history does not record the receiving or obeying of any requests or orders of Force 136, and clearly intends to indicate that the decision was entirely its own.

Apparently because of the MPAJA guerrillas' non-compliance of the order of 16 August, SEAC headquarters had no choice but to rescind that order and to endorse the MPAJA headquarters' order of 22 or 23 August. On receipt of this message on 23 August, Force

136 officers began to readjust their positions. They now reported that despite the new attitude, some MPAJA groups were friendly, others hostile. The friendly guerrillas were said to be in central Perak, Selangor, Malacca, and south Johor. The attitude of MPAJA central headquarters was reported to be friendly and cooperative. This was evident in the amicable relationship established between headquarters representative Chin Peng and John Davis. In upper Perak, Kedah, north Johor, and parts of Pahang, Force 136 officers encountered hostility and non-cooperation from MPAJA guerrillas.[16]

These different reactions were due to two factors. First, in many areas MPAJA units had no liaison contacts with Force 136, so that when Force 136 officers parachuted into their camps after the surrender, they were treated as unwelcome guests who had dropped in without any introduction or advice from central headquarters. Second, the initial attempts of Force 136 officers in contact with MPAJA groups to restrain the guerrillas from leaving their camps to take over towns and villages incurred their hostility and were apparently regarded as attempts to rob them of the fruits of Japanese defeat.

Since a full central MPAJA command hardly existed, how each unit was to react to a local situation depended on individual MPAJA area commanders. The question of how successful each Force 136 officer was in exercising any tactical command over the MPAJA guerrillas depended on his relations with the MPAJA area commander. It would seem that in the first week of the Japanese surrender, the officers found it very difficult to confine the guerrillas to their camps. The high incidence of MPAJA guerrilla attacks on the Japanese and local police between 15 and 31 August also suggests a further defiance of orders of the Force 136 officers.[17] SEAC headquarters had explicitly instructed that military engagements between the guerrillas and the Japanese should be avoided at all costs because they might escalate and disrupt the landings of the British occupation forces.

These acts of defiance meant either that there was a breakdown in communications between Force 136 and MPAJA headquarters, or that the latter, while agreeing to cooperate with the British, intended to utilize the situation following the surrender to its own advantage as much as possible — such as seizing towns and setting up People's Committees.

After SEAC headquarters had authorized guerrilla takeovers of areas vacated by the Japanese, it refused to define any further tasks they should undertake on re-entry of British forces to Malaya. Before the Japanese capitulation, SEAC had in fact planned to launch Operation Zipper to invade and recapture Malaya either in late August or in September. For that military operation the MPAJA's agreement had been sought and obtained. The MPAJA had wholly supported the British desire to drive the Japanese out of Malaya. It was ready to cooperate with any planned British invasion of Malaya, and be allotted specific tasks such as sabotage and diversionary engagements with Japanese forces to facilitate the landing of British forces. But the sudden surrender of the Japanese and their apparently docile acceptance of Allied terms, rendering the role of the MPAJA no longer necessary, presented a different picture entirely. The question arose at SEAC headquarters whether the MPAJA would now be more of a hindrance than a help to British occupation forces. The attitude of SEAC is best summed up as a wish that the MPAJA would simply get out of the way. It should also avoid any hostilities with the Japanese troops in order to prevent unnecessary bloodshed and disruption of landing plans. The failure of SEAC to give a clear order to the MPAJA to assist in its reoccupation of Malaya has been blamed by Force 136 headquarters for being responsible in allowing the MPAJA guerrillas to do virtually whatever they liked in the areas they took over in the interval before the British forces arrived.[18] It is necessary to follow the deliberations at SEAC headquarters to see how they viewed the MPAJA threat to British reoccupation plans.

Mountbatten and the Resistance Movements in Malaya

Since July 1944 Mountbatten had taken a special interest in Malaya's political problems, paying particular attention to the resistance movements and to the Chinese and MCP problem. The Secretary of State for the Colonies, Oliver Stanley, in a secret memorandum presented to the War Cabinet on 9 December 1944 recorded Mountbatten's views as follows:[19]

> I have been in correspondence with the Supreme Allied Commander South East Asia, who has strongly represented to me the importance of making known our future plans in general to the peoples whom these plans will affect.* Admiral Mountbatten holds

---

* These plans included the formation of the Malayan Union and proposals to give the Chinese citizenship and equality of status with Malays.

that the proper reception of our future policy in Malaya depends upon its being fully explained beforehand, and that the time is now ripe to do this.

In advancing this point of view, the Supreme Allied Commander is thinking not only of long-term considerations, but also of the creation of a favourable atmosphere for the setting up of a military administration for which he will be responsible. Moreover, those responsible for present operations of a social character within his Command have made the same case for their own reasons. So much so that the organisation [i.e., SEAC] has had to be given certain general guidance on the subject for the use of its agents....

To the requests of Mountbatten and his staff, the minister had replied that he was not yet convinced that "the time has come for our plans to be divulged in full, since this would involve committing ourselves to every feature of those plans at a time when many relevant facts are by force of circumstances unknown to us".[20]

On 11 May 1945 Mountbatten sent a telegram to the British chiefs of staff requesting them to urge the British government to publicize its proposed Malayan Union policy. He did this while asking the chiefs of staff for instructions on the resistance movements in Malaya. Mountbatten argued that publicity of the Malayan Union policy would greatly increase his power to use the Chinese resistance movement, that is, the MPAJA. As he explained to the Chiefs of Staff:

The best chance of military action against the Japanese lies in my supporting the largely Chinese movement known as the Anti-Japanese Union and Forces [AJUF].

The political implications of this are governed by the fact that the Chinese in the greater part of Malaya did not in the past enjoy equality of status. Consequently support of this movement might invite pressure to secure these privileges once hostilities are over.

The potential danger will be minimised if HMG's [His Majesty's Government's] policy for the future of Malaya is disclosed now. This policy offers the local Chinese something concrete and if its disclosure is deferred until after liberation we may well appear to be making concessions to the Chinese under pressure. Whereas if it is disclosed now the AJUF can be told that no additional undertakings as to post-war status can be given to any resistance movement as such but that their objective must be limited to the expulsion of the Japanese.[21]

This is one of the clearest official statements in support of some British offer of rewards or political concessions to the MPAJA guerrillas in particular, and to the Chinese community in general. In the same memorandum Mountbatten also suggested that Force 136 should offer increased support to the MPAJA and the Malay resistance movements, but that British attitude towards the Kuomintang guerrillas should be the subject of further consideration. According to him, the KMT guerrillas present "a political problem of their own, since as members of the Kuomintang, they are affiliated with China proper and may well be used as a nucleus to spread in Malaya the strong Chinese nationalism which is manifesting itself in China today".[22]

On 11 May itself, Mountbatten again wrote personally to the Secretary of State for the Colonies, explaining the background to the request he had made through the British chiefs of staff. It is an important document as it expresses succinctly his liberal political aspirations for Malaya and contains little-known details of the British Colonial Office's plans to prepare post-war Malaya for self-government. These included the formulation of common political identity and multi-racial integration among the three major races of Malaya. His letter reads *in extenso*:[23]

> In the case of Malaya, there is of course the difficulty that the Resistance Movements are largely composed of Chinese elements and that the Chinese in the greater part of Malaya did not in the past enjoy equality of status. If we back them to any appreciable extent, and accept their cooperation, we shall owe them a special debt and this will give them a strong case if they choose to ask for special privileges.
>
> I feel, however, that this point is already largely covered in the Directive on HMG's policy for Malaya, forwarded to me by the War Office in their letter 098/4335 (CA4) of the 10 July 1944 (WD) which in the first para states that "our declared purpose of promoting self-government in colonial territories should provide for a growing participation in the Government by the people of all the communities in Malaya". I also feel that you personally strongly back the implementation of this aim, since in your letter to me of the 21st August 1944 you state that "our pre-war experience offered *hardly any sign of a conception amongst the three peoples*

that they were Malayans. Our plan is to proceed both from the top and the bottom in fostering the growth of such a conception — viz. by a single representative legislature at the top, and at the same time the institution of local bodies which will not be purely Malay but more broadly based and representative of the country."

If HM Government's policy is made public, it becomes possible to tell the Chinese elements that we cannot guarantee any additional privileges on account of services rendered in the Resistance; but we can point to the fact that the policy offers them concrete advantages.

I am aware that publicity may be regarded as prejudicial to the negotiations, which we are contemplating with the Sultans, following our reoccupation of Malaya. But it seems to me that if we are convinced of the rightness of the solution we propose, and are backed by world opinion, we can afford to risk that complication.

I very much hope that the War Cabinet will see their way to agreeing with my new proposals. The question of Resistance Movements within the British Empire is in a special category. Presumably we have not previously found Colonial Subjects rising to fight on our behalf when we were about to occupy their territory, and the fact that they are doing so today seems to me a wonderful opportunity for propaganda to the world in general, and to the Americans in particular, at a time when we are being accused of reconquering colonial peoples in order to re-subjugate them.[24]

Although there is no record of a reply from the Secretary of State to the Colonies being received by Mountbatten, there is a telegram sent to him by the British chiefs of staff on 7 June 1945 stating that since the British Cabinet had not given its final approval, no advance publicity could be made on the Malayan Union policy. The telegram stated:

Post-war constitutional policy on Malaya has only received provisional approval of Cabinet for planning purposes and is liable to modification. Until this has been decided no publicity of policy can be made and you should ensure that your clandestine organisations impress upon the resistance movements that any association with them is purely military.[25]

The British chiefs of staff approved Mountbatten's earlier proposals in his telegram of 11 May on the use of the "AJUF" and the Malay resistance movement. They also agreed that their attitude towards the KMT guerrillas should be subject to further consideration, after investigations into the scope and extent of their organization. However, they urged him to obtain such intelligence as he could from the KMT guerrillas "without prejudice to any decision we may wish to make in future regarding our recognition of this movement".[26]

On 4 August 1945, after Force 136 investigation had provided SEAC headquarters with the relevant information on the nature of the three sections of the resistance movement in Malaya and their relationship to each other, Mountbatten recommended further to the British chiefs of staff that he should be authorized to accept the "fullest cooperation" of the MPAJA and the MPAJU, that he should try to induce the Malay resistance movement to cooperate with the former, but that he should be released from any obligation to the KMT movement.[27] His reasons for these proposals were:

> that the MPAJA and the MPAJU had expressed enthusiastic "pro-Malayan" sentiments, whereas the Kuomintang stood for the strengthening both of the Chinese community as a separate community in Malaya, and of the bonds between this community and China; that there was great hostility between the two sections of guerrillas so that it would be difficult to back both; that he trusted the Communist Party's undertaking to cooperate with the British during the period of military administration; and that clandestine operations yielding valuable intelligence were entirely dependent upon the friendship and support of this section. True, the "pro-Malayan" sentiments of the Communists involved the expulsion of the British, the establishment of a Communist-dominated Republic of Malaya, and without doubt, the dominance of the Chinese; but Admiral Mountbatten still felt that the rank and file of the Communist guerrillas could probably be weaned from these views if other methods could be devised of granting to them the equality of status with Malays which was what they most desired; for this purpose he pressed again for the publication of the British plans for the future constitution of Malaya, which included the creation of Malayan Union citizenship....[28]

Mountbatten's proposal that he should be released from any obligations to the KMT guerrillas appears to have had no effect. As F.S.V. Donnison points out, his proposal was soon crowded out by the many problems surrounding the imminent surrender of Japan. There is also no record of any decision by the British chiefs of staff. As a result, Force 136 officers continued to be attached to KMT resistance forces in Malaya.

SEAC's Post-Surrender Expectations

On 15 August, with Japanese surrender imminent, Mountbatten received a conference paper prepared by SEAC's political and intelligence divisions on appropriate actions to be taken by Force 136 and the resistance movements in Malaya, Burma, Siam, and Sumatra, all within Mountbatten's jurisdiction. With regard to Malaya, the paper made a fairly perceptive assessment of the MPAJA guerrillas and how they were likely to act in the interval before the arrival of British forces. This was presented as follows:

(1) The Malay movement and the KMT guerrillas are of little account and the policy to be adopted should, therefore, be based on the AJUF.

(2) The AJUF are first and last anti-Japanese and not pro-British except insofar as such an attitude might be of advantage to them. They would very easily become anti-British if differently handled.

(3) British and American officers with AJUF are by no means in command, and can only exercise a limited controlling influence. They might easily become casual prisoners.*

(4) The desire of the guerrillas to kill Japanese will not stop in the event of capitulation. By restraining them, we will to some extent be cheating them of their prey. They will undoubtedly busy themselves in paying off old scores, and in liquidating "collaborators".

(5) The guerrillas are hungry and cut off from supplies by the Japanese; they are, therefore, likely to do their best to take advantage of Japanese inactivity to improve their lot.

(6) Guerrillas are "fair game" for the Japanese, whether the latter have capitulated or not, since their activities can clearly be considered offences against law and order.

(7) Unless the AJUF are given clear instruction which it suits them to observe they will be potential troublemakers. They are a

---

* The American clandestine organisation, the Office of Strategic Services (O.S.S.) had parachuted several agents into MPAJA camps in Johor and Pahang in 1945 and worked with Force 136 officers. Their presence in Malaya was nominal, since Malaya was not within the American sphere of operations. However, the O.S.S. agents were despatched into Malaya at O.S.S. headquarters' own request to collect intelligence for their own use. During the war O.S.S. compiled several informative reports on Malaya that are now available in the U.S. Archives.

menace to civil authority from the point of view of long-term policy. There is little doubt that the Communist Party and Union [that is, the MPAJU] will seize every opportunity during the period, which is bound to set in following the Japanese capitulation to further their political ends. They may use force.[29]

The paper considered that if the guerrilla forces were to be properly used to SEAC's advantage, then they should be kept in their areas and remain as far as possible under the control of the Allied Force 136 officers. They should avoid clashes with the Japanese, and should be ready to carry out whatever tasks were considered necessary, such as the provision of intelligence, guides, and interpreters, or making contacts with Allied prisoner-of-war camps.

The conference paper had incorporated the main points raised in a separate Force 136 headquarters memorandum. The objects of the memorandum were stated as: "To prevent seizure of power in Malaya by AJUF and to avoid unnecessary bloodshed before the arrival of regular forces."[30] Force 136 headquarters in Kandy reckoned that no regular forces would reach Malaya for at least 14 days. There were, however, about 80 British officers with about 200 support staff liaising with the MPAJA and communicating with SEAC headquarters through about 40 wireless telecommunications sets. The MPAJA reportedly had about 3,000 guerrillas, mostly Chinese communists, and containing elements "desirous of preventing a permanent return of British rule".[31] All were violently anti-Japanese, and had agreed to SEAC's orders with the object of throwing the Japanese out of Malaya. More than 2,000 arms had been sent to them since May 1945. Experience had shown, particularly in Greece, that resistance movements should be given clear instructions on what to do when their country was liberated, otherwise they would inevitably cause trouble, and might well attempt to "seize power in the principal towns".[32] The Greek communist rising,* which had taken place about eight months before the war with Japan had ended, had taught the British what to expect from communist resistance movements in Southeast Asia in the event of a Japanese capitulation.

---

* The Greek communist resistance movement ELAS (National Popular Liberation Army) had begun an insurrection in December 1944, following withdrawal of German occupation forces from Athens and other towns. It was British military intervention, which helped the royalist forces to stem the communist tide. See C.M. Woodhouse, *The Struggle for Greece, 1941–1949* (London, 1976), pp. 129 –31.

At the same time, Force 136 Headquarters stated:

AJUF have been very nearly our only friends during the occupation. We are under an obligation to them and do *not* wish to
give them the impression that we are ready to drop them now
that we *no* longer have any use for them.[33]

Considering the courses of action open to SEAC, Force 136 said
that to do nothing pending the arrival of regular forces would be
to allow what had happened in Greece to take place. On the other
hand, to tell the MPAJA to cooperate with the Japanese in the administration of the country, pending arrival of Allied troops would
certainly not be understood by violently anti-Japanese guerrillas.
Force 136 suggested that British liaison officers should be instructed
as follows: (1) prevent contact between the MPAJA and the Japanese;
(2) keep the MPAJA in the country districts where there were no
Japanese; and (3) give the MPAJA the task of keeping order generally
in such districts.[34]

On 15 August, the date on which the Japanese Emperor broadcast acceptance of the Allied surrender terms, Mountbatten's staff
meeting at SEAC headquarters approved the recommendations
outlined in the above conference paper.[35] On the 16th, at another
meeting, Gen. Sir William Slim, Commander-in-Chief, ALFSEA,
suggested that the resistance forces in Malaya, Burma, Siam, and
Sumatra should not come out into the open until it was beyond
any doubt that the Japanese would comply with Allied surrender
orders. Mountbatten agreed with this view.[36] On 18 August, as an
indication of the great concern felt in Whitehall, the War Office in
London wired Mountbatten, expressing its views on likely developments in Japanese-occupied territories in which Britain had an
interest. On Malaya, the War Office said:

Much depends on how successfully we disarm the AJUF. These
appear to consist mainly of Chinese communists with anti-British
tendencies. We consider AJUF elements more likely further
source of trouble than the Kuomintang Chinese ....[37]

Since 11 August, directives were going out to Force 136 officers in
Malaya. A telegram, undated but believed to have been communicated on 11 August, said:

It will be some days before regular Allied Forces arrive. In interval
it is essential to avoid clashes between AJUF and Japanese and *to*

prevent AJUF seizing power. At the same time we do not wish to give AJUF impression that we are preparing to discard them now that they have served their purpose. You should therefore inform AJUF as follows:

1. Victory is now at hand and your contribution has been important and appreciated.
2. Allied troops will shortly arrive but meanwhile to prevent clashes and unnecessary bloodshed you should avoid all towns and other districts where Japanese are present.
3. Where there are no Japanese you should in conjunction with Allied officers attached to you take over responsibility for ensuring law and order until Allied Forces arrive.[38]

However, Col. John Davis, chief of the Force 136 mission in Malaya, was unhappy with these instructions. In a very blunt telegram to Force 136 headquarters on 19 August, he said:

Your recent telegrams are disturbing. Following must of course be obvious to you. Controlled AJUF are soldiers under command of SACSEA. They expect and await specific orders and not vague directives. I am satisfied they will obey such orders provided they are reasonable. Orders for them to remain half starved in the hills while the Allies leisurely take over the administration from the Japs will not be reasonable.

Some arrangement must be made with the Japs for controlled AJUF to emerge during the interim period though they need not interfere with the Japs administration. AJUF must be given full share in the honours of victory: Controlled AJUF should now be limited to those already armed by us plus other armed men who will accept our control. They must be fully equipped, rationed and used by us at the earliest opportunity until time for disbandment.

Good treatment of controlled AJUF will have an excellent effect on uncontrolled AJUF many of whom may later be absorbed. Do your utmost to preserve and strengthen central control otherwise discipline will collapse. The alternative to all this is chaos and anarchy, which may take decades to eradicate. The matter is very urgent. There is serious risk of a disastrous anticlimax.[39]

Davis was most anxious that MPAJA central headquarters be accorded a proper status, that its guerrillas be treated as Allied soldiers (this did not happen until 4 September) and used jointly with arriving British forces to liberate Malaya. Worried that SEAC might still view the MPAJA with suspicion, Davis sent another message on 21 August:

> You must not give SACSEA [i.e., Mountbatten] impression that MPAJA are threatening to break out. Nothing could be further from the truth. The danger is that SACSEA may irreparably damage MPAJA discipline and cause such a breakout by failing to exercise the control and give the support, which MPAJA have been led to expect.[40]

On the same day, a meeting chaired by Mountbatten discussed the guerrilla activities in Malaya. Captain Garnon-Williams, head of the Political Division, who shared the sentiments expressed by Davis, presented the reports from Davis. He suggested that definite tasks should be allotted to guerrilla forces when the Allied reoccupation forces landed in Malaya. If this was not done, he feared it would be very difficult to control "men who, up to now, had obeyed the standstill order and were very short of food".[41] Gen. Sir William Slim, however, opposed this view. He said that if the Japanese behaved correctly and British landings went off without incident, any guerrilla activities might upset a situation, which would otherwise be under control. The guerrillas should only report, as formed bodies under British officers, to arriving British forces, and then be given certain tasks as part of the regular reoccupation forces. Colin Mackenzie, Commander, Force 136, said that although such a course of action would be suitable where it was easy for the guerrillas to make contact with British forces, he thought that it would not be easy to prevent sporadic guerrilla hostilities with the Japanese, particularly in the more remote areas of northern Malaya. He suggested that the guerrillas be given some definite tasks. In the end Slim had his way. Mountbatten, however, directed the Head of the Political Division to consult with Slim and to prepare a paper formulating the actions, which guerrilla forces should be instructed to take upon re-entry of British forces to Malaya. He also directed that a note be prepared on the local political and military problems, which SEAC was likely to face on re-entry.[42]

Mountbatten was understandably very anxious to land British forces as quickly as possible in Malaya. He was unable to do so, however, because of General MacArthur's request that landings be delayed until 31 August.[43] As MacArthur had rightly predicted, Field-Marshal Terauchi made it clear on 22 August that he would not obey Mountbatten's orders until he had heard from the Emperor.[44] British occupation forces, therefore, could not begin landing at Penang until 3 September, and were delayed from landing elsewhere in Malaya because Japanese naval mines in the Straits of Malacca had to be cleared first.

In the meantime, SEAC decided to increase the strength of Force 136 personnel in Malaya to prevent the MPAJA guerrillas from usurping the functions of government. One of those who volunteered to return to Malaya by parachute at the end of August was Col. Spencer Chapman, who had returned to Colombo on 19 May by submarine. He was parachuted into Pahang, where it was feared the guerrillas might get out of hand.[45] He was asked to assist Force 136 Maj. J.R. Leonard, a former Malayan Game Warden. Leonard had dropped blind some distance from a district MPAJA headquarters, and had reported that the MPAJA guerrillas were unhelpful, even hostile. As a result of these reports, SEAC decided to drop one or more support groups to assist Leonard in controlling these "refractory" guerrillas.[46] Force 136 officers in other areas also reported meeting with MPAJA non-cooperation and hostility, especially those in Kedah and north Johor.

Meanwhile, civil affairs officers who were to run the British Military Administration (BMA) in Malaya were making their own careful analysis of what to expect from the MPAJA guerrillas. Ralph Hone, the Chief Civil Affairs Officer (CCAO) designate, along with other senior civil affairs officers, feared that "the communists in the jungle at the time of the Japanese surrender had every intention of taking over control in Malaya".[47] On 22 August, a SEAC headquarters forecast of expectations of disturbances in the Far East stated that in Malaya the MPAJA was the likely source of trouble because its "hard-core elements" were "communists who hold extremist and anti-imperialistic views and are known to support the idea of an Independent Republic of Malaya".[48]

On 24 August, apparently owing to the worsening guerrilla situation in Malaya, Colin Mackenzie, Commander of Force 136, wrote a memorandum to the senior staff at SEAC headquarters stating that the inevitable delay between the ceasefire and the re-occupation of Malaya was rapidly "increasing the difficulties with which we shall be faced in connection with the AJUF". He urged that the British government should now be asked to disclose the relevant details of its Malayan Union policy for post-war Malaya.

Mackenzie said the new policy would remove two important grievances connected with the AJUF.[49] He discussed these two grievances as follows:

> It must be borne in mind that the AJUF is:
>
> (a) Almost entirely composed of domiciled Chinese whose status as citizens has been inferior to that of Malays in various important respects, and
> (b) Contains within its ranks Communists who have undoubtedly widened their influence considerably during the last three years. The Communist Party was treated before the war as an illegal association and as such was subject to the attention of the police.
>
> The new Colonial Office policy almost entirely removes these two grievances.[50]

Mackenzie earnestly urged that Mountbatten be requested to send a further signal to the British government stressing the importance of an immediate authorization to disclose the relevant details of the policy. Mackenzie also suggested that Force 136 officers in Malaya be authorized to release relevant details of the Malayan Union policy to the AJUF and to the Sultans:

> Every hour increases the danger of some occurrence, which may place the AJUF irretrievably in the wrong and subsequently lead to the embitterment of relations after the necessary counteraction has been taken by the British.
>
> Moreover, any further delay in disclosing essential details of this policy will expose us to an increasingly serious risk of it appearing that the policy has only been extorted from us by fear of further AJUF activity which might be detrimental to order and good government.
>
> The best chance we have of avoiding these problems is to strengthen the hands of the Liaison Officers now with AJUF. One of the best ways of doing this is to be able to authorise them to inform the members of the AJUF of the Government's new policy.
>
> It is understood that one reason given for the delay in announcing the policy is that it is necessary first to inform the Sultans that the new policy will involve some loss in their powers etc. If, as we suppose, it is not a question of negotiating with the Sultans but simply of informing them for the sake of courtesy of the incidental effect on their position, we urge that the information

it is desired to pass to the Sultans be set out in a fixed form and communicated to the appropriate Force 136 officers who could quickly arrange for the communication to reach the various Sultans.

We again urge the increasing and serious dangers of further delay.[51]

A few days later Mountbatten was to take action. By then, however, the situation involving the MPAJA had become clearer.

SEAC's broadcasting stations were now instructed on the new propaganda to disseminate to Malaya. The line to be taken was (1) maintenance of law and order; (2) emphasis on Britain's strength and confident determination to carry out its mission to Malaya; (3) presentation of Britain's aims through an approach likely to be sympathetic to "progressive elements" in Malaya; and (4) avoidance of over-optimism regarding return to peace-time conditions.[52] The Dominions Office in London also issued to the Australian government similar guidelines on broadcasting to Malaya.[53] It said that "trouble being caused by armed Chinese communists in Malaya" should be the first consideration in any propaganda to the people of Malaya.

> In any event we should cater for the worst possible contingency. These bands, which are formed from a pre-war nucleus, have a controlling influence in the resistance movement in Malaya, which has cooperated loyally with us. A small element has announced their intention to establish a Malayan Republic ....[54]

Because of Australia's geographical proximity to Malaya, its radio stations were to put out as fully as possible stories from Britain on planning for a post-war world, pointing out in commentaries that Malaya had no small place in these plans, and that Britain envisaged "a prosperous Malaya which will eventually enjoy self-government within the British Commonwealth by a representative government regardless of race".[55]

On 25 August SEAC headquarters broadcast a radio talk to the resistance movements in Malaya.[56] The guerrillas were told that in some areas their first orders would be to move into parts of the country the Japanese had left. Their first duty would be to keep order, to prevent looting, burning, and stealing, and to guard roads, railways, bridges, and other important places from attack by bandits or by collaborators "who want to stir trouble, so that they will be able to disappear in the confusion that follows".[57] As soon as British troops arrived in Malaya the guerrillas should put themselves under the orders of the local British commander. If there was no British force nearby, they should keep on ensuring peace and order in their areas. British officers already with them would become responsible, when British forces arrived, for the guerrillas' support and rations. The BMA, which was to take over from the Japanese, would help the guerrillas take their place in Malaya. The guerrillas would be found work, and those who wanted it would be able to secure training for a trade or occupation. They would receive subsistence while they were being found work, or while in training. Provision would also be made for their wives and families. The broadcast ended with this appeal:

> Keep close contact with the British officers. Carry out carefully the orders they pass to you from the Supreme Allied Commander. Above all, see that life in your district goes on smoothly and quietly until the British forces arrive.[58]

Although the Force 136 minute at Kandy states that the broadcast was to be issued in Malay, Chinese and English, it was heard in Malaya only in Malay and English. This struck Capt. Alastair Morrison, a Force 136 officer listening to the broadcasts in the MPAJA camp in Ulu Yam (Selangor) as absurd since the bulk of the MPAJA guerrillas was Chinese.[59] This apparently was an oversight for a similar message was also included in SEAC's newsletter, *Victory Herald*, dated 25 August, which appeared in Malay, Chinese and English.[60] Thousands of copies of this newsletter were airdropped into Malaya before the reoccupation began. The radio talk and newsletter, while allotting guerrillas specific tasks, were directed at all resistance movements in Malaya and not specifically to the MPAJA. Both fell far short of the request of Davis and Force 136 headquarters that only the central control of MPAJA headquarters should be used, and that MPAJA guerrillas should be regarded as SEAC troops. SEAC conceded this recognition only on 4 September, when Japanese surrender delegates at Rangoon were asked to treat them as Allied forces. By that time the MPAJA guerrillas had taken the law into their own hands in many places. It appears that only about 11 September was authority given for guerrilla forces to enter Japanese-occupied areas to maintain order, if the Japanese were not already doing this.[61] The chief Japanese surrender delegate at Rangoon, General Numata, cabled Field-Marshal Terauchi on 10 September informing him of the SEAC order that the MPAJA in Malaya should be accorded treatment as Allied forces. They were to be distinguished by a green uniform and a green French-style beret and on occasion a tiger badge.[62]

MPAJA and Other Guerrilla Takeovers

The areas taken over by the MPAJA and other guerrilla groups were quite extensive. One source says that about 70 per cent of the small towns and villages throughout the peninsula fell into guerrilla hands,[63] and another states that the MPAJA "virtually held complete control" of the peninsula, especially the more remote inland regions.[64] The actual size of the areas taken over is difficult to establish with any certainty. But clearly a vast political and military vacuum existed for the guerrillas to fill as Japanese troops evacuated outlying districts.

The specific movements of Japanese troops into larger concentrations will perhaps give an indication of the outlying districts, which fell to the guerrillas. Japanese troops in the northern area (i.e., Kedah, Perlis, and Kelantan) began concentrating in three directions: those in northern Kedah moved to Sungei Patani, troops in Kelantan moved into Siam, and the remainder in Kedah withdrew to Alor Star or further south to Bukit Mertajam.[65] Troops in the central area (Perak) joined Hq. Twenty-ninth Army at Taiping or moved to Ipoh and Kuala Kangsar. In the southern area (that is, Selangor, Negeri Sembilan, Malacca, and Pahang) troops began to concentrate at Kuala Lumpur, the base of Hq. Ninety-fourth Division, or moved to Kuala Lipis, Bahau (near Seremban), and Malacca. About 5,000 troops were concentrated in the naval garrison of Penang. The Hq. Seventh Area Army moved its troops in Singapore to Jurong, about 20 miles from the city centre, and then withdrew them further into Johor where they rejoined the remainder of the army in Johor, either at Kluang or Kota Tinggi, and finally at Allied orders were concentrated at Rengam, about 40 miles northwest of Johor.[66]

The withdrawal of the Japanese was carried out slowly and without fanfare. In areas such as Kluang, Bentong, and Kuala Terengganu the troops slipped out at night, so that the local population did not know until the next morning that the Japanese had gone. In other areas the Japanese left in broad daylight and were watched silently by the local population. At Raub and Fraser's Hill, both small towns in Pahang, a few people in the largely Hainanese Chinese community began to boo and shout the Japanese terms of abuse "Baka daro! Baka daro! (You fool!)" after the troop convoy was on its way out of town.[67] As one informant recalled the scene:

> Most of the Hainanese at Fraser's Hill were communists or communist sympathisers, so this accounted for their boldness. A few people, however, feared that the troops would turn back. When the trucks kept going, more people took up the cry. It was clear to everyone that the Japanese were leaving the town for good as the trucks were loaded with their bicycles and other belongings. An Indian who stood beside me yelled, "The shorties [a derogatory term referring to the height of the Japanese soldiers] have gone! The shorties have gone!"[68]

The disappearance of the Japanese was usually the signal for the jungle or hill people (the local terms for the guerrillas) to come out into the open — often within a matter of hours.

Except for Kota Bharu, which fell to KMT guerrillas, most of the towns on the east coast of Malaya were taken over by the MPAJA. These included one or two towns such as Kuantan and Pekan where a token force of Japanese remained apparently at Allied orders to maintain order. These token forces of Japanese preferred to confine themselves to barracks so as not to provide provocation to the guerrillas who were allowed to take over the town.[69] Although the Japanese were more numerous on the west coast, they still pulled out from many smaller towns in that area, such as Kluang, Batu Pahat, Tampin, Klang, Bidor, Lenggong, and Kroh.

The MPAJA guerrillas, however, attempted to seize several towns still under Japanese occupation. Guerrilla attacks on Japanese positions were quite serious. Force 136 officers did all they could to avoid clashes between the guerrillas and the Japanese, but with limited success. The general tactical pattern of the MPAJA was to start scattered shooting in various parts of a town and then to attack the Japanese post or police station on the main road outside the town.[70] It is indicative of the feverish guerrilla activity about this time that literally overnight barricades, roadblocks and fortified posts appeared in and around most small towns. Main roads were obstructed with fallen tree-trunks. Inter-district traffic was paralysed. Cars, lorries, and vehicles belonging to Japanese were commandeered.

Many local policemen and Japanese soldiers and civilians were killed in the fighting. Between the date of surrender and 31 August the guerrillas launched 212 attacks on the Japanese army, police, railways, factories, and stores. During the same period the Japanese suffered 135 casualties, including 63 killed. Local police casualties were 31 dead or wounded and 357 missing. The MPAJA guerrillas suffered 78 killed and 48 arrested.[71]

CHAPTER 7

Outbreak of Violence and Reign of Terror

News of the surrender emboldened the guerrillas to come out of the jungle…. There was terror and slaughter.

– Mamoru Shinozaki, *Syonan – My Story*, 1975

…Now I dare not go out. You might ask why this is. I say, quite honestly, because there is violence in the land, because in the small towns and villages of Malaya, the gun and pistol rule.

– Letter describing experiences of the transitional period
in *The Sunday Times*, Kuala Lumpur, 3 Mar. 1946

Something of the turbulent conditions prevailing in the countryside in Malaya, when shots were heard day and night, can be conveyed by the violent incidents which erupted during the two-week breakdown of law and order, especially the conflict between the MPAJA guerrillas and their rivals.

The Malay Groups

The Malay resistance forces, Askar Melayu Setia (AMS), which operated in north Perak, and Kedah, and the Wataniah in Pahang were separate and autonomous units under British Force 136 control. They had very few dealings with the MPAJA before the Japanese surrender, but soon afterwards antagonisms developed between them and the MPAJA over control of areas. Because the AMS was a smaller force than the MPAJA, its members sided with the KMT groups in Perak and in Kelantan. The MPAJA took the field against some units of the AMS guerrillas and succeeded in breaking them up.[1]

In Pahang, about 17 August, after learning about the Japanese surrender, the Wataniah guerrillas informed Force 136 that they feared Sultan Abu Bakar of Pahang might fall into communist hands. In that event he would either be killed or forced to aid communist plans for a takeover of the state. A radio message was sent to SEAC headquarters advising them of the situation. A day or two after this, when the Sultan and his party arrived at the Ng Tiong Keat plantation on their way from Kuala Lipis to Pekan to collect food supplies, he was approached by six armed members of Force 136, three Americans, and three Nationalist Chinese under the command of Lieutenant Betoise. After explaining the situation to the Sultan, Lieutenant Betoise revealed that his orders, which had been radioed from Ceylon, were to take the whole party into the jungle and keep them in a safe place.[2]

The next day the Japanese, who thought that the communists had kidnapped the Sultan, sent out regular troops to investigate. They killed a number of innocent Chinese and caused the remainder of the estate workers in that area to flee into the jungle. In the meantime the Japanese posted notices in Malay claiming that the Sultan had been abducted and murdered by Chinese communists. Fearing that this would produce racial clashes, members of Wataniah under instruction from their headquarters followed the billposters around and tore down the inflammatory notices when no Japanese were in sight.

On 8 September Captain Dorrity of Force 136 arrived at the camp and conducted the whole party to the main road, where Colonel Headley and a detachment of Wataniah in full uniform were waiting to escort the Sultan back to his capital. The ruler, wearing a colonel's uniform supplied by Force 136, received a tumultuous welcome in every town and village through which he passed. The Wataniah, backed by Gurkha paratroops of Force 136, then took over control of large areas of Pahang from the Japanese and remained on the alert to frustrate any attempt by the MPAJA to seize control, until a detachment of regular troops landed from destroyers at Kuantan.[3]

Force 136 probably did not allow the royal party to emerge until 8 September because the situation remained unsafe. Until that date, neither Force 136 nor Wataniah was in a position to do much to check the MPAJA, which had entered Bentong, Raub, Kuala Lipis, and Jerantut, the main towns in Pahang. Brig. L.H.O. Pugh, sent to Pahang to take control of the state in September, found these towns virtually in the hands of the Chinese guerrillas of the MPAJA. In Raub they flew the hammer and sickle flag above the Union Jack. "I refused to let them participate in the Victory Parade in the town unless the position of those flags was reversed," Pugh said. The communist flag soon fluttered below the Union Jack.[4]

Despite Wataniah's precipitate action in asking Force 136 to "kidnap" the Sultan, there is no evidence that the MPAJA was inclined to seize any Malay ruler anywhere in the country. However, the action is important in showing the extent of Malay fears of a communist takeover.

In early August the Malays in Kedah heard ominous reports that on the day of surrender communist guerrillas would emerge from the jungle and take possession of Kedah towns and villages. It was reported that they would lower the Japanese flags and hoist their own three-starred red emblems. A secret Malay political association called Saberkas (Unity), which operated under the guise of a cooperative store, decided to organize Malay youths to prevent Alor Star, the capital, or any Kedah town or village from falling into Chinese communist hands.[5] The leaders of Saberkas were Tunku Abdul Rahman, who was then Superintendent of Education (later to become Malaysian Prime Minister), and his friends Mohamed Khir Johari and Senu Abdul Rahman (both later to become his ministerial colleagues). A few days after, the MPAJA was reported to have taken over Kedah police stations at Kepala Batas, Alor Janggus, Takai, and Simpang Empat and seized the weapons.[6]

Saberkas members warned the MPAJA that there would be inter-racial trouble if the MPAJA guerrillas attempted to take over the capital. In some villages in Kedah, communist units had begun to run affairs openly, which raised tensions between Malay and Chinese inhabitants. Malays prepared for counteraction. *Parangs* (the long Malay knives) and axes were sharpened in anticipation. In Alor Star itself members of the Chinese Chamber of Commerce, apparently members of the MPAJU, were reported to have walked into the police station and said that they would take control. Tunku Abdul Rahman rushed to the station.

> He [the Tunku] found Malays milling outside. He stood on a table and urged them to keep calm. Inside the station he found some extremely worried Chinese. Their audacity, brashness, and

arrogance had been pricked like a balloon. They asked for assistance to get home safely. They were given safe conduct, and the immediate threat of racial troubles in Alor Star disappeared.[7]

Saberkas also contacted the AMS guerrillas under Force 136 command in Kuala Nerang in north Kedah, and urged them to enter Alor Star quickly to forestall the anticipated entry of MPAJA guerrillas. The local Japanese garrison commander was also informed. Japanese troops were sent from Jitra, where the communist troops were reported ready to start their triumphant march to Alor Star. The Japanese took up positions, but agents were said to have reported back to the communists, who cancelled their march. When Force 136 officers and AMS guerrillas arrived at Alor Star the Kedah flag was flying from the masthead outside the Balai Besar, the royal audience hall in the heart of the capital. It had been hoisted by Saberkas youths who had armed themselves with wooden staves and who stood guard around the building.[8]

The Malays appear to have been fully alert to the possibility of a Chinese or MPAJA/communist takeover of the country — an event that they were determined to prevent. While takeovers of predominantly Chinese towns and villages went off with little trouble, takeovers of largely Malay areas led to inter-racial conflicts, for example, in the districts of southwestern Johor and the Sungai Manik district of lower Perak. In each case the MPAJA takeover was opposed by Malays and led to Malays attacking Chinese. The inter-racial conflicts in southwestern Johor were more extensive and started earlier than the Sungai Manik conflicts. Both incidents will be discussed later.

Chinese Secret Societies, KMT Guerrillas, and Bandit Gangs

This was a time when the pistol and knife reigned. While the MPAJA played the role of heroes in many places, their arrogant and ruthless behaviour also antagonized people who sought protection from other groups such as the Chinese secret societies. In times of crisis, such as the post-surrender interregnum, people were concerned with survival and with obtaining protection from any group considered strong and willing to protect them. With rumours of a Japanese surrender surfacing in early August 1945, not only collaborators had reason to fear the vengeance of the MPAJA but also anyone politically opposed to a communist regime.

In Perak, at least, all these elements combined to turn people to the Triad societies, of which the Ang Bin Hoey was the most prominent. Shortly before the Japanese surrender, when MPAJA retribution in these areas seemed imminent, the Ang Bin Hoey members were said to have received secret permission from the Japanese officer in charge of Kuala Kurau district to organize all Triad elements in the area for mutual protection.[9] Seven *bagans* (estuarine fishing villages) were organized with the headquarters, the Ang Bun Tua Kongsi, covering and controlling the whole area from Province Wellesley to Pantai Remis. New members joining the Hoey at this time were informed that the purpose of the society was protection from communist attacks. Support came too from Penang Triad members who had taken refuge in Krian and Larut during the occupation, and from the Kwangsai gangs in the Kuala Kangsar hills. Arms were obtained (possibly at Simpang) from stocks that the Japanese rapidly consolidated after the surrender, and were distributed to Triad groups in every coastal village. Some, however, also filtered through to the nearby communist sympathizers at Selama from their contact in Kuala Kurau.[10]

The Triad also recruited about 100 Malays, mainly Banjarese with a reputation for belligerency, from the district between Kuala Kurau and Tanjong Piandang. The Malays who joined the societies did so for mutual protection, later extended to include protection from the MPAJA. They underwent a special form of initiation ceremony, such as swearing on the Koran.[11]

As the MPAJA surged out of the jungle to take over control of areas in Perak they were opposed in turn by the Chinese secret societies, the OCAJA guerrillas, and the Kwongsai bandit gangs. The MPAJA forces from Sitiawan took over the outskirts of Taiping as the centre of control for Larut, and other troops from Selama made Bagan Serai their headquarters for the control of Krian. These operations were accomplished without difficulty, but the MPAJA were not alone in the field, for their rivals, the OCAJA guerrillas, also came swiftly down from Lenggong and established themselves in Kuala Kangsar, where they were reinforced by Kwongsai gangs who had also spent the occupation in the hills in the district.[12]

There are some indications of armed clashes between the two groups, as the MPAJA attempted unsuccessfully to disarm the OCAJA. When the MPAJA attempted to extend their control to the fishing villages of the Perak coast they were met with armed opposition from the Ang Bin Hoey. At Kuala Kurau, where their suggestion

that the Hoey should cooperate in setting up a communist government was rejected, and where the Triads refused to hand over their
arms, two Triad members — the leading Chinese trader of the
village and his brother — were arrested and taken to Bagan Serai,
and their shop looted. Their prosperity under the Japanese had made
them obvious targets. They were subsequently released in exchange
for a prominent MPAJA leader captured by the Ang Bin Hoey near
Trong.[13]

The fighting was intense, but eventually MPAJA troops pre-
vailed. After their arrival in Malaya, British troops stopped the
fighting, arrested Triad members and disarmed some MPAJA units.
Blythe gives a dramatic account of the fighting:

> Both sides began an armed fight for control. Several severe clashes
> took place at Kuala Kurau, in one of which some ten MPAJA
> men were killed, and alarmed at probable retribution both from
> the MPAJA and the returning British, about 100 Triad members,
> including many who had taken refuge during the occupation,
> fled to Penang…. At Kuala Gula a young leader, Tan Leng Lay,
> proved a fierce fighter, and from Port Weld the Triad veteran,
> Yeoh Ah Bah, drove the communists out of Matang and back to
> Taiping. Further south again fierce fighting took place in the Trong
> area, where some of the MPAJU are said to have been attacked
> by Triad members with nibong spears. Eventually, however, the
> MPAJA groups prevailed, and the Triad fighters took refuge in the
> inaccessible swamps of Pasir Hitam, where KMT guerrillas joined
> them. Throughout September the struggle continued, and as late
> as the 28th two boatloads of wounded Triad men sailed across to
> Penang Island to seek succour from their Brethren.[14]

On the east coast of Malaya a force of 170 KMT guerrillas who had
been confined to the Thai border by Force 136, following clashes
with the MPAJA in early 1945 were now able to enter and occupy
Kota Bharu, the capital of Kelantan. For several weeks about 150
MPAJA guerrillas from a base in Terengganu besieged them. A Force
136 officer, Colonel Headley, who requested the MPAJA to remain
in Terengganu, eventually established a truce. On 21 September the
KMT guerrilla leaders agreed to hand over all prisoners arrested by
them and to work in the future with the police under orders of the
BMA.[15] One account, which mistook the Chinese KMT guerrillas in
Kota Bharu for those of the MPAJA, describes what had happened:

> In Kota Bharu … the Chinese guerrillas occupied the town and proclaimed themselves masters. They terrorized the local peoples, robbed them, and looted their homes. They put up roadblocks, examined every vehicle and all passengers and stopped every pedestrian. They exacted a toll and a salute. Only firm handling by British forces when they arrived put an end to MPAJA terrorism.[16]

Bandit gangs were also rampant after the surrender. They claimed to be anti-Japanese armies, but in fact used the term as a cloak to rob, extort, and intimidate the public. One example was a group of lawless Chinese elements, which operated at Ampang, a Chinese settlement about eight miles from Kuala Lumpur. During the Japanese occupation members terrorized the inhabitants of Ampang and committed their robberies, extortions, and ruthless murders. The gang was heavily armed. In 1944, after complaints from the local inhabitants, the MPAJA started a drive to exterminate the gang. After the Japanese surrender, the gang became aware of the change in circumstances and started to call itself the "Kee Tong guerrillas" (Kee Tong in the Hokkien dialect meaning Public Service). At the same time, the gang sent representatives to negotiate with the MPAJA, which, thinking it had turned over a new leaf, accepted its cooperation. Members were sent to guard a police station and to help maintain peace and order before the arrival of British troops. Instead, they used the MPAJA cloak to their advantage to carry out further criminal activities. Later the MPAJA was forced to disband the gang and help the British police take its leader into custody.[17]

Roving bandit gangs also operated in remote and isolated areas. They usually picked Chinese squatter settlements existing along the jungle fringe. An eyewitness account of one of these roving bands in Pahang shows how they would descend suddenly on farming communities:

> I was about 10 years old when the war ended. My father, uncle and elder brothers had been butchers in Kuantan, but we fled to open a farm near the jungle fringe. We supported the MPAJA because they had saved one of our relatives from the Japanese. The family fled into hiding because it was feared that the Japanese would round up everyone of the family.
>
> Our farm was among four farms in the area. Since the Japanese surrender became known, there were a lot of troublemakers roaming the countryside, robbing and killing. One day, after the

surrender, the MPAJA unit in our area headed by my uncle had just left our house after their meals. Probably about 15 minutes had elapsed, when we saw about seven or eight armed men entering the path leading to our hut. We did not recognize these men. My mother quickly herded us children into the hut and bolted the door.

The men surrounded the hut. A thin bearded man holding a gun knocked at the door, asking to be allowed in. My mother said there were only women and children in the house and asked them not to bother us. They said they were anti-Japanese people. They needed food and money, as they were hungry, otherwise they threatened to confiscate our pigs, poultry and vegetables, and even burn our hut down. We were terrified. This was not the talk of the MPAJA who were always respectful to the people and would pay for the things they bought. My grandmother tearfully appealed to them to spare our lives. They kept throwing their bodies against the door to break it down. Suddenly, there was some commotion outside and shots were fired. The exchange of firing went on for some time. Finally, the armed men withdrew, and I saw my elder brother and the MPAJA men outside the house. They had returned in time to save us from the bandits. The bandits had been able to inflict some injuries on the MPAJA men before fleeing but one of them was shot and captured. He was immediately executed.[18]

Pattern of MPAJA Takeovers

Areas vacated by the Japanese would be entered immediately by a column of uniformed guerrillas marching down the main street under triumphal arches erected by supporters to welcome them. The Chinese population always with enthusiasm greeted the MPAJA units. There was clearly Chinese admiration for their endurance in facing the rigours of jungle life and resisting the Japanese. However, areas still under Japanese occupation did not provide such easy glory. They involved Japanese resistance, so that guerrillas had first to attack and overrun Japanese military or police posts. It is conceivable that in some instances small detachments of Japanese troops under siege handed over their posts to the MPAJA without a skirmish, after negotiating a safe withdrawal from the area. Where Japanese troops were deployed in strength in an area, such as Ipoh and Taiping, the MPAJA would not attack. Their usual strategy was to infiltrate behind Japanese positions and carry out sabotage missions and looting of army stores and arms depots. Probably because of the increasing scale of these attacks, the Japanese were forced to accelerate withdrawal of their forces from many areas.

In both categories of takeovers, the first site to be occupied was usually the police station. There were reported instances of police stations being seized, ransacked, and burnt down. Where the Japanese had evacuated, the remaining Malay and Sikh policemen would either run away or barricade themselves inside the police stations or quarters. They were often fair game, the first victims of revenge meted out by guerrillas to collaborators. If the policemen did not surrender, their police station would be attacked. If they gave themselves up without a fight, they would be disarmed, victimized, or killed. In big towns such as Ipoh, Taiping, and Seremban, Japanese troops confined themselves to barracks in the last few days preceding the arrival of British forces in September, and local policemen too barricaded themselves within the police headquarters, usually a large fortress-like building.

The treatment meted out to policemen, detectives, Kempeitai informers, and profiteers began what many Malays have described as the "reign of terror".[19] Actions of the guerrillas encouraged people to take the law into their own hands. Many began to settle old scores. In fact anyone accused of profiteering, causing harm or death to people, robbery, or rape was liable to be abducted, dragged out into the streets, and given a "people's trial". Many were summarily executed. Instances of mob violence were also reported. Mobs would vent their anger on the victims as they were paraded in the streets. The hands of the victims would be tied behind their backs, or their hands and legs would be tied up and strung over a pole. Then, either in the face of persistent demands from the crowd, or in response to a MPAJA command, the victim would be made to kneel. The trial commenced immediately. This was an opportunity for those with any grievances to hurl allegations at the victim. When the crowd or the MPAJA had had enough of the tirade, someone would yell out for the death sentence. The victim would either be spirited away to be shot, or, more commonly, killed on the spot, in a most callous and brutal manner. Shooting the victim was often rejected by the crowd as being too simple and painless a way to die. Every hideous form of torture imaginable would be tried out — beating with sticks, iron rods, or any sharp object, bayonetting, stabbing, and finally mutilation or decapitation. Victims cried out in agony, and sometimes the ritual continued even after life had been extinguished. Eyes would be gouged out, genitals cut off, the lower body disembowelled.

Often it was not the guerrillas themselves but those with the most grievances against the victim who perpetrated these acts. Public approval seems to have been quite commonplace, as this contemporary account shows:

> The most gruesome part of the "Communist" programme was the cleaning up of traitors and running dogs. Those informers, detectives, blackmailers, sub-inspectors, sergeants, and "third-degree-experts" that failed to "disappear", were combed out. The "hill-people" had agents in all railway stations, border towns and boundary posts, and, many informers and detectives attempting to escape, were caught. They were given a "trial". Village head-men and peoples' representatives were present at the trials, and according to people who had witnessed these assizes, they were "democratic and fair".
>
> When the verdict was "Guilty of Death!" the convicted were cold-bloodedly executed in public. In certain places in Selangor and Perak, certain "condemned dogs" were put into pigs' cages, carried round the town, and then butchered before the crowds. Indian and Malay "Communists" had also participated in such executions, and what is significant is that the crowds condoned the vengeance of the "Communists"! Even the slaughter of mistresses of the Japanese, especially MP's paramours, received public approval. Such was public hatred against the "oppressors of the people".
>
> Where the verdict was "Guilty, but not amounting to death", the convicted people were put through varying degrees and forms of punishment. In the case of policemen and detectives, they were given the third-degree, just as they had meted it out to others. It was nothing short of "an eye for an eye, and a tooth for a tooth."[20]

Many British personnel who had lived with the MPAJA guerrillas in the jungle had seen the tortures carried out on traitors or offenders. They had considered these practices both revoltingly cruel and unnecessary. Often the traitors and informers caught deserved to be punished by death, as they had brought death and suffering to many people. But the MPAJA turned the execution into an elaborate exhibition of terror to serve as warning to future offenders.[21]

At Titi, a small town in the Jelebu district of Negeri Sembilan after Japanese troops had withdrawn, some ten, pale, rough-looking

Chinese MPAJA guerrillas appeared in the main street of the town. All were armed with machine-guns and rifles. They immediately went into the houses of three Chinese detectives, dragged them out, and bayoneted them to death.[22] Revenge was the dominant theme of the new regime during its first week of control. For several days no one was allowed to leave Titi. In the meantime public notices in Chinese appeared, asking people to report complaints against Japanese collaborators to the MPAJA. A few days later a "public court" was held on the same spot where the detectives were killed. Eight prisoners, tied from hand to foot, were carried from their place of captivity suspended from a pole. They were made to kneel before the crowd.

> The embittered ones began to rush forth to the accused and kicked and spat at them for the "crimes" done. One by one, the accused were pushed forward and each person's "crimes" (ranging from blackmail to false accusations of residents resulting in their imprisonment or death) read out aloud with the final question: "Does this man deserve death?" Eyewitness informants said that the crowd present was in such a revengeful mood that everybody shouted out "Death sentence, death sentence" to every one of the prisoners. Each was bayoneted to death and the victims "squealed like pigs being slaughtered".[23]

At Fraser's Hill, a holiday resort in the Pahang highlands, three Sikh policemen were abducted in the night and killed, after the MPAJA guerrillas had entered the town. The Sikhs and Malay policemen had barricaded themselves in the premises of the police station soon after the Japanese troops had left in the morning, on 22 or 23 August. A few hours later the MPAJA guerrillas, between 10 and 15 in number, men and women, armed, gaunt, lean, and deathly looking, stalked into the town. They surrounded the police station but did not attack it straightaway. They ordered the policemen to come out. The policemen inside were so terrified that none dared fire a shot. Instead they cried out for mercy. A few shots were then fired into the police station, followed by an announcement from the guerrillas: "We only want the three Sikh policemen." The three Sikhs were alleged to have been brutal in their treatment of the local population during the Japanese occupation. Once the targets had been identified, the Malay policemen quickly extricated themselves from the premises and made good their escape, abandoning the Sikhs to their fate. That night, after having waited long enough to scare the life out of the three men, the guerrillas walked into the premises, and escorted them away. Their mutilated bodies were hanging outside the building next morning — a macabre sight to the residents of the little town.[24]

At Bidor, a town on the main north-south highway in Perak, immediately after the Japanese had evacuated, the MPAJA guerrillas marched into the town to the tumultuous cheers of the Chinese population. The police station was occupied, many of the Malay policemen killed, and the MPAJA's three-starred emblem flown beside the Communist Party's hammer and sickle flag atop the police station and other buildings. Among local residents arrested was a communist supporter accused of being a profiteer. An informant described how this incident occurred:

> I was nine years old when the war ended, but I still remember vividly what happened in Bidor. I don't think I can ever forget the incident. Self-confident and overbearing, the MPAJA guerrillas swaggered about the town. Most of the time, they were marching and drilling, in response to orders being shouted at them by their commanders. A middle-aged woman, the wife of a *Kempeitai* informer, was tied to a lamp post. Other men and women, believed to be informers and police detectives, were being paraded around the town, with their hands tied behind their backs. I did not see the woman, or the other prisoners killed. But I learnt later they were killed in a most horrifying manner. Some people pushed me out of the way and advised me to go home, "Children should not see these things."
>
> Later, my father, a proprietor of a provisions shop, was also arrested. He was taken away from our house. The guerrillas accused him of being "a capitalist who had harmed the people". Someone had given false information against my father. Fortunately, one of our relatives was a communist. He immediately spoke to an official in the local communist party, and explained that though my father was a shopkeeper, he had secretly contributed money and food to the resistance movement. The guerrillas who arrested him were from another district. There were witnesses to vouch for my father's record. The intervention was timely. We thought my father had already been executed. But he was freed, and told to reform his capitalist attitudes. He was badly shaken when he came home.[25]

Unlike this informant's father, other Chinese who went through a similar experience of walking to the brink of death "turned over a

new leaf" and became communist activists. This was what happened
to Osman China who, though born a Chinese, was reared by a
Malay family. He regarded himself as Malay. He rose to become the
MCP's chief propagandist in the Malay language in Pahang until his
surrender to British security forces in 1955. He recalled the incident
when his life was spared during the interregnum:

> ... When the Japanese surrendered I was working in a Japanese
> office in Kuala Terengganu. I was only seventeen years old. I was
> arrested by the communist guerrillas and taken with two others
> into the jungle. Here we were told that we were Japanese colla-
> borators and had been sentenced to death. We were led away from
> the camp and told to dig our own graves. The other two were
> shot and I, very much shaken, was led back to the camp. There
> I was told that I had been spared and that if I studied hard and
> cooperated I would be let off, if I refused I would be shot. I was
> kept in the jungle from September 1945 until January 1947 when
> I was led out of the jungle and given a job in the General Labour
> Union offices in Kuantan.[26]

Malay stories of the MPAJA's harsh treatment to Malay policemen,
detectives, informers, and other collaborators are also common. The
effects of these actions on Malay-Chinese relations will be discussed
more fully in the following chapter. They all paint the same picture:
the MPAJA guerrillas, or the Bintang Tiga as they were called by
the Malays, had got in two or three weeks ahead of the BMA and
had made the most of their opportunity to pay off old accounts. The
Malays in Jelebu (Negeri Sembilan), according to one source, saw
the post-surrender interregnum as "fifteen days of terror.... These
two weeks under the Three Stars seem to have frightened the Malays
more than the whole period of Japanese rule."[27]

At Temerloh, a predominantly Malay rural town in Pahang,
Ishak Haji Mohammed, a member of the Kesatuan Melayu Muda
(KMM), was an eyewitness to the MPAJA guerrillas' high-handed
behaviour. Although he was to become active in the Socialist movement after the war and be detained by the British for alleged pro-
communist activities, Ishak never forgot nor forgave what Chinese
MPAJA guerrillas did in his *kampung*. After the Japanese forces
pulled out, about 20 MPAJA guerrillas emerged in Temerloh. Their
intention was not merely to mark the Allied victory over Japan,
Ishak said, but "to show off their Chinese chauvinism".[28] Soon they

led a predominantly Chinese procession through the town. Several Chinese carried aloft a roast pig, "whose sight is repugnant to the eyes of the Muslim Malays, who are forbidden by their religion to touch or eat it". There were also several Chinese banners and slogans, and smoking joss sticks to celebrate the event.

After the MPAJA had taken over control of Temerloh, they began arresting a number of Malays and Indians on a variety of charges, some considered by the Malays to be extremely trivial, such as non-settlement of small debts owed to Chinese small traders. Those arrested were detained at Temerloh police station. Some were tried, tortured, and executed. Ishak recalls:

> Within those seven days the lock-up at Temerloh police station, where I was born and brought up, was full of Malays and Indians. Pak Uda Kia had been arrested. Usup Kampar was there too. So was Alun, the elephant hunter (his real name was Harun).[29]

Ishak and other Malays in the town could no longer endure what they regarded as the MPAJA's "injustice and cruelties". They decided to act. A large crowd of Malays gathered and marched to the police station. There, to their surprise, they were able to gain entry to the police station without opposition and free the prisoners.

Next day, the local commander of the MPAJA called Ishak to his office. He suspected a trap to kill him but went nonetheless. He was asked to explain why he had organized the procession. Ishak replied that the MPAJA was not only chauvinistically Chinese but also unjust and discriminatory to the other races. Ishak said that he had read an MPAJA newsletter, which urged Malays, Chinese, and Indians to regard themselves as brothers and sisters, yet the MPAJA had arrested and tortured only Malays and Indians. Why had the MPAJA sided with the Chinese traders? The local commander, an English-educated Chinese who spoke Malay, apologized for what had happened. He said that the arrests had been carried out at the instigation of elderly Chinese who were in fact "imbeciles and chauvinists". He hoped the matter could be settled with a feast, towards which the MPAJA would contribute seven buffaloes. The objective would be to promote inter-racial goodwill and solidarity. The celebration was held, attended by a large number of Malays, but Ishak himself boycotted the function, as he still felt very bitter over the incident. A Malay historian's survey of the MPAJA's reign of terror sums up the Malay memory of this period:

Within those two weeks, the Bintang Tiga guerrillas had taken prisoners, tried, sentenced and murdered anyone they suspected of being Japanese supporters or lackeys. Within that period many Malays, Indians, Eurasians, Chinese and others, especially members of the police force, were taken away and killed by the MPAJA guerrillas in a cold-blooded and cruel manner.... The Malay States and the Straits Settlements were under an inhuman regime. There were no longer any proper laws and human lives no longer had any value.[30]

The MPAJA 'System of Government'

After taking over an area, the communist guerrillas' first preoccupation was to "administer justice". Only after this had been done were "people's committees" set up and the reins of local government taken over by the Communist Party. The communist administration was given different names. In Muar and Batu Pahat they were known as "Soviets",[31] and at Titi in Negeri Sembilan and other towns they were simply called the "People's Communist Government".[32] Usually a one-storey or two-storey shop house on the main road was requisitioned as headquarters of the Communist Party. The party's flag and the MPAJA flag would fly side by side in front of the building. Similar flags were displayed by supporters on the windows of shop houses and other buildings, such as the police station, which would be normally occupied by MPAJA guerrillas if still intact and not burnt down. The people's committees consisted of farmers, workers, shopkeepers, and leading citizens with an unblemished record of non-collaboration. Unlike the "state people's committees", there is little evidence of Malay and Indian representatives being on the town and district people's committees. In distributing rice and foodstuffs to the people some "committees" and MCP cadres in the Perak districts were alleged to have been discriminatory towards Malays and Indians. When complaints were made to party leaders, they immediately attempted to set it right, but much damage had already been done.[33]

Meanwhile, some guerrillas were assigned to police duties. These guerrillas spent their time marching or drilling up and down the main street, while at both ends of the street other guerrillas stood. Vehicular traffic was stopped and checked. Any Japanese-owned vehicle was immediately seized. Much of the inter-state traffic passing through such towns was disrupted,[34] while Japanese troop convoys passing through were subject to sniper fire or ambush. Anyone entering or leaving the town was checked.

A public gathering would be held in the form of a meeting, or a dinner, at which party officials delivered speeches. Supporters and the town's citizens in the people's committees would organize the dinner, to entertain the officials as well as to celebrate the MPAJA's "liberation" of the town. The theme in the speeches was always the Communist Party and the MPAJA guerrillas as liberators, under the guidance of the former, which had liberated the country from Japanese rule. The people would be told that the British were returning to rule Malaya, but that the party had grown in strength and the British would find a new political spirit among the people. The people should be vigilant. It remained to be seen whether the British intended to carry out democratic reforms. A few people were unhappy about cooperating with the British. But generally everyone got the message that the British were to be welcomed back. However, the ground was well prepared by the party's cadres to build up support among the people.[35]

By the end of the first week after taking over a town, the Communist Party would have successfully imposed its authority and eliminated all opposition. It asked for the cooperation of all, and none dared to refuse. There is evidence that in some areas the communists fixed prices of commodities, eliminated all traces of Japanese influence,[36] established Chinese schools, and took over the properties of profiteers and Japanese collaborators. Regulations were also handed down banning gambling, opium smoking, and prostitution. Public notices in Chinese were pasted on walls of buildings, warning that thieves and robbers would be caught and punished.[37]

At Kupang, about five miles from Baling in Kedah, a group of MPAJA guerrillas took power. They refused to allow a British Force 136 officer, Major Hislop, to enter Kupang, so that he and his group had to remain in their jungle camp until invited by a Japanese unit in Baling to take over Baling town.[38] Tension arose in Baling in the evening after Hislop's arrival, as news was received that the Kupang guerrillas intended to attack Baling. Hislop radioed SEAC headquarters for reinforcements, and was told that he could expect none. British and Japanese forces combined to defend the town. They waited behind defensive positions until daybreak, when it was clear that the attack was not forthcoming. In the morning Hislop dispatched two KMT technicians in his group, both dressed in Chinese Nationalist Army khaki uniforms, with a single blue star on their caps, to Kupang to parley with the MPAJA guerrillas. MPAJA animosity towards the KMT guerrillas was known, yet the two men were to present themselves as representatives of the Chinese government of Chiang Kai-shek. It was a risky mission, but one which the two men were quite willing to undertake. They were allowed in apparently on the assumption that they were the advance party of Chiang's Army rumoured to arrive in Malaya.

J.M. Tsang, one of the men, describes the communist regime, which they encountered in the town:

> We drove in a car to Kupang to meet with the MPAJA commander. On entering the town, we saw the Communist Party's red flag, with the hammer and sickle, flying on top of several buildings. Many guerrilla patrols were marching on the street. A poster stuck on the wall of a Chinese shop house proclaimed that a People's Communist Government had been established. Several regulations were announced to enforce law and order. The "People's Committee" which issued these decrees, warned that thieves and robbers would be punished. Gambling and opium smoking were prohibited.
>
> We stopped outside the office of the Communist Party, which was indicated by a large sign in Chinese characters. We met the MPAJA commander, a stern looking man in the top storey of the building. There were two MPAJA guerrillas standing guard. On his table was draped the Communist Party flag. We communicated Hislop's request to him to try and maintain order until the arrival of British troops. He scoffed at Hislop's attempt to impose some measure of authority over him. He would take orders from MPAJA Headquarters and from no one else. He questioned our role, and said we should have nothing to do with the British.[39]

At Titi in Negeri Sembilan, after MPAJA guerrillas had liquidated the three Chinese detectives and taken over the town, they requisitioned an empty shop house on the main street for their headquarters. A large sign in Chinese characters, which read "Office of the Communist Party", was displayed in front of the building. Inside the office were gathered party officials and senior ranking officers of the MPAJA, who constituted the "People's Communist Government of Titi". After the first public trial and killing, speeches were made by the officials declaring that Titi was now a liberated area and that the "People's Communist Government of Titi" was going to look after the rights and interests of the people without interference from "outsiders" (meaning the British, should they return).[40] It was made clear to all present that the new government in Titi was communist, and that no reactionary factions would be tolerated. Before the war many Chinese businessmen were known to have been members of the KMT, and it was now obvious to these businessmen that the Chinese population of Titi was completely with the communist government, and that the wisest thing for them to do was to follow suit. A "people's committee" was formed, with two representatives from each area. Most of these representatives were Hakka farmers, tin miners, or rubber tappers. Educated representatives were appointed as secretaries and teachers. Education was given top priority in the new government's reform programme. More than twenty teachers, mostly young men and women, were employed by the new government to teach children and adults alike to read and write. There were also classes on communism and politics. The Malays in the surrounding areas were left out of the programme, partly because the revenge, which the MPAJA had taken against several Malays, had alienated that community. The new government did not have time to proceed further, as news soon reached Titi that British troops had arrived at the nearby district town, Kuala Klawang, and would soon take over Titi.[41]

At Fraser's Hill in Pahang, after MPAJA guerrillas had executed the three Sikh policemen, they proclaimed a communist government. That evening, after occupying the town, a public meeting was held at the Rest House, requisitioned as the Communist Party headquarters. All residents were ordered to attend, including Malays and Indians and workers on the government experimental vegetable farms a few miles away. A former resident recalled what happened at the meeting:

> I was the highest-ranking Government civil servant around. The Malay District Officer, appointed by the Japanese, had fled. A Hainanese houseboy, a friend of mine, came with a message from the communists asking me to attend. As Chief Clerk in the Superintendent's Office, or 'CC' as everyone called me, my presence was regarded as important. At the Rest House I saw the guerrillas pale and deathly looking from living in the jungle arrogantly basking in their glory. They were cordial but curt to me, apparently thinking that I was nothing but a government lackey. They knew through the Hainanese houseboys that I did not support the Japanese. I nearly paid with my life for listening

to the BBC on the shortwave radio. I was saved by my wife who saw a Japanese officer and convinced him with the aid of family photographs that she was half-Japanese. Her uncle married a Japanese woman.

At the Rest House meeting, the communists declared, "We have freed Malaya from the Japanese. Do not be afraid. We will look after you all. The British won't be coming back. We will set up a communist government throughout the country. Give us your whole-hearted cooperation." These words were delivered in Mandarin, which I do not understand, but the Hainanese house-boy interpreted them to me. I don't think the Malays and Indians present understood either what was said, but their Chinese friends must have explained the meaning to them. The communists made no speeches in Malay or English, but one of the Indian labourers had been asked to speak. He spoke in Malay and said he supported the communists and hoped they would improve the lot of everyone by distributing enough rice and foodstuffs to the people. A few days later, at the Selangor Club up on the hill, a dinner was held to which every resident was asked to contribute money. The Communist Party officials made similar speeches. This time it was a mainly Chinese affair.[42]

This MPAJA group in Fraser's Hill, which clearly belonged to the Seventh Regiment (East Pahang), had little or no contact with MPAJA central headquarters or Force 136. For such isolated groups the 27 August statement of the MCP's CEC would mark the first evidence of a shift in party policy.

The communist takeover at Fraser's Hill lasted about three weeks at the most, beginning about 28 August. On about 15 September the first contingents of Indian troops, the Hyderabads, was sighted at the Gap, a mountain pass about 12 miles from the town. A few lorry-loads of Indian troops under British officers soon entered the town to shouts of welcome of a small mixed group of people, which had gathered. The uniformed MPAJA guerrillas were nowhere in sight, but communist flags were still fluttering on the rooftops of the police station and the post office. British officers immediately ordered these to be taken down and the Union Jack flown in their place.[43] The residents, witnessing power changing hands, saw the Hyderabads move up higher into the hills, and there, it is said, they stopped and seized vehicles driven by MPAJA guer-rillas attempting to remove property from government bungalows. The Hainanese community at Fraser's Hill, the majority of whom were known to be sympathetic to the communists, were forced to accept the fact that the British had returned to rule Malaya. When a Force 136 officer showed up later at Fraser's Hill, the MPAJA recovered some prestige when MPAJA guerrillas were allowed to retain their arms and were employed on guard duty. But the humiliation, which the Hyderabads had inflicted on them, was not lost to the town residents.[44]

On 3 September, Chapman and three other Force 136 officers (Richardson, Headley, and Leonard) were the first British officials to enter Raub, the nearest town to Fraser's Hill. On the 5th they entered Kuala Lipis, the capital of Pahang, where there were still some Japanese troops. They decided to protect the Japanese from the Chinese guerrillas, if they agreed to stay as far as possible in their camps and help Force 136 guard supply dumps in the towns. The MPAJA, on the other hand, were to keep to the smaller towns and country districts, and to prevent lawlessness there. On 6 September Chapman drove over to Kuala Lumpur to meet John Davis, and returned with a Gurkha Support Group "to add a little prestige" to Force 136 headquarters in the rest house at Kuala Lipis.[45] On 8 September he and Headley entered Kuantan, and the next day met the Sultan of Pahang at Pekan.

Kuantan presented a clear picture of MPAJA hostility to Headley and Chapman. It had been taken over by the Seventh Regiment, MPAJA. Except for Chapman, who had met three of their men at Mentakab in December 1942, there had been no British contact with their unit since the Japanese occupied the country. Even MPAJA central headquarters had lost contact with the Seventh Regiment for three years. These guerrillas had been able to dominate the local Malay government at Kuantan and had grown quite powerful. The Malay district officer, Dato Mohamed, was reported to be on the verge of mental breakdown.[46] The guerrillas had emerged from the jungle at the end of August, taken control of the town, and summarily tried and put to death some inhabitants alleged to have collaborated with the Japanese. Chapman and Headley were initially helpless, and had to turn to Davis and MPAJA central headquarters for help in gaining any influence over the Seventh Regiment in Kuantan. Chapman recalls:

> When we entered the town, the situation was rather delicate as the Japs, who seemed to consider the cessation of hostilities as a mutual agreement rather than surrender, were very truculent and

still went about the town fully armed. The MPAJA were at first equally uncooperative. They felt that they had opposed the Japs for so many years without any help from the British (and the 7th Regiment had killed many hundreds of Japs in large-scale skirmishes in the jungle) and had restored order in Kuantan before we arrived. It was not until I had taken their leaders over to Kuala Lumpur to parley with Davis and members of their own headquarters that they would agree to obey my orders....[47]

One by one the communist takeovers collapsed in the face of the arrival of British forces. There was no open opposition, the guerrillas either withdrawing from the towns or remaining passively to welcome the British forces. In some instances guerrillas were immediately disarmed and harassed by British troops, who searched their premises and seized any printed materials critical of British policies. These acts of suppression naturally increased the anti-British mood of the MPAJA.

At Titi in Negeri Sembilan, the Chinese population appeared unhappy with the news of the impending British arrival. A public meeting debated the question of whether the British should be welcomed back. It was decided to send a man to Kuala Klawang, where the British had already taken over, to ask them to leave Titi alone. The request was rejected, and the next day a land-rover carrying BMA officers arrived with a loudspeaker announcing monetary offers to the MPAJA guerrillas and asking the people to cooperate with the BMA to restore law and order. Residents recalled that the people in Titi watched in stony silence until the officials' voices were hoarse and the land rover faded into the distance towards Kuala Klawang. A day later a number of BMA officers arrived with troops and began questioning people.

This "survey team" (as the Titi people then called them) left the area in disgust for no one had given them anything important. The following morning, a whole battalion of troops turned out in Titi town and ordered all the town residents to come out of their houses. They were to assemble at the central open space (site of the present police station) and their homes searched. The British troops were alleged to have been very rude and rough to the residents when they were assembled for questioning by some British military officers who questioned many people through a Chinese interpreter. In the meantime, the soldiers searched the houses (probably for firearms). The British officers were said to be very hot tempered and shouting at the ones they singled out for questioning. On that occasion, the British authorities managed to get three or four former AJA guerrillas to sign a form and a couple surrendered their rifles....

It was considered a very humiliating experience and many in Titi began to appreciate the local communists' anti-British talk and were even prepared to assist the MCP financially whenever they needed it....

Unlike the local communists who were sensitive to the emotions and characteristics of the Chinese, the British military officials had hurt the feelings of the Titi residents, and worst of all, by crude questioning of the towkays and leading figures of the community in public, the British had caused their best allies to turn against them.[48]

It would appear that only in predominantly Chinese towns like Titi where communists had earlier done their groundwork well that any high-handed manner of the British officials and troops helped to turn the Chinese population against the British.

SEAC's Reaction to the MCP's 27 August Statement

On 28 August Force 136 officers in Malaya wired to SEAC headquarters a copy of the eight points of the MCP CEC's statement that was issued on 27 August. Capt. G.A. Garnon-Williams, head of SEAC's Political Division, commented:

I think this appears to be a very reasonable and liberal document. It is a great pity that our own Colonial Office did not wake up some weeks ago. It is presumed that action with SAC [i.e., Mountbatten) will be taken by C.P.A. [Chief Political Adviser].[49]

On 3 September, after consulting Mountbatten, the CPA, M.E. Dening, wrote to the Colonial Office informing it of the MCP's eight-point programme and urging it to give "the speediest and fullest practicable publicity" to the Malayan Union policy.[50] Dening feared that unless this was done "uncertainty and distrust should lead the resistance movements (the great majority of whose numbers are Communists) to adopt an attitude towards the return of British Administration from which it might be difficult for them to withdraw and which might unnecessarily complicate our post-war tasks in Malaya". He added that it was the view of Mountbatten and concurred to by General Hone, the CCAO-designate for Malaya, that an early announcement of the Malayan Union policy "even in the most general terms, is necessary if we are not to create for ourselves a very difficult situation upon re-entry into Malaya".[51]

Commenting on the MCP's statement, Dening said, "The sentiments expressed in this manifesto are irreproachable" and added:

> It will be seen that the Communist Party have rather stolen our thunder and that we have lost that element of surprise for our progressive policy, which would politically have been so valuable. Much of the programme could be subscribed to by His Majesty's Government with very little amendment.
>
> The population is of course not yet ready for a full electorate system but our policy does envisage a larger measure of participation in Government by the people.
>
> The reference 'freedom of societies' reflects anxiety of Chinese as to whether societies to which they belong will be declared illegal. A decision has already been taken on this point and it would be to our advantage to make this clear at once.[52]

On the same day, the newly elected Labour Cabinet approved the Malayan Union policy. Mountbatten was informed of the decision on 17 September — five days after he had accepted the official surrender of the Japanese armed forces in Singapore. The urgent need for publicity as expressed by Dening appeared to recede as more and more areas in Malaya were successfully occupied by British troops — with little resistance from the MPAJA guerrillas. Nonetheless, his cable had now awakened Whitehall fully to the need for publicity on the Malayan Union Policy.*

The liberal policy of Mountbatten towards the MCP/MPAJA and the Chinese was immediately put into force by the BMA (Malaya).

---

* See Memorandum to the Cabinet by the Secretary of State for the Colonies, G.H. Hall, "Policy in regard to Malaya", C.P. (45), October 1945, in C0273/675/50823 Pt. I. In the memorandum, Hall stated: "In proposing the early inception of a programme of publicity, I am influenced by very recent information as to the present state of affairs in Malaya. This information indicates that politically the most difficult body of Chinese in the Peninsula (the main group of the Resistance Movement and largely Chinese 'Communists') have set before themselves a goal which corresponds in very many respects with our own policy. It is not too much to say that the whole of our relations with the Chinese population of Malaya may be fundamentally affected by a timely statement of our intentions." Hall (Labour) had replaced Oliver Stanley.

But the BMA (Malaya) was not directly under Mountbatten's personal authority unlike the BMA in Burma where Mountbatten was responsible for making important political concessions to Brigadier Aung San and the Burma National Army, the counterpart of the MPAJA.[53] In Malaya, the initial liberal policy of the BMA encountered opposition from British army field commanders who saw the MPAJA guerrillas as a nuisance in their tasks of establishing law and order in the country and who were anxious to demobilize the MPAJA as quickly as possible.

Fearing that the MPAJA might challenge British authority, the British army first ordered all MPAJA units to concentrate in certain centres and to come under its overall command. Force 136 officers were allowed to continue as liaison officers. Second, the British army declared the MPAJA to be no longer operational after 12 September. However, the MPAJA units were allowed to remain intact and armed, while negotiations proceeded for their disbandment. They could no longer act on their own without authority from army officers. This meant that, while their activities before 12 September, particularly the arrests and executions of collaborators, were regarded as justified by military exigency and not to be pressed in BMA courts, such acts were prohibited after 12 September. In the months thereafter, between five and ten MPAJA guerrillas or commanders were arrested and arraigned on killings reported to have been committed after 12 September.[54]

The most well-known cases were those of Chu Kao, a Johor MPAJA deputy commander arrested for execution of a collaborator in Kluang on 15 September, and Lai Kam, arrested for a double killing committed in Bentong on 16 September. Chu Kao was later sentenced to death for murder, but the charges against Lai Kam were subsequently dropped on the grounds that witnesses had disappeared and others were being "terrorized".[55] The arrests and trials of these men (as well as others such as the Selangor MPAJU leader Soong Kwong on charges of extortion and intimidation) marked the resumption of conflict between the communists and the British administration.

CHAPTER 8

The Malay/MCP/Chinese Conflict

Che Salleh has gone a step further than most traditional preachers of Holy Wars who merely promised Paradise to those who died killing the infidel. He has appealed to the pre-Muslim background of Malays with the promise of invulnerability.

– British military intelligence report, 11 June 1946

Of all the branch organizations and movements of Islam, the mystical and semi-secret Sufi *tarekat* (brotherhoods or orders) are regarded as the foremost missionary vanguard. Their members comprise holy men and the Islam they represent is often called "popular Islam" different from that of the *ulema*, the established religio-legal scholars and officials. In Africa and Southeast Asia where the *tarekat* have been most active in the past few centuries, their followers have proselytized and successfully converted peoples of different races and tribes to Islam. Usually, they achieved conversion through a ruling family who then converted their subjects. Because of their individualistic approach the Sufi mystics also tolerated variations in local religious practice among their converts.

This is not the place to go into a history of Islam in Malaya and Southeast Asia,[1] but suffice it to say that it was not until the nineteenth century that the Sufi brotherhoods in the Middle East and in Southeast Asia began moving towards political action, to make calls for the defence of Islam, and to participate in what has been called primary resistance against European colonialism. A pan-Islamic movement came into being, which had as its goal the defence of Islam, and consequently a religious revival simultaneously got underway. Muslims throughout the world rallied around the Pan-Islamic banner of the Ottoman Sultans. In Indonesia and in several countries of Africa, militant Muslims launched *jihad* (holy wars) against the European powers. The Java War (1825–30) against the Dutch, led by Prince Diponegoro was fought under the banner of Islam; so was the Padri War of 1832/3 in Sumatra. The Tjilegon risings in Banten (Java) of 1888 were initiated by the Qadiriyyah *tarekat*.[2]

However, not all *tarekat* were violent or militant; nor were all *jihad* led by *tarekat*. None the less, several *tarekat* like the Qadiriyyah were among the foremost anti-colonialist fighters. In the nineteenth century in Africa, the Nigerian Sufi mystic, Usuman dan Fodio, gave a new expression to the doctrine of *hijra* (migration) and *jihad*. In theory, migration must precede a conflict against powers inimical to Islam. With Usuman, Muslims who were under foreign colonial pressures or attacks from "unbelievers" must migrate, regroup them-selves under their own leaders, then fight back to defend their own societies and culture and prevent their values from being over-whelmed and destroyed by the armed intrusions of non-Muslims.[3]

Jihad is thus the war against unbelievers, not necessarily against the colonialist enemy only. It may be launched to expand the terri-tory of the Islamic state, convert unbelievers by force, or to resist attacks on the Islamic state or society from outside or within, in which case it may be conducted against Muslim rebels of the state. The participation of a Muslim in a *jihad* is considered a pious act that stands on the same level as asceticism and other good works, and in the Koranic verses and traditions Paradise is promised to those who fall in battle.[4]

In Malaya, the first known Malay rebellion, which was described as a jihad, was the anti-British rebellion of 1928 in Terengganu. It is believed that a *tarekat* was involved, but its identity has never been clearly established. This chapter will describe the involvement of the Qadiriyyah *tarekat* in the inter-racial conflict between Malays and Chinese during the Japanese occupation, which began in the Batu Pahat district of Johor in May 1945. The violence spread to other parts of the south-western Johor, increasing in intensity after the Japanese surrender. Similarly, inter-racial violence occurred in the district of Sungai Manik in lower Perak and in other states. The Perak clashes were not coordinated with the Johor incidents, but they had many factors in common. The Malay struggle took on the character of a religious movement, a *jihad fi Sabilillah* (literally War in the Path of Allah), or Holy War.[5]

The Causes of the Conflict: The Malay View

The most bitter Malay experience with regard to the Chinese was the humiliation, degradation, and physical torture which the MPAJU/ MPAJA was said to have inflicted upon them. As one Malay described it:

> The psychological fermentation of mistrust, anger, and frustration of the Malays stemming from insults, scorn and arrogance thrown upon them, had to reach its saturation at a point in time.[6]

The offensive behaviour of the Chinese in the MPAJU/MPAJA is said to have taken many forms. They are alleged to have forcibly collected taxes (such as "head taxes", "commodity taxes") as well as supplies and intelligence from Malay villagers, as they also did from Chinese. The local Chinese MPAJU members, sometimes accompanied by armed Chinese MPAJA guerrillas, would enter Malay villages to recruit young and able-bodied Malay men to join them as guerrillas.[7] They would also demand Malay women for the kitchen work in their camps. Some of the Chinese men would abduct Malay women, molest them, or keep them as mistresses. All the time the Chinese would use threats and insulting language, and look down on the Malays. The MPAJA and the MPAJU Chinese are also said to have slaughtered pigs in the mosques, and forced Malays to eat pork.* Without trial Chinese guerrillas would kill Malays on the slightest suspicion of being collaborators. Many Malay policemen, *penghulu* (district headmen), *ketua kampung* (village headmen), and government officials were said to have been tortured and executed in a cruel and inhuman manner. Wives and children would also be shot along with the suspected collaborators. Bodies of victims were

---

* A story was told to Kenelm O.L. Burridge, while he was doing research in Batu Pahat, of how a Malay *kampung* was surprised by the MPAJA guerrillas one evening. All the inhabitants were herded together in the space by the mosque, and then, bringing some pigs, the guerrillas slaughtered them in the mosque, cooked them, and forced the Malays to join them in a feast. See Kenelm O.L. Burridge, "Racial Relations in Johore", *Australian Journal of Politics and History* 2, no. 2 (1957): 163.

said to have been mutilated beyond recognition, an act that offended the Islamic religion. Sometimes the victims would be killed in their houses, which would then be burnt down. The Chinese would also prevent the Malays from congregating and attending Friday prayers, for fear that the Malays were gathering to attack the Chinese.[8] This list of acts that the Chinese in MPAJA are said to have perpetrated is by no means exhaustive. These stories have assumed the form of myths. As Burridge has observed:

> Insofar as the story is told and retold, cannot be checked as a matter of historical fact, and has no co-ordinates in space or time, it has the force of a myth, a symbol, expressing pertinent points in a social relationship. The villain is a Chinese and his first and most immediate victims are Malay women. To the question "Why should the Chinese kill these women?" the answer was, "To obtain their clothing". There is no economic issue as between the murderer and the Malay. The motive for the murder is seen as robbery, a rather ferocious killing for a meagre profit — sheer greed. In other words, there is no competitive issue as such, merely a unilateral condemnation of the Chinese by the Malays for ruthlessly working for their own profits to the exclusion of the ordinary human interests of others....
>
> Whether these things actually occurred as matters of historical fact seems irrelevant in the present context. Either they were figments used as propaganda, which could be relied on to touch the Malays most vitally, or, assuming them to be untrue, they are stories invented after the event, which account precisely for the events themselves. Thus, if the Chinese really had done the things they are accused of they might reasonably expect some kind of rough handling; and since, in fact, there were incidents, and many Chinese were killed when they occurred, it is logical to explain the killings by relating them to actions which would have invited this kind of retaliation. In short, certain things were worth fighting for.[9]

Although many of these stories have become myths, even myths have their origins in real events. How to distinguish myth from fact in this instance is a difficult task — given the fact that either side in an inter-racial conflict always blames the other for causing the trouble. It is sufficient for the purposes of this study to indicate the general Malay perceptions of the Chinese in the MPAJU/MPAJA to offset the MPAJU/MPAJA perceptions of Malays given in Chapter 3.

Such perceptions are important to indicate why people decide to fight, and how they justify fighting after the fact.

Perceptions of Malay novelists and short-story writers also reflect popular Malay images of the Chinese in the MPAJU/MPAJA. To give just one example, Muhammad Haji Kidin, in his 1965 novel *Kerana Si Kuntum* (Because of Si Kuntum), does not mention the MPAJA nor the racial identity of the villains of his story.[10] They are just described as *pengganas* (bandits) and *perompak* (robbers) who pillage and burn down a Malay *kampung* near Kluang in Johor. Nevertheless, in case the reader is unsure about the racial identity of these bandits, the author inserts two illustrations showing them wearing Chinese hats.

Kamaruddin, the hero in the story, is the only survivor of the bandits' massacre of the *kampung*'s population of 70. Most of the inhabitants are killed in their sleep, their homes looted and burnt down. Kamaruddin vows revenge. Opposed equally to both the bandits and to the Japanese administration, he seeks refuge with an aboriginal tribe, the Sakais, whom he converts to Islam and trains for warfare. The story reaches its climax in the clash between the Sakais and the bandits. A Japanese army unit under Lieutenant Yamaguchi arrives in time to rescue Kamaruddin and the Sakais.[11]

Stories of the lack of respect shown by such Chinese towards Malay custom, religion, and Malay women increased Malay hostility towards the latter. When Malays saw these actions they failed to distinguish between Chinese "communists" and "non-communists". All Chinese were seen as the same — the enemy of their race and their religion. Once aroused to this point the Malays began to organize themselves and to retaliate. All that was needed was a misunderstanding or concrete incident to set them off.

The *Kiyai* Phenomenon or the New Leader

In 1928 in Terengganu a Malay Islamic leader led a peasant revolt against British rule. In playing this role he took over from the traditional Malay chief. Malay chiefs had launched a series of abortive revolts against the British between 1875 and 1911, but thereafter no longer attempted to lead any further opposition to British rule. In all the past Malay revolts the religious-mystical elements were prevalent and the Malay military commanders were always said to be men in possession of "secret powers and religious knowledge". It was the uncertain times of the Japanese occupation that again threw up such Malay leaders with magical qualities.

Under Japanese rule, Malay society continued to rely on the weakened Malay aristocracy and the British-trained bureaucratic elite. At the beginning the KMM non-aristocratic elite had risen to safeguard Malay positions in the rural areas. But when they fell from power the mantle reverted again to the weakened aristocracy. However, when rural Malays found themselves continually harassed and threatened by Chinese in the MPAJU/MPAJA, they discovered that neither the Malay aristocracy, the Malay police force nor the Malay Giyu Gun were of any help. Every strata of Malay society appeared helpless in facing this new foe. Even the Japanese found it difficult to suppress the Chinese MPAJU/MPAJA. It was by turning to their religion, Islam, that the Malays found their new leaders. They arose from among the ranks of the local Muslim "holy men".

The World of the Sufi *Kiyai**

The Malay struggle against the MPAJA/Chinese in Batu Pahat was organized mainly by the Javanese *kiyai* who were leaders or members of the local Sufi *tarekat*.† Islam provides the basic worldview and

---

* At the *kampung* (village) level, a *guru* is a religious teacher who is different from a *che'gu* or *guru sekolah* (school teacher). The *guru* may be a *Haji* who has spent several years in Mecca, yet *Tok guru, Tuan guru,* or *kiyai* is the form of address the Malay villagers use for him. The Javanese have a preference for the term *kiyai*, the Banjarese the term *Tuan guru*. *Tok guru* is also common, especially in Kelantan and Terengganu. Since the inter-racial incidents to be discussed occurred in areas in which the Javanese and other Indonesians predominated, the term *kiyai* is preferred.

† The term *Sufi* means "mystic", while the term *Tasawwuf* expresses what is understood by the word "mysticism". There are believed to be nine *Sufi* orders existing in Malaya, of which only three are said to be really widespread and popular among the Malays — the *Qadiriyyah*, the *Naqshbandiyyah*, and the *Ahmadiyyah*. Dr Syed Naguib al-Attas (who hails from Batu Pahat) is the leading Malay authority on Sufism in Malaya. He writes: "Although there are various orders scattered throughout Malaya, there is no single *Shaykh* or leader exercising absolute authority over any particular one of them. Such being the case, we find there are many *Shaykh* to a single *Tarekat*, and these are local *Shaykh*, their leadership-being recognised by members of their respective *Tarekat* in particular localities...." See Syed Naguib al-Attas, *Some Aspects of Sufism: As Understood and Practised among the Malays* (Singapore, 1963), pp. 1, 33–4.

action of the Malays through a combination of canon and theo-
logical instruction. Yet the non-Islamic traditional segment of the
Malay worldview is also obtrusive. Sufi mysticism seems to harmo-
nize and accommodate both worldviews.

It is easy to confuse the Sufi mystic with the shaman because
both profess knowledge of supernatural powers. The occult powers
of shaman such as the *pawang* and the *bomoh** are not unknown to
the Sufi mystic, who will occasionally perform some of the functions
of either the *pawang* or the *bomoh*, when required to do so.[†] Yet in
many ways they are different from one another. The Sufi mystic is
within the newer Malay worldview or system, which is Islam, and
his role and actions are devoted to Islam. The *pawang* or *bomoh* is of
the older Malay worldview of animism and *adat* or tradition. Spirit
worship is frowned upon by Islam, which sees it as worship of the
devil. Because of this, the office of the *pawang* and the *bomoh* is said
to be falling into abeyance; yet they are still regarded by Malays as
a relevant part of their constituted order of society, without whom

---

* *Pawang* means "magician or wizard" and *bomoh* "local medicine man or doctor,
versed in traditional medicine". The *pawang* was formerly required to perform
agricultural rites in order to ensure good harvests of crops, or fish, or even
ore during mining. The *bomoh* usually practise their art for the cure of human
disease. Both terms are, however, often used as though they are interchangeable.
See W.W. Skeat, *Malay Magic* (London [1900], 1965 reprint), pp. 56–7. In 1955/6,
in a village in the *mukim* of Batu Pahat, only the office of *bomoh* was still in
use when Kenelm O.L. Burridge visited it. He comments: "The activities associated with a *pawang* should be no concern of a good Muslim; they are, in the
main, occult, and the more power of this kind a *pawang* has the further he re-
treats from the community and from Islamic values. He lives alone and 'concen-
trates' on his expertise: only a lesser *pawang* lives in the village." A single man
may combine the functions of *pawang* and *bomoh*, but Malay villagers still seek
a *bomoh* if it is impossible to get a Western-educated doctor. See Burridge,
"Managerial Influences in a Johore Village", *JMBRAS* 30 (May 1957): 99–100.
[†] The late Haji Fadil of Johor (died 1956), a *Shaykh* of both the Qadiriyyah and
Naqshbandiyyah orders, was Sultan Ibrahim's favourite *pawang* or "spiritual man".
He studied in Mecca, was a well-known teacher of several Sufi *tarekat* and was
estimated to have 4,000 followers in Johor, among whom the most famous was
Kiyai Salleh bin Abdul Karim of Simpang Kiri, Batu Pahat. Haji Fadil lived at the
Pasir Plangi Mosque, which belonged to Sultan Ibrahim. It was said he received
ample allowance from the Sultan who had "always patronised and kept spiritual
men about him". Naguib, *Some Aspects of Sufism*, pp. 34–5, 52–4.

no village community is complete.* Local Malay perceptions of the Sufi mystic and the shaman are somewhat complicated by the view of the orthodox religious authority of the state, as represented by the Jabatan or Majlis Ugama (Religious Department or Council), which disapproves of many of the magico-mystical practices of both the Sufi mystic and the shaman. The clearest distinction between the Sufi mystic and the shaman is that they differ in their "intention" and in the relationship in which they stand to their followers. Naguib draws the distinction well:

> The Magician [shaman] would force the "spirits" to grant what is desired, which may be that which guards against evil, or that which procures favours from the "spirits". The Sufi does not demand what is desired, rather he submits to the Divine will upon which man feels dependent ....
>
> The Magician's followers, or audience, ask for favours and their relation to him is temporary in contrast with the more permanent relationship that exists between the Sufi and his followers. Further, the authority of the Magician is not so much based, like that of the Sufi, upon personal charisma.[12]

In the *kampung* of Batu Pahat, the Sufi *kiyai*, mostly of Javanese peasant origin were highly venerated by the local Malay population. They command prestige and popularity because of "their charismatic powers, and the alleged miracles they are believed to have performed, the depth of their learning, the efficacy of their teachings as experienced by their followers and the disciples who will propagate them to others".[13] In times of crisis and social turmoil the local Malays turn to their Islamic religion and to their religious leaders for advice and spiritual guidance. In such an event, the charismatic Sufi *kiyai* can help them to take measures for their own self-protection and, if necessary, organize and train them for battle. It is the Sufi *kiyai* who can invoke supernatural powers in the cause of Islam, such as a *jihad*, and lead his followers into battle as the

---

* The standing of the *bomoh* among the Malays was given a big boost by Tunku Abdul Rahman when he was prime minister of Malaysia (1955–70). As a patron of the Malaysian Football Association, he frequently sought the services of the *bomoh* to ensure a rainless day for any big soccer matches. The Tunku and his successor, the late Tun Abdul Razak, were known to have their personal *bomoh* and *pawang*.

Khalifah, the delegate of the *Shaykh* [the founder] of the Qadiriyyah Sufi order. He is invested with certain of the *Shaykh*'s powers and represents him in areas remote from his base.[14] The "secret powers" which the Sufi *kiyai* are said to possess include the *ilmu batin* (spiritual or mystical knowledge), *ilmu ghaib* (knowledge of becoming invisible and inaudible), *ilmu pencak silat* (knowledge of martial arts), and *ilmu kebal* (knowledge of invulnerability). Among the well-known Sufi mystics of Johor are the late Kiyai Salleh, whose supernatural powers and fighting prowess are legendary, Haji Muhammad Shah, former Chief Kathi of Johor, and Haji Othman bin Haji Muhammad Amin of Mukim Simpang Kiri in Batu Pahat.[*]

A war between Muslims and non-Muslims turns into a *jihad* only if it is so declared by any *imam* or religious leader. The *imam* has to consider carefully whether the threat to Muslims and to Islam is so great that he has no other alternative but to issue the *fatwa* (the summons) that all Muslims in the land should go on a *jihad*. *The Shorter Encyclopaedia of Islam* puts it as follows:

> ...If a Muslim country is invaded by unbelievers, the *Imam* may issue a general summons calling all Muslims there to arms, and as the danger grows so may the width of the summons until the whole Muslim world is involved. A Muslim who dies fighting in the Path of Allah (*fi sabil Allah*) is a martyr (*shahid*) and is assured of Paradise.... Such a death was in the early generations regarded as the peculiar crown of a pious life ... any war between Muslims and non-Muslims must be a *jihad* with its incitements and rewards....[†]

The *Mukim* of Tanjong Sembrong and Simpang Kiri

Batu Pahat district in Johor was divided into at least 15 *mukim* before the war. The *mukim* is the smallest territorial and administrative unit demarcated by the Land Office. In Johor a *mukim* consists of a number of *kampung* varying in size from about 10 square miles to 90 square miles, and has a population of between 3,000 and

---

[*] Not every Sufi *kiyai* would possess all this knowledge, but he who does would emerge the outstanding charismatic leader. Naguib, *Some Aspects of Sufism*, pp. 34–5.

[†] *Imam* generally refers to both the congregational prayer leader and any Islamic religious leader. Gibb and Kramers, *A Shorter Encyclopaedia of Islam*, p. 89.

35,000. The head of each *mukim* is the *penghulu*.[15] Although little evidence is available on *mukim* administration during the Japanese occupation, it appears that the Japanese did not alter the division of the *mukim* areas and retained the bulk of pre-war *mukim* administrative officials.

The inter-racial clashes first started in Tanjong Sembrong known as Mukim VII, and these were followed by clashes in Simpang Kiri, or Mukim IV. In both *mukim* Indonesians heavily outnumbered indigenous Malays. In Tanjong Sembrong, Banjarese (from Banjarmasin in Indonesian Kalimantan) were said to have constituted about 40 per cent of the Malay population, and in Simpang Kiri Javanese constituted the majority. Other Indonesian elements found in both areas were Bugis and Acehnese.[16] The Banjarese, Bugis, and Javanese have a reputation in Malaya of being belligerent when aroused. The Javanese especially are noted for millenarian movements and Sufism, and have a tendency to produce leaders with magical qualities.[17] It is probably for this reason that these Indonesians were the first to oppose the Chinese/MCP/MPAJA in the area. Kiyai Salleh was locally believed to be of mixed Javanese and Indian Muslim parentage, although a British report described him as being of Sumatran Malay extraction.[18]

The Chinese population of both *mukim* in 1945 was reported to have been fairly equal to the Malay population, although demographic figures in the *mukim* for 1945 are not available. The 1947 British-conducted census of Malaya, which includes *mukim* population statistics, has to be used with caution to establish the demographic picture of the two *mukim* in 1945. The inter-racial clashes in 1945 caused many Malays and Chinese to become displaced from their homes. In areas where their ethnic group constituted a tiny minority before, most Malays or Chinese did not return even after the area had been pacified. Only in areas where Malays and Chinese were of roughly equivalent numbers was it likely that both groups would remain, stand their ground and fight.

The 1947 census gives the total population of Tanjong Sembrong as 14,170, of which the Malays numbered 8,674 and the Chinese 5,147. In Simpang Kiri the total population was reported to be 10,715, of which the Malays comprised 10,320 and the Chinese 284.[19] It is clear that the Simpang Kiri figures cannot be taken to reflect the situation in 1945, as it shows that the whole *mukim* ended up practically 100 per cent Malay. Simpang Kiri was the military stronghold of Kiyai Salleh and the 1947 statistics reflect Malay supremacy in the fighting. On the other hand, the figures of Tanjong Sembrong can probably be taken to indicate that the demographic picture had remained roughly unchanged despite violent inter-racial clashes. The resilient Chinese presence in the *mukim* in 1947 was probably due both to their ability to withstand Malay attacks in 1945 and to the efforts of the BMA to encourage large numbers of Chinese settlers to return to their homes in Tanjong Sembrong after the British had regained administration of the area.

The Sabilillah Movement

Malay self-defence measures in Batu Pahat district, and later in Muar district, finally coalesced into the Sabilillah movement. I prefer to use the term Sabilillah, meaning the Holy War, to describe the movement because there is evidence to indicate that it was so called at the time. Halinah Bamadhaj, who has studied the racial clashes in Mukim IV Simpang Kiri, Batu Pahat, calls it the Muhammadiah movement. It is said to have got its name from the Muhammadiah organization formed by the *penghulu* of Simpang Kiri, Mohd. Kari.[20]

The Sabilillah was not an organization but a loose religious movement based on Sufi mysticism.* Its objects were basically to arouse the Malays, to encourage them to overcome Chinese/MPAJA domination, and to strengthen Malay self-confidence. These teachings naturally fostered widespread antagonism towards Chinese and encouragement to kill Chinese because it was difficult to draw a line between the Chinese and the MPAJA. In short, its object was purely

---

* It was Naguib who first revealed that the Sufi *tarekat* played a role in the Malay struggle in Batu Pahat. Although the Sufi *tarekat* in Malaya have been peaceful and non-militant, yet they are said to have definitely influenced the outlook of the Malays with regard to their system of political and social order. Naguib adds, "They [the Sufi orders] have never been known to exhibit a religious militarism except perhaps during the Batu Pahat uprising which threatened the whole of Malaya with communal strife." However in some countries, the Naqshbandiyyah and Ahmadiyyah orders have exerted their political role and tended towards militarism. In Sumatra, for example, the Naqshbandis are said to have shown themselves capable of tending to militancy or aggressiveness whenever the circumstances permit. Naguib, *Some Aspects of Sufism*, pp. 64, 99. < correct title ?> For Naqshbandiyyah activity in Java in the 19th century, see Sartono Kartodirjo, *The Peasants' Revolt of Banten in 1888* (The Hague, 1966).

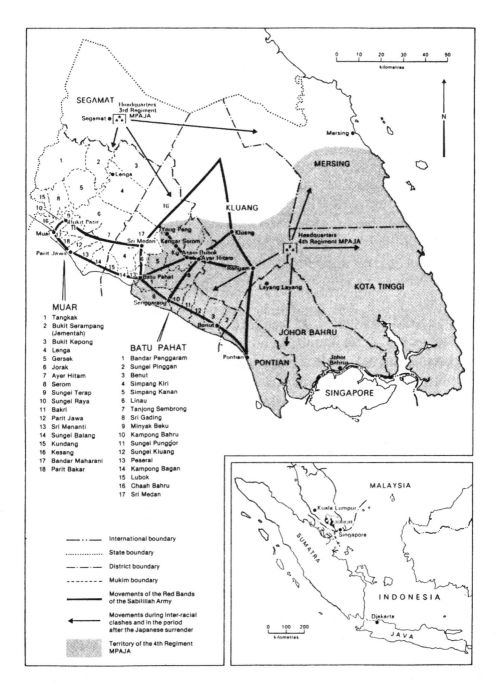

Fig. 4. The *Mukim* of Muar and Batu Pahat and the Separate Movements of the Third and Fourth Regiments, MPAJA, and the Red Bands of the *Sabilillah* Army During the Period May–August 1945

and simply anti-Chinese. It was religious because "the best way to arouse and to unite the Malays was through their Islamic religion".[21]

The Sabilillah teachings took the form of congregating Malays to recite verses of the Koran, as a result of which they were supposed to become invulnerable during warfare.[22] Charms were also used to confer invulnerability, the chief one being a gold needle or a piece of stone known as *delima*, which was blessed and then pierced into the forearm of the convert.[23] Drinking a potion blessed by the *imam* or *kiyai* was also said to give the convert invulnerability. These teachings had a great effect on Malays in Batu Pahat, even though many Malays were killed in the fighting that ensued.[24] The method practised by the legendary Kiyai Salleh and his followers was said to consist of the recitation, several hundred times repeated, of certain verses of the Koran after each of the five prayers obligatory every 24 hours. Disciples were warned that attainment or failure of invulnerability depended on their own behaviour and that success would only be achieved if they faithfully followed the teachings. Above all, they were forbidden to steal, rape, torture, or kill anyone innocent, or to provoke action. The disciple who failed to follow these instructions scrupulously would lose his invulnerability.[25]

Kiyai Salleh first came into prominence in May/June 1945 when he organized Malay resistance effectively in his Simpang Kiri area and led Malays in attacking the Chinese/MPAJA. His fame began to spread throughout the entire Batu Pahat district. Malays were particularly impressed by the real or exaggerated stories of his supernatural powers. He is said once to have subdued, single-handed, a group of about 200 Chinese. At another time, to the amazement of his men, he alone lifted two huge coconut trees, which barred his line of advance.[26] A BMA intelligence report has described his other known supernatural powers:

> Che'gu [Teacher] Salleh himself — it is popularly claimed — cannot be killed by bullets; he can walk dry-shod across rivers; he can burst any bonds that are put upon him; his voice can paralyse his assailants, making them drop their weapons; and were Chinese to take him and set him in a cauldron of boiling water he would emerge alive and unharmed.[27]

These powers Kiyai Salleh had also delegated to two principal assistants who, together with himself, had the ability to confer "invulnerability" upon devotees who faithfully observed the ritual he had laid down. The power, however, lasted "only as long as the Faith of the Initiate in his own safety is firm".[28]

Kiyai Salleh is said to have been born in Parit Jawa, a few miles south of Muar town. He was a disciple of Kiyai Haji Fadil, a *Shaykh* of both the Qadiriyyah and Naqshbandiyyah Sufi orders and the *pawang* of Sultan Ibrahim. He was believed to have been a leader of gangs of robbers before the war, for which he spent a period in prison.[29] Naguib describes him as an enigmatic personality, of short stature and dark complexion, who sported a goatee and had small beady eyes that could "at times glow with boyish mischief, or glare with a fury that has been known to strike terror into the hearts of his enemies".[30] At the height of the fighting in Batu Pahat he is said to have had constant visions of Shaykh 'Abdul-Qadir Jilani, the Founder of the Qadiriyyah order, who warned him of imminent dangers and aided him many times in overcoming his enemies in various supernatural ways. Naguib records a story, which Kiyai Salleh told him:

> One day in the month of Ramadhan [fasting month], he had a vision of Shaykh 'Abdul-Qadir Jilani who appeared dressed in black. The Shaykh warned him of imminent attack by the Chinese "Bandits", revealing to him their position and their line of advance. The Panglima [Kiyai Salleh] at once rounded up his men and surprised the "Bandits" whom he found exactly as described in the vision, and who were preparing to launch their attack. It was reported that the Chinese "Bandits" feared Panglima Salih very much.[31]*

During the interview he showed Naguib his famous sword (*parang panjang*), which had claimed 172 heads. Despite his known exploits, Kiyai Salleh was never arrested after the British returned. The reason will become evident later in this chapter.

Tentera Sabil Selendang Merah (Holy War Army of the Red Bands)

This was the military organization of Kiyai Salleh,[32] which took its name from the *selendang merah* (a band or sash of red cloth) worn

---

* The month of *Ramadhan* refers to Aug./Sept. 1945. The title of *Panglima* means Chief Warrior or Commander-in-Chief.

on the arms of the followers, the majority of whom were said to be Javanese and Banjarese.[33] Kiyai Salleh and his commanders wore a wider red band across their chests. The weapon which he and his men usually carried was the long sword or machete known as the *parang panjang*, though other known weapons used were the *lembing, kris, pedang,* and *tombak.** The Red Bands attacked only with these weapons, and the MPAJA would meet them with guns and bullets. Chinese accounts confirm that though few of their Malay attackers were armed with automatic weapons, they were able to inflict heavy casualties among the Chinese. This attests to the fighting courage and religious fanaticism of the Sabilillah Army. In fact, the Chinese commonly called the Malay bands, which attacked them *shou dao* (long knives), referring clearly to the *parang panjang*. The Sabilillah army under Kiyai Salleh's leadership had not come into existence when the Malays began their attacks on the Chinese in May 1945. Independent Muslim groups had arisen first in Tanjong Sembrong. One group, the Barisan Islam (Muslim Front) under *Tuan Guru* (teacher) Haji Mokhtar of Tanjong Semberong, was said to have led the initial attack on the Chinese.[†]

Because of his popularity, Kiyai Salleh was urged to bring the various groups in Batu Pahat under his central command, and the Sabilillah army came into being probably in June or July 1945. It became most active during the interregnum after the Japanese surrender but before the arrival of British troops in the area. Most Malay accounts focus on its activities during this interim period, regarding its appearance as the rival of the MPAJA. It meted out retaliation for the widespread MPAJA abductions, tortures, and executions of Malays regarded as informers and collaborators.

The structure of the Sabilillah Army and its Kiyai commanders during the interim period was said to be as follows:

---

* These are different types of Malay knives and spears used during Malay warfare in the past, which were apparently revived for use of the Sabilillah army. For description of each of these weapons, see Donn F. Draeger, *Weapons and Fighting Arts of the Indonesian Archipelago* (Tokyo, 1972).

† *Tuan Guru* Haji Mokhtar was said to have assumed the Commander's role of *Khalifah* in the Holy War. See Musak Mantrak, "Sejarah Masyarakat Majemuk di Mukim VII, Batu Pahat", pp. 64, 68; and his article "Anchaman Komunis, 1945–1946", pp. 21–2.

Commander-in-Chief	Kiyai Salleh Abdul Karim
General commissioner	Kiyai Wak Joyo
South Johor	No. 1 commander, Kiyai Kusin
	No. 2 commander, Kiyai Mashudi
	No. 3 commander, Kiyai Mayor (Moh)
East Johor	No. 1 commander, Kiyai Saudi
	No. 2 commander, Kiyai Maskam
	No. 3 commander, KiyaiSarbini
North Johor	No. 1 commander, Kiyai Mustahir
	No. 2 commander, Kiyai Haji Shamsuddin
	No. 3 commander, Kiyai Haji Shukor[34]

The Inter-racial Clashes

The origins of the inter-racial clashes in Tanjong Sembrong and Simpang Kiri are difficult to establish with any certainty. This is due to a problem of sources. There are more Malay than Chinese accounts of these clashes. These and other sources — especially Japanese and MPAJA — are also so contradictory that it is best to introduce each account separately as rival perceptions of the same incidents, and then to attempt a judgement.

The Malay Version

Trouble is said to have begun in April 1945 in the *mukim* of Tanjong Sembrong, when a *ketua kampung* (headman) named Daud was abducted by the MPAJA while travelling to Yong Peng. He was believed to have been killed, but his body was never recovered. The disappearance of three more Malays in the *mukim*, one after another, began to cause real concern to the Malay population. It was believed that they had each been abducted secretly, and were either tortured or killed in connection with their failure to collect the various "taxes" which the Chinese MPAJU officials had imposed on the Malays.[35]

The *mukim* had a mixed Malay-Chinese population. The Malays were all of Indonesian stock, the majority being Banjarese. Each adult in the village was asked to pay a contribution of $3, which was regarded by the Malays as excessive. The *penghulu* and *ketua kampung* were held responsible for collecting the money every month from the Malays. The Chinese villagers were also forced to contribute, but apparently paid up with little protest. MPAJU threats were frequently issued to those who refused to contribute money or to provide other needs such as supplies, intelligence, and recruits.

The head of the Chinese MPAJU in the *mukim* was Seng Nga, his assistant was Ah Koi, and their headquarters was in Kangkar Serom. As early as 1942 they had tried to persuade the Malays in the *mukim* to join the MPAJA, and finally succeeded in getting several Malays to establish the Malay section. A schoolteacher, Chik Gu Jamain b. Abdul Hamid, was appointed president of the section. The "Justice of the Peace" was Shahran bin Abdul Ghani, and the treasurer Salleh bin Yunus. The Malay section would work with the *penghulu* and *ketua kampung* to raise contributions among the villagers towards financing the activities of the MPAJU and MPAJA. Race relations were said to have been peaceful until the Chinese MPAJU officials began behaving arrogantly towards Malays in the latter part of the Japanese occupation. By April 1945, the Malays found MPAJU insults and harassment so unbearable that the Malay section refused to cooperate any more.

Soon after this there was an incident in which two Sumatran Malays were abducted by the MPAJU/MPAJA. One escaped back to his *kampung* with the news that his friend had been killed. It was then that the Malays realized what the fate of the other missing Malays might have been. This discovery greatly angered the Banjarese, who had suffered more than the others and who could no longer bear the Chinese harassment. The Malay section enquired of the MPAJU headquarters the whereabouts of the missing men, but drew evasive answers. The *penghulu* of Tanjong Sembrong reported the disappearance to the Japanese authorities, but no immediate action was taken. This soon led to the abduction and killing of the president of the Malay section of the MPAJU, Chik Gu Jamain. A group of armed Chinese guerrillas appeared at his house one night in April 1945, bundled him into a gunnysack, and carried him away. Other Malays witnessed the incident. Although he screamed for help, no one dared to go to his rescue. There had been a struggle in the house, as evidenced by bloodstains on the walls and broken property all over the place. He was never seen again.

On 3 May a group of MPAJA men appeared at Parit Khalid to abduct two more Malays. Again, one of the Malays escaped and fled to the home of a *ketua kampung*, Haji Talib, who was a disciple of the Sufi mystic *Tuan Guru* Haji Mokhtar. This led to resistance against the MPAJU/MPAJA being organized. Haji Mokhtar immediately assumed leadership and began preparations to train and

The Malay/MCP/Chinese Conflict | 211

form a fighting group with him at the head. The news also spread
that the MPAJU had ordered a ban on gatherings for Friday prayers.
Apparently the ban was imposed to prevent the Malays coming
together with those in other districts to organize any resistance.
The MPAJU must have learnt that some organized resistance was
already underway. *Tuan Guru* Haji Mokhtar issued the *fatwa jihad*
(the call to wage the Holy War). On 5 May Malays reported to the
district officer (DO) of Batu Pahat, Ismail bin Dato Abdullah, and
also to the Japanese authorities, rumours of MPAJU/MPAJA plan to
attack the Malay population. The DO discounted the rumours, but
the Japanese took the reports seriously this time. They decided that
the Malays and the Japanese would coordinate their attacks on the
MPAJU/MPAJA. At 11 p.m. the Malays attacked an MPAJA detachment in Asam Bubok, and during the skirmish killed the MPAJU
leader Seng Nga. On 6 May, Japanese Kempeitai officers and troops,
assisted by two Malay youths, arrived in the *mukim* and rounded up
a lorry-load of Chinese. The MPAJA carried out raids against the
Malays in retaliation. Malay attacks were said to be well planned,
each group comprising forty men from a particular *kampung*, but
most of the Chinese who fell victim to the blades of the *parang
panjang* were believed not to have been involved in the MPAJU at
all.[36] No Chinese or Malay in the *mukim* could any longer escape
from the conflict.

The clashes soon spread to Mukim IV Simpang Kiri whose
penghulu, Mohd. Kari, invited Kiyai Salleh to lead the Malays against
the Chinese. He also formed an organization, the Muhammadiah,
to unite Malays against the MPAJA. It included all influential local
officials, religious and secular.[37] In other *mukim* trouble had also
started over misunderstandings between Malays and the MPAJA/
Chinese. The MPAJA/Chinese behaviour was regarded as arrogant
and unbearable. Reports of communist atrocities spread. The MPAJA
was said to have butchered, gunned down, or beheaded Malays
and administered the "water treatment" — pumping water into the
victim's body until the belly swelled, immersion in a tub of water
until drowned, or scalding with hot water. MPAJA/Chinese "revenge"
killings were said to have taken their toll of Malay officials — DO,
ketua kampong, *penghulu*, and policemen.[38]

On 10 June, the MPAJA killed the DO of Batu Pahat, Ismail
bin Abdullah, at Benut.[39] The MPAJA is said to have made a determined effort to track him down.[40] A dramatic account of the assassination by an observer reveals that besides the DO, a Ceylonese

doctor and a Japanese officer were also gunned down at a public function:

> The killing of our District Officer, Inche Ismail and Dr Woodhull by MPAJA terrorists in Benut in July 1945 was a tragedy. Inche Ismail was a brilliant officer who had borne the weight of office through the trying and difficult years of the Japanese Occupation with conspicuous success. Dr Woodhull was a Jaffna Tamil and was my friend and neighbour. He had accompanied Ismail, the District Officer, Dr Ng Giok Seng and two Japanese officials to Benut to do relief work among flood victims.
>
> The visit was widely advertised to ensure the attendance of as large a number of destitutes as possible from the interior and thus afforded the MPAJA the opportunity to lay an ambush. It would appear that Dr Woodhull had a premonition that he would not return alive and did not want to go at first but later changed his mind and went.
>
> After the party arrived in Benut they were entertained to a reception by the Chinese Chamber of Commerce. Soon after the entertainment started, someone rang a bell and the building was surrounded by a detachment of the MPAJA.
>
> Despite Dr Ng Giok Seng's plea to the District Officer and Dr Woodhull not to run away, they followed the Japanese officers and tried to run the gauntlet of gunfire which greeted their effort. The District Officer, Dr Woodhull and one of the Japanese officers were shot and killed instantly while the sole surviving Japanese dived into the Benut River and swam to safety.
>
> Dr Ng Giok Seng was taken to a jungle hideout where he remained till the liberation of Malaya. It was he who gave me an account of the incident recounted above and said that his captors had told him that Dr Woodhull's life would have been spared had he not attempted to run away. This was certainly true for soon after Dr Woodhull's death, his widow received a letter from the MPAJA expressing regret for killing her husband and forwarding a sum of money by way of compensation.[41]

It was this type of vengeance killing of Malay officials, which incited Malay religious leaders to call on their followers to *berjihad* and to defend themselves.

The Japanese Version

A Japanese newspaper account[42] has described how Malays in the *kampung* of Seri Medan (Mukim 17) in Batu Pahat district took up arms against "communistic bandits" on 11 May 1945. Seri Medan is 15 miles northeast of Batu Pahat town, or Bandar Penggaram, as the Malays prefer to call it. The *Penang Shimbun*, taking what it called a "grand stand view" of the incident, reported that trouble had started as early as 15 February 1945, when the MPAJA held a big meeting at Seri Medan to which all villagers, Malays and Chinese, were forced to attend. Thereafter the MPAJA levied "commodity taxes", "head taxes", and "property taxes", not only on Malays but also on Chinese. The guerrillas also allegedly committed "all kinds of mischievous acts including assaults on mosques" in Barisan Bubok (Asam Bubok):

> Enraged by these assaults [on the mosques] a Malay leader in Seri Medan called on the villagers to arm. He told them of the bandits' assault and they started a campaign to conquer them. They killed a few bandit leaders and deprived them of their arms and ammunition. Against this retaliation, the bandits attempted to revenge themselves and on 11 May, about 100 of them were sent to the kampong to terrorise the villagers. This started a general conflict between the innocent villagers and bandits.
>
> The villagers with the "Rising Sun" flag at the head of their procession and carrying parangs succeeded in carrying out death-defying attacks on the communists.
>
> Thus, the cry of "Kill the Bandits once for all" movement was relayed to all the neighbouring districts, and on 14 May in Barisong they killed two among ten attackers. The innocent inhabitants in Parit Tiga then began to take refuge in other districts and consequently became separated from the bands of Communistic bandits.[43]

Soon after this incident, the report said, the Japanese army intervened and launched attacks on the MPAJA in coordination with the Johor Jikeidan and the Batu Pahat police force. The Japanese were concerned with what they described as "false propaganda" spread by the MPAJA that the incident was a racial conflict fostered by the Japanese. To rebut these accusations, the Japanese "carried out such schemes as would calm the situation, in addition to helping the innocent refugees by providing them with homes, etc.". The tension was said to have eased subsequently and, impressed by these schemes, the public started to reconstruct their homes, "voicing at the same time their firm determination to cooperate with the authorities". The Johor Seicho (administrator) gave a donation of

$200,000 to both Chinese and Malay refugees, "having given strict orders to the Jikeidan to smash the bandits".[44]

In the meantime, Chokan Kakka (the governor) also sent his view of the situation officially to the "pro-Japanese" Batu Pahat Overseas Chinese Association proclaiming that "this conflict was not a racial one, but one between the bandits and the good public". At the same time the Sultan of Johor, "from the religious point of view", was said to have given stern orders to his followers "to destroy the enemy of religion once for all".[45]

Despite the Japanese measures, *Penang Shimbun* said, bandits continued to be active, so that the authorities could no longer stand by, and "firmly determined" in late June to carry out a big-scale anti-communist operation from three directions — Muar, Batu Pahat, and Keluang — simultaneously. The main body of the Japanese army moved north from the Batu Pahat-Pontian highway through jungles, while a unit from the Yong Peng-Batu Pahat highway marched eastwards. This was to be a "pincer movement", which would close in and destroy an estimated 1,000 bandits in Parit Taja. The northern Japanese army unit lined up along the Muar–Yong Peng highway was a blocking element, waiting to cut off any of the guerrillas fleeing from the dragnet. The Japanese were so confident they had the MPAJA guerrillas trapped that a great deal of publicity was given to the operation. They were sure that it was only a matter of time before they had all the guerrillas captured or killed. The army's propaganda corps followed up in the rear of the fighting units "with all means of publicity to help ease the living conditions in the rear".[46]

The operation began on 22 June, and was reported to have gained some successes. After marching for a few days through jungles, which had become an awful muddy swamp owing to heavy rain, the Japanese troops swooped on the MPAJA base. "Taken off their guard", another Japanese newspaper reported, "the enemy bandits dispersed in all directions into the jungle, leaving behind 40 corpses and a large amount of provisions".[47]

The report went on:

> A flying party, which started from Api Api, west of Pontian, succeeded in surprising the enemy on a hill north of the Southern highway, and taking the commander of the second section prisoner, captured many weapons, including one automatic 13-millimetre gun manufactured in England, as well as clothes.

Moreover, the northern units which had occupied an essential line in the north, seized enemy bandits who fled northward, along the line or surrounded the rest in the jungle. They also attacked the bandits on the Southern hill, midway between Yong Peng and Ayer Hitam, as a result of which they accounted for 19 enemy corpses, 20 prisoners, and a booty of weapons and much ammunition.

Meanwhile, the western units surprised and destroyed the bandits on the northwest hill of Seri Medan (14 miles from Yong Peng) early on the morning of 24 June, and launched an attack against the enemy who fled westward on the Yong Peng-Batu Pahat highway.

Simultaneously with these big successes of our units, the *Syu Boetai* [Local Peace Preservation Unit specially trained for fighting and combing out communists], which was formed by the inhabitants, has occupied the important eastern line, and a unit from this body is guarding the Batu Pahat-Ayer Hitam highway.

It looks as if the bandits have completely lost their spirit to fight, and having thrown away their weapons are escaping through our ranks, wearing plain clothes.

For the present, the armed bandits have disappeared in this area, and a lull prevails, but our units, determined to continue the operations, are preparing their next strategy.

The results achieved by our side which have been confirmed at present are as follows: Enemy corpses abandoned: 64; Enemy taken prisoner: 28; Booty: One automatic 13-millimetre gun, seven rifles; 1,273 rounds of ammunition, 21 automatic pistols; 142 rounds of ammunition; 17 hunting guns; 87 rounds of ammunition; 180 rounds of ammunition for automatic rifle; four hand grenades, 15 explosives, and many types of bayonets, spears, bicycles, parts of weapons, provisions and clothing.[48]

Anxious to show that the incidents in the Batu Pahat district were not racial, and that the Japanese army had not gone into the area merely to help the Malays, *Malai Sinpo* also reported an incident on 10 June 1945, in which the MPAJA had attacked Benut in Batu Pahat district, a town with a predominantly Chinese population of 3,000. The guerrillas were alleged to have raided the village and kidnapped "about 2,000 innocent people, mostly women and children, including the wife and child of Mr Yu Jin Nim, *Sibutyo* (branch chairman) of the Overseas Chinese Association as well as looted their properties". The report, which made no mention of the killing of the Malay DO, concluded:

This wicked deed is clear proof that the communistic bandits dare to violate their own compatriots and as a result even the Chinese inhabitants in the Batu Pahat and Pontian areas, who hitherto were said to be not cooperating with Nippon authorities, are now extremely angry with them.

The Overseas Chinese Association of Batu Pahat is also fully cooperating with the State Government in affording relief to the evacuees by means of controlling prices, collection and transportation of provision, and endeavouring devotedly to restore public peace.

Under the present strained war situation, it is evident that this trend should have a great influence on the 2,000,000 Overseas Chinese in Malai.[49]

The MPAJA Version

The MPAJA's Fourth Regiment (south Johor) claims that the Japanese, after their plan "to provoke racial discord had backfired on them", changed their plans and launched a systematic offensive against the regiment.[50] It said that the Japanese army successfully carried out operations between June and July 1945 against its headquarters, in which the regiment lost "some of our best commanders — equal to half our losses in the past".[51] On 17 June, the Japanese were reported to have mobilized more than 1,000 troops and attacked the regiment's main base from three directions. The Japanese advanced along "four lines of encirclement", in an attempt to destroy the whole regiment "at one stroke". The four major offensives occurred as follows: the first and second in September 1944, the third offensive in April 1945 and the fourth "grand offensive" in June-July. But the MPAJA combatants "bravely crushed the enemy plot and broke through the encirclements". The heroes of this campaign were Sieh-pai and Cheng Wen, whose courage and fighting ability were regarded as "noble and exemplary" in the face of enemy fire. One of them was seriously injured. Both fought their way out of the encirclements.[52] Many of the guerrillas preferred death to imprisonment, and fought to the last.

The regiment appears more concerned with describing its military engagements with the Japanese in detail and in glorifying its heroes. Not much information was given to what happened in the racial clashes in Johor. The record of the central military headquarters of the MPAJA is equally reticent, making only a brief reference to the racial clashes. The headquarters claims that because the war was going badly for Japan in 1945, the Japanese decided to attack the Chinese anti-Japanese movement in Malaya, that is, the MPAJA. In Johor the Japanese resorted to stirring racial ill will. They armed the Malays and instigated them to attack the Chinese, thereby making Malays and Chinese fight and kill one another.[53]

With regard to the racial clashes, Chin Peng in his autobiography says that the clashes had begun before Tokyo's surrender. He doubted that the Japanese officers even knew that their troops were responsible for igniting tension between Malay and Chinese communities. He said: "As early as July — before the first of two atomic bombs dropped on Japan — Japanese troops disguised as AJA guerrillas — went to a mosque in Johore and slaughtered a pig. This immediately inflamed Malay sentiments and they turned on the local Chinese villagers.... Trouble spread from Batu Pahat to Yong Peng. The Malays were armed with *parang panjang* — the long knife. The Chinese villagers who became their targets were unarmed and desperately called for the AJA for support.... In the end, many [British] liaison officers had no option but to move with us. We set up a line and told the Malays not to cross it. The Malays, believing their magic amulets would shield them from bullets, charged our lines ... we chased them into nearby kampongs and arrested the ring leaders."[54]

The Chinese Version

Very few Chinese accounts provide details of how the racial clashes in Batu Pahat started. It is usually narrated that the Japanese instigated the Malays into attacking and slaughtering Chinese. The Chinese government, in a post-war memorandum to the British government, claimed that it had received reports that between May and August 1945 there were several occasions when Malays in Johor, "instigated by the Japanese Army, massacred Overseas Chinese there, the victims numbering over 4,000 and refugees 20,000 and losses of property being very large".[55]* It gave no details of the incidents. However, one Chinese account, when explaining the Japanese motive

---

* The ministry expressed concern that most of the "criminals" were not punished after the British army reoccupied Malaya, and noted that there was an outbreak of further incidents when Malays massacred Chinese in November 1945.

for instigating the Malays, alleged that it was a part of the grand design of the Japanese military administration to carry out anti-Chinese operations in the country. It said the decision was taken in 1944 before the German collapse (Germany surrendered unconditionally on 8 May 1945), to fan anti-Chinese feelings among the Malays and then to instigate them to attack the Chinese. It was believed that the Malays would obey the Japanese because the former always followed those in authority.[56] Another Chinese account claims that anti-Chinese hatred among Malays was whipped up by the Kempeitai and its Malay informers in Johor a week or so before the Japanese surrender:

> The Malay *mitoys* [informers] were instructed to return to their *kampung* and warn their people of a Chinese take-over of their country. They should stir up a Holy War against the "pig-eaters" who would rob them of their heritage. Whether the Holy War against the Chinese would succeed or not was secondary. The important thing was to hit back at the Chinese and discomfort them.
>
> Once the first clashes were known, the communists in the MPAJA alerted the Chinese in the villages and towns all over the country, to be ready for the Malay rampage. The cry was: "The Malays are out to kill — so, kill before you are killed". This created fear in the hearts of the people and made them dependent on the MPAJA for their safety.[57]

According to Chinese accounts, the first Malay attack on Chinese in Batu Pahat was said to have occurred on 10 May 1945, when a car carrying Chinese was stopped on the Batu Pahat–Pontian road.[58] The driver was killed instantly, while the owner of the car escaped with some injuries. The Malays rifled the contents of the car, and then set fire to it. At the Senggarang police station, the Chinese survivor made a report in which he alleged Malay villagers, assisted by Malay policemen, had committed the crime. A Chinese detective from this police station subsequently leaked the information to some Chinese that the Malay officers at the police station had not passed the report up to their Japanese superiors, but instead had fabricated a report in which they claimed that the robbers and assailants were communists.

This was the beginning of a series of attacks and massacres of Chinese by Malays in the Batu Pahat district. The Chinese seemed to have been caught entirely by surprise and were baffled by the tenacity of the Malay attacks. Derogatory terms used to describe their Malay attackers, such as "rascals" and "gangsters", are not very helpful in establishing the true identity of the latter. However, many Chinese identified the presence of Malay policemen within each attacking group, and said that the police station was frequently used both as the army headquarters and as a place of refuge for their attackers. It was noticed that policemen seldom used their weapons, and seemed to have been content to remain at the rear to cover the attackers whenever the latter charged forward. The policemen would intervene and open fire only if they saw MPAJA guerrillas. The attacking Malays, wielding only long knives (*parang panjang*) and spears, hurled themselves into Chinese houses and settlements, screaming and killing men, women, and children in their path and those who could not escape or resist them. After pillaging Chinese houses, the Malays usually set them on fire. Massacres were also reported in Parit Gumong, Parit Kecil, and Parit Kali.

It was at Parit Kali that the Chinese first put up resistance. But one night the Malays gathered there in great strength and attacked. Chinese resistance collapsed and the Chinese suffered huge losses. It became impossible for Chinese to remain in any settlement where the Malay attacks did not cease. Hence many Chinese settlers burnt their houses down and moved to seek refuge in the nearest town or settlement with a larger Chinese population. The MPAJA appeared briefly on the scene. The guerrillas captured a few Malay "gangsters", told them Malays and Chinese should live in peace, and released them, so that they could return to their *kampung* with the message. But the MPAJA was rebuffed. The Malay attacks continued. At Parit Raja, about 200 Chinese were believed to have been massacred. The Malays began to strike terror into the hearts of the Chinese who were forced to retreat from town to town.

One reason for the high casualties suffered by the Chinese was said to be the initial Chinese reluctance to abandon their homes and move immediately out of the rural areas:

> Because their families and love of property tied the Chinese down, they were not united together to resist the Malays and therefore suffered great losses in lives…. On the other hand, the Malays abandoned their occupations and turned into murderers, all led by headmen in each district. As they went from one district to another district, they rallied more and more Malays, saying to one another, "The Chinese are powerless to resist us. We have

the Japanese forces to back us. Soon we shall be able to share the Chinese property amongst ourselves". Some Malays took the attitude of "wait-and-see", while others participated including many Malays who had been good friends of Chinese.[59]

By 23 May the attacking Malays had swept through all the *mukim* of Batu Pahat and were beginning to march into the Muar district. More and more Chinese settlers fled to the bigger towns. Unconsciously the Malays had applied the Maoist guerrilla strategy of the countryside surrounding the cities. The Malays were said to be very happy. Whenever they saw Chinese refugees they made the gesture of chopping heads. The Malays began to control all the key highways and roads, "making trouble everywhere, killing Chinese at will".[60] If the Chinese thought they had escaped death by running to the towns, they still had to suffer starvation, as very few Chinese supplies could now get through. The countryside was dotted with the charred ruins of hundreds of Chinese houses and the corpses of Chinese. The only Chinese who dared to move about in the rural areas were armed groups or the guerrilla bands of the MPAJA. They attempted to go to the rescue of Chinese stranded in isolated farming settlements. These groups began to wage guerrilla warfare on the Malays. They avoided strong Malay areas, and attacked the weak and isolated ones. As a result, the Malay toll began to rise. It was a retaliatory attack on Benut on 10 June that was said to have killed the DO of Batu Pahat, Ismail bin Dato Abdullah.

It was also the retaliatory attacks of the MPAJA, the Chinese believed, which forced the Japanese to intervene militarily on the side of the Malays. Both Japanese and Malays regarded the Chinese counter-attack as the work of the communist bandits. The Japanese organized a large-scale campaign, using their own armed forces together with the Johor Jikeidan (Self-Defence Corps) and the Batu Pahat police force. The Japanese troops were said to have been more courageous than the Malays because they dared to penetrate deeper into the jungles to search for the MPAJA. Any highway that had a sidetrack would be penetrated by a Japanese army detachment, using Malays as guides. Before committing their own forces the Japanese had thrown in several reinforcements of Malay police from Perak and Malacca, but their performance had been unsatisfactory. A stalemate continued for more than a month, until the beginning of August when the Japanese resumed operations. A week later, however, they were forced to cease their attacks because the Japanese

Emperor had surrendered. Even after the surrender the Malay-Chinese clashes continued, but soon contacts were established between both sides, during which the "Malay chief", i.e., Datuk Onn Jaafar, asked for peace and so ended the fighting.

The British Version

The Malay massacres of Chinese in the Batu Pahat area had not only alarmed the Japanese authorities and struck terror in the hearts of the local Chinese population, but also caused concern to Mountbatten's SEAC. Force 136 officers in the field relayed the news to SEAC. SEAC leaflets (bearing an emblem of the British flag) were airdropped into the affected area, urging people to stop fighting. The leaflet, dated 20 July, was in Malay and English. The Malay text carried the heading "Jaga Baik-Baik" (Take heed), and said that it had come to the attention of the British that certain people in the villages of Benut, Senggarang, Rengit, Pontian Kechil, Yong Peng, and Parit Jawa had "attacked and oppressed their neighbours in accordance with the wishes of the Japanese who are trying to turn one race against another".[61] It warned that the BMA would severely punish the guilty persons. The inhabitants were urged to remember the names and misdeeds of these people. The leaflet in Malay read:

> Macham mana pun Kerajaan British Dapat tangkap orang salah.
>
> Jaga baik-baik orang di-Johore! Hari balasan nanti sampai!*

Directing its appeal at the Malays, SEAC circulated another leaflet dated 25 July, in the Malay Jawi script, entitled "Bersatu Melawan Jepun" (Unite against the Japanese). It was written in the form of an appeal from a Malay individual. The English translation reads:

> Before the treacherous Jap attack on our country we Malays lived at peace like brothers with the other races of Malaya and the Government looked after the people of every race, even the Japanese barbers and shopkeepers, without oppression and cruelty.
>
> How different under the Jap oppressors! They do not care who starves as long as Japanese bellies are full. They try to make us

---

* The English translation reads: "No one can escape British justice. Take heed People of Johore! The Day of Repayment will come."

Malays hate our fellow Asiatics and to turn one race against another. They do this because they hope that while people dispute the Japanese will remain on top.

Do not be deceived my brothers.

We Malays must join with people of every race who are prepared to assist. All races must unite to free Malaya.

The Day of Repayment will come. Whoever helps to free my country is my friend.[62]

The meaning of these propaganda leaflets was clear to Malays in Batu Pahat who read them. There would be British punishment for those Malays involved in the racial clashes. It also meant that the British had taken the side of the MPAJA and the Chinese in the conflict.

From all these different accounts, the following conclusions emerge. It is clear that some MPAJU/MPAJA actions, such as abductions of Malays and attacks on mosques, were initially responsible for arousing Malay hostility and resistance in Tanjong Sembrong and other *mukim* in Batu Pahat district. Although this picture emerges largely from Malay sources, it conforms to the general known picture of MPAJU/MPAJA behaviour throughout the Japanese occupation (see Chapters 2 and 3). As some Malay accounts admit, the MPAJU/MPAJA actions were not gratuitous, but represented reprisals for Malay non-cooperation and hostility.

Chinese, MPAJA, and British accounts blame the Japanese for starting the inter-racial clashes, but there is no real evidence to substantiate this. It is possible that the Japanese did instigate Malays and give backing to the Sabilillah movement *after* the trouble had started. Certainly they added their own military support to the Malay onslaughts, inflicting great suffering on the Chinese in the Batu Pahat district.

15 August: The Japanese Surrender

The combined Malay and Japanese onslaughts on the MPAJA and the Chinese reduced the Chinese population in south western Johor to a state of siege and despair. The Chinese were now haunted by the prospect of starvation, as food supplies dwindled rapidly because of strict Japanese controls. The movement of goods, vehicles, and people on the highways of southwestern Johor was curtailed in order to prevent foodstuffs from falling into guerrilla hands. Armed Malays roamed the countryside and their attacks were unceasing.

The news of Japanese surrender was most welcome to the Chinese population in south-western Johor, who were now confident that relief would arrive soon. Before long the guerrillas of the Fourth Regiment (south Johor) came down from the hills and emerged from the jungles to take over most towns in the region. Japanese troops either withdrew from the towns or were confined to barracks, leaving the MPAJA guerrillas with virtually a free hand. The Chinese guerrillas, in their green uniforms supplied by SEAC, with the three-red-star emblem on the crest of their five-cornered caps, and with guns strapped to their bodies, were greeted lustily by the Chinese population, who came out into the streets in large numbers to show support, to welcome the guerrillas as liberators and saviours.[63] MPAJU supporters erected triumphal arches along the main streets through which the guerrillas marched. It was a great moment of jubilation for the Chinese, whose morale was further boosted by rumours that Chiang Kai-shek's army would soon arrive with the British army to help reoccupy Malaya temporarily.

The feeling rapidly gained ground among the Chinese in south-western Johor that the situation had changed to their advantage already. The MPAJA in particular, and the Chinese in general, now began to take the law into their own hands. After taking over control of most towns, they began savagely to settle old scores with the Malay police and others who had worked under the Japanese. The assumption of political authority by Chinese, and their lack of respect for Malays, immediately produced further deterioration of race relations. The political power exercised during this interim period and the brutal nature of communist and Chinese vengeance was to be the last straw for the Malays. Malay attacks had, in fact, ground to a complete halt. Their driving impetus seemed to have been lost momentarily with the news of the Japanese defeat. The British, who had airdropped leaflets to the people warning against massacres of Chinese, were soon to return. Speculation spread that the Chinese and the MPAJA would be pampered by the British and would become "more superior and more arrogant than ever".[64] The Malays in south-western Johor came under a cloud of uncertainty and despair.

Revenge was the operative principle during this transitional period. Anyone suspected of collaboration with the Japanese became a public enemy. Charges of traitors, informers, and "running dogs" were hurled at all those in authority and all those who had served the Japanese *Kempeitai* — Malays, Chinese, and Indians. In Batu Pahat, however, it was predictable that the MPAJA and the Chinese would exact revenge on Malays. Malays from the interior of the district were slowly coming into the towns to discover the situation for themselves. Apparently, without Japanese support, they needed to re-establish contacts with other areas and to collect food supplies, which were being discharged rapidly from Japanese stores and food dumps. The guerrillas had taken over control of the main interstate trunk roads, checking, seizing, or destroying any vehicle that belonged to the Japanese. Malays who entered MPAJA and Chinese-dominated towns came instantly under attack. As no truce in the racial clashes had been declared, Chinese and the MPAJA considered the fighting still on. MPAJA guerrillas and armed Chinese also attacked surrounding Malay villages, and abducted and killed many *penghulu*, *ketua kampung*, police officials, and *Kempeitai* informers. The Chinese reign of terror now began.[65]

To retaliate against the MPAJA, the Tentera Sabilillah Selendang Merah (Sabilillah Army of Red Bands), under the command of Kiyai Salleh, began to carry out reprisals on Chinese and the MPAJA guerrillas. Batu Pahat "again witnessed terrible bloodshed during this interregnum". Malay attacks were said to be more ferocious than those of the Chinese, and surpassed their earlier level. They fought more determinedly and with greater religious fanaticism.[66] The Red Bands launched numerous raids, attacking in groups, chanting prayers, and wielding *parang*, *kris*, bamboo spears, and iron rods (some bearing Koranic verses). For the second time in the racial clashes, Chinese and the MPAJA could neither stop them nor understand the drive behind them.

The intensity of the Malay resistance was now partly due to Malay fears that the Chinese would seize political power in Johor and throughout the country. Rumours had spread among Malays, and were generally believed, that the British government had promised the Chinese and the MPAJA that Malaya would be handed over to them after the Japanese surrender.[67] Apparently Malays began to realize that if they did not fight back the Chinese would get whatever political rights they asked from the British. At this critical moment the Sultan of Johor is believed to have turned to Kiyai Salleh as the Malays' saviour. Kiyai Fadil, the *pawang* of the Sultan and *guru* of Kiyai Salleh, arranged for the Sultan to meet his now famous student. During the meeting at Pasir Plangi palace the Sultan embraced Kiyai Salleh, kissed his hand, and thanked him for his deeds. He asked Kiyai Salleh to "menjaga negeri kita" (guard our country). The Sultan then sat down and shared a meal with Kiyai Fadil and Kiyai Salleh.[68]

Datuk Onn bin Jaafar — The Peacemaker

Datuk Onn returned to Johor Bharu from the KRIS conference on 18 August aboard a Singapore-bound train, which also carried three other KRIS delegates from Singapore — the KRIS secretary-general Hassan Manan, lawyer Sardon Haji Zubir, and journalist A. Samad Ismail (see Chapter 4). At Labis, Johor, their train was derailed as a result of an MPAJA ambush, during which gunfire was exchanged between Japanese troops and the guerrillas. Later that day a train from Singapore arrived to pick up the passengers, and Datuk Onn and Sardon Haji Zubir alighted at Johor Bharu. There are no recorded accounts of Datuk Onn's thoughts or plans at that moment, but in the next two weeks he was to emerge as a brave, astute, and far-sighted Malay leader. Soon after his return, Sultan Ibrahim appointed him as DO of Batu Pahat. The post had remained vacant since the assassination of the last incumbent, Ismail bin Datuk Abdullah, in June. It is said that the Japanese authorities had repeatedly asked for Datuk Onn to fill the post, but Sultan Ibrahim had refused because he required Datuk Onn at court.[69]

Why did the Sultan finally agree to Datuk Onn's appointment at this late hour (after the Japanese surrender had become known)? No evidence on the Sultan's considerations is available, but the most probable reason seems to be that the communal violence in the Batu Pahat and Muar districts had presented serious post-war implications for the Malay aristocracy in Johor. The British had already warned in their airdropped leaflets that they would investigate and take action against Malays responsible for instigating the racial clashes. The implication was that the Malays were culpable. There was therefore a need among the Johor aristocracy to disavow any responsibility in the matter. It would look good if Datuk Onn, whose son Hussein was in the British army in India,[*] was seen by

---

[*] Hussein Onn (the former Malaysian prime minister) was educated at the Military Academy, Dehra Dun, in India. He had joined the Johor military forces as a cadet in 1940 and was commissioned in the Indian army, seeing service in Egypt, Syria, Palestine, Iraq, and India where he served at general headquarters in New Delhi. After the Second World War, on attachment to the BMA he became commandant of the police depot at Johor Bharu.

the returning British administration as the DO appointed to settle the communal dispute. If he succeeded in his efforts as a peace-maker, it would redound to his ruler's credit.

Meanwhile, on or about 21 August, when the MPAJA guerrillas were taking over Muar and Batu Pahat towns, Kiyai Salleh's Sabilillah Army of Red Bands were launching widespread attacks on Chinese in the towns and neighbouring areas. Kiyai Salleh himself led attacks on the Chinese strongholds around Ayer Hitam, while his com-manders attacked Chinese in the area around Batu Pahat town.

The Sabilillah Army planned its biggest attack on Parit Jawa, a predominantly Chinese town, a few miles south of Muar. It was agreed that all the commanders including Kiyai Salleh himself, Kiyai Mashudi, and Kiyai Wak Joyo would lead their regiments into attack.[70] Most of the commanders picked a certain Saturday, probably 25 August, as the most auspicious day for the attack, that being the month of Ramadhan. But disagreement appeared in the form of Kiyai Mashudi, who argued that the day of attack should be the Wednesday before the Saturday suggested. When the other commanders demurred, Kiyai Mashudi said he and his army would carry on alone. His conduct is inexplicable unless he was setting himself up as a rival to Kiyai Salleh. On Tuesday night, the eve of Mashudi's attack, Mashudi and his forces assembled at Parit Gantong, a quarter mile from Parit Jawa. They spent the whole night chanting prayers and reciting verses from the Koran. But the Chinese in Parit Jawa heard about his planned attack, and before dawn a large number of Chinese families evacuated to Muar town. Those who remained behind in Parit Jawa were armed with guns and knives and supported by an MPAJA force well equipped with machine guns. Mashudi attacked at 9 a.m. but his force was repulsed. What was worse for him, none of the other Sabilillah army commanders joined in the fighting He was forced to withdraw his men from the town. Both sides in Muar and Parit Jawa concluded that Mashudi's offensive had been an abysmal failure. The Malays attributed it to his arrogance. In retaliation the MPAJA and the Chinese counter-attacked Malays in a nearby area, taking ten Malay lives.

Mashudi's failure strengthened the need for Malay unity and reaffirmed faith in Kiyai Salleh's leadership. It was Kiyai Salleh him-self who now picked the next target for attack — Batu Pahat town (or Bandar Penggaram), the largest Chinese stronghold in south-western Johor. He would lead the attack. The Red Bands gathered in the *mukim* of Kampung Bagan and then marched in columns into the *mukim* of Peserai, bordering the *mukim* of Bandar Penggaram. The Red Bands were on the march when Datuk Onn bin Jaafar, accompanied by Datuk Abdul Rahman, an *Orang Kaya* (local chief), caught up with them to stop the attack.[71]

Before he appeared in Peserai, Datuk Onn had taken office as DO, was living in Malay territory, and was identified with the Malay side. He took the initiative of going personally to MPAJA (or Bintang Tiga) headquarters in Bukit Pasir to parley for peace, although Chin Peng says he and his assistant were "arrested," or "kidnapped" by the MPAJA and forced to mediate in the conflict.[72] He said, "…Datuk Onn helped bring the violence to an end by speaking to the Malays. It was a very emotional time and nobody was willing to listen coolly to details of how the racial trouble began. The killing was on a very large scale. At least 1,000 died. Naturally, propaganda had it that the MPAJA was the primary cause. This is patently untrue."

Datuk Onn rationalized that since it was the MPAJA that had caused the racial trouble, the MPAJA had to agree to a truce first. His role was only to play the intermediary. One morning, with great fortitude, he climbed on his bicycle and rode towards Bukit Pasir.[73] He had arranged with Kiyai Salleh to follow him a short distance behind and had instructed the latter that if he (Datuk Onn) succeeded in reaching MPAJA headquarters, Kiyai Salleh should join him inside. Kiyai Salleh did not fully concur with Datuk Onn's mission, but agreed to go along to protect him.[*] After meeting two shocked Chinese and introducing himself as the DO, Datuk Onn was taken to MPAJA headquarters. Soon after, Kiyai Salleh himself appeared beside Datuk Onn. The "peace" talks lasted the whole day. They agreed on a truce and that further talks be held to iron out any misunderstandings between Malays and the MPAJA/Chinese.[74] It was the month of Ramadhan, when Muslims go on a daily fast, and for Datuk Onn this was a most auspicious achievement.

While the talks went on, violence continued in other parts of the district. Not long after returning home from the talks, Datuk Onn received news that the followers of Kiyai Salleh had gathered

---

[*] Anwar Abdullah describes it as an extremely dangerous journey. No Malay dared to travel alone in the Batu Pahat-Bukit Pasir road. Kiyai Salleh was said to have advised Datuk Onn not to embark on the mission, but he was determined and headstrong. He was prepared to go even if Kiyai Salleh did not accompany him. Datuk Onn was then 50 years old.

in Kampong Bagan and were about to attack Batu Pahat town.[75] He began to suspect that Kiyai Salleh had betrayed him. He immediately contacted Datuk Abdul Rahman Musa, a Johor chief, and together they rushed to Kampung Bagan. He feared that he might be too late, and that his peace settlement with the MPAJA would be shattered.

There are various accounts of what actually took place during the confrontation. Anwar Abdullah's account says that it was with some trepidation and anger that Datuk Onn caught up with the columns of the Red Bands and singled Kiyai Salleh out. The confrontation was charged with tension.[76] Datuk Onn was bent on stopping Kiyai Salleh's attack at all costs, even in the presence of Salleh's 1,600-armed supporters who had already worked themselves into frenzy.* Onn's biographer Anwar Abdullah records how his hero, with great courage and skilled oratory, administered a public rebuke to Kiyai Salleh, the folk hero, and subdued the tempers of his followers.

> "What is the meaning of this, Salleh," Datuk Onn asked of him. "You can't do this sort of thing. Such an action is against the law. You should have consulted with me first. I am the District Officer here. This gathering has been inspired by you."
>
> "Here is my breast", Datuk Onn offered him. "Plunge your dagger into it if you do not wish to obey me. After you have struck me down then you may do what you wish. So long as there is life in this body, I shall stop you. I, as the DO and the representative of the Sultan and the *ra'ayat* [the people] am responsible for what happens in this district. I do not want to be held responsible later for any major disaster such as you have planned."[77]

Kiyai Salleh was reportedly glum as he listened to Datuk Onn's speech. He did not say a word, but his followers who were swayed by Datuk Onn's oratory, spontaneously cried out their readiness to obey his advice, to cease their warfare against the Chinese and to help him restore peace.[78]

Another account says that Datuk Onn arrived at the scene with two leaders of the Batu Pahat Chinese. Datuk Onn is said to have recognized Kiyai Salleh's authority and flattered him; he warned the crowd that British troops would soon arrive, and that if order were not restored by then Malay blood would flow; and he indicated that

---

* Musak Mantrak in "Sejarah Masyarakat Majemuk di Mukim VII, Batu Pahat", gives the figure of "1.604 followers", p. 87.

the Malays had achieved their goal, when he forced the Chinese leaders to promise the crowd that no more Malays would be killed. Kiyai Salleh promised the Chinese that if another Malay was killed all the Chinese in the town would be slaughtered.[79] Another account has Datuk Onn telling the crowd that they had succeeded in their objectives by teaching the Chinese an unforgettable lesson. He assured them that the Chinese would not commit any further attacks on the Malays.[80]

Such assurances by Datuk Onn seemed necessary to soothe the heated tempers of the crowd. Besides, Datuk Onn's flattery of Kiyai Salleh seemed appropriate, given the latter's reputation and standing. Whatever the versions, however, they all agree that the aristocrat came out master of the situation. Soon after the incident, Kiyai Salleh became a faithful supporter of Datuk Onn. In the next few days Kiyai Salleh and Datuk Onn travelled around the various Selendang Merah areas in Muar and Batu Pahat, to appeal for calm and peace, and to attend *kenduri* (feasts).[81]

Racial peace had been achieved before the arrival of British troops in Johor. The peace settlement probably occurred on 1 or 2 September (Hari Raya Puasa), the Muslim festival. The first civil affairs officers of the BMA arrived in Johor Bharu on 8 September, and a few days later extended their detachments to Batu Pahat and Muar, where they found 4,000 and 10,000 refugees respectively.[82] British security officials investigating the Batu Pahat incidents were anxious to take Kiyai Salleh into custody, but Datuk Onn successfully blocked their efforts. He interceded on Kiyai Salleh's behalf, and is said to have sought and obtained Sultan Ibrahim's authority. Datuk Onn is reported to have told the British Resident Commissioner: "Salleh has now been accepted and acknowledged leader of every Malay in the *mukim* of Simpang Kiri before and since the commencement of the trouble between Malays and Chinese in the kampungs."[83] Datuk Onn did this because he had come to realize that he could secure Kiyai Salleh's support for his own future ambitions. When the *penghulu* of Simpang Kiri died in September, Datuk Onn appointed Kiyai Salleh the new *penghulu*. Kiyai Salleh reciprocated with political support. When in January 1946 Datuk Onn formed his own political party, Pergerakan Melayu Semenanjung (Peninsular Malay Movement), the president of the Simpang Kiri branch was Kiyai Salleh. He continued as president when this organization merged with the United Malays National Organization to follow Datuk Onn who had become president of UMNO in June.

The Sungai Manik Incidents (15 August–15 September 1945)

In the *mukim* of Sungai Manik (lower Perak) after the Japanese surrender racial violence there continued sporadically into the BMA period. Unlike Batu Pahat, where the three parties involved — Malays, Chinese, and the MPAJU/MPAJA — reached a peaceful settlement, no truce was achieved at Sungai Manik because Malay attacks had cleared all Chinese settlers from the area before the British returned.

The Sungai Manik incidents are indirectly linked to the incidents in Batu Pahat. The majority of Malays in the *mukim* of Sungai Manik are Banjarese, many of them related to the Banjarese in several *mukim* of Batu Pahat district. When the racial trouble in Batu Pahat raged between May and August, the news quickly spread to their Banjarese brethren in Sungai Manik, who themselves were experiencing similar problems with the Chinese in the MPAJU/MPAJA. The MPAJU's attempts to recruit young Malay men and women in Sungai Manik to work in nearby MPAJA camps had been rebuffed. When the MPAJU suggested to the Banjarese headmen that they should change their Friday prayers to Sunday (as was suggested also by the MPAJU in Mukim VII of Batu Pahat), this was deemed an unpardonable insult and a sacrilege to the Islamic religion.[84] Spurned by the Banjarese, the MPAJU stepped up their harassment by making demands for cash contributions and supplies of rice and foodstuffs. Stories of MPAJU/MPAJA abductions and murders of recalcitrant Malays filtered through the Banjarese population. It soon became necessary for the Banjarese to organize themselves for self-defence. Several *tok guru* emerged who were prepared to teach the *silat* (martial arts) and the *ilmu kebal* (knowledge of invulnerability).

A gathering of the Banjarese men in the *mukim* took place at the house of Imam Haji Bakri at Parit (irrigation canal), Sungai Manik. Village religious men present were Haji Shukor, Imam Haji Bakri, and Haji Marzuki, the last two having been appointed by the congregation as their *khalifah*, each empowered to issue the *fatwa* (the call to wage Holy War). Haji Shukor was deputy *khalifah* to Imam Haji Bakri. The *ilmu kebal* classes became known to other areas in the Banjarese basin of lower Perak, and a deputation of men from Telok Banjar, ten miles away, came to Sungai Manik to learn the martial arts and the magico-mystical powers of invulnerability.

The Japanese surrender on 15 August fell during the month of Ramadhan (the Muslim fasting month). When the news became known the MPAJU/MPAJA became openly active and attempted to establish control in Sungai Manik, as they had done in smaller towns in lower Perak. When the *penghulu* and *ketua kampung* refused to cooperate, attempts were made to abduct them. The *penghulu*, Haji Hassan Ibrahim, was an adept exponent of the *silat*, and when a group of armed Chinese MPAJU/MPAJA men came to take him away he attacked them first. With powerful blows and kicks he is said to have floored three men, who died instantly.[85] The other Chinese fled, and Hassan gave chase, killing one more. He decapitated the four dead men and carried their heads in a sack to the nearest Japanese military office in Telok Anson. After narrating his story he asked the Japanese for arms. The senior Japanese officer was not in, but two soldiers accompanied him to the Japanese military headquarters in Ipoh, where permission was given him to obtain arms. He was provided with four rifles, a pistol, and a box of ammunition. The Japanese sent a patrol of 24 soldiers to accompany Hassan back to his house, where they exchanged gunfire with the communists, which lasted three days.[86]

This incident emboldened the Banjarese to launch reprisals on the MPAJU/MPAJA hideouts and Chinese settlements in Sungai Manik and in the neighbouring *mukim* as well. Chinese settlers in these areas were forced to flee to Telok Anson, which had a larger concentration of Chinese. When British troops arrived on the scene, much of the countryside in lower Perak, especially the Banjarese basin, had been denuded of Chinese who had become refugees in Telok Anson.

The organization and pattern of Malay attacks in Sungai Manik was very similar to those in the Batu Pahat and Muar areas of Johore. It had the characteristics of the Sabilillah movement, although the initiative, planning, and organization was not coordinated with those in Johor. Stories of the MPAJU/MPAJA takeover in Batu Pahat in the interim period brought by Banjarese relatives did, however, fan the flames of violence. The BMA succeeded temporarily in controlling the trouble, but soon it erupted again.

The BMA Period: The Conflict Spreads

The prolonged racial ill will and conflict during the BMA was partly aggravated by the MPAJA guerrillas' pursuit of Malay collaborators

in particular. The situation was worsened by British policies, especially the BMA's extension of preferential treatment to the Chinese
and to the MCP/MPAJA to the detriment of Malay interests. Consequently, Malays found their role, status, and institutions in decline,
if not suppressed by the BMA. In contrast, the Chinese seemed to
be in the ascendancy and to have everything their way. The latest
British threat to Malay rights was represented by the British government's announcement of the Malayan Union policy on 10 October,
which aimed at taking away the Sultans' sovereignty and granting
equal citizenship rights to the Chinese. The disclosure of the
Malayan Union plan and the beginning of MacMichael's mission to
strip the Malay rulers of their sovereignty promoted further Malay
hostility toward Chinese, and built up resentment against the British.
Consequently, Malays resorted to further violence against Chinese.
The struggle continued as the Sabilillah (Holy War).

Racial tension and minor clashes were reported in Malacca,
Johor, Pahang, Kedah, and Kelantan in September and October. A
Force 136 field intelligence report of 11 September disclosed that
the situation in the vicinity of Batu Pahat was difficult. Malays were
still active. A witness had reported 30 Chinese killed and their
houses burning at Simpang Lima, while the Chinese population in
Batu Pahat panicked. The first report received by telephone at Hq.
Fifth Indian Division had said 500 Chinese were killed. An investigation showed that the figure was exaggerated, but confirmed there
had been trouble. A column of British troops was despatched to
Batu Pahat to restore order.[87] Meanwhile, other Force 136 reports
indicated that the Malay population in several areas was terrified
of the MPAJA. One unconfirmed report said that Chinese executed
the Malay district officer (DO) at Mersing on 2 September. Another
quoted a senior Malay police officer at Kluang as saying that the
area's DO and police chief had been arrested by the MPAJA and
were believed killed. The Malay officer appealed for protection for
the remaining police at Kluang, as he feared disturbances.[88]

On 19 September, Malays in Kota Bharu (Kelantan) petitioned
the Sultan to prevent an outbreak of violence against the Malay
population. The KMT guerrillas who controlled the town were said
to be massing for an attack, and there was a reported plot (apparently by the KMT) to kill the deputy Mentri Besar of Kelantan,
Datuk Nik Ahmad Kamil. Two Gurkha support groups were immediately despatched to Kota Bharu. At Kuala Krai, in spite of the

promises made to the Force 136 officer attached to the Malay resistance unit, the MPAJA tried 11 Malays and sentenced 3 to death. The MPAJA leader Wong Lit was warned that while the BMA had no objection to his apprehending suspects, he was on no account to try or execute them.[89]

On 26 September, Malay-Chinese clashes occurred in Alor Gajah (Malacca), in which one Malay was killed and two Chinese seriously injured. The following day armed Malays were reported attacking Chinese in Senggarang (Johor), one of the areas of racial violence during May to August 1945. Two Chinese were reported killed, but the trouble was quickly localized. After this incident, Force 136 considered that it would be better for the army to use regular British troops rather than the MPAJA to suppress any trouble there.

On 29 September, Force 136 reported that frightened Malays were arriving in Pekan (Pahang) with stories of MPAJA killings and intimidation. On 12 October, a Malay chief of Negeri Sembilan, the Datuk Mentri of Jelebu, was arrested by the MPAJA on charges of instigating the Japanese to kill Chinese and British troops found sheltering in his village. On 26 October, tension was reported between Malays and Chinese in Merbok village (Kedah).

Although these racial incidents were assuming serious proportions, neither the MCP, the BMA, nor Malay leaders did much to defuse the overall tension. On 6 November there occurred the worst racial incident since the BMA takeover: at about 6 a.m. a party of Malays armed with *parang* and *kris* descended on the Chinese settlement at Padang Lebar, near Kuala Pilah, and killed 35 women and children and 5 men. According to Victor Purcell, who rushed to the spot with the SCAO, Colonel Calder, the Malay attackers had buried the bodies except for those of the children, which they threw down the well. Ten Malays were arrested immediately and seven others later. They said during interrogations that the Chinese had coerced them to join the Communist Party, and that threats were used to obtain subscriptions.[90]

A Malay view of the incident was that the BMA failed to contain these racial clashes because it was too weak in its early phase. This same source revealed that the Sabilillah movement of Batu Pahat was directly involved in the Padang Lebar massacre. Kiyai Selamat, of Batu Pahat, one of the chief disciples of Kiyai Salleh, was said to have led 1,000 Malays on the rampage from Batu Kikir to Padang Lebar, killing about 170 Chinese. British military intelligence subsequently found that Kiyai Selamat had been to Segamat, to Lenggeng, and as far afield as Mantin in Negeri Sembilan to spread the teachings of Kiyai Salleh and to recruit followers. He was thought to be of North Borneo origin.[91]

The next day there was a clash at the nearby village of Batu Kikir between Malays and MPAJA guards posted there to restore order. Four MPAJA guards were killed, while Malay casualties were six killed and two injured. On 8 November, Purcell and Calder toured Kuala Pilah and Bahau, towns in the neighbourhood, to comfort Chinese refugee families who had been placed under military protection. Both assured the refugees, especially the women, that the situation was in hand, enumerated the places where troops were stationed, explained that tanks and soldiers were patrolling, and told them that a meeting to prevent further bloodshed was to take place the next day to which the Malay and Chinese headmen had been summoned.[92]

At Batu Kikir Colonel Calder addressed a large crowd of Malays in the course of which he rebuked those who had taken part in the massacre. As Purcell reported it:

> Colonel Calder made them assemble in one spot and made a long and eloquent speech to them in Malay. He told them, with several references to their own proverbs, that they had lost in one day the reputation it had taken years to build. He rebuked them as cowards and criminals who had slaughtered innocent women and children. They listened intently and were now obviously sobered. When asked by Colonel Calder to do so they signified their intention of keeping the peace according to the Koran of which he reminded them.[93]

Purcell said he spotted one Malay among the crowd carrying a *parang* in a sheath. The man was seized and disarmed, and his case was used as an object lesson to the crowd. "Others no doubt carrying concealed *parangs* or knives edged to the outside of the crowd," Purcell added.[94] The firm action taken by the BMA, such as arrests of ringleaders, brought the situation temporarily under control.

On 7 November, the MCP held a meeting in Seremban, the capital of Negeri Sembilan state, to discuss the situation. The communist leaders were obviously shaken by the events, and among the resolutions passed was one that they should change their attitude regarding Malays to one of conciliation.[95] The Chinese reaction generally was panic. Chinese settlers from Padang Lebar and the outlying areas were reported to be pouring into Seremban.[96] The situation in the local areas was so bad that in talks with the CAO Malay villagers in the Ulu Berenang area stated that the Malay-Chinese feud was of too long standing for them to guarantee their own good behaviour to allow the evacuated Chinese to return to their village.[97]

Chinese in Singapore and elsewhere in the country viewed the Padang Lebar massacre with horror and urged the British authorities to take steps to prevent Malays from attacking Chinese. The *Nanyang Siang Pau*, a Singapore daily, reported that the KMT party in the city and its branches had jointly despatched telegrams to British Premier Attlee, appealing for an order to the BMA to protect effectively the lives and properties of Chinese. The newspaper noted that for the last few months' cases of wholesale massacre of Chinese by Malays had flared up in rapid succession in Johor and Negeri Sembilan, resulting in enormous loss of Chinese lives and property.[98] As an indication of the desperate plight the Chinese were now in, on 20 November a joint telegram was sent to Mountbatten by the southern Johor branches of the MCP, the KMT, the people's committee and Chinese associations of Johor, to express Chinese concern over the Padang Lebar massacre, to blame the BMA for allowing it to happen, and to demand protective measures from the local garrisons for the Chinese population.[99]

The Padang Lebar massacre had repercussions not only in the whole of Negeri Sembilan and the neighbouring state of Malacca but also in Selangor, Kedah, Pahang, and Johor. It encouraged Malays to step up attacks on Chinese. According to military intelligence reports, Malay over-confidence was based on exaggerated Malay accounts of the Padang Lebar incident. At Gemas (Johor), Malays boldly staged a procession through the Chinese quarter, but no incidents were reported.[100] All Malays now seemed united in their struggle to prevent Chinese political domination of their country. A BMA intelligence report indicated Malay thinking behind the struggle:

> ... There appears to be an appreciable concern among educated Malays regarding the future status of Malays in Malaya [following publication of the Malayan Union policy] and there is a fairly widespread belief that the Chinese are securing an economic grip of the country which, if unchecked, may eventually lead to poli-

tical control. Thus any movement designed to rouse Malays to take greater interest in securing their position is sure of support and reports from all regions refer, in a lesser or greater degree, to the prevalence of inter-racial feeling.[101]

In view of the increasing inter-racial conflicts, the proposed disbandment of the MPAJA and KMT guerrilla movements on 1 December was naturally viewed with much disfavour by the Chinese population and, conversely, welcomed by the Malays, even though a few Malay guerrilla units such as the Wataniah were also being disbanded. The ratio of Chinese guerrillas to Malay guerrillas was somewhere in the region of 20 : 1. In Alor Star and Sungei Patani, both in Kedah, the local Chinese population was reported to be unwilling to let the MPAJA disband because it regarded the MPAJA as protection against possible trouble from the Malays.[102] The MPAJA supreme headquarters was also not happy to disband; but since the MCP had taken a decision in favour of it, it agreed to carry it through. In Kota Bharu, the KMT guerrillas refused to disband on 1 December, giving as their reason Chinese demands for protection against attacks from Malays. Several groups of KMT guerrillas, totalling about 40 people, fled the town with their arms and withdrew to the Malay-Thai border. The BMA had rejected the KMT guerrillas' request to be allowed to keep their arms.[103] A few days later, however, Malay-Chinese trouble broke out in the state. The KMT guerrillas in upper Perak also refused to disband and absconded with their arms to the Thai-Perak border, where they teamed up with their Kelantan comrades and terrorized Malays in the countryside. KMT guerrillas now branded "bandits" by the military, held sway at the Thai–Malay border for eight months. They did this mainly by obtaining the tacit support of Thai border police and military through suitable inducements and a share of their spoils gained by highway robberies, kidnappings, murders, and raids on helpless Malay, Chinese, and Thai farmers and settlers on both sides of the border. It was only in July 1946, after several fruitless attempts to negotiate with the leaders of the KMT guerrillas, and the intervention of the Chinese consul-general in Malaya, that the British authorities finally succeeded in inducing a large portion of the KMT guerrillas to disband and disarm.

Throughout December, inter-racial tension increased in every state throughout the country. It was thought by British military intelligence that the areas of greatest danger were those where the Malays were smaller in numbers or of equal proportion with Chinese. Areas and states where the Malays were in overwhelming majority, such as Kelantan and Terengganu, reported fewer inter-racial clashes, although tension existed. But after the Padang Lebar incidents, there were reports of Malays in Terengganu and Kelantan attacking Chinese. The *Kin Kwok Daily News* of 19 December reported Malay attacks on Chinese in Besut (Terengganu) and urged the BMA to protect Chinese lives and property. Inter-racial friction in Kota Bharu (Kelantan), culminating in clashes on 20/21 December. Three Chinese were killed and one wounded, and one Malay was killed and three wounded. Malays attributed the friction to the arrogance of the Chinese before the disappearance of the KMT guerrillas.[104]

In Perak inter-racial trouble erupted again with the murder of four Chinese women at Ayer Tawar on 27 December, followed the next day by the murder of six women at Layang Layang Kiri, which is northeast of the Perak River. These clashes reached serious proportions when 41 Chinese were killed, 32 others reported missing, and 32 Malays killed. The centre of the trouble was Bruas. About 100 Chinese took counter-action on 30 December, attacking the Malay village of Lambor Kanan, further down the Perak River. Casualties in these clashes amounted to nearly 50, more Chinese than Malays being killed. The Chinese also attacked another nearby riverside village the following day and killed 16 Malays, including 7 children who were deliberately burnt to death.[105]

Chinese residents in the area began evacuating south to Telok Anson for fear of Malay reprisals. South of the Bernam River, 30 Chinese families living near the Malay village of Bagan Nakhoda Omar left their homes and withdrew into a local Chinese settlement. The general state of tension was indicated when a British patrol visited Kampong Gajah, on the Perak river north of Telok Anson, and reported Chinese having been cut up by Malays in the market. They found the whole Malay population armed with *parang*, swords, and spears. They remarked that though Chinese reports claimed that the Malay gangs had carried firearms and even automatic weapons, all Chinese casualties had been inflicted with cold steel.[106] Chinese newspapers reported that because of the inter-racial clashes Chinese traders in Sitiawan and the Dindings had suspended business.

For the remaining period, January through March 1946, only a brief summary of the major inter-racial incidents is necessary to show the deteriorating situation throughout the country. The following summary is taken from a BMA report:

… There were later outbreaks in various parts of the country, especially in Lower Perak where in the first three weeks of January, the death toll amounted to approximately sixty Chinese and thirty Malays, and in the Raub district of Pahang where on the 11th of February the Malays made a sudden attack on the Chinese and killed thirty and wounded sixteen, two of them-selves being killed and ten wounded. The first big incident in which the Chinese were the aggressors was at Bekor, on the Perak River, on the 2nd of March when seventy-six Malays were massacred in a surprise attack made at dawn.[107]

In the Raub incidents the Sabilillah was very much in evidence. The disbanded elements of the wartime Malay guerrilla force Wataniah were said to be involved. Trouble between the MPAJA and Wataniah was of long standing, but as usual ordinary people were the chief sufferers in the clash. On 11 February, the Acting DO, Encik Annuar, arrived at the village of Batu Malim, wartime headquarters of Wataniah, to collect rent due on state lands. He found racial trouble brewing and "religious fanatics" inciting a mob to violence.[108] Annuar tried repeatedly to persuade the hostile gathering to disperse. But members of the mob who were in various stages of religious ecstasy that led them to believe they were invulnerable, refused to be calmed. The following account narrates what occurred:

> A few minutes after he [Annuar] had returned to the area head-man's house to send off a messenger to collect reinforcements of police, Annuar heard the frenzied beating of the mosque drum, followed almost immediately by terrified shouts and screams. When he tried to break up the riot that was then raging he was resisted, and as he had too few police available to help him, drove off to collect a more effective force. By the time that he returned with an adequate party of armed policemen, however, the fighting had ended and thirty Chinese and two Malays lay dead, while sixteen Chinese and ten Malays had been wounded. His own career was an extra casualty.[109]

More signs of the Sabilillah appeared in the Malay attacks on Chinese in Telok Anson in early March. The Chinese reported that the attacks were well planned, well organized, and very extensive, marked by vigorous bell ringing in mosques from the 13th milestone to the 28th milestone of the Bagan-Natul Road.[110]

After the incidents in March Malay attacks suddenly ceased, and calm was gradually restored throughout the country. There are two reasons for this. First, the British authorities had finally started to use the Sultans to restrain their subjects. In mid-December, the Sultan of Selangor came out exhorting his subjects to restrain themselves and to maintain inter-racial harmony. The Sultan attributed blame for the trouble on wartime conditions created by the Japanese. In January and February, the Sultans of Perak and Pahang toured the affected areas in their respective states, urging their subjects to remain calm. The Sultan of Perak helped the BMA to set up goodwill committees. The MCP also joined in with the Chinese Chambers of Commerce to appeal to Chinese to keep calm. Second, the Malay anti-Malayan Union campaign had now reached its climax on 1 March, with the meeting of the All-Malay Congress at the Sultan Suleiman's Club at Kampung Bharu in Kuala Lumpur. This congress decided to form a national Malay political organization, the United Malays National Organization, to rally Malays throughout the country to crush the Malayan Union plan. Henceforth this campaign was to take priority over all other matters, and it was now neither the Chinese nor the MCP but the British government which became the main target of Malay hostility.

CHAPTER 9

Conflict between the Communists and the BMA

Today Malaya has become a British colony again. The British have replaced the Japanese as rulers of Malaya, so the target of the national liberation struggle is once again the British.

– Lai Te in his report to the Eighth Conference of the
Central Committee of Malayan Communist Party
in Singapore, 22–27 Feb. 1946

One of the first policies adopted by the BMA was the granting of the fullest freedom of speech, publication, and association in the country — one of the eight demands of the MCP's manifesto of 27 August 1945. By also adopting the policy that the prewar Registration of Societies Ordinance would not be reimposed, the BMA extended the official recognition which had been accorded at the last minute by the governor of the Straits Settlements, Sir Shenton Thomas, in December 1941 to the MCP, the KMT, and other Chinese associations which had previously been illegal.[1] It also meant that Chinese labour organizations could now be freely organized, whereas before the war they had been hindered and checked at every stage. Even the criminal Chinese secret societies could now come out into the open.

Although Victor Purcell, the Chief Chinese Affairs Adviser to the BMA, was to make several speeches declaring that the BMA allowed freedom of speech, publication, and association,[2] he did not specifically state that the MCP, the KMT, and other banned pre-war organizations could now operate freely. The fact that they were allowed to exist without any police hindrance was to be taken by those organizations and the public as an indication that such freedoms were permitted. Consequently, although the MCP had many branches established throughout the country, it did not emerge completely into the open and maintained a semi-underground status. An apparent reason was that they could never be sure when unstated freedoms might be taken away again.

The BMA's policy towards societies, in particular, was determined by several considerations: (1) the fact that the MCP had been recognized by the governor during the Japanese invasion; (2) that the Supreme Allied Commander, Mountbatten, had made an agreement with the MPAJA which was under the control of the MPAJU; (3) that the MPAJA would continue to be in existence on the British return and would not be disbanded until some time later; and (4) that Chinese public opinion, if not the MCP and the MPAJA, would have been alienated by any premature restriction of the rights of freedom of speech and of association.[3] The most important consideration was that Mountbatten had found the MCP's eight-point manifesto of 27 August 1945 unobjectionable. The MCP had made promises of cooperation, which he accepted at their face value. Mountbatten personally attached considerable importance to the MCP and Chinese questions.

The favourable attitude of Mountbatten towards the Chinese and the MCP was immediately transformed into policy by the BMA. Mountbatten was anxious to shift his headquarters to Malaya but until then, he maintained a personal interest in Malayan affairs and kept in close touch with Hone, the CCAO, whose Chief Chinese Affairs Adviser, Victor Purcell, saw things very much in Mountbatten's liberal way. The upshot of this was that at the beginning of the BMA period Chinese affairs assumed a far greater importance than Malay affairs within the BMA.

But the BMA civil affairs staff did not have it easy. The MCP began making a determined bid for political influence, the young militants in the MCP were restless and indulged in various forms of agitation against the BMA, while the party leaders seemed unable or unwilling to control these militants and appeared to vacillate between cooperation and non-cooperation with the BMA. On the other hand, the British field commanders and their officers were hostile if not intolerant towards the MPAJA guerrillas and the MCP elements, which they regarded as a nuisance and a threat to law and order. The BMA civil affairs staff and the military commanders were frequently at loggerheads over how to deal with the Chinese guerrillas and political activists. The military frequently did not hesitate to use tough and coercive measures such as shootings, arrests, and detentions to deal with the communist groups, while the BMA staff preferred diplomacy and negotiations. On the side of the BMA civil affairs staff the Force 136 officers continued to maintain good liaison with the guerrillas.[4] Eventually, first Hone, then the Force 136 officers, and finally Purcell became disillusioned with the intransigent communist attitude and supported the military's tough measures towards the communists.

As shown in Chapter 3, the party's CEC had announced very moderate policies on 27 August 1945 to deal with the return of the British administration. Top British officials found most of the MCP's eight demands unobjectionable, except the demands for an elected national assembly and the right to vote, for which the British had no immediate plans. Throughout the BMA period the party's moderate leadership under Lai Tek put aside its ultimate goal of an independent Democratic Republic. Whether this was a temporary tactic, a reflection of honest expectations of British support, or an anti-party manipulation by Lai Tek is difficult to say. It may have been all three simultaneously. As a programme, however, the 27 August manifesto proved inadequate and shortsighted. Consequently, the party's leadership would amend and issue, in piecemeal fashion, a variety of specific demands to the British administration.

This is evident in the MCP's statement on 7 November 1945, when it put "six proposals" to the British government, including the demand for self-government, which was not one of the eight demands in the 27 August statement, although it had hoped that the British government would consider granting self-government to Malaya. In the 7 November statement the MCP "proposed" that Malaya be granted the right to determine its own administration, judiciary, and legislature, as well as the right to solve its political and economic problems, national defence, and foreign relations. Other "proposals" related to less government interference with the people's freedoms of speech, publication, and assembly, general increases in wages, and the abolition of restrictions relating to trade, travel, and transportation.[5]

Successive policy statements were largely repetitive in their emphasis on the need to raise living standards, improve working conditions, and secure freedoms of speech, publication, and assembly, and a representative form of government. The party would add increasingly detailed demands. Later statements reflected reactions of the communists to the Malayan Union plan, their growing awareness of the United Nations, and support of the Republics of Indonesia and Vietnam. It began adopting Mao's concept of "New Democracy" as a slogan and to set up one or two organizations with "New Democratic" in their names, such as the New Democratic Youth League and the newspaper *Sin Min Chu* (New Democracy). MCP propaganda continued to be anti-imperialistic. On questions of foreign policy the party's propaganda emphasized support for Soviet foreign policy and world peace.

Between August 1945 and January 1946, the party worked towards certain interim goals, that is, the organization of labour unions, political pressure groups and the political education of the masses. Its actions were very much influenced by the local situation, such as riots and workers' strikes that broke out spontaneously throughout the peninsula owing to rice shortages, gross inflation, and low wages. Party members immediately stepped in to take over these grievances "and to organize the dissatisfied local population and workers. In the tasks of organization, young militants of the MCP were very much to the fore, but they made matters worse for the MCP's moderate leadership by taking to the streets and inevitably clashing with the British military.

While the militants were challenging the MCP's leadership, moves were underway to expose Lai Tek, the secretary-general. An article published in a Penang Chinese newspaper in September 1945 denounced him as a traitor to the party during the occupation. Ng Yeh Lu, who had been the party's representative in 1941 and had been a known agent of the Kempeitai, wrote it.[6] Although the allegation was regarded as incredible and ignored by the Central Executive Committee, it led party members to rethink past episodes. The rumours continued and gained in strength when they came to the attention of Yeung Kuo, a Selangor member of the Central Standing Committee who had been virtually banished to Penang by Lai Tek. Apparently as a result of consultation between Yeung Kuo and other Central Committee members Lai Tek found himself relegated to the political bureau and barred from the organization committee which, under Yeung Kuo, became responsible for the organization of the party.[7]

Lai Tek fought back. In a campaign at the end of 1945 his role as supreme leader of the party was made public and he was hailed as saviour and preserver of the MCP. Beginning at the end of November and extending throughout December, letters and telegrams addressed to Lai Tek or Light or Wright (his aliases) were published in the local press, all expressing admiration for his leadership of the party in the past ten years. On 27 November the Negeri Sembilan Women's Union, in its published letter to Lai Tek, exhorted him to greater efforts and assured him that members would unite under the leadership of the MCP to work for the liberation of the people and the emancipation of women.[8]

At a tea party organized by the Perak branch of the MCP in Ipoh on the same date, the state MCP representative, Miss Eng Ming Chin, attacked the "conspirators" against Lai Tek as "remnant Fascists" who were against the MCP. She urged public bodies to send letters and telegrams giving him their support and to enquire after his health.[9] One telegram, which best reflects the orchestrated campaign to boost Lai Tek's standing was sent in December 1945 by 13 Chinese public bodies in Singapore and southern Johor. After a warm salutation to Lai Tek, the telegram said:

> We the people in Southern Johor have in the past been consi-
> dered backward politically, economically and culturally with an
> equal lack of unity and understanding. Today we are known as
> "a strong force in the emancipation of the anti-Fascist people of
> Malaya". At the same time, we have set up in a short period after
> the Japanese surrender the Southern Johor People's General
> Committee, the highest organ representing the sentiments of the
> people.
>
> Truth tells us that we are indebted to your able guidance for
> this success. In other words, we realise that had there been no
> MCP, we would not have been united today. Continuous growth
> in strength of the MCP, therefore, is the best guarantee for the
> emancipation of the Malayan races and its existence represents
> our most necessary weapon.
>
> As leader of the MCP as well as the saviour of the five million
> people of Malaya to win democratic freedom, your life and your
> health are of deep concern to all. Existing side by side with the
> New Democratic movement in Malaya are remnants of reac-
> tionary Fascists now in the stage of their last struggle. But we are

firmly resolved to exterminate them with racial unity. We give our support to the Eight Points and the Six Proposals of the MCP, and we request you to give us more guidance and encouragement towards their realisation.[10]

This campaign was most timely. It took place just before the central committee met for its Eighth Enlarged Plenum from 21 January to 3 February. This meeting, which Lai Tek chaired, re-elected him secretary-general. A new central committee was also elected. However, the seven-man Central Standing Committee now included both Chin Peng and Yeung Kuo, who had combined to investigate Lai Tek's past and present activities.[11] Lai Tek was still too strong to be dislodged, and no one yet had dared to challenge him or raise any criticism of him at the meeting. It was not until March 1947 that Chin Peng and Yeung Kuo amassed sufficient information to unmask him. They then convened a special session of the central committee in Kuala Lumpur. But Lai Tek, who had learnt of their intentions, failed to appear.[12]

The campaign to boost Lai Tek's standing attracted the attention of the British intelligence services, which immediately began investigations into his wartime conduct. The scanty evidence in the open official records in London suggests that it was not until late December 1945 that the British intelligence authorities realized that their pre-war agent was alive and still leading the Malayan communist movement. Probably because he was unsure of British attitudes towards him, Lai Tek had not immediately re-established contacts with them and had ingeniously concealed his true identity.

He had in fact appeared in Singapore on 24 September at a meeting with the DCCAO Singapore, Brigadier McKerron, and other senior BMA officers, apparently arranged by Force 136 headquarters. Lai Tek had introduced himself as Chang Hong, the name he had used as one of three members of the MPAJA supreme headquarters who had negotiated and signed the MCP-SEAC anti-Japanese cooperation agreement with John Davis of Force 136 in January 1944.[13]

At this meeting, "Chang Hong" expressed his desire to assist the BMA in Malaya. He referred to his connections with the MPAJU and the MCP, both of which had supported the MPAJA in the field during the occupation. However, he emphasized that he was not in a position to speak for either the MPAJU or the MCP, as both were quite separate organizations from the MPAJA, their only connection

being that they had all been anti-Japanese and had mutually supported one another during the occupation. "Chang Hong" agreed to
use his influence to bring about a meeting between the BMA and
responsible leaders of the MPAJU and the MCP. A later meeting
with the commissioner of police was regarded by Force 136 headquarters as having achieved little, but it was considered that "Chang
Hong" would use his influence with the Chinese communities to
prevent arrests and abductions by Chinese societies which were
taking the law into their hands.[14] On the same day, "Chang Hong"
introduced the Singapore AJU leader, Lee Soong, and the local
MCP leader, Wu Tian Wang, to the DCCAO. Both promised the
BMA their whole-hearted cooperation. It should have been obvious
to Force 136 and to the Field Security Section that the influential
"Chang Hong" who displayed such authority was none other than
their old friend Lai Tek. Lai Tek was certainly ill at ease but astute
in disguising himself and concealing his identity.

However, in late December a Maj. R.J. Isaacs of Field Security
Section began to interrogate several MCP witnesses to establish the
identity and whereabouts of Lai Tek.[15] It transpired that one important witness in what was described in the confidential file as the
"Wright case" committed suicide in Isaacs's house on 21 December.
The fear arose that Isaacs and other witnesses would be put in the
box at the inquest, in which case there would be serious danger
of exposure of British investigations into Lai Tek's activities. SEAC
headquarters was informed, and in a message to headquarters
Malaya Command said: "If this occurs probably we shall be forced
to arrest him [Lai Tek] and make a case."[16] Isaacs was reported to
be seeking legal advice to determine the best way to minimize the
exposure of British activities. This message was addressed "personal"
to four top officials in the BMA including Major Blades of the
Malayan Security Service, who subsequently became Commissioner
of Police, and Victor Purcell, the Chief Chinese Affairs Officer. The
availability of this important evidence in the open files can only be
regarded as an oversight, because no more was to be found about
the "Wright case" in the subsequent correspondence.

With regard to the "Wright affair", John Davis has now revealed
that Major Isaacs was in the midst of investigations of Japanese war
criminals, when "highly sensitive" facts emerged about Lai Tek.
Isaacs wanted corroboration from Davis, who had been Lai Tek's
case officer before the war, about revelations, unknown even to Innes
Tremlett, Davis' superior in Force 136, of Lai Tek's collaboration

with the Kempeitai. Davis, however, still took the line that "if Force 136's European officers had come through the war unscathed, it was because of Lai Tek's residual loyalty to his British spymasters."[17]

Probably in January, Lai Tek resumed his contacts with the British Special Branch in Singapore. The Special Branch records, including the reports of Lai Tek seen by Anthony Short, while they appeared to him unsatisfactory, categorically confirmed Lai Tek's role as a Special Branch agent:

> One could hardly expect a formal record of all the subsequent transactions; but the ones that exist are curiously impalpable and remote: hardly what one would expect of a highly efficient and presumably ruthless double agent. It can only be assumed that material facts transmitted were never committed to paper. Even so, the air of mystery in which he thrived, indeed that was essential for his survival, is hardly dispelled by the record of his dealings with the Special Branch.[18]

Probably after contacts had been re-established with the Special Branch, Lai Tek attended the Eighth Enlarged Plenum of the Central Working Committee, which began on 21 January 1946. This meeting was important in two respects. It re-elected Lai Tek as secretary-general, and adopted the new policy, which he had formulated, called the "Malayan Democratic United Front" policy, whereby the MCP was to seek alliances with other political parties while building up its mass organizations such as trade unions and youth movements.[19] In a nine-point "democratic" programme the party would establish the basis of the United Front; it was a more specific repetition of earlier demands for self-government, an elected National Assembly, and guarantees for basic civil rights. The United Front against imperialism and for the advancement of democratic principles of government was part of the communist pre-war programme. During the United Front, the participating parties were to preserve their political independence.[20] In fact, this United Front policy had been put into practice a few months earlier when the MCP sponsored the formation of two political parties as "fronts" — the Malay Nationalist Party (MNP) in November and the Malayan Democratic Union (MDU) in December.[21]

Lai Tek in his 22-page report to the Plenum had pre-empted criticism from the militants by declaring that he was in favour of revolutionary struggle, but he urged the party to adopt the United Front policy for the present phase of struggle. In his analysis of the colonial problem and the world situation, Lai Tek saw two ways of resolving the problem: (1) to use bloodshed and revolutionary struggle, as in Vietnam and Indonesia; or (2) to use the United Front of the whole nation, through an alliance with all parties and coordinated with the peace forces of the world, including the United Nations.[22] When he discussed the Malayan situation, Lai Tek noted that British imperialism had become repressive again since the British return to Malaya. The struggles of the Vietnamese and Indonesian peoples were influencing the Malayan people, and the bitter conflicts between the MCP and the BMA were now preparing the MCP and the people for a "revolutionary high tide" and a Malayan nationalist movement. In view of this, the MCP must stand for revolutionary struggle, but the correct line for the present situation was for the MCP to establish a "national United Front" to unite the people and to fight for democracy. Lai Tek expounded it further as follows:

> Today the basic demands of the people have still not been fulfilled. The Malayan people are under colonial rule. The struggle of the Malayan revolution remains — complete liberation and complete independence of the country. Therefore, we the MCP must continue to propose the revolutionary struggle for national liberation and we the MCP must carry on a "New Democratic" movement. Based on this basic task, and under the new historical circumstances of today, the MCP and the Malayan people must, firstly, carry on the correct line for a national liberation movement to establish the National United Front for democracy based on the common interests of all parties and alliances, and act together on a common democratic programme, and oppose British colonial rule and fight for democracy and a better livelihood.[23]

In other words, Lai Tek had now agreed that a return to armed struggle in the future was inevitable, but prior to launching the armed struggle the MCP should prepare the people by means of struggle for particular concessions within the British system. Lai Tek himself admitted that the eight-point manifesto of 27 August 1945 and the six proposals of 7 November 1945 were "partly out of date". For the new circumstances, he said, the Central Committee had "taken back" the eight-point programme and introduced the nine-point "democratic" programme, which was adopted at its Eighth Plenum.[24] These moves by Lai Tek should be understood as concessions to the militants, who were mounting increasing pressure on him to adopt a more revolutionary line.

Communist Activities, September through January 1946

After the Japanese surrender, the MCP and the MPAJU/MPAJA acted quickly to consolidate their position as a leading force in post-war Malaya and to organize popular support to influence the returning British to grant the people a democratic form of government. Communist propaganda corps travelled extensively, particularly in the states of Perak and Johor, urging the various races to unite in the cause of a "New Democratic" Malaya. The MPAJU and the MPAJA had taken over most of the small towns evacuated by the Japanese troops. Force 136 officers worked with those guerrillas with whom they had contact to maintain law and order, while attempting to bring outside groups of guerrillas under their influence.

Communist-sponsored committees were established by the MCP/MPAJU/MPAJA alliance to run local administrations in the towns until British troops arrived. Many different types of associations were formed, controlled either directly or indirectly by the communists. Among them were cultural and social clubs, people's associations, self-governing committees, women's unions, and labour unions. MCP workers did not necessarily staff the various associations formed, but the ties were such that communist policies provided political guidance. These and other activities were designed to gain recognition for the communists by the British and a voice in the post-war government of Malaya.

The Selangor state committees of the MCP, the MPAJU, and the MPAJA took the lead and jointly called a Selangor State Congress of People's Representatives on 25 September, at Kuala Lumpur. The Selangor Congress, the largest and most successful of several state and district congresses, apparently represented an effort to set up a representative assembly that would then obtain recognition from the British authorities. A call was sent out to all racial communities to send delegates, but response was unenthusiastic except from Chinese, who therefore had a disproportionately large number of delegates. The ostensible purpose of the meeting was somewhat vague. The congress was to form the Selangor People's State Committee, but this committee, the organizers said, "neither serves as a government nor a corporation but is a public body to express public views represented by peoples of all nationalities and all caste [*sic*] thereby protecting the interests of the people".[25]

An executive committee composed of 91 members was chosen, and from this body a working committee of 45, the real governing body, was appointed. Twenty-three resolutions were passed by the congress and sent to the BMA. Most of these were of an economic or social nature, intended to improve the livelihood of the people, to lower prices, and to establish better labour conditions. Others were of a political nature, such as those requesting the BMA to: (1) put into effect the Atlantic Charter with regard to self-government and democracy; (2) support the programme of the Malayan Communist Party; (3) realize self-government in Malaya and establish central and regional representative organizations for the exchange of people's ideas which were to be expressed through the medium of the Anti-Japanese Union; (4) guarantee absolute freedom of speech, press, public organization, publication, belief, and congregation; and (5) legalize and encourage the position of the anti-Japanese organization.[26]

The Selangor committee's structure was the most elaborate and its work the most widely reported of all the state committees. It had several departments such as culture, social welfare, and general affairs. The chairman was Phang Sau Choong, a representative of the Selangor state committee of the MCP. There were also a few Malays and Indians on the committee but they did not hold any key posts. As representatives of their communities they were required to attend meetings with BMA officials, and to translate certain declarations into Malay and Tamil. The offices of the working committee and the Selangor Congress were sited at the Chinese Assembly Hall in Kuala Lumpur. The upper Pahang, Negeri Sembilan, and southern Johor state committees were also set up, each taking its cue from the Selangor committee. But in almost every town in each state there was already a smaller people's committee or people's association, under the dominance of communists. The BMA recognized the committees by welcoming the representations they made on various problems affecting the people's livelihood.[27]

September passed with the overall political situation generally quiet, though conditions throughout the country were far from stable. Widespread looting, banditry, and other crimes were reported, as well as numerous cases of abduction and murder of collaborators.[28]

The first week of October passed very much in the same fashion, but in the second week several important developments took place. On 10 October, the Secretary of State for the Colonies announced the Malayan Union policy in the British Parliament. The next day, when the local newspapers reported the announcement, Sir Harold MacMichael arrived in Malaya to begin his mission to interview the Malay rulers and to obtain their signatures to new treaties. The real significance of these British moves did not hit the local population of all races and political persuasions until a few weeks later. Meanwhile, 10 October or the "Double Tenth" (China's National Day) was celebrated on a national scale with large Chinese processions and mass meetings jointly organized by the communists, Chinese guilds and organizations, and the Malayan Kuomintang. The leading part played by the MCP/MPAJU/MPAJA and their members in these celebrations attested to the fact that they saw themselves as Chinese and as Chinese organizations and Chinese patriots owing a loyalty to China.

On 12 October, the Royal Air Force police arrested Soong Kwong, the Selangor AJU leader, on a charge of extortion for an offence committed on 10 September — before the establishment of the BMA — without prior reference to the BMA police. Before this arrest nine minor labour and MPAJU/MPAJA officials had been arrested by the British army on a variety of charges, some with and some without BMA approval. The result of Soong Kwong's arrest was a large protest demonstration at the Kuala Lumpur *padang* (public field) on 15 October. The DCCAO (Malaya), Brigadier Willan, met a delegation. In reply to questions he explained that, while the charges against those arrested were a matter for the courts, all except two had been released and the other two, including Soong Kwong, had been granted bail. The delegates were not satisfied, but after a while departed.[29] In the next two weeks there were sporadic labour stoppages, strikes, political meetings, demonstrations, and minor disturbances throughout the peninsula. The immediate causes of these disturbances were shortages of food, lack of work, and in-adequate wages, but the BMA authorities were unsure whether there were any links between these disturbances and Soong Kwong's arrest.

The charges against Soong Kwong are of significance because they related to an incident, which occurred before British administration was re-established on 12 September. Soong Kwong, the general secretary of the MPAJU in Selangor, was alleged to have attempted on 10 September to extort money from a Chinese named Chan Sau Meng, who was seized by the MPAJU and kept tied up in a room for a week. Soong Kwong interviewed him and accused Chan of profiteering and extortion during the occupation. The punishment for this was death for himself and his family, Soong Kwong said, but Chan would be released on payment of $300,000. A promissory note was signed. Chan was released and in due course brought

$32,000 in cash, together with jewellery and other property. The BMA's attitude on such cases arising from any incidents before 12 September was that they would not be taken up, as the MPAJU/MPAJA was to be regarded as operational up to 12 September and its activities before that date were to be regarded as justified by military exigency.[30] It was in this context that the arrest by the RAF provost, without reference to the BMA police, complicated matters for BMA officials. Other MPAJU/MPAJA members had been arrested on charges of allegedly commandeering military vehicles or trespassing on prohibited areas without proper authority or possessing stolen property. These charges were connected with what Purcell has described as the "change-over from a war to a peace footing".[31]

By January 1946, about 30 members of the MPAJA had been arrested in Selangor, Johor, and elsewhere, on charges ranging from illegal possession of stolen property to murder. Besides Soong Kwong, two other well-known cases which aroused widespread leftist agitation were those concerning Choo Kow, who was arrested on 1 January on a charge of murdering a Japanese-employed special policeman at Kluang on 15 September 1945, and Lai Kim, described in an intelligence report as one of the notorious MPAJA executioners who was arrested in August 1946 in Bentong for a double murder committed on 16 September 1945. MPAJU/MPAJA officials accused the BMA of injustice in arresting AJA members instead of stepping up arrests of collaborators of the Japanese. This line was echoed by the MCP's semi-official newspaper *Sin Min Chu*:

> Arrests of Anti-Japanese elements are happening in other places. In view of their frankness in speech and their antagonism towards evildoers, these elements are hated by the BMA and the Chinese collaborators of the Japanese, and consequently their life is in danger. The British are treating the Japanese collaborators leniently, while they make arrests of anti-Japanese elements, who ought to be well treated. This must be rigorously opposed.[32]

On 21 October began what became known as the weeklong Perak disturbances associated with the shortage of rice. These were organized through the people's committees. The following is the reported chronology of events based on British intelligence reports:[33]

21 October: At Ipoh, a large demonstration was held on the *padang*, consisting of 3,000 people, mostly women. After a talk by leaders of the people's committee, demands were made for five *gantang* of rice and a dole of $20 per person. The meeting dispersed quietly.

At Sungei Siput (25 miles east of Taiping), there were similar demonstrations by a crowd of 5,000. The British liaison officer of Force 136 was surrounded. Two other BMA officers, Colonels Harvey and de Crespigny, who came to the scene, were also prevented from leaving by the crowd and were roughly handled. After the crowd had been warned to disperse, the troops opened fire. As a result one person was killed and three wounded. Order was finally restored the next morning.

At Parit Buntar (15 miles north-east of Taiping), there were similar demonstrations of 7,000 people demanding rice and work. Fifty people were arrested and detained in Taiping gaol.

22 October: A fairly successful general strike and closing of shops occurred throughout Perak. At Ipoh, another demonstration of 1,000 people gathered outside the civil affairs offices, armed with staves, and started a sit-down strike. On arrival of a company of troops the crowd was given 30 minutes to disperse, followed by two periods of five minutes' grace. The leaders of the crowd persuaded them not to disperse, and six shots were fired. Three in the crowd were killed, three wounded. The crowd dispersed and the ringleaders were arrested.[34]

At *Taiping*, a large crowd gathered and demanded release of those arrested in the previous day's demonstration. Troops opened fire. Four persons were killed.

Colonel Harvey, the Civil Affairs Officer, met a People's Committee deputation from Ipoh, which submitted five demands as follows:

> (i) An issue of four *gantangs* per head for November (once and for all); (ii) a cash payment of $20 per head; (iii) cancellation of order restricting movement of foodstuffs; (iv) exemption from payments of water and light dues for October, November and December; and (v) raising of rubber and tin prices to a reasonable level.

Force 136 officer Colonel Broome undertook to return to Kuala Lumpur to get Brigadier Willan's replies to these demands, but in the meantime the latter came to Ipoh himself.[35]

23 October: Brigadier Willan addressed a meeting on the *padang* at Ipoh. Before his arrival, speeches and the singing of communist songs worked up the crowd of about 3,000. Brigadier Willan made a speech in which he dealt with every aspect of the situation and made the following replies to the demands:

> (i) There would be a free issue for October of one *gantang* of rice per head; (ii) there would be relief for all destitutes and work for all able-bodied men at pre-war wages; (iii) the restriction of the movement of foodstuffs was for the protection of the people against profiteers. It would not be cancelled; (iv) no light or water charges would be made for October. If and when charges were made those genuinely unable to pay would be let off; (v) no price was fixed for tin. The rubber price was fixed at the highest level, which would enable Malaya to compete with the synthetic article.

After his speech, the leaders expressed dissatisfaction. Brigadier Willan and his staff now left. In half an hour the crowd dispersed.[36]

At Parit Buntar and Sitiawan there were also disturbances. In Sitiawan the BMA Civil Affairs officer was surrounded and made to sign a document agreeing to demands. In Bagan Serai there was an incident in which shooting occurred.

At Kuala Kangsar, 18 arrests were made when a crowd collected.

At Batu Gajah (10 miles south of Ipoh), a crowd of 5,000 collected outside the Court House. Some penetrated the building and destroyed files before being ejected. The leaders later saw the SCAO, who had to be rescued by troops, as he was being stoned.

24–26 October: Minor disturbances at various places in Perak.

27 October: Fourteenth Army reported that it was rumoured the strikes might spread to Selangor coincident with the imminent trial of Soong Kwong.[37]

Elsewhere, between 21 and 31 October, strikes and minor disturbances also occurred: a dockers' strike in Singapore over complaints of inadequate pay started on 21 October, followed by strikes of the city's municipal and bus workers on 25 and 27 October; a strike by 6,000 workers at the Batu Arang (Selangor) coalmines began on 13 October and continued until mid-November; minor disturbances also took place in Pahang, Johor, and Malacca. But by 2 November the situation had improved considerably, with the exception of the dock and municipal workers, who were reported to be returning to work slowly.

The verdict of the BMA on the situation on 30 October was that the main cause of the recent disturbances was the lack of rice. The food situation was not yet satisfactory, and rice stocks were not large. In some areas there was widespread malnutrition, and in many areas wages were still low despite a shortage of labour.[38] In assessing the part played by the MCP in these disturbances, the BMA concluded that the MCP's influence had been present in varying degrees in most areas, and was probably strongest in Selangor and north Perak. In Perak, it observed, incidents had been centrally controlled, but the central agency had not yet been detected. However, on 1 December 1945 the BMA established for the first time that, despite propaganda put out by the communists, the MCP, its many associations, the MPAJU, and the MPAJA were in fact all one. The general headquarters were believed to be at Lintang, between Ipoh and Taiping (Perak).[39] The controlling influence in Chinese politics was undoubtedly the MCP. It became clear to the BMA that there was now a need for some official contacts with the MCP's real leadership. Victor Purcell interviewed the Perak communist leaders, including the fiery and attractive Miss Eng Ming Ching, between 4 and 6 December, after having earlier met the Singapore MCP official, Wu Tian Wang. But these interviews convinced Purcell that none of these people was the genuine controlling authority.[40]

The Lai Tek personality cult appeared in the Chinese newspapers around this time, and it is my belief that the attention of the BMA's intelligence services was now drawn for the first time to the presence of the former British agent. Accordingly, military intelligence units throughout the peninsula were alerted to look out for him, for henceforth reports frequently appeared in the weekly intelligence summaries of a person who fitted his description being seen in many places as far apart as Johor and the northernmost Thai-Malay border regions.[41] According to one reliable source, Lai Tek regained contact with British officials in early 1946 and was periodically interrogated in 1946 and 1947. Interrogations of Lai Tek were said to have been held in October 1946, but it is not known whether this was the first time since the war.[42] It is most probable that the first contact with the Special Branch was re-established some time in January before the Eighth Enlarged Plenum of the central committee, which began on 21 January.

The semi-underground status of the MCP throughout BMA rule makes it difficult to assess properly the party's activities during this period. The MCP maintained this status because it was sceptical of British intentions. In the few reports it published during this period, the MCP was extremely guarded and reticent about its role in the labour movement. It did not indicate whether it encouraged any of the strikes or disturbances, nor what the rationale might be for creating such social and economic unrest. However, subsequent reports issued by the MCP as a post-mortem on the post-war situation, after the removal of Lai Tek in 1947, suggest that the MCP under Lai Tek had made a mistake in not fulfilling its role as the vanguard of the proletariat and had in a sense betrayed the trade unions by not acknowledging leadership. This confirms my view that the strikes and disturbances in October, far from being inspired by the MCP's moderate leadership under Lai Tek, were in fact initiated by the MCP's young militant elements. A Fourteenth Army intelligence report had, in fact, said that many of the October 1945 incidents were the work of "hot-headed youth elements who are acting with more impetuosity than older men would advise".[43] The militant wing of the MCP, led by Chin Peng and Yeung Kuo had begun its investigations and was apparently encouraging communist agitation and labour unrest to oust Lai Tek or make him change his moderate policies.

Meanwhile, the party accepted invitations from the BMA to appoint representatives to serve on the advisory councils set up throughout the country. These councils were formed at the suggestion of Mountbatten to enable the BMA officials to consult and discuss problems of each territory with representatives of local communities and interests. There were usually two left-wing representatives among fifteen members in the council — one from the MCP and another from one of its associations such as the GLU or the New Democratic Youth League. Other members of the council were from the KMT, the MNP, business associations, and professional groups. These councils paralleled the pre-war Sultan's State Executive Councils or the Straits Settlements Legislative Council except that they had no legislative powers. General Hone inaugurated the first meeting of the Singapore Advisory Council on 14 November.

Because of the unprecedented representation given to the MCP and other political groups in the Singapore Advisory Council, Purcell remarked in his diary that it "marked an epoch in the history of Singapore".[44] He noted that the communist members particularly did good work during the discussions, which "covered everything from supply, trade and industry, and prostitution to education and the Press". The criticism of the composition of the council by the MCP representative, Wu Tian Wang, and his comments on BMA administration were said to be "usually to the point". As a result, standing committees were afterwards set up on which the various members of the council were asked to serve. However, the official attitude of the MCP towards the council was quite different — that this fell short of the party's demand for democratically elected Legislative Councils. Purcell observed:

> The Leftist Press took a carping and condemnatory line regarding the Council but generally among the Chinese the reception of the Council meeting and of the Deputy Chief Civil Affairs Officer's [Brigadier McKerron] speech were favourable.[45]

The disbandment of the MPAJA carried out on 1 December 1945 presents another example of the conflict between Lai Tek and the militants in the MCP. When Force 136 on behalf of the BMA and the British army presented the proposal for disbandment, as early as September, the Standing Executive Committee debated the issue. Lai Tek was in favour of the proposal, but the rest of the committee strongly opposed it.[46] Yet Lai Tek got his way. It can only be assumed that Lai Tek argued that the MCP, having opted for constitutional struggle, was now in the invidious position of having a standing army without a role. To defy the British meant confrontation. A better strategy was to deceive the British. Not all weapons should be surrendered; the ex-MPAJA servicemen should form an association so that, if necessary, demobilized men could be easily mustered for armed struggle. These measures were, in fact, put into effect.

The negotiations between John Davis of Force 136 and representatives of the MPAJA supreme headquarters were long and drawn-out. Originally, the Fourteenth Army decided that the MPAJA should be disbanded on 1 November, but when this date approached there was still no agreement in sight. Talks bogged down over the payments of gratuities to the guerrillas. The MPAJA guerrillas within and outside Force 136 influence were called the old guard and the new guard respectively. The idea of the military commanders was that Force 136 should persuade the new guard to bring their weapons in and join the old guard. Both would then be disbanded. An inducement was to pay the guerrillas in the old guard a monthly salary of M$30 plus rations from 15 August to the date of disbandment. In November it was provisionally agreed between the MPAJA and the Fourteenth Army that this force would be disbanded on 1 December and that members would hand in their arms on disbandment. Each man would be paid a gratuity of M$350 in two instalments, M$250 on disbandment and a further M$100 three months later. Each disbanded person was free to enter civilian employment or to choose service with the police, volunteer forces, or the Malay regiment.[47]

On 1 December the MPAJA was formally dissolved, but it was rumoured that only a portion of the MPAJA had disbanded. The main force, British intelligence suspected, would remain in the jungles or continue operating under the guise of clubs and similar organizations. After the disbandment formalities, carried out with much ceremony, in which British military commanders took the salutes and paid tributes to the MPAJA's services, it was reported that only old-type weapons had been turned in; newer weapons had been concealed, mostly in the jungles.[48] It was later reported in early May 1946 that two regiments — one in Perak, the other in Johor — still approximated a state of mobilization. Information about communist arms dumps began to appear increasingly in military intelligence reports. Searches were ordered to be carried out. In one raid on an old MPAJA hideout at Bekor (Perak) the British army came across a Chinese village "commune", dominated by a Self-Governing Association, flying a red flag and complete with drilling ground and a "people's militia". The villagers opened fire at the sight of the British troops, and in the exchange of fire one man was shot dead by the army. The village was then searched. Seven men were detained.[49] Several KMT guerrilla groups in Perak and Kelantan had also refused to lay down their arms on 1 December, although their leaders in talks with Force 136 had agreed to this. One reason given was that they needed the arms to protect the Chinese, as Malay-Chinese tensions had been increasing in their areas. By May 1946, the KMT guerrillas were still reported to be holding out at the Thai-Malay border.[50]

After the formal demobilization of the MPAJA, associations for demobilized personnel were formed in the areas where regiments had operated. A central association, known as the Pan-Malayan Federation of Anti-Japanese Army Ex-Servicemen's Associations, was established at Kuala Lumpur on 8 December. Area branches were established in Selangor, Negeri Sembilan, northern Johor, southern Johor, Perak, and Kedah. It was also planned to establish branches for upper and lower Pahang. In addition, numerous sub-branches were established. The president and vice-president of the central association, together with the presidents of the eight area branches, constituted the working committee of the central association, and were, in general, the same men who had commanded the headquarters and the eight regiments of the MPAJA.[51] Thus the top-level direction of the ex-guerrilla clubs paralleled that of the former MPAJA. The stated aims of the central association included cultivating ties of friendship among ex-guerrillas, recommending work to them, assisting them in their difficulties, and improving standards of education. The organization, aims, views, and progress of these ex-guerrilla associations were publicized in a newspaper, *Charn Yew Pau* (Combatant's Friend), which appeared under the sponsorship of the MPAJA Ex-Servicemen's Association and was printed at the communist-owned Min Sheng Pau press. In general the tone of the newspaper was pro-communist, anti-Kuomintang, and anti-imperialist.

Although there is no direct evidence that all the leaders of the ex-guerrilla associations were members of the MCP, or that the party issued directives, their policies were parallel and representatives of ex-guerrilla associations participated in meetings with various communist-sponsored groups that adopted political resolutions. Some sort of working agreement had certainly been reached before the 1 December demobilization, when communist influence was dominant in the MPAJA. These ex-guerrilla associations provided a potentially well-organized military arm for the MCP, which would be ready for use, whenever necessary, as happened in the MCP's insurrection in June 1948.

On 6 January, at an impressive military ceremony on the Singapore public field, Mountbatten presented campaign medal ribbons to eight MPAJA commanders, including Chin Peng, Chen Tien, and Liu Yau. Surprisingly, "Chang Hong", alias Lai Tek, like Liu Yau one of the three top MPAJA commanders, was not among those decorated. Evidently he was still keeping out of sight.[52]

Events were now moving towards a showdown between the MCP and the BMA. The militant elements of the MCP found the social and economic situation in the country to their advantage and were resolved on further agitation. There was increasing evidence during the months October to December 1945 of a determined campaign by these elements, waged through the trade unions and other MCP-controlled organizations, to cause embarrassment to the BMA and to the MCP's moderate leadership. Every move was designed to stir up conflict between the communists and the BMA, and it appeared to the BMA that the communists were attempting to bring the government down.

The communists held up the conviction of MPAJU leader Soong Kwong and of Perak GLU officials, in January 1946, on charges of extortion and sedition as typical examples of British injustice.[53]* There was continued criticism in the Chinese press, and at many meetings held during these months, of the BMA's failure to consider the welfare of the people, its refusal to implement promises made under the United Nations Charter, its interference with freedom of speech and assembly, the ruthless behaviour of British troops towards the local populace, and "imperialistic determination" of the British to impose the reactionary conditions of former colonial rule. Accusations were even made that conditions were worse than they had been under the Japanese. Because of such criticisms the BMA suspended the publication of six leftist newspapers.[54]

The climax came when the militant communist elements, working through the Singapore GLU, decided to call a general strike in January, unless their demands for the unconditional release of Soong Kwong and other party and labour officials received a satisfactory answer. Hone and his senior staff briefed Mountbatten, who had moved his office to Singapore, on Soong Kwong's case. He considered that in the circumstances Soong Kwong should be set at liberty, lest his continued detention constitute preventive arrest, which was contrary to Mountbatten's policy.[55] In fact, he was critical of Hone's handling of the disturbances in October, which had resulted in casualties.[56] Mountbatten now gave orders for Soong Kwong's release. But when it was brought to his attention that the

---

* The manner in which the trial of Soong Kwong was conducted lent itself to criticism. Soong Kwong had been charged with intimidation and extortion, but, for lack of evidence, had not been convicted until 3 January, although he had had more than one retrial. A British judge had presided over the court with two Malayan assessors, but there was a split verdict. The judge found him guilty, but the assessors voted for his acquittal. A second trial had the same result, and it was deemed that the assessors were intimidated. At the third trial an entirely British panel convicted him and he was sentenced to four years' imprisonment. Donnison, *British Military Administration in the Far East*, p. 389; Richard Clutterbuck, *Riot and Revolution in Singapore and Malaya* (London, 1973), p. 50.

threatened general strike was coupled with the demand for Soong Kwong's release, Mountbatten promptly cancelled the release. "I considered he [Soong Kwong] should be set free," Mountbatten recalled, "but I was not prepared to encourage lawlessness by allowing the instigators of direct action to suppose that their threat to paralyse the life of Singapore had in any way contributed to his release."[57]

A general strike of 24 hours, nevertheless, took place on 29 January. It was estimated that 170,000 came out in Singapore alone. In the peninsula sympathetic strikes of a day's duration also met with considerable success. In certain places such as Ipoh, however, where a strong line was taken by the authorities in advising shops to remain open and promising protection in the form of police and military patrols, the strike was broken. The extent of the strike, Mountbatten observed, "bore witness to the efficiency and the ramifications of the directing organisation [the MCP]".[58] On 3 February the review of Soong Kwong's sentence was published, and he was released on sureties.

It might not have been sheer coincidence that the first trial of strength with the BMA chosen by the militant communist elements coincided with the 14-day meeting of the Eighth Enlarged Plenum of the MCP's central committee. It had been apparent that Lai Tek's policy of moderation was unpopular with the militants, but also that they had not been able to change it, as he was well entrenched within the CEC. Lai Tek's general authority during much of this period was nevertheless tenuous. Militancy was a revolutionary activity dominant in the party within the policy of its "peaceful and legal" struggle, and to curb or dampen such activity was against that rising spirit. At the conference, Lai Tek briefly noted the widespread agitation throughout the country and flattered the militant elements by regarding such agitation as the prelude to "a high tide of anti-imperialism". He added:

> During these past four months in Malaya, there has been an outbreak of strikes, demonstrations, and economic struggles of the 500,000 peasants, workers, youths and intellectuals, manifesting their desires and demands for a democratic system and a better livelihood. The Malayan workers are asking for higher wages, democracy and protesting against the arrests of anti-Japanese elements. During these struggles, Chinese and Indians formed two friendly alliances [apparently a reference to Indian labour in the GLUs] in this democratic movement. Therefore, Malaya's

revolutionary movement of today is preparing conditions for a high tide of anti-imperialism, and the MCP is calling all people to unite together to defeat the plot of imperialism.[59]

A second general strike was called for 15 February. The day chosen was the anniversary of the fall of Singapore; the reason given was that the strike would commemorate the abandonment of the city to the Japanese. The intention to discredit the BMA was clear.

In anticipation of this trouble, the British field commanders, BMA officials, and Mountbatten met on 9 February to discuss the situation. Differences arose between Mountbatten and the other officials on appropriate counteractions. As the BMA historian Donnison describes it:

> ... Admiral Mountbatten was reluctantly persuaded by the DCCAO Singapore [Brigadier McKerron], supported by Lieutenant-General Sir Miles Dempsey, the Commander-in-Chief, ALFSEA, and the Chief of Staff, South East Asian Command, Lieutenant-General Sir Frederick Browning, that this was a serious challenge which must be met if British administration was to continue at all, and that the only way to meet it was to strike at the Communist leaders. He refused to act by preventive arrest, but agreed, still reluctantly, to expel the leaders who, being alien Chinese, were liable to banishment under the pre-war Banishment Ordinance. His reluctance proceeded not only from his personal conviction of the advantages to be gained from a liberal approach but from the knowledge that it was at that time a part of the British Government's policy for the future of Malaya that the power to banish should not be used....[60]

On 13 February Mountbatten ordered a ban on all processions or meetings and issued an official statement, repeated throughout the country, that defiance of this order would not be tolerated and that aliens who flouted the order would be liable to repatriation to their places of birth or citizenship. On the night of 13 February, some hours after the warning had been issued, 24 MCP members and officials, 10 of them Chinese nationals, were arrested in several raids in Singapore in connection with the proposed general strike.

The names of the ten Chinese nationals were submitted to Mountbatten, with the recommendation that they be repatriated to China as prominent organizers and troublemakers. Mountbatten refused to do this, however, because he did not consider that these ten men "could reasonably be held to have had time to profit from the warning which had been issued; nor that they could since that warning have committed any misdemeanour which would qualify them for expulsion".[61] The commander-in-chief, ALFSEA, and Mountbatten's chief of staff strongly represented that there should be no release of the arrested men. Mountbatten was firm in his refusal to expel without trial in court, but eventually agreed to the leaders being kept in custody until the return of civil government on 1 April 1946.[62] The ten were then promptly deported without legal proceedings to China where, it was later claimed by the communists, they were subjected to severe punishment by Chiang Kai-shek's government.

In spite of the arrests, on the morning of 15 February a public meeting took place in front of St. Joseph's Institution, Singapore, and a procession formed. When the police tried to disperse the procession, they were resisted and allegedly attacked by a crowd armed with crowbars, sticks, and bottles. The police opened fire, and two people were killed. In the peninsula demonstrations also took place. At Labis (Johor) 15 people were killed when the police opened fire on a crowd, which was allegedly attacking them. In Penang a crowd was dispersed with spraying from a fire hose. A few days later a demonstration at Mersing (Johor), in sympathy with the victims of the Labis incident, resulted in a further clash with the police and further fatalities.

On the whole the militants were badly trounced in the showdown. Not only were more MCP leaders arrested and banished, but also their actions had caused the death of at least 20 supporters. The MCP elements now realized that the administration intended, and had the means, to take a strong line to maintain order. The lesson was learnt. The MCP's militants withdrew into the background. The party was forced to devise a new strategy and to reorganize itself, based on three major considerations: (1) the party was to take greater measures to ensure security by not exposing too many of its organizations and officials and to reduce its open activities; (2) the United Front organizations were to be the only ones to step up their activities as a cover for the party's underground activities; and (3) the party was to prepare for the eventuality of armed struggle, the timing of which was to be determined by the extent of further government repressive measures.[63] Thus, for most of March through August 1946, the party was involved in closing all its 12 open branches and ordering them underground. The party was to have only two open offices, one at Kuala Lumpur and the other at Singapore. This was the situation until the government's declaration of an Emergency in June 1948 prompted the MCP into launching its uprising.

Victor Purcell, the Chinese Affairs Adviser in the BMA, had now reached the end of his patience as far as the MCP was concerned. The 15 February incident convinced him that no other course remained than to adopt a tough policy. As he noted in a memorandum:

> We must accept the fact then that no compromise can be made with the MCP. Its aims and those of the British Government are in ineluctable opposition.... What we are confronted with at present is the threat of small but resolute elements to terrorise the entire community with the undermining of the administration as their sole end....
>
> Therefore, on due consideration, I recommend that all the leaders or any other persons who have directly or indirectly conspired to create the recent disorders and to defy the administration shall be pursued and dealt with, with all the resources at our disposal. When any of them are liable to expulsion under the existing law an expulsion order should be made and carried out....
>
> We cannot honour our trusteeship if we are unable to maintain the authority of the administration whether it is military or civil and we cannot move towards universal education and representative government while we are under the threat of a group of gangsters and thugs.[64]

Purcell, however, argued for the retention of the advisory councils but suggested that for new councils yet to be set up, the BMA should only appoint left-wing representatives who would "cooperate and obey the law".[65] This was an apparent attempt to split the communists.

CHAPTER 10

The Malay-British Conflict

The Malays have always been looked upon as a simple and law-abiding people and we propose to live as such, but at the same time, like every other race or every other nation, we hope we still claim a place in our country.

> – Datuk Onn bin Jaafar in a speech at a dinner
> to mark the end of the All-Malay Congress at
> Suleiman Club, Kuala Lumpur on 4 Mar. 1946

Under the BMA the whole of Malaya, including the nine Malay states, came under one direct and unified administration identical to what the Japanese had established during their occupation. The British had failed to introduce such a system of administration in Malaya before the war. Although martial law was not declared, the BMA operated in much the same fashion as if this had been done. All legislative, executive, and Sultan's state councils were suspended. The Sultans also could not function until civil government was reintroduced. Rights and properties acquired during the Japanese occupation, however, were subject to investigation and to such action as the BMA considered necessary.[1]

One of the first acts of Brigadier Willan, the DCCAO (Malaya), was to contact the Malay Sultans and to check on their records during the Japanese occupation. The British Army's Field Security Unit had been supplied with the lists of principal suspects, which included the Sultans, but none of its officers were empowered to deal with the Sultans.[2]

Of the British-appointed Sultans, only five had survived — the Sultans of Johor, Selangor, Perak, and Pahang, and the Yam Tuan of Negeri Sembilan. In Terengganu the Sultan had died on 25 September 1942 and his eldest son, Raja Ali, had been appointed by the Japanese to succeed him. In Perlis the Raja died on 1 February 1943 and was succeeded by his half-brother, Tengku Syed Hamzah. The Japanese chose Tengku Syed Hamzah, although Tengku Syed Putera had been the heir apparent elected by the state council of Perlis in April 1938 with British approval. In Kedah the Regent, Tengku Badlishah, had been appointed Sultan in place of the Sultan who died in 1943. He had been Regent since 1938 owing to the illness of the Sultan. In Kelantan, Tengku Ibrahim, whose title was Rajah Kelantan, the heir apparent and brother of the Sultan, was installed as Sultan on 25 June 1944, the day of the Sultan's death. The Thais, with Japanese consent, had allowed Tengku Badlishah and Tengku Ibrahim respectively to take their places.[3]

The Japanese had deposed the Sultan of Selangor, Tengku Sir Hishamuddin Alam Shah, on account of his being a British favourite, and in his place had installed his eldest brother, Tengku Musa-Eddin, whom the British had previously debarred from succession.[4] The Japanese removed Tengku Sir Hishamuddin on 15 January 1942 soon after their forces overran Selangor. Probably out of gratitude to the Japanese for recognizing his claim to the title, Tengku Musa-Eddin became the most outspoken royal supporter of the Japanese regime. He was also one of the Sultans who patronized the KMM leader Ibrahim Yaacob. British army intelligence described him as "black" (meaning "a security risk") and marked him down to be detained on reoccupation of Malaya. Likewise, Tengku Syed Hamzah was considered "pro-Japanese or otherwise of ill-repute",* but the latter was not arrested.[5]

---

* The security classifications used by the British Army were as follows: "Whites" were those who were considered to be of no security danger and therefore did not require to be detained; "Operational Blacks" were those who, though "White", were not allowed to return to their homes because they had unavoidably seen or might see Allied dispositions, which information would be of value to the enemy; "Greys" were those considered to have been imbued with enemy propaganda to an extent which would be a liability to security if released; "Blacks" were irreconcilables who were a danger to security and must be locked up. See "Classification of Suspects", in Principal Civil Affairs Directives for BMA of Malaya, 6 Aug. 1945, in W0220/565.

Willan questioned each of the pre-war Sultans to determine their attitudes towards the Japanese. The attention paid to the question of collaboration can be established from the following extract of Willan's report of his interview with Sultan Ibrahim of Johor:

> The Sultan went on to say that whatever speeches he had made during the Japanese Occupation had been done on their orders. They always composed his speeches and he had merely been used as a mouthpiece as ordered by them.... All the Sultans had been forced by the Japanese to contribute 10,000 dollars to the Japanese cause and they had done so on orders, not voluntarily. To sum up, Col. Hay [the Senior CAO for Johor] and myself came away with the impression the Sultan was delighted that the British had come back, and that he had disliked the Japanese intensely. He appeared to have no guilty conscience when the question of collaboration with the Japanese was mentioned. He was undoubtedly satisfied with the setting up of the BMA.[6]

Willan remarked in the same report that he did not think MacMichael's future mission would face any problem from Sultan Ibrahim: "I would say that if the policy of the British Government is to proceed with the new constitution and the necessary new treaties, the sooner the Sultan of Johor is approached in his present state of mind the better."[7] In a later telegram to SEAC and to the Colonial Office, Willan said that he had forgotten to mention that during the interview Sultan Ibrahim was "very nervous" of the Chinese resistance forces in his state. They were said to be causing "a lot of trouble" to Malays. Willan's telegram continued:

> It is obvious from the way he spoke that he had no idea that the Force 136 element of the Chinese Resistance Forces is officered by British officers. He [the Sultan] said that if the BMA would authorise him he would arm 20,000 Malays to quell the Chinese. I informed him that he should do nothing.[8*]

Willan interviewed Sultan Abu Bakar of Pahang on 28 September. He described the Sultan as "being nervous" when he was encouraged to talk of his experiences during the Japanese occupation. The Sultan

---

* In raising the issue of the Chinese resistance forces, Sultan Ibrahim appears to have been testing Willan's attitude on the Malay-Chinese conflict, which was not raised during the interview.

stated that he had kept aloof from the Japanese as much as possible and had only contacted them upon orders, which he could not refuse. From all reports that he had received, Willan said that the Sultan had in no way actively collaborated with the Japanese.

> Force 136 during the time they were operating in Pahang spoke well of the Sultan's conduct during the Occupation. The Sultan said his speeches had been composed by the Japanese. He was genuinely pleased at the British return.[9]

When Willan had satisfied himself that each of the pre-war rulers whose legitimacy was not in doubt had not actively collaborated with the Japanese, he extended nominal recognition to each ruler. In this way he extended nominal recognition to first the Sultan of Johor, then the Yam Tuan of Negeri Sembilan, the Sultan of Selangor, the Sultan of Perak, and the Sultan of Pahang. Each Sultan was told that as a result of the BMA, neither he nor his state council could function, but each would be paid a monthly allowance at pre-war levels.

On 14 September, at the royal town of Kelang, just before he interviewed the pre-war Sultan of Selangor, Tengku Sir Hishamuddin, Willan arrested the Japanese appointee, Tengku Musa-Eddin, and exiled him to the Cocos Islands. In order to counter rumours, which he feared would spread quickly, he released a terse press communiqué on the arrest, in which he explained that Tengku Musa-Eddin had been installed by the Japanese, but had already been passed over before the war in the succession of the Sultanate of Selangor with the approval of the British government. When Willan met Tengku Sir Hishamuddin, the latter was so overcome with joy that he had tears in his eyes and could not express himself for a few moments. After receiving Willan's warm regards, he disclosed that some of the Malay notables had been loyal to him. On discovering that Musa-Eddin had possession of the crown, Willan promised to recover it. Willan, in extending nominal recognition to Tengku Sir Hishamuddin as Sultan, told him he could not carry out any of his royal functions during the BMA. The Sultan said he understood and was pleased that the British had returned.[10]

Willan's encounter with, and treatment of, the remaining four Japanese-appointed rulers was somewhat different. The Raja of Perlis, Tengku Syed Hamzah, voluntarily relinquished his office after encountering hostility from Willan during their meeting in Perlis on 17 September. Willan's attitude towards him, like his attitude towards Tengku Musa-Eddin, was influenced by the pre-war British policy of favouritism. His handling of Tengku Syed Hamzah reveals this clearly:

> There had been adverse reports about Syed Hamzah by successive British Advisers in Perlis. I asked Major Burr [Force 136 officer in Perlis] the whereabouts of Syed Putera, who in April 1938 was, on proposal of the Raja, nominated as *Bakal Raja*, i.e., heir or prospective successor of Raja, by votes of all members of the State Council except Syed Hamzah who did not vote but pressed his own claims in opposition to those of Syed Putera. Major Burr said Syed Putera was living in a small shack near the railway station ....
>
> Syed Hussein, younger brother of Syed Hamzah, then told me that Syed Hamzah wished to write a letter stating he had abdicated from the position of Raja. I replied that if Syed Hamzah wished to write a letter I would take it back with me but it must be understood that he did so of his own volition and not by any request or order of mine. I added that in any view Syed Hamzah could not in any case abdicate from a position he had never legitimately occupied.[11]

When he had found and interviewed Tengku Syed Putera, Willan extended the BMA's nominal recognition of him as the Regent of Perlis. Willan sanctioned that he be paid the pre-war Raja's full monthly allowance of $6,000. He described Tengku Syed Putera as an intelligent young man and pro-British.[12]

Willan told Sultan Ibrahim of Kelantan and the other rulers that the BMA could not recognize any Sultan who had been appointed during the period of the Japanese occupation. He also instructed them to cease flying their personal royal flags. When Willan met the Sultan of Kedah, Tengku Badlishah, he addressed him as Regent, the title he held before the war. As further indication that he approved of him, Willan sanctioned that he be paid the pre-war Sultan's allowance of $6,000. However, Willan adopted a hostile attitude towards the Sultan of Terengganu, Raja Ali, because of military intelligence reports describing him as "grey" and alleging that he had committed certain discreditable acts (not specified) during the Japanese occupation. But since Willan was not empowered to remove him, he was granted nominal recognition. His state council however, deposed Sultan Ali on 5 November 1945, just before MacMichael visited the state. The reconvening of the state council was improper, as it had already been suspended by the BMA in a proclamation, yet Mac-Michael and the BMA recognized its decision later. The decision to remove Sultan Ali was widely believed to have been inspired by the BMA, but the state council explicitly denied any BMA interference. It gave the reason for his removal as "certain crimes" committed by Sultan Ali during the Japanese occupation which rendered him unfit to be Sultan. His younger brother, Tengku Ismail, or the Tengku Raja Paduka, younger brother of the dead Sultan, replaced him.[13]

The Malay Elite Demoralized

The confidence of the Malay aristocracy was badly affected by the BMA's suspension of state councils and the interviews Willan had conducted with the Sultans. As Willan moved from state to state, uncertainty developed among the Malay aristocrats with regard to their respective ruler's position. At each interview Willan had forbidden the Sultan's court advisers to attend. Willan's confirmation or deposition of a ruler led to divisions within court circles. Sultan Ibrahim of Johor, before being confirmed ruler by Willan, made the most surprising comment to Willan that "the only person he knew who had collaborated with the Japanese" was his Mentri Besar, Ungku Aziz, whom he described as "90 per cent pro-Japanese".[14] He also told Willan to watch his brother ruler, the Japanese-appointed Sultan of Selangor, Tengku Musa Eddin. Sultan Ibrahim was reported to have said that Sultan Musa-Eddin had been asked by the Japanese to kill his brother, Tengku Sir Hishamuddin, but "the only good thing about Musa-Uddin was that he refused to do so".[15] Sultan Ibrahim's behaviour, if correctly reported by Willan, should be understood as either an attempt to win official favour from the BMA or a continuation of his frequent disagreements with his volatile Mentri Besar. In Selangor, and in Perlis, a realignment of loyalties followed within court circles. In Terengganu, Willan's hostility to Sultan Ali soon led to court intrigues, and the state council met, apparently under the inspiration of the BMA, to oust him.

The Malay aristocracy was clearly divided and weakened by the stigma of collaboration, which hung over the heads of rulers and Malay notables who held high office. In addition to Ungku Aziz of Johor, the Mentri Besar of Kelantan, Datuk Ahmad Nik Kamil, was another under a cloud of suspicion.[16] Investigations into the conduct of other Malay aristocrats were reported from time to time.

Like the Malay aristocracy, the Malay bureaucracy was also badly affected by the BMA's attitude towards collaboration. Willan had told Sultan Ibrahim during their interview:

> ...It would be one of the duties of the BMA to enquire into the conduct of Government servants and State notables during the Japanese Occupation. Their continued employment would depend on whether they had collaborated with the Japanese. I explained that a policy of clemency would be adopted but, at the same time, ringleaders of collaborationists would be brought to justice and punished.[17]

As a result of the investigations a reaction set in, and senior Malay civil servants came to feel rebuffed and disillusioned. The wounding enquiries prescribed for the detection of those who had collaborated with the Japanese, and the resultant delay in making full and immediate use of recovered officials, were felt to spring from an underestimate of Malay loyalty and ability.[18]

Thirdly, the Malay Police Force had disintegrated. A BMA enquiry revealed that the force was "the only public service of Government which has completely fallen down as a result of their activities under the Japanese rule".[19] Since the post-surrender rise of power of the Chinese guerrillas, all manner of reprisals had been carried out against active members of the police force. Many Malay policemen had been killed and kidnapped. As a result of these retaliatory actions by the Chinese the police force was utterly discredited and demoralized. Most policemen were afraid to show themselves outside stations or barracks, and police work and duties generally were non-existent. The BMA concluded that this state of affairs was likely to continue for some time, and that the police could not resume their normal duties until the situation altered and the animosity that the Chinese community had for the Malays lessened. The BMA realized that they had to build up the police force quickly, because, without it, law and order at the local level would not prevail. It was decided to act in two ways: (1) to raise public confidence by weeding out suspected collaborators and appointing new officers under British officials; and (2) to instil self-confidence and self-respect in the police officers and men by making transfers of state police personnel. For instance, officers and men drafted into the police depot from Perak were to be sent to Negeri Sembilan or one of the other states in which they had not served for some years.[20]

However, there did not seem to be any systematic recruitment of Chinese into the police force.

Investigations began on suspected Malay police involved in the racial clashes in Batu Pahat, Muar, and Johor Bharu. It was decided that until all the bad hats had been weeded out, the police would not be re-armed. Major A.J.A. Blake, the Civil Affairs (Police) Officer in Batu Pahat, reported on his investigations:

> I have found the feeling against the Malays here was so strong that I had to make a plunge and do something about it. I held an identification parade of all the Police and one by one the people whose husbands, father, etc. had been slaughtered by the Police including one Sergeant were picked out on specific charges of Murder so I have them all in custody. I hope to finish brief details against each charge by tomorrow morning and bring the accused down to Johor Bahru in the afternoon for trial there.[21]

These arrests were being carried out after widespread Chinese demand for action against collaborators, especially from left-wing Chinese newspapers and organizations. Special courts were set up in Singapore and in major towns in the Malay Peninsula to deal with collaboration offences.* Suspects were not confined to Malays. But prosecution, as had been foreseen by the BMA, was a difficult problem. A large proportion of cases had to be withdrawn for lack of sufficiently reliable evidence. Many accused persons had to be released when it was established that accusations were being made with little foundation and frequently for motives of personal spite. By January 1946, complaints of collaboration under investigation in the peninsula numbered 1,393, though roughly half the cases, which came up before the special courts for investigation were dismissed.[22]

Politically, the Malays were in limbo. Many KMM activists during the Japanese occupation were apprehended, such as journalists A. Samad Ismail and Ramli Haji Tahir in Singapore, and others like Idris bin Hakim and Mohamed Sidek in Kuala Lumpur.[23] Ishak Haji Muhammad, Mustapha Hussein, and other KMM leaders who

---

* These special courts were set up because in the early months, the police could not cope even with ordinary crimes. If the special courts found that a *prima facie* case was established, a further preliminary enquiry was held before a district court, after which the accused could be committed for final trial by the appropriate superior court. Donnison, *British Military Administration in the Far East*, p. 303.

had gone into hiding appeared on "arrest on sight" lists of the Field Security Section:

> Look out for the following members of the KMM. Hassan bin Abdul Manan. Javanese-born, Selangor Malay language teacher. Believed in Java. Ishak bin Haji Mohamed born Pahang some time in Malay Administrative Service, former editor *Warta Malaya*. Believed in Temerloh, Pahang. Mustapha bin Haji Hussein vice-president of KMM, born Perak lecturer Serdang Agricultural School. Believed in Ipoh 20 August under protection of Professor Itagaki....[24]

Mustapha Hussein was subsequently taken into custody, but several months later after petitions were made to the BMA from former members of the Malay Regiment whose lives he had saved from the Japanese, he was released. Ishak Haji Mohamed, however, went into hiding and was able to emerge two months later without being arrested.[25] Ibrahim Yaacob's name also appeared on the wanted lists, but the Field Security Section had learnt from the Kempeitai that Ibrahim, accompanied by his wife, brother-in-law Onan Haji Siraj, and Hassan Manan, had fled in a Japanese military aircraft to Java, where it was believed that he had contacted the Indonesian leader Sukarno.[26]* The KRIS movement, inaugurated on 17 August with Dr Burhanuddin AI-Helmy as chairman, had gone underground. The leaders of this movement were quietly surveying the political situation to see how far the BMA would go in punitive action against collaborators. They would be the first Malay group to make a re-entry into politics — with the assistance of the Chinese-led MCP.

Resurgence of Malay Nationalism

On 10 October 1945 the Secretary of State for the Colonies announced in the British Parliament the details of the Malayan Union policy. The statement was carried in full in the local newspapers the following day. Briefly, the British government proposed to negotiate fresh agreements with the Sultans for the purpose of creating the Malayan Union, which would consist of the nine Malay states and

---

* British intelligence feared that, even though Ibrahim Yaacob had left the country in August, he was likely to remain in contact with his comrades in Malaya by means of couriers. There had been several reports of small parties of Indonesian agitators from Sumatra infiltrating into Singapore, Malacca, and Taiping.

the British settlements of Penang and Malacca. Singapore would be governed separately as a Crown Colony. The new agreements would enable the British monarch to "possess and exercise full jurisdiction" in the Malay states.[27] The British government appointed Sir Harold MacMichael as its special representative to conduct negotiations with the rulers for this purpose. When the British monarch possessed jurisdiction, it was intended by Order-in-Council to constitute the Malayan Union. It was also announced that while Malays would automatically become Malayan Union citizens, non-Malays could be eligible for it on the basis of birth or a suitable period of residence. As citizens, they would enjoy equal rights with Malays.[28]

The statement in the British Parliament was timed so that MacMichael arrived in Malaya the day after it was made. On 18 October he held his first interview with the Sultan of Johor, virtually following the same route Brigadier Willan had traversed the previous month. Like Willan's interviews, MacMichael's also followed a pattern. He sounded out each Sultan for his views on the Malayan Union policy. When he was satisfied that the Sultan would sign the new agreement, MacMichael handed him a secret memorandum from the Secretary of State for the Colonies, explaining the Malayan Union plan in greater detail.

The memorandum gave assurances that the other races would not submerge the Malays. Side by side with the Malays, it said, the other races whose real identification was with Malaya would be able to reap the reward of their loyalty, for Malayan Union citizenship would carry with it the qualification for public and administrative service in the union. "This will strengthen the Malays and the country," the memorandum reassured. "Great Britain has learnt the richness of such an infusion of new blood and talent and it is one of the foundations of her strength."[29] The Malayan Union would have a legislative council, which would include, besides the governor of the union, official and unofficial members, nominated by the governor. There would also be an executive council. In deciding to establish this system, the British government had constantly borne in mind "the special position of the Malay Rulers as traditional and spiritual leaders of the Malay people".[30] Each ruler would be provided with an advisory Malay council to be presided over by the ruler. It would not only have the task of reviewing all legislation relating to the Islamic religion but also on other matters with the agreement of the governor. The dignity and prestige of the rulers would be fully maintained; so too would the policy to "safeguard the rights of the Malay people in matters of land reservation and in their facilities for education and progress".[31]

MacMichael gave each ruler two days to digest the document and make comments. They were asked not to reveal the details of the document to anyone. Each ruler was also made to understand that at their next meeting he was expected to sign the new treaty, transferring jurisdiction in his state to the British Crown. If he refused, MacMichael was empowered to refuse him official recognition. When each ruler had signed the new treaty, he was asked to promise that he would not disclose to anyone privately or publicly what he had done. This disclosure was to be the prerogative of the Secretary of State for the Colonies.[32]

It is clear that MacMichael had used, and was authorized to use, coercion to achieve the purpose of his mission. The Secretary of State for the Colonies, G.H. Hall, in a secret memorandum to the British Cabinet, had stated that he would accept nothing less than full compliance from the Sultans in transferring their jurisdiction to the British Crown. Hall said:

> ... We cannot allow ourselves to be deterred by an obstinate attitude on the part of any or all of the Malay Rulers with whom Sir Harold MacMichael will have to deal in his forthcoming mission. I regard it, however, as very essential, quite apart from the matter of publicity, that His Majesty's Government should now affirm their intention to carry through, in spite of obstruction on the part of any particular Malay Ruler, the policy which they have approved [i.e., the Malayan Union plan]. All our plans for the Malay States depend upon the success of Sir Harold MacMichael's efforts to secure jurisdiction in each and all of the States....[33]

Although MacMichael did not raise the question of British recognition of each ruler at every interview, the rulers themselves knew of the threat that hung over their heads. Willan had already done his groundwork well. The impact of Tengku Musa-Eddin's arrest and deposition, the voluntary resignation of Tengku Syed Hamzah as the Raja of Perlis, and the Terengganu state council's moves to oust Raja Ali were all examples of BMA power and manipulation, which could be applied to any recalcitrant ruler. Most of the rulers later claimed that they were intimidated and, fearing to lose their thrones, had signed the new treaty MacMichael presented.[34]

With the exception of the Sultans of Johor and Selangor, the other rulers were tough going for MacMichael. The strongest opposition came from the Regent of Perlis, the Sultan of Kedah, and the Sultan of Kelantan — the rulers who had yet to be officially recognized by the British government. It is significant that MacMichael sought Colonial Office approval on the appointment of Sultans only in regard to four states — Tengku Badlishah, the Regent of Kedah; Tengku Ibrahim, the Raja Kelantan; Tengku Syed Putera of Perlis; in the case of Terengganu, MacMichael considered the incumbent, the Japanese-appointed Raja Ali, as unsuitable and favoured Tengku Paduka, brother of the late Sultan.[35] This request for Colonial Office advice and approval indicates that conferring of official recognition, as a means of manipulation was to apply only to these four rulers and not to the others. In the end, MacMichael found that he needed to formalize only two appointments — the election of Tengku Syed Putera by his state council on 3 December and the installation of Tengku Paduka as Sultan of Terengganu on 19 December. Willan's appointment of the Regent as the Sultan of Kedah and his nominal recognition of the Raja Kelantan as the Sultan of Kelantan were accepted. It would seem that the question of extending formal recognition was a very arbitrary one — to be used whenever convenient to suit MacMichael's purposes. During the stormy sessions he had with the Sultan of Kedah who refused to sign the agreement Mac-Michael presented him, he reminded the ruler that he had not yet been recognized. "Perhaps", MacMichael is reported to have said, "Your Excellency would prefer to return to your friends in Siam?"[36] Visibly upset, the ruler signed, under protest. After that, the question of recognition was not raised again.

MacMichael accomplished his mission by collecting the signatures of all the nine Malay rulers. The Malay subjects of the rulers did not immediately know the behind-the-scenes pressures and arm-twisting that he had resorted to. However, on 15 December, a week before he concluded his interviews with the rulers, MacMichael was met in Kota Bharu by a peaceful demonstration of Malays opposing the Malayan Union. As news of some of his methods of coercion on the rulers spread, the Malay demonstrations increased in size and force. The Malay campaign against the Malayan Union will be dealt with after the following discussion of the Malay Nationalist Party.

The Malay Nationalist Party

It was in the wake of the inter-racial clashes and the announcement of the Malayan Union plan that the wartime radical pro-Indonesian groups were invited by the MCP to come out into the open and enter into a united front alliance. These groups, still obsessed with the idea of *Indonesia Raya*, were keen to continue with their unfinished struggle at the end of the Japanese occupation. The Indonesian revolution was now underway, and these Malay radicals were hoping that they could arouse widespread Malay support for their cause. The MCP appears to have become aware, too, of its need to rally some Malay support in view of the increasing Malay-Chinese tensions throughout the country.

In early September, the MCP through a Malay or Indonesian communist named Moktaruddin Lasso, initiated efforts among a group of non-communist Malays on the staff of the Ipoh newspaper *Suara Rakyat* (Voice of the People) to form a Malay political party. The newspaper's editor, Ahmad Boestamam, was asked to convene a meeting for this purpose by Moktaruddin, who had earlier contributed some money towards the newspaper on behalf of the MCP. Moktaruddin did not tell the editor and his staff where the money came from, but the latter guessed it was from the MCP because Moktaruddin was in the MPAJA.[37]

To this meeting Moktaruddin brought his leftist friends Arshad Ashaari, Baharuddin Tahir, Rashid Maidin, and Abdullah C.D. Arshad Ashaari proposed the name of the new party as Partai Sosialis Malaya (Socialist Party of Malaya). Ahmad Boestamam suggested the Partai Kebangsaan Melayu Malaya (Malay Nationalist Party of Malaya), the name bearing a similarity with Partai Nasional Indonesia (Indonesian Nationalist Party) of Sukarno, whom Boestamam admired greatly. Boestamam's proposal won the day. The meeting elected Moktaruddin as *pro tem* chairman, Dahari Ali, a friend of Boestamam, as secretary-general and Arshad Ashaari as treasurer.

The MNP's inaugural congress was held on 30 November 1945 at Ipoh. There the party's eight-point programme was produced and adopted. It was similar to the MCP's eight-point programme of 27 August except that in addition to the MCP's demands for the basic freedoms of speech and the press, the raising of the people's livelihood, increased wages, and reforms in education, the MNP also urged the fostering of friendly relations among the races, equal rights for all races, emphasis on the development of agriculture and the abolition of land taxes, and support of the Indonesian nationalist movement.[38]

The tone of the speeches was leftist. Many shades of Malay opinion were represented, however. There were even some members of Malay royalty, although all the rulers had declined invitations to attend. An official of the MCP-dominated People's Association, Chen Tian Wah, and a representative of the MPAJA, Fifth Regiment (Perak), addressed the delegates during the speeches of welcome, each urging Malays and Chinese to unite in the interests of the country's political advancement. These speakers also referred to the recent Malay-Chinese clashes, and said Malay-Chinese differences should be resolved amicably. The Malay communist, Abdullah C.D., also stressed the need for unity of all races in the fight against colonialism. It was reported, too, that one of the points made by a speaker (not identified) that to maintain that Malaya belonged only to the Malays was to disseminate narrow nationalism. A greater front incorporating other races was urged. Moktaruddin, who had been nominated as chairman, did not turn up.[39] Dr Burhanuddin, the acting chairman, made a strong speech advocating support for the independence movements in India, Indonesia, and Indochina, and proclaimed that Malaya must be considered a part of Indonesia, for the ultimate independence of which everyone was urged to work whole-heartedly.[40] The congress adopted the Indonesian flag as the MNP's banner. Resolutions passed by the delegates appreciated the principles behind the British government's Malayan Union policy, affirmed that the MNP desired to cooperate with all races in Malaya, and declared that Malaya was a division of the Indonesian state. Within the MNP's executive committee Moktaruddin was elected chairman, Dr Burhanuddin AI-Helmy (formerly of KRIS) vice-chairman, and Dahari Ali secretary-general.

There appeared to be two themes running through the congress. One was that of racial harmony and racial unity and the lack of any anti-Chinese or anti-MCP criticisms, which was presumably due to the MCP influence behind Moktaruddin. The other was the strong propaganda links with the Indonesian nationalist movement. It was reported that considerable communist propaganda had been dis-seminated during the congress, which was not favourably received by Malays present. Many of the MNP's supporters were former members of Ibrahim Yaacob's KMM and KRIS movement, which had advocated *Indonesia Raya* as the ultimate Malay ideal to check Chinese economic and political domination in Malaya. It therefore is difficult to see how the MCP could reconcile its own long-term aims with those of the MNP. There is no evidence to show that the predominantly Chinese MCP had given any support to the idea of a proposed union with Indonesia. In fact, after the congress, there was reported to be a pronounced uneasiness among the Chinese, who regarded the proposed union with Indonesia with much disfavour, as it would place them in the undesirable position of a minority in an Indonesian-dominated state.[41]

The MNP's support of the Malayan Union policy seems a curious aberration in Malay thinking. There are two possible explanations for the MNP's support of the Malayan Union. One is the radical and republican nature of the MNP leadership. Yet they knew that the Sultans retained the traditional loyalties of most Malays, which was presumably why they had extended invitations to the rulers to attend the congress. It was possible that these radicals thought the KMM connections with some of the rulers during the Japanese occupation should be exploited. It was also possible that they regarded the British removal of the Sultan's sovereignty as facilitating the creation of a republican state. The other reason was probably tactical, to make their re-entry into local politics by supporting a British policy which seemed favourable to them, thereby preventing any British action against themselves.

It was soon reported that the Kelang (Selangor) branch of the MNP decided on 8 December to sever all connections with the MNP at Ipoh.[42] The reason given was the strong communist influence at the Ipoh congress, which was not allowing the party to be truly representative of Malay opinion. Another reason probably was the MNP's support for the British Malayan Union policy, which, as we have seen had become increasingly unpopular with the Malay ruling class. A proposal to form a new party, the Malay Nationalist Party of Selangor (MNPS), was carried at the Kelang branch meeting on 8 December, despite strong opposition from one participant, Abdul Latiff, and from others with communist sympathies who had organized the original Kelang MNP branch. It was intended that the MNPS would be a political and social body covering the whole of Selangor state with the following objectives: to protect the traditional rights and religious dignity of the Sultan as the sovereign Muslim ruler; to encourage political and social reforms; to safeguard the privileges of the Malays; and to cooperate with the BMA in working for the development of ultimate self-sufficiency in Malaya. The branch committee included individuals from aristocratic and Islamic groups with strong anti-Chinese and anti-communist views.[43]

While this incident did not help the MNP's image, the role of Moktaruddin himself was a shadowy one. Moktaruddin appeared to be working for the MCP, but he was also at heart an ardent Indonesian nationalist. It was said he constantly expressed a strong desire to go to Sumatra to help the Indonesian guerrillas fight the Dutch.[44] Known as *Lang Lang Buana* (Javanese for the traveller) by his close MNP colleagues, he was described by British military intelligence as a former schoolteacher, a Moscow-trained communist, a disciple of Sukarno, the leader of the Malay section of the MPAJA, and a member of the MCP for the past three years.[45] Soon after the congress Moktaruddin disappeared and was not seen again in Malaya. His position as MNP chairman was taken over by Dr Burhanuddin Al-Helmy. In July 1946, British intelligence concluded that Moktaruddin was, in fact, the "notorious" Indonesian communist Tan Malaka.[46] It was believed that after the KMM leader Ibrahim Yaacob fled to Indonesia, his proposed plan for the linking of Malaya to Indonesia after the latter had proclaimed its independence was still to be pushed through. After Sukarno had proclaimed the republic, contact with Malaya was lost. Tan Malaka, however, visited Malaya and, in conference with the MCP organized the MNP.[47] There is a gap in information concerning the whereabouts of Tan Malaka in late September. He is known to have disappeared suddenly from Jakarta at this time, having met Sukarno, Sjahrir, and others during August-September 1945.[48] However, the available evidence seems to refute the claim that Tan Malaka was Moktaruddin Lasso, or vice versa.[*]

The Formation of UMNO

After MacMichael's return to London with the signatures of the Sultans on the new treaties, the Secretary of State for the Colonies

---

[*] In January 1981 the Malaysian government released a photograph of Moktaruddin Lasso in connection with a TV "confession" of MCP chairman Musa Ahmad who had allegedly defected to Peking in 1980. Moktaruddin was said to be one of the leading lights in the post-war Malay left-wing movement who had influenced him to support the MCP. Musa was then in the MNP.

presented to the British Parliament on 23 January a White Paper outlining details of the plan, which included the points in the secret memorandum MacMichael had earlier handed to each ruler.[49] It was the publication of this White Paper, which "changed the affair from a private conflict to a much-publicised open controversy".[50] It is not proposed to go over the details of the anti-Malayan Union campaign, as this has already been adequately studied by scholars, except to present some Malay (and, later, Chinese) perceptions of the Malayan Union, which set Malays and Chinese on different political directions.

The White Paper announced that MacMichael had successfully concluded treaties with the Sultans, in which they ceded full jurisdiction to the British monarch to enable the latter to legislate in their states. The purpose of MacMichael's mission had already been disclosed on 10 October, and therefore did not come as a surprise. What surprised the Malays was that the whole mission had been a *fait accompli* and had been done secretly and, in some cases, without proper consultations and approval of the respective Sultan's state councils. The deep resentment especially felt by the Malay elite throughout the Malay states to the Malayan Union plan was aroused by two main factors: (1) objection to transfer of jurisdiction to the British Crown and to the creation of the Malayan Union; and (2) the offer of equal status of Malayan Union citizenship to Chinese and other races.

The Malay press generally voiced strong criticism at the transfer of jurisdiction by the Malay rulers to the British Crown. *Utusan Melayu* of 24 January described it as "a blow for the Malay Rulers and their subjects". It refused to believe that the new agreements between the Sultans and the British government were made in a friendly spirit. In Kelantan, Kedah, Terengganu, Johor, and Selangor, thousands of Malays demonstrated and strongly protested against the Malayan Union plan.

Clearly, the second reason for the Malay opposition to the plan was the granting of equal citizenship rights to Chinese and other races in Malaya. *Seruan Ra'ayat* of 25 January 1946 declared, "The British Labour Government must realise that the giving of citizenship rights to all those domiciled in the proposed Malayan Union is an act of injustice to the Malays, the native inhabitants of Malaya." On 25 January a big demonstration at Alor Star affirmed that Malays did not want a Malayan Union if it meant, "sharing their inheritance with alien races".[51] This same point had been made by the *Seruan*

Ra'ayat on 24 January in a leader which energetically urged all Malays to do their best to preserve "our children's birthright so that they can hand it on to posterity as our forefathers handed it down to us". *Seruan Ra'ayat* said that this legacy was now more seriously endangered than it had ever been in the past and exhorted the Malays to strive "with all their might and main to preserve it".

Between September and December 1945, the Malay traditional leadership in the country had seemed weak and incapable of leadership. The Malays could only turn to the rural religious leaders like Kiyai Salleh in their struggle against the Chinese and the MPAJA guerrillas. The weakened state of the traditional Malay leadership was due to the stigma of collaboration with the Japanese, the terror activities of the MPAJU/MPAJA guerrillas and Willan and Mac-Michael's actions against the rulers. Even the non-aristocratic urban political elites in the KRIS were in hiding and did not dare to emerge until the end of November, when they formed the MNP with the assistance of the Chinese-dominated MCP.

In late December and early January, however, the traditional state leaders in response to the Malayan Union policy revived most of the pre-war state associations, such as the Persatuan Melayu Selangor and the Persatuan Melayu Johor.[52] Although these associations basically pandered to Malay state parochialism, there was now a realization that the strength of the Malays lay in their unity. With the exception of the radical MNP, which had given Malay nationalism a peninsula-wide appeal, no other group had yet done so. Just before the war the various state associations had discussed the idea of merging their associations into a pan-Malayan federation, but separate state feelings were so strong that they could not be submerged and the attempt foundered. Disgusted with this parochial bickering, radical young Malays led by Ibrahim Yaacob had formed the KMM, which made both a peninsula-wide, and an Indonesia-wide appeal to the Malays.

The more recent failure of the MNP to win any widespread Malay support to its pro-Malayan Union policy allowed rival groups of Malays to initiate their own peninsula-wide organization. In late November Datuk Onn and his small circle of friends, decided to overcome the causes of Malay weakness, which they attributed to ethnic, state, self-interest, and factional differences. They agreed that the Malays needed a national association, which could submerge all these differences in the interests of Malay unity. The group chose Datuk Onn to lead the Malays. On 3 January they set up the Pergerakan Melayu Semenanjung Johor (PMSJ, or the Peninsular Malay Movement of Johor).[53] It only required an opportune moment for Datuk Onn to make his entry into the national political limelight.

Two other Malay associations in Johor were the Lembaga Melayu Johor and the Persatuan Melayu Johor, but unlike them the PMSJ specifically aimed at higher goals than Johor interests. Its constitution stated that its aims were to unite the Malays, and to strive for and defend the special position and privileges of the Malays, so that they would "cultivate a love for their country, and cooperate with the Government and among themselves".[54] Within Johor, the movement would attempt to assure the security of Malays, as sporadic Malay-Chinese clashes were still reported in Batu Pahat and other areas.

British military intelligence, which was interested in this new party, reported that the aims of the PMSJ were, in fact, to unite the Malays of Johor to counter the policy of the MNP and to achieve the betterment of conditions of peninsular Malays. It said the party was gaining a strong following in Batu Pahat, as Datuk Onn had wide influence there as the DO.[55] A later report said his influence had now spread to neighbouring parts of Johor, chiefly the districts of Muar, Pontian, and Johor Bharu. Though no direct connections could be proved, British military intelligence attempted to identify a similarity of views and aims between Datuk Onn's party and other parties, which had recently sprung up among Malays in other states. It began to appear that the movement, under various names, was of very considerable extent. In Pontian and Johor Bharu it was known as Persatuan Melayu; in Pahang the Wataniah was thought to conform to Datuk Onn's party, and that he had conversations with its leader, Major Yeop Mahidin.[56]

After the PMSJ was formed, Datuk Onn openly broke with his former KMM colleagues in the MNP. As we have noted in Chapter 5, Datuk Onn had been critical of the KRIS movement and its form of Malay independence. Although he had been a member of KMM, he is said to have refused to join KRIS. British intelligence was doubtful of his anti-British tendencies, even though he had joined the KMM and been editor of Ibrahim Yaacob's pre-war newspaper *Warta Malaya*. In an interview with British intelligence, Datuk Onn said he was opposed to both the MCP and "Indonesian interests" in Malaya.[57] He said he had refused to join KRIS and that there was no question of independence in his programme. He regarded the Malays as "unfit at present to maintain a separate existence outside the sphere of British protection".[58] Datuk Onn further stated:

> My plan is to get Malays to put their own house in order and to keep away from communists and Javanese. Their affairs are no concern of ours.[59]

British intelligence was quite impressed by his statements, and thereafter was to urge for complete support of Datuk Onn and his party as a counter to the MNP. Their comments were:

> There is no reason to doubt the sincerity of his [Datuk Onn's] intentions. He wishes to improve the conditions of the Malays and their position in the country, and his plan is to start in the *kampungs* by persuading people to help themselves and to work for their own improvement. His opposition to communism and Indonesian interest is clear ....[60]

Although MNP officials, such as Ishak Haji Mohammed, made attempts to get Datuk Onn to work with them, his party, the PMSJ, refused to come together with the MNP.

The publication of the White Paper on 23 January, and the outcry, which immediately followed, gave Datuk Onn the chance he had been waiting for. He wrote a letter to the leading daily *Utusan Melayu* and to other Malay newspapers, which appeared on 24 January, and supported the idea advocated by the *Warta Negara* several weeks earlier, that a congress of Malays be held as early as possible not only to resolve differences which existed between the Malay associations themselves but also to discuss the fate of the Malays in the peninsula.[61]

The idea was very timely. Not only did it receive wide support from all shades of Malay opinion, including the MNP, but also the convening of the congress helped to check further divisions from taking place within Malay society. On 1 February a meeting of Johor Malays convened by the Persatuan Melayu Johor at Sultan Abu Bakar Mosque condemned Sultan Ibrahim for his unilateral signing of the treaty with MacMichael ceding the state's jurisdiction to the British monarch. Johor, like Terengganu, had written constitutions expressly forbidding the ruler to surrender the state to any other power or country. The anti-Sultan Ibrahim meeting was punctuated with cries of "Down With the Sultan!", a cry which had never been heard before by Malays. The anti-Sultan Ibrahim move was spear-headed by a close friend of Datuk Onn, Datuk Abdul Rahman bin Mohamed Yassin. Datuk Onn had been invited, and had originally said he would not attend. But suddenly, when the meeting was underway, he appeared and rose to his ruler's defence. He criticized the move to denigrate Sultan Ibrahim. His eloquent speech, however, failed to sway the gathering from voting in favour of the resolution to send a protest to the British government and also a protest to the Sultan for accepting the Malayan Union on behalf of the people.

But soon the momentum was lost. It is believed by one of the "conspirators", Dr Awang bin Hassan, that Datuk Onn must have been intercepted by M.C. Hay, the Johor Resident Commissioner, and came to Johor Bharu with instructions to save Sultan Ibrahim's throne for him.[62] Seven leading Johor Malays, all civil servants, who took a leading part in the anti-Sultan Ibrahim movement were thereafter suspended from government service by Hay, and barred from leaving Johor without Hay's permission. Elsewhere, in Selangor, Perak, and in other states similar Malay rumblings and protests were heard criticizing the rulers for ceding their respective state's jurisdiction to the British Crown, but in none did the movement reach the level it did in Johor.

On 1 March 1946, 41 Malay associations, including the MNP, from all parts of Malaya including Singapore, came together at the Sultan Sulaiman's Club in Kuala Lumpur. The ceremony was opened by the Sultan of Selangor and attended by senior BMA officials. It was an emotional ceremony, and the conference, which followed, was a success.[63] Datuk Onn was elected chairman. One of the resolutions was to form a pan-Malayan Malay political organization to organize a countrywide Malay opposition to the Malayan Union. It was to be called the United Malays National Organization, and was duly set up at the next meeting of the congress in Batu Pahat on 11 May. With the All-Malay Congress, Malay unity was achieved with the single purpose of frustrating the Malayan Union; and with the creation of UMNO this unity was consolidated and strengthened. For the first time the Malays had a genuine mass political movement that combined all the necessary ingredients based on traditional patron-client relationships. It was a movement supported by every key group of Malay society — the aristocrats, the radicals in the MNP, the lower rural leaders such as the *penghulu* and *ketua kampung,* the Islamic groups, businessmen, the civil servants, and the police and ex-servicemen.

The MNP had been forced by the tide of Malay resentment against the Malayan Union plan to attend the All-Malay Congress and to affiliate itself to UMNO. The MNP now became preoccupied with promoting race consciousness among the Malays, and in resisting the growth of Chinese political influence in Malaya. Symptomatic of this was its emphasis on Malay language, Islam, Malay special privileges, the position of the rulers, and also the adoption of the Indonesian red and white flag, the last because the MNP considered Malaya a part of a Greater Indonesia. It was over the issue of UMNO's flag, which consists of a *kris* within a circle set against yellow and green that the MNP withdrew from UMNO. The MNP leaders wanted the Indonesian flag to be UMNO's flag. It was in fact the MNP leaders' own political style and commitment to the Indonesian revolution which made them break with the conservative, aristocratic UMNO leadership under Datuk Onn. Their ideal of a Greater Indonesia was too radical, too republican, and far above the heads of the Malay peasant, while Datuk Onn and UMNO's appeal was set very much in terms of the traditional Malay society and current Malay fears of Chinese domination, and hence was more successful.

Chinese and MCP Perceptions of the Malayan Union Policy

The offer of Malayan Union citizenship as outlined in the White Paper would benefit about 1.6 million local-born Chinese, or 62.5 per cent of the total Chinese population in Malaya, who would automatically become citizens. Although this is based on the figures of locally born Chinese in the 1947 census,[64] which were not published until 1949, the British government must have roughly estimated the percentage of local-born Chinese in Malaya, based on projections of the 1931 census. Of the remaining 980,000 Chinese, or 37.5 per cent, who were born in China or elsewhere, many could qualify residentially for Malayan Union citizenship. It was this lot of 37.5 per cent Chinese whose case was to be championed by the MCP and various Chinese guilds and associations. Otherwise, the Chinese population was generally quite satisfied with the Malayan Union citizenship provisions, as indicated by Chinese press reactions.

The Chinese newspapers had no objections to voice against equal citizenship for all. In fact, they welcomed it whole-heartedly. Comments from the Chinese Press — *Sin Chew Jit Poh* and the pro-communist *Sin Min Chu* (New Democracy) of 24 January and the *Hua Ch'iao* (Overseas Chinese) of 26 January — ranged between scepticism of the Malayan Union's practicability and expressions of satisfaction about the proposed citizenship rights. All Chinese newspapers voiced resentment over the separation of predominantly Chinese Singapore from the Malayan Union. The *Sin Min Chu* of 24 January, however, stood out from the others as the White Paper's most vehement critic. It argued that far from enhancing the political status of Malayan people, the White Paper would only "consolidate Britain's hold on Malaya and Singapore". The *Hua Ch'iao* of 26 January was jubilant over the intention of granting equal citizenship rights to all. The Penang *Chung Hua* (China Press), however, was cautious in its attitude. In its issue of 24 January it said that the Chinese would have to make up their minds now about the question of their citizenship. Malaya is "the second mother country" of the Chinese but before they could apply for Malayan citizenship they had to recognize Malaya as their only mother country. It continued:

> If we want to have rights of citizenship in Malaya, we must either openly declare or quietly consent that we are separated from our mother country. We are still doubtful about the detailed contents of the White Paper, whether the people of Malaya are allowed to legislate their own laws or be allowed time to determine their status as to where they stand. We hope that such detailed contents of the White Paper can be made clearer in connection with these two points on the rights of citizenship, affecting Overseas Chinese.[65]

In short, the problem for most Chinese appeared to be simply a matter of choice. The Malayan Union proposals were favourable to the Chinese and had aroused sufficient interest among them. They were now eager to obtain further details of the scheme. Certainly, there were mixed feelings and doubts about what "Malayan Union citizenship" meant — a similar attitude also emerged in local Indian press reactions.[66] Many of the proposals of the Malayan Union were so ambiguous that it was impossible for the non-Malays to be really enthusiastic about the plan as a whole. Some scholars have described the general non-Malay attitude *vis-à-vis* the Malayan Union as apathy and indifference, in comparison with the outspoken and militant opposition of Malays to the plan. It is said that had the

Chinese been more enthusiastic and loud in their support for the Malayan Union, they might have been able to salvage many of the liberal citizenship terms offered therein.[67] It is debatable whether such Chinese support could have stopped the British giving in to Malay demands. More pertinent to an understanding of the political crisis of that time, however, is the fact that both Malays and non-Malays were dissatisfied with various aspects of the plan. This situation reflected a plural society in which each community jealously sought and fought for its own rights and was indifferent to the claims and rights of others.

At the time of the British return the leadership of the Chinese community in Malaya had passed, temporarily at least, to a younger generation of men and women in the MCP and in the MPAJU/ MPAJA. The old Chinese business leader or *towkay* had been discredited during the Japanese occupation. With the gradual return of some of the former Chinese business and community leaders, such as Tan Kah Kee, Lee Kong Chian, and Aw Boon Haw, who had been refugees in India, Indonesia, and Thailand, the pre-war Chinese associations were revived. Attempts were now made by these returned Chinese leaders to consolidate the strong bonds of ethnic unity, which had developed among the Chinese in Malaya when they faced the common Japanese threat. In these efforts the MCP was to lend its support.

Besides its conflict with the BMA, the MCP continued to pay attention to Chinese interests over those of Malays and Indians. On 24 October a Singapore MCP official, Wu Tian Wang, expounded the MCP's position on the question of Chinese unity and multi-racial unity. He said that the party believed in multi-racial unity, but felt that each race in Malaya should also build up its own unity. At the same time they should all work towards inter-racial unity, cooperation, and Malaya's progress and prosperity. He welcomed the return of Tan Kah Kee from Indonesia and expressed the hope that "Tan Kah Kee will continue to be our leader in our present fight for democratic freedoms".[68] He urged the "Overseas Chinese" to unite with the other races in the struggle for self-government:

> The Overseas Chinese [Hua Ch'iao] contribution towards the liberation of Malaya can be said to be the greatest, for they have not only fought and sacrificed their lives but have also suffered most enormous losses materially and culturally. But they have now been almost excluded from the proposed constitution of self-government in Malaya. Overseas Chinese must all realise

that the constitution for self-government will decide the future interests of the Chinese economically, politically and culturally. Today, the interests of the Overseas Chinese are inseparable from those of the Malay and Indian brethren. Therefore only through the strengthening of cooperation and complete unity amongst the five million people of the different Malayan races could the establishment of a true and democratic self-government be guaranteed.[69]

The MCP's ambivalent position on nationality meant that it still had not resolved the question of how to make its struggle a truly Malayan one. By using the term "Overseas Chinese" (*Hua Ch'iao*) instead of the term "Malayan Chinese" (*Ma Hua*), which the MCP had preferred in 1940, Wu was pandering to the nationalism of the Chinese in Malaya. Apparently the movement towards Chinese unity, which had arisen during the Japanese occupation, and had been consolidated in mid-1945 during racial conflict was so strong that the MCP had to come to terms with it. Soon, however, the growing CCP-KMT conflict in China would be extended to Malaya and to cause a political rift among the Chinese.

The idea of Chinese unity in Malaya crystallized with the formation of the General Association of Overseas Chinese in Singapore on 24 February 1946. Its constitution declared that it would take a strong interest in China's politics and strive to check the civil strife between the CCP and the KMT and help them bring about peace and democracy. Locally, its major objectives were to promote racial harmony, eliminate the barrier of regionalism among Chinese, help the local government, and safeguard the interests of the "Overseas Chinese".[70] Although the White Paper had appeared on 29 January, the association had no comments to make on its details.

On 7 February, a week before the party's second showdown with the BMA, Lai Tek, the MCP's secretary-general, sent a telegram to the British Communist Party condemning the White Paper for perpetuating British colonial rule instead of granting self-government as demanded by the MCP. He again reiterated demands, which he knew the British Government was unlikely to concede:

Establish the Pan-Malayan Unified Self-Government with Singapore as the centre of control administratively and commercially. Formulate Pan-Malayan and unified democratic constitutions granting absolute freedoms of speech, publication, organisation, assembly, strike, demonstration, belief and civic liberty.

Safeguard and promote Malayan national economy and culture.

Stipulate Malayan citizenship on absolute equality enabling all domiciled peoples in Malaya above 18 years of age to become Malayan citizens.

Grant equal rights of vote, election and administration and equal opportunity in social and economic reconstruction to all irrespective of period of domicile, property, social status, education, sex and belief, with only the following two exceptions:

(a) Those who collaborated with and assisted the Japanese Fascists in administrative control;

(b) Those immigrants who came to Malaya during the Japanese Fascist regime.[71]

The details of this letter did not become public until 9 March, when it appeared in the party's English-language publication, *The Democrat*. By then the positions of the MCP and BMA had become totally irreconcilable. Although the party's militants were badly trounced by the BMA, Lai Tek's moderate policies had also proven to be unsuccessful. According to a 1948 MCP document, it was Lai Tek's 1945/6 efforts to postpone the revolution in Malaya, which led to his being unmasked and deposed. "His directing policy gave rise to dissatisfaction by his comrades, and at two meetings he was severely criticised," it said. "He was forced to escape because the post-war environment no longer afforded him the opportunity of putting his deceptive and traitorous tactics into effect."[72] As the MCP receded further into the background as an underground organization following the debacle in February 1946, its policy statements became increasingly irrelevant and unrealistic, as they failed to take note of the full consequences of the British concessions to the Malays in July 1946.

Postscript: British Government Gives in to the Malays

As the anti-Malayan Union agitation spread, gathering support not only among Malays in Malaya but also among MPs and former British civil servants who had served in Malaya — the "ex-Malayans" in Britain — the decision was taken to drop the Malayan Union plan. In taking this decision, the Colonial Office in London had also been influenced by the Malayan Union Governor, Sir Edward Gent, who took office on 1 April when the BMA came to an end.

Gent had said there was absolutely no prospect of Malay cooperation so long as the union plan stood. He advised London to reach agreement with the Sultans. He regarded the MCP and the MNP, as well as the Chinese and Indians in general, as being of little consequence.[73]

More details of the considerations, which led the Colonial Office to drop the Malayan Union, have become known due to the 'restricted' confidential British official records being opened after the 30-year ruling.[74] Certainly there were British fears, from the security point of view, that if the Malay campaign failed, the Malays might turn to Indonesia for leadership and thereby help the MNP to recover from its weakened position.[75] Between the traditional Malay aristocracy and the Malay radicals in the MNP, the British evidently preferred the former. Furthermore, the MCP's militant agitation had disillusioned the British; it appeared to be interested in creating trouble and chaos and seizing power, and posed a direct threat not only to British interests but also to the economic and political future of Malaya. Lukewarm support for the Malayan Union proposals from the Chinese in general was interpreted as indifference or a lack of interest in Malayan affairs. Like the Chinese, the Indians were also considered to be too committed to a home-land focus.

On 24 and 25 July the British Governor-General, Malcolm MacDonald, and Gent jointly held private conversations with the Malay rulers and UMNO representatives on the latter's joint draft constitutional proposals. During these secret talks both sides made key concessions. The British governors agreed to restore sovereignty to the rulers, recognize the special position and rights of the Malays and guarantee prospects of ultimate self-government to Malaya. In return, the Malays agreed to the British demand for a strong central government to ensure economic and effective administration of the country and were willing to discuss a common form of citizenship "which would enable political rights to be extended to all those who regard Malaya as their real home and as the object of their loyalty".[76] These principles formed the basis of discussions of a 12-man working committee, which the three parties set up. The committee comprised five British government representatives, four representatives of the Malay rulers, and two representatives of UMNO, including its president Datuk Onn bin Jaafar. The committee whose formation was publicly announced was authorized to examine the constitutional proposals put forward by the Malay rulers and UMNO and to work out in detail "fresh constitutional arrangements in the form of a provisional scheme *which would be acceptable to Malay opinion*".[77] In short, the British government had given in to Malay demands to abandon the Malayan Union plan. All that remained to be done was for the working committee to work out the details.

CHAPTER 11

Conclusion

The facts of history are... facts about the relations of individuals to one another in society and about the social forces which produce from the actions of individuals results often at variance with, and sometimes opposite to, the results which they themselves intended.

– English historian Professor E.H. Carr,
in *What is history?* 1976

The eventful period covered by this study — 1941 to 46 — is central to an understanding of post-war political developments in Malaya. It was during this time that the die was cast. This period marked the first real contest for political power in Malaya between Malays and Chinese — the two major races in the country. The privileged status of Malays as the indigenous people, which had been taken for granted before the war, was for the first time challenged during the Japanese occupation by Chinese communists, Chinese guerrillas, and supporters. But pre-1941 Malaya had already displayed how far apart the various races were. Because of their different economic, social, and political interests and status, they were only prevented from getting at one another by the British colonial regime. The danger signs of future conflict had appeared as British policies gradually aroused Malay resentment and led to a build-up of Malay nationalism. The Japanese occupation widened their differences further. As the occupation forcibly cut them off from China, Chinese residents for the first time were forced to look inwards to Malaya and to fight, lay down their lives and defend the country. It was this orientation that made them stake political claims, leading inevitably to a contest with Malays for power in post-war Malaya.

293

The Japanese occupation also led to a resurgence of Malay nationalism, especially through the KMM and its leader Ibrahim Yaacob. It led to an overall upliftment of Malay morale, confidence and political consciousness, which asserted itself not only in the Heiho, Giyu Gun and Giyu Tai, but also in the civil service, especially in the local district and village government. The occupation set the stage for the political contest between Malays and non-Malays for post-war Malaya — a contest that was in one sense inevitable, yet was also unintended or unplanned. The inter-racial clashes generated a momentum all their own and unleashed unexpected consequences.

Japanese repressive measures against the Chinese had led to a mainly Chinese resistance movement, the MPAJA, dominated by the Chinese-led MCP; their "pro-Malay" policy created an undercurrent of resentment and distrust among Chinese towards Malays. Malay cooperation made Malays appear a chosen instrument of the Japanese. Consequently, inter-racial conflicts developed as the MPAJA became distrustful of Malay villagers, government officials and policemen whom they regarded as collaborators — just as they regarded Chinese and other groups who worked or allied themselves with the Japanese.

The post-surrender interregnum allowed the MPAJA guerrillas to take over a large number of small towns and villages in the country following the withdrawal of Japanese troops from outlying areas. Although the MCP leadership had decided against forming a communist government and declaring a republic, the MPAJA guerrillas in many localities seem to have wanted to exercise the prerogatives of new power. In most cases they did it in a very crude and counterproductive fashion, focusing on settling scores against Japanese informers and collaborators, brandishing weapons, threatening people, and generally creating a mood of fear, even a reign of terror. Local MPAJA guerrillas thus expended their energies on secondary objectives and wasted precious political capital. Their short administration left an indelible impression on the minds of most people of how frightening communist rule might be. For Malays especially, fear and distrust of Chinese was intertwined with fear and distrust of communism.

The inter-racial clashes seemed inevitable when large numbers of Malays became victims of Chinese MPAJA killings. In retaliation, Malays by their own peculiarly unique methods of warfare, which combined traditional Malay martial arts, Islamic religious fervour, and faith in supernatural powers, successfully withstood guerrilla attacks and launched their own reprisals against Chinese communities. They were able to slaughter and terrorize Chinese villagers without check forcing survivors to flee to larger Chinese settlements for refuge. Neither Chinese villagers nor the MPAJA guerrillas could stop the attacks nor understand their fanatical force. The Chinese retreat, which occurred between May and August in Johor and Perak and also in other parts of the country from September to March 1946, demonstrates that the Malays had effectively countered the MCP/MPAJA's attempts at political domination in the country. In addition to being defeated militarily by the Malays, both the MCP and Chinese were also unprepared for politics in post-war Malaya. The MCP had not shed its Chinese character and Chinese were still unclear about their loyalties, while the British government's Malayan Union policy required them to shift their political orientation fully to Malaya. They were not yet ready to do this. For this reason, they did not give enthusiastic and full support to the policy, although apparently they stood to gain from it.

Malays saw the Malayan Union policy as a threat to their privileged status in Malaya and to their rulers' sovereignty and opposed the granting of equal citizenship rights to Chinese and other non-Malays. The anti-Malayan Union movement, organized by the Malay elite, successfully presented the British move as one favouring the Chinese at the expense of the Malays. The British capitulation to the Malay anti-Malayan Union campaign resulted in them making extensive concessions to Malay demands. The rights and privileges that the Malay rulers and UMNO secured meant that the Malays would inherit political power when the British finally left the country. Several factors had led to the British concessions. One was British fears that if Malay demands were not met, the Malays might accept union with Indonesia in order to resist Chinese and non-Malay domination in the country. There was also a British sense of injustice in their abrogation of pre-war treaties with the Malay states, in which they had previously offered protection and advice to the Malay rulers in all matters except on Islam and Malay customs. To introduce the Malayan Union the British had pushed the rulers aside in order to unify the Malay states and the Straits Settlements and centralize their administration of Malaya. But in their negotiations with the Malay rulers and the UMNO leaders, they finally were able to restore the rulers' sovereignty and secure their agreement to the idea of federation. This was also a turn-about by the

Malay rulers who before the war had rejected the idea of a wider federation.

There was British realization that the Chinese were still in a dilemma over their dual nationality, and that the Chinese problem had to be resolved gradually through a citizenship, which the Chinese would have to work out with the Malay representatives. There was also British disillusionment with the MCP's failure to fulfil its promises of cooperation in the BMA period; as well as surprise at the less than total enthusiasm of Chinese for the Malayan Union policy. In the first instance, one may say that the willingness of many British administrators to cooperate with the MCP was only skin-deep, as indicated by Mountbatten's lack of success in liberalization. In the second instance, the British failed to appreciate that the Chinese were not quite ready to give qualified endorsement to a Malayan Union citizenship. In any event, British agreement to restore the Malay rulers' sovereignty and curtail citizenship rights to non-Malays ensured that the pre-war privileged status of the Malays would be restored.

The MCP's failed position deserves a more critical look. Since its inception in 1930 the MCP had lacked Malay support. Predominantly Chinese, it had attempted but failed to reorientate the perceptions of its Chinese members to a Malayan situation and to the realization that without Malay and even Indian support its Malayan revolution would remain an essentially Chinese revolution. From September to December 1945, the MCP found the adjustment from the wartime armed struggle of the Japanese occupation to peacetime politics in BMA-administered Malaya extremely difficult. The party's members virtually were left to do whatever they liked due mainly to the lack of new, clearly defined objectives and to the continuing focus on wartime enemies of the party — the local Japanese informers and collaborators. The pursuit of revenge and rough justice had led to the continuation of the inter-racial clashes between Malays and Chinese. The guerrillas and MCP members generally treated Malays with distrust, if not with hostility.

Clearly, for the post-war period, the MCP lacked a liberal and far-sighted programme, one that would enable it also tactically to deal with the British. This resulted in the party dealing in piecemeal and half-baked fashion at different times. The 27 August policy had dropped the goal of a "Malayan Democratic Republic", and pressed for basic freedoms and the raising of living conditions. In November 1945 the party pressed for self-government but ignored national independence. It was always one or two steps behind political developments. This meant that it was unable to make any headway in its professed policy of cooperation with the British. These inconsistent policies were, in fact, manifestations of internal divisions in the party. A militant faction was opposing the ambivalent leadership of Lai Tek, the "arch-traitor". They had refused to endorse his call to cooperate with the British as British suppression of MPAJA and MCP activities increased and became overt. Beset with these internal problems, the party thus lagged further behind political developments following the "deal" between the British and the Malay rulers and UMNO to scrap the Malayan Union and replace it with a federation. Now realising the importance of coming to terms with Malay nationalism, it sought an alliance with the leftwing Malay Nationalist Party, but the MNP failed to secure for it any immediate political gains. Consequently, the MCP was left without any alternative solution other than that of a belated armed revolution from its militant wing.

In 1946, the Malays were the real victors in the political contest with the MCP/Chinese and the British. Their struggle seems to have gone through several phases with different elites emerging in each phase. At the beginning, under Japanese rule, the KMM non-aristocratic elite had risen to safeguard Malay interests. But when they fell from power, the role reverted again to the weakened aristocracy. However, when rural Malays were continually harassed and threatened by Chinese in the MPAJU/MPAJA, they discovered that neither the Malay aristocracy, the Malay bureaucracy, the Malay police force nor the Malay Giyu Gun were of much help. Every strata of Malay society seemed helpless in facing this new foe. Even the Japanese found it difficult to suppress or eliminate the Chinese MPAJU/MPAJA. It was by turning to their religion, Islam, that the Malays found their new leaders. They rose from the ranks of the local Muslim "holy man". Malays recovered from their state of despondency, frustration, and outrage to fight back against the MCP, the Chinese, and the British. Earlier setbacks and humiliations had only re-awakened their spirit of nationalism and resistance. They realized that they were in danger of losing their political rights, and probably sensed that the Chinese position was more vulnerable and therefore fought back. Malays discovered the need to sink their differences and to build up their unity. With this unity they were able to take on successfully first the Chinese and the MCP challenge, and then the British challenge in the form of the Malayan Union plan. UMNO was the key to their new unity. In contrast, the MNP's crusade for *Indonesia Raya* struck an irrelevant chord in the political temperament of the Malays, and to the more urgent Malay need to fight off the threat posed by the Malayan Union.

The Malay-Chinese clashes also meant that Malays would resort to widespread extremist violence if pushed. The long-term implications of this extremism were very great: the overall Malayan polity might always be held subject to ultimate Malay recourse to mass bloodshed. If so, then the Chinese would have to either accept this threat perpetually and make concessions whenever demanded, or develop their own capability to at least make the violent Malay option very debilitating. Otherwise, talk of pan-ethnic cooperation would usually be at Chinese expense.

What of the British position *vis-à-vis* the political contest between Malays and non-Malays? British policy concerning the interracial clashes was apparently one of stepping in where needed to restore order, but the fact that these clashes were allowed to drag on for so long (at least six months) casts some doubts about British ability to end the disturbances. The Malayan Union policy failed to stop Malays and Chinese getting at each other's throats, and, in fact, aggravated the conflict. British ambivalence finally gave way largely due to their fears that Malays would resort to more militant action and turn to the Indonesian Republic for support if the Malayan Union policy was not scrapped. Their decision to restore to the Malay rulers their sovereignty ensured that Malays would emerge victorious in the political contest for post-war Malaya.

Finally, a historian is tempted to conjecture with the help of hindsight on whether the post-war scene would have been any different if either the KMM or the MCP had seized that moment of history in the post-war interregnum to come into power. Such a conjecture may seem quite unfair on the two organizations concerned. The KMM's major weakness was the lack of initiative by their members in a moment of crisis, unlike the *pemuda* in Indonesia, who seized control of radio stations and key government buildings in many areas of towns in Java and in the other islands. The KMM leaned too heavily on the Japanese and on the Indonesians to achieve their goal of Malay independence within *Indonesia Raya* instead of on their own strength. The MCP, tied by a pact to the British, had been weakened by purges and led by a man with a record of collaboration with police authorities. Although its guerrilla army, the

MPAJA was willing to offer armed resistance to the British, the party's leader Lai Tek had denied it this role.

Even if these were missed opportunities for the Malay nationalists in the KMM and the Chinese communists and guerrillas in the MCP/MPAJA to strike out on their own paths to power and national independence, it is doubtful if the other group or ethnic community would have accepted the *fait accompli*. There was bound to be Chinese opposition to *Indonesia Raya*, just as Malays would have resisted a communist republic. Neither the KMM nor the MCP had the vital ingredient — Malay-Chinese unity or multi-racial unity as a whole — to forge a combined spirit of struggle for independence and national liberation.

The need for the different races in Malaya to think of themselves as one nation did not come easily. This only came about after a period of conflict and resolution. It was in the wake of the 1945/6 conflicts that a pan-ethnic Malayan nationalist movement was born. The first pan-ethnic movement for self-government was the united front forged between the MNP and the MCP, in the AMCJA-PUTERA* in 1946–8. From 1948 to 1955 the various races in Malaya would seek various formulae to achieve pan-ethnic co-operation and independence. Among those who would rise to champion such a cause was Datuk Onn bin Jaafar, who made the personal sacrifice of resigning his presidency of UMNO after its refusal to open its doors to Chinese and non-Malays. He formed the multi-racial Independence of Malaya Party to seek independence for Malaya, but it failed to get support from the various races. Eventually it was the Alliance of three ethnic-based parties — the UMNO, the Malayan Chinese Association, and the Malayan Indian Congress under the leadership of Tunku Abdul Rahman — that successfully negotiated with the British government in 1955 for independence.

Both UMNO and the MCA in 1955 adopted a compromise formula which has been described as the "historic bargain" — a "special position" for the Malays in return for citizenship for qualified Chinese and other communities, Malay as the national language, the Malay rulers as constitutional monarchs, Islam the official religion, and freedom for all races to practise their religions, customs,

---

* AMCJA (All-Malaya Council of Joint Action) consisted of non-Malays, while PUTERA was a Malay organization.

and languages. This agreement had become necessary to create national unity and demonstrate to the British that pan-ethnic co-operation was viable and that national unity and integration was their ultimate goal. However, since independence some Chinese groups have described the terms as "unequal and unfair" and they have asked that they be amended to enable Chinese and other citizens to achieve full equality of status with Malays.

The communist insurgency, which began in 1948, was financially expensive and socially disruptive, but proved to be a catalyst to national independence. It forced the British government to expedite self-government and grant independence and cultivate the non-communist elites of the three major races to deprive the communists of any political victory, which they feared might otherwise ultimately accrue to them. In 1955 the communist leaders were still in the jungle as hunted men trying to gain a foothold in the independence talks but rebuffed. On 31 August 1957 the UMNO-MCA-MIC Alliance government, which was elected into office in 1955, obtained independence for Malaya from the British government.

Achieving independence was one thing. Building a truly pan-ethnic society and nation was quite another, an effort that is still far from complete. The May 1969 inter-racial clashes demonstrated once again that a Chinese political challenge could result in bloodshed. The clashes were caused by a stalemate in the Selangor Legislative Assembly elections because opposition Chinese strength equalled UMNO's. The May 1969 clashes, however, have again reaffirmed the UMNO-MCA-MIC "historic bargain" as the corner stone of the new Malaysian nation. Whether the "bargain" will continue to form the basis of Malaysian politics and society indefinitely in the future remains to be seen.

APPENDICES

Appendix A

Translation of Memorandum entitled "Marai dokuritsu mondai" [On the problems of Independence for Malaya] by the Political Affairs Section, Ministry of Foreign Affairs, Tokyo, dated 20 February 1945

1.   It is expedient to grant independence to Malaya, Britain's former territory (except the four states, Kelantan, Trengganu, Kedah and Perlis which were incorporated into Thailand's territory by the Japan–Thailand Treaty of 20th August, 1943) by the most efficient measures taking into consideration the composition of its population and the former system of rule, etc. Accordingly problems concerning Malaya's independence are, in brief, as follows:

2.   Composition of Population

     According to 1936 estimates the total population of the British territory, Malay Peninsula (including the population of the previously mentioned four provinces which were incorporated into the territory of Thailand in 1943) was 4,694,166 and the racial composition is as follows:

     Malays: 2,095,217 (a little over 44.6%)
     Chinese: 1,821,750 (a little over 38.8%)
     Others: 777,299 (a little under 16.6%)

     Taking this year's population, the composition without the four provinces which were incorporated into Thailand is as follows:

     Malays: 1,210,718 (a little over 34.3%)
     Chinese: 1,699,594 (a little over 47.7%)
     Others: 651,948 (a little over 18%)

According to the above figures, apparently the main race in Malaya, excluding four provinces incorporated into Thailand, is Chinese rather than Malay and it is presumed that the old racial composition has changed little, even taking into account considerable population increases. Therefore, in granting independence to Malaya it is impossible to ignore the Chinese on population grounds alone, even without taking into consideration their economic activities. Out of the total population of Malaya in 1936, Malays and Chinese show a ratio of 57% to a little over 43% and in the 1941 census, a ratio of a little over 54% to a little under 46%. That is, the ratio of racial composition has hardly changed in those five years so that it is assumed that in the last eight years from 1937 up to the present, the figures have hardly changed or at least the rate of increase of the Chinese is greater than that of the Malays. These days, the present Malayan military government is starting to show signs of changing the policy enforced in the early stages of military administration and which had been claimed to stand for principles emphasizing the position of Malays, because it has become impossible to ignore the power of overseas Chinese merchants in various areas such as commerce, industry and labour.

3. The System of Administration under British Rule

Britain divided Malaya into three parts; the direct control area (the Straits Settlements), Federated Malay States and Unfederated Malay States. She ruled the Straits Settlements as her territory and the Federated Malay States and Unfederated Malay States as her protectorates. The difference between the above is not so clear but it seems to be a difference of the level of protection so that in recent times Malaya has not been really independent. According to the above conditions, it is difficult to grant independence to Malaya by repealing the present military government and replacing it with a new system of government. Therefore, in conclusion, the only alternative methods which can be adopted are as follows:

(a) To incorporate the four provinces, Kelantan, Trengganu, Kedah and Perlis into Thailand and the rest into China.
(b) Rule through the creation of a political organization with the cooperation of the Chinese, the main race in

Malaya, and Malays. (For instance, like Sino-Malay Mixed Administration)

(c) To make Malaya a state of a Federated Indonesia.

Source: Microfilm No. 16-30 in the Nishijima Collection, Waseda University, Tokyo. Also appears as Ms. Film 50, item no. 5 in the Wason Collection, Cornell University, New York. Translated by Mr Shun Ikeda of the Japanese Department, A.N.U.

Appendix B

Statistics of Casualties during the Resistance Campaigns (according to GSI Hq 29 Japanese Army)[*]

(a) *Under the Japanese 7th Army*

Japanese	Total	400	about 175 killed
Police		1,000	
Resistance Army		2,200	700 dead and 1,500 arrested

(b) *Under 29 Army: February 1944 to 14 August 1945*

	Dead	Wounded	Missing	Total
Japanese	15	20	5	40
Para-Military	--------- 16 ---------		—	16
Police	--------- 350 ---------		100	450
				506

	Killed	Arrested	
Resistance Army	150	400	550

(c) *From the surrender to 31 August 1945*

	Dead	Wounded	Missing	Total
Japanese	63	54	4	121
Para-Military	3	—	11	14
Police	--------- 31 ---------		357	388
				523

	Killed	Arrested	
Resistance Army	78	48	126

(d) *Consolidated Totals*

Japanese	approx.	600 casualties
Police		2,000
Resistance		2,900

Source: 25 Indian Division Weekly Intelligence Review No. 11, dated 28 Nov. 1945, enclosure in *MU Secret 335/46 Vol. 1.*

---

[*] The statistics for Johor are not included because Johor fell within the command of the Japanese 7th Area Army based in Singapore.

Appendix C

Statistics of Attacks made by the Chinese Resistance Army (15 Aug. 1945–31 Aug. 1945) (according to GSI Hq 29 Japanese Army)

State	Against the Army	Against the Police	Against the Railway	Against Cars	Against Factories & Stores	Misc.	Total
Perak	28	40	6	17	3	27	121
Selangor	10	5	3	10	5	5	38
Negri Sembilan	—	7	1	7	—	5	20
Pahang	3	5	—	1	1	4	14
Kedah	1	4	1	1	—	3	10
Malacca	—	4	—	2	—	—	6
Trengganu	—	—	—	—	—	1	1
Kelantan	—	—	—	—	—	1	1
Penang	—	1	—	—	—	—	1
TOTAL	42	66	11	38	9	46	212

Source: 25 Indian Division Weekly Intelligence Review No. 11, dated 28 Nov. 1945, enclosure in *MU Secret 335/46 Vol. 1*.

Appendix D

Statement of the Selangor State Committee
The Communist Party of Malaya, dated 27 Aug. 1945

A manifesto to the compatriots of the various nationalities of Selangor to celebrate the glorious victory of the Anti-Fascist struggle in the Far East and to materialize the present 8 principles of the Communist Party of Malaya.

Dear compatriots of all nationalities of Selangor.

On the 9th of August, Soviet Russia declared war on Japan, and on the 15th of the same month, Japan surrendered unconditionally to the Allies.

Hence, the Far-Eastern Anti-Fascist struggle has now achieved complete victory. The period of war and its horrors and atrocities has now passed. Peace prevails today in the Far East and in the whole world.

Let us celebrate this inestimably bright and glorious victory with our greatest jubilation. Let us applaud with loud cheers of joy and with zealous sentiments welcome the arrival of peace and freedom.

This grand victory is achieved through the merits of the Governments, Armies and Peoples of Soviet Russia, China, Britain and United States respectively; through the merits of the Japanese peoples, who are Anti-Fascist and Anti-war; and also through the merits of the Far Eastern Communist Parties, the Anti-Japanese armies and the peoples of the Far Eastern small nations. Therefore we must extend our highest and most respectful salute to those countries and peoples, who in these few years, have been ever persistent in the Anti-Fascist struggle. We must also bemoan deeply those fallen warriors who sacrificed their lives in the Anti-Fascist struggle.

The victory of the Far Eastern Anti-Fascist struggle is of great historical significance: —

(1) Wiping out the chief perpetrators of the Far Eastern war — The Japanese Fascists; ending the Far Eastern war totally; reducing the sacrifices and losses of the Far Eastern peoples and eliminating the calamities, pains and hardships of the Far Eastern peoples; all of which result in the Far Eastern peoples attaining peace and happiness as well as freedom and democracy.

(2) This is the first time that the domination of the barbarous Japanese has been overthrown. This will greatly encourage the struggling sentiments of the huge masses, strengthen their confidence of victory, and help and propagate the liberation movements of the Far Eastern small nations. These will make the liberation movements achieve victory easier, a victory both absolute and secure.

(3) Russia's entry into the Far Eastern war is the cause of Japan's unconditional surrender. This makes a change to the nature or characteristic of the Far Eastern situation, whence all the Far Eastern small nations are running along the path towards New Democracy, just the same as in Europe. The Far Eastern problem is not the singular affair of one particular country. It has become an international affair. Therefore, the Far Eastern problem will be settled in the forthcoming Far Eastern Conference.

Now the world situation has greatly changed: War has ended completely and absolutely; the era of fear and senseless slaughter has passed and mankind has achieved freedom, peace and happiness. Those evil perpetrators of war, who are instrumental in causing the destruction of the civilization of the world have now been liquidated. The peoples of the world are on the preliminary step towards establishing a New Society and a New World. The slave system of Fascism has been completely abolished. The peoples of every country of Europe, Asia, Africa and America had surged on the roaring tides of New Democratic Movements. New Democratic countries have been set up one after another. Small nations have achieved liberation and the peoples have attained freedom, peace and democracy.

Old generations have gone and passed. The history of mankind is on the threshold of a new generation. The peoples of the world have never before experienced such a day as today, so grand and glorious, so free and happy. This is the newest page in the history of mankind.

More than 3 years have come to pass, we, the five-million compatriots of Malaya had suffered indescribable calamities, hardships and pains under the barbarous domination of the brutal Japanese. Innumerable compatriots had been tortured and imprisoned, robbed, slaughtered, passed semi-starving and death-struggling lives, and rendered homeless. Innumerable aunties and sisters have been outraged, molested and raped and still more brothers had been driven to the battle-fronts to serve as cannon-fodders. However, every of these blood debts has now been settled. The tyranny of the Fascists has thereby ended.

Today Malaya is located in a new situation and in a new generation. New Democratic movements of the world have been widely circulated, and the new International Organization has approved the principles of democracy, self-government and human rights. The problem of Malaya has become a part of the International problem. All advanced countries of the world and their peoples will certainly help us. On the other hand, in these several years, the Communist Party of Malaya has from the very beginning been persistent in their struggle. Their capabilities and intelligence as leaders in the Anti· Japanese struggles have greatly won the zealous support of the compatriots. In these three odd years of painful struggle, the compatriots of all nationalities of Malaya have greatly elevated their struggling spirits and strengthened the unity of all the people.

As a result, the National Liberation of Malaya has obtained more beneficial terms, and is certain to be successful and victorious in the end. The future prospect of Malaya is unlimitedly bright.

In these three odd years, under very extremely painful and difficult conditions the Communist Party of Malaya, the Malayan Peoples' Anti-Japanese armies and the Anti-Japanese Unions have suffered undescribable pains, but for the welfare of all the compatriots of Malaya, they have never for a moment relaxed in their duty.

In these three odd years, the Communist Party of Malaya has led the compatriots of Malaya in innumerable struggles, frustrating every impudent intrigue of the enemy. The Peoples' Anti-Jap Armies have on several hundred occasions, engaged the enemy in big and small battles, in which the enemy suffered several thousand casualties. The Anti-Japanese Unions have educated and united the compatriots on a vast scale, and have helped them to settle many difficulties and disputes and have maintained the order of the respective place. All these are well known to the compatriots of Malaya.

Now that the Japanese have surrendered, the British Government will return to dominate Malaya. Under this new situation, we must clarify and stress to the compatriots of all nationalities of Malaya that WE, THE COMMUNIST PARTY OF MALAYA, WILL CERTAINLY SERVE THE NATION LOYALLY, WE WILL CERTAINLY CONTINUE TO LEAD THE COMPATRIOTS TO STRUGGLE FOR THE REALIZATION OF THE DEMANDS OR WISHES OF THE PEOPLE.

For the purpose of safe-guarding the interests of the compatriots and struggling for the realization of the new Democratic System of Malaya, the Central Committee of the Communist Party of Malaya under the new situation, hereby suggests the present 8 Principles to the compatriots of all nationalities of Malaya: —

(1) Support the Democratic Alliance of Soviet Russia, China, Britain and America. Support the new International Peace Organization.

(2) Materialize the Malayan Democratic polity. Establish organs of peoples' wish for the whole of Malaya as well as the respective States by universal suffrage of the various nationalities and Anti-Japanese organisations of Malaya.

(3) Abolish the political structure formed by the domination of the Japanese Fascists in Malaya. Abolish all Japanese laws and decrees.

(4) Practise the absolute freedom of speech, publication, organisation, public meeting and belief. Assure the legal position of all parties and organizations.

(5) Relinquish the old system of education and exercise democratic education with the respective national languages. Expand national culture.

(6) Improve the living conditions of the people; develop Industry, Agriculture and Commerce; relieve the unemployed and refugees; increase wages universally and practise the "8 hours" work system.

(7) Reduce the prices of goods to the level; stabilize the living conditions of the people; punish corrupt officials, profiteers and hoarders.

(8) Treat the Anti-Japanese armies kindly, and help the families of the fallen warriors.

We had suggested before "Establish Malaya into a Democratic Republic". Today we are not deviating from this programme, because it is the object of our struggle. We have been persistent for 20 years, because we want Malaya to be established into a Democratic Republic. But in order to cope with the demands of the present situation, we again suggest the present 8 Principles. These 8 Principles are to realize the preliminary steps of the Democratic Republic, because they are part of the requirements of the Democratic Republic.

Consequently we hereby zealously exhort:

Compatriots of all classes who love peace, protect the interests of the people with national conscientiousness. Strengthen the unity of all nationalities on a wider scale and establish a new juggernaut force. Support vehemently the present 8 Principles of the Communist Party of Malaya. With the fullest strength, struggle for the complete realization of these Principles. Double our energy and struggle persistently to realise the New Democratic System of Malaya.

All police, detectives and Government servants! The period of Japanese domination has now passed. You have previously betrayed the interests of the compatriots. Your crimes and misdeeds will not be considered by us now, unless you still possess National Conscientiousness, and repent sincerely for your past misdeeds. Henceforth, you must serve truly the interests of the nation. Love and protect the compatriots, and we will consider you as compatriots as well. We ardently hope that you will support the Principles of the Communist Party of Malaya in serving for the interests of the compatriots.

All robbers and gangsters! With the help of the enemy, you have previously committed innumerable infamous deeds. Now, Japan has surrendered unconditionally. We hope that you will earnestly repent for your past misdeeds, and we will not consider you as our enemy unless you love and guard the interests of the people; respect and consider the lives and properties of the people as well.

Britain is a member of the United Nations. We hope that the British Government will end their dominating policies on colonies; genuinely execute the decisions of the San Francisco Conference by giving "Self-Government" to the Malayan people, establish an organ according to the wishes of the people; practise democratic politics and wholly realize the 8 Principles suggested by us.

Dear compatriots of all nationalities! In these 3 odd years of Anti-Japanese Struggles, you have by your shining examples displayed the wonderful courage and gallantry of the Malayan people. Now, you should learn from the people of Europe, and keep up your gallant spirit. Our dear compatriots! The new generation has arrived, we must unite on a far wider scale, and form into files and fall in under the New Democratic Flag, struggle to the last.

Let us hail loudly:

ALL NATIONALITIES OF MALAYA!
BE MORE WIDELY UNITED!
MATERIALIZE THE 8 PRINCIPLES!
MATERIALIZE THE NEW DEMOCRATIC SYSTEM!
LONG LIVE THE FAR EASTERN ANTI-FASCIST VICTORY!
LONG LIVE THE PEACE AND DEMOCRACY OF MALAYA!

Issued by:
The Selangor State Committee
The Communist Party of Malaya.
Dated this day 27th August, 1945.

Source: Sel.C.A.162/45, 8.M.A. (Malaya), Arkib Negara Malaysia.

Appendix E

"Bandits Attempt to Disturb Peace of Malai:
Series of Serious Incidents Reported from All Parts of the Country",
Malai Sinpo, Monday, 3 September 1945

One of the biggest obstacles to the peaceful progress of Malai, since its occupation by the Japanese forces, has been the trouble constantly caused by bandits.

From the day it was announced that hostilities had ceased in East Asia these bad elements have been more active in Malai. That their depredations have been confined to a few incidents in remote parts of the country, is mainly due to the rigorous steps taken by the Japanese military, who have been entrusted with the maintenance of peace and order in the country till the arrival of the British forces.

The Japanese military authorities feel it their duty to the Malaian public to ensure their safety and an act of their good faith to the Allies to mete out severe punishment to these bandits. In the proclamation published on Saturday the Japanese army in Malai stressed that it would not permit the existence of such bandits, nor would the Allies when they come. These bandits, therefore, would be destroyed in the near future.

The public of Malai are strongly advised not to believe in the falsehoods circulated by the bandits but instead to co-operate with the Japanese Army to ensure the security of their homeland.

Should there be any who have been misled into joining the bandits, they are advised to come forward and to help in the preservation of peace and order for the sake of the happiness of the people.

BANDIT ACTIVITY

Since Aug. 15 there have been many cases of bandit activity throughout the country some of which are summarized below:

On Aug. 15 in the neighbourhood of Kuantan, 20 bandits attacked 12 police constables, several of whom were killed and wounded, but the bandits were repulsed with casualties and some ammunition captured.

On the same day in the suburbs of Kuala Lumpur, bandits attacked the house of Nippon-zin residents, but were repulsed, while 50 bandits wearing Nippon Army uniforms, attacked a factory in Batu Cape, Negri Sembilan, and made their escape after plundering some arms and other things.

Near Bentong, Negri Sembilan, on Aug. 17, 30 bandits made an attack. After some fighting they escaped leaving a prisoner. On the following day 10 others reappeared when one was killed and another arrested. 30 bandits who attacked the town of Bentong were repulsed, leaving a prisoner, and at Karaku, in the same state, several of them attacked the Sultan, and escaped without achieving their purpose.

At Rengam, also in the same state, a very powerful group of bandits attacked the police but were repulsed after many casualties. On the Japanese side the Shidekan and some others were killed and wounded. A Nippon-zin pedestrian in Furega (Negri Sembilan) was fired upon by bandits, but he gallantly counter-attacked and repulsed them.

At Ninberis, in Pahang, 15 Nippon soldiers repulsed a party of bandits who attacked them.

On Aug. 18 about 10 p.m. 10 bandits attacked the police station at Jerantut, and were repulsed after a 30 minute struggle. After reinforcing their number to 30 they attacked again and were repulsed a second time leaving behind several dead.

IN SELANGOR

At Kampong Gajah, in Selangor, 13 Nippon soldiers, including Sub-Lieut. Miyake were attacked, also labourers employed by the army at Rawang. At Batu Arang, a group of bandits attacked the railway station and the telephone and other materials were looted. At Kepong military engineers were attacked.

A group visited the house of Nissan Norin and Co, 3 miles south of Kuala Lumpur and demanded a lorry. A Nippon army unit went into action upon receipt of a message and repulsed the bandits.

At Telok Anson one group attacked the telephone exchange and another the police station at about 8 p.m. but after fighting they were repulsed leaving four dead and some arms and ammunition.

On Aug. 19 they attacked a motor-car belonging to the Pahang Government, 3 miles north of Mentakab, while another group carried out anti-Nippon propaganda among labourers in the same place.

Near Klang four constables were attacked by bandits and seriously injured. On the same day they attacked a police station in Malacca and the next day 40 bandits attacked the headquarters of the Volunteers Corps. They were repulsed by a crack police squad.

Near Runketua in Perak a powerful group of bandits encircled and attacked the police station twice. Receiving an urgent message a Nippon army unit rescued the police and repulsed the bandits. At Tanjong Toh Alang, two bandits surrendered after serious fighting.

At Nibong Tebal, in Kedah, a group of 30 bandits attacked the police station but all surrendered after a furious counter-attack.

The Asahan police station in Johore was attacked on Aug. 20 and on the same day a powerful armed group of bandits attacked the police station at Semenyeh but escaped without gaining their objective.

At Seremban 14 bandits attacked a Nippon residence in the day, but as a Nippon army unit took immediate action they escaped leaving four dead and two motor lorries. They repeated their attack on the Seremban police station without success.

On Aug. 21 bandits attacked the Tanks police station in Malacca and at Ketan Island, Selangor, they attacked the volunteer head-quarters without success.

A group of 100 bandits attacked the Kamotu-Syo at Rasa and escaped after receiving serious injuries. About 200 bandits attacked the barracks of the Indian National Army in Tapah, Perak. They attacked a Nippon-zin residence at Lahat and a Nippon civilian at Tindal.

The police station at Kuala Kangsar was attacked on Aug. 22 when they unsuccessfully demanded the policemen to deliver their arms. At Rimba Panjang, they destroyed the railway and a train crashed. All communications were destroyed checking transport. Senda and Co. at Kurankan, in Kedah was attacked.

At Mantin they compelled about 200 inhabitants to assemble and collected information from them. Sixty bandits on the same day and 40 the following day attacked Malai [Malay] villages at Sungei Ton, Sungei Man and three other areas in Perak.

On Aug. 23 seven bandits blew up a ferry on the Pahang river at Jerantut and 10 unsuccessfully attacked the Kati police station in Perak. The police stations at Bagan Serai and Parit Buntar were attacked on Aug. 24.

In addition to the above, an armed group of 100 bandits attacked merchants recognised by the Gunseikanbu and caused a dynamite incident at Kemanan, in Trengganu, kidnapping local constables.

In several punitive expeditions there were glorious deaths of Nippon-zin civilian officers, and casualties among local policemen. The local inhabitants are grateful to the Japanese military for the protection afforded to them.

NOTES

Chapter 1

1. Rupert Emerson, *Malaysia: A Study in Direct and Indirect Rule*, first published in 1937 (Kuala Lumpur, 1964), pp. 35–7.
2. For details on the peasant and modern sectors of the pre-1941 Malayan economy I have drawn heavily from Lim, *Peasants and Their Agricultural Economy*, pp. 21–7; Ness, *Bureaucracy and Rural Development in Malaysia*, pp. 28–39; and Emerson, *Malaysia*, p. 42.
3. Victor Purcell, *The Chinese in Malaya* (London, 1948), pp. 231–4.
4. For a good summary of educational policies prior to the Second World War, see the Malaysian Government's *Report of the Royal Commission on the Teaching Services* (Kuala Lumpur, 1969), pp. 15–6, and Ho Seng Ong, *Education for Unity in Malaya* (Penang, 1952).
5. William R. Roff, *The Origins of Malay Nationalism* (Kuala Lumpur, 1967), pp. 57–8.
6. I.K. Agastja (alias Ibrahim Yaacob), *Sedjarah dan Perdjuangan di Malaya* [History and Struggle in Malaya] (Jogjakarta, 1951), pp. 70–1.
7. W.R. Roff, "The Persatuan Melayu Selangor: An Early Malay Political Association", *JSEAH* 9 (Mar. 1968). See also Roff, *Origins of Malay Nationalism*, pp. 235–47.
8. Wang Gungwu, "A Note on the Origins of Hua-Ch'iao". Paper presented at seminar in the Department of Far Eastern History, Australian National University, 2 Mar. 1976.
9. Yen Ching Hwang, *The Overseas Chinese and the 1911 Revolution, with Special Reference to Singapore and Malaya* (Kuala Lumpur, 1976), pp. 154–6.
10. Wang Gungwu, "Sun Yat-sen and Singapore", *Journal of the South Seas Society* 15, 2 (Dec. 1959): 55–68; see also Yen, *The Overseas Chinese*, pp. 95–8.
11. Purcell, *The Chinese in Malaya*, pp. 214–6.
12. There seems to be some confusion in the MCP regarding the date of its founding. According to C.C. Too, the Malaysian government's psychological warfare expert, who had access to archival MCP documents, the

party had claimed on different occasions, the years "1930" and "1931" respectively as the years of its inauguration. He said one MCP document claimed, "in 1930 the South Seas Communist Party held its second congress during which the central committee of the Malayan Communist Party was inaugurated". On the other hand, a party booklet, issued on 1 January 1952, said, "On 1 July 1931 Malayan communists held their first congress under the leadership of the Communist International [Comintern] and officially founded the Malayan Communist Party." See C.C. Too, "Notes on the History of the Communist Party of Malaya", p. 137, in Tan Sri C.C. Too Papers, University of Malaya Library. Scholars generally regard "1930" as the actual date, but the party did not make a full recovery after a series of police raids in 1930 and 1931 until 1932.

13. Gene Z. Hanrahan, *The Communist Struggle in Malaya*, first published in 1954 (Kuala Lumpur, 1971), pp. 28–9, 31. A more detailed history of the MCP is given in Chapter 3.

14. T.H. Silcock and Ungku Abdul Aziz, "Nationalism in Malaya", in *Asian Nationalism and the West*, ed. William Holland (New York, 1953), pp. 287–8. See also Usha Mahajani, *The Role of Indian Minorities in Burma and Malaya* (New York, 1960), pp. 22–8; and Sinnapah Arasaratnam, *Indians in Malaysia and Singapore* (Kuala Lumpur, 1970), pp. 96–102.

15. Donald R. Snodgrass, *Inequality and Economic Development in Malaya* (Kuala Lumpur, 1980), p. 42.

16. Gordon P. Means, *Malaysian Politics* (London, 1970), p. 44.

17. J.M. Gullick, *Malaysia* (London, 1969), p. 85.

Chapter 2

1. Key participants on both sides of the military campaign have written accounts to explain the reasons for the British defeat. See Lt.-Gen. A.E. Percival, *The War in Malaya* (London, 1949) and Col. Masanobu Tsuji, *Singapore: The Japanese Version* (Sydney, 1960).

2. *Malay Mail* (Kuala Lumpur), 10 Dec. 1941.

3. For details of the last minute preparations to defend Singapore, see Png Poh Seng, "The Kuomintang in Malaya, 1912–1941", *Journal of Southeast Asian History* 2, 1 (Mar. 1961): 1–32; Virginia Thompson and Richard Adloff, *The Left Wing in Southeast Asia* (New York, 1950), p. 130.

4. See the memorandum on Dalforce by Brig. P.A.N. McKerron, Deputy Chief Civil Affairs Officer (Singapore), BMA, n.d. (c. Nov./Dec. 1945), in BMA MLF/261.

5. See the British Army's intelligence reports in the file "Fifth Column" in CO 273/671/50790.

6. Harry Miller, *Prince and Premier* (London, 1959), pp. 57–9. See also the Tunku's (Prince's) article, "Memories of the Japanese Occupation", in the English-language newspaper; *The Star* (Penang), 25 Aug. 1975.

7. Chin Kee Onn, *Malaya Upside Down* (Kuala Lumpur, 1976), pp. 17–24.

8. Li Tieh Min *et al.*, *Ta-chan yu Nan-ch'iao* (*Ma-lai-ya Chih pu*) [The World War and the Overseas Chinese in Southeast Asia (the Malaya section)] (Singapore, 1947), pp. 68–9, 93, 97, 102–7; Chin, *Malaya Upside Down*, pp. 98–9; and Yoji Akashi, "Japanese Policy towards the Malayan Chinese, 1941–45", *Journal of Southeast Asian Studies* 1, 2 (Sept. 1970): 66–8.

9. Mamoru Shinozaki, *Syonan: My Story* (Singapore, 1975), pp. 20–1. After the war, the prominent Chinese leader, Tan Kah Kee, blamed both the British authorities and the Malayan communists in Dalforce for putting up the Chinese resistance, which provoked the Japanese later to punish the Chinese by launching the *sook ching*. See *Sin Chew Jit Poh* (Singapore), 30 Oct. 1945.

10. Akashi, "Japanese Policy towards the Malayan Chinese", pp. 66–8.

11. Shinozaki, *Syonan*, pp. 20–1; Chin, *Malaya Upside Down*, p. 21.

12. See Domei news agency report, 3 Mar. 1942, in Office of Strategic Services (OSS), State Department, U.S.A., *Programs of Japan in Malaya* (Intercepts of shortwave broadcasts from Radio Tokyo and affiliated stations from February 1942 to June 1945), originally classified "Restricted", published in Honolulu, 10 Oct. 1945, p. 15.

13. Shinozaki, *Syonan*, pp. 22, 25.

14. The story of the massacre at E-Lang-Lang was published in the newspaper, *New Thrill* (Kuala Lumpur), 23 Oct. 1976. The report followed the discovery by miners of mass graves containing the remains outside the village. *Sook Ching* also occurred in Malacca and Penang, where monuments have been erected to commemorate the massacres of large groups of Chinese.

15. Akashi, "Japanese Policy towards the Malayan Chinese", p. 69.

16. Y.S. Tan, "History of the Formation of the Overseas Chinese Association and the Extortion by the Japanese Military Administration of $50,000,000 Military Contribution from the Chinese in Malaya", *Journal of the South Seas Society* 3, 1 (Sept. 1946): 1–2. See also Document 47, "Principles Governing the Implementation of Measures Relative to Chinese, 25th Army Group", Apr. 1942, in *Japanese Military Administration in Indonesia: Selected Documents*, ed. Harry Benda *et al.* (New Haven, 1965), pp. 178–81.

17. Tan, "History of the Formation of the OCA", pp. 7–10.

18. Goh Kok Leong, "A Legal History of the Japanese Occupation in Singapore", *The Malayan Law Journal* (Jan. 1981): xx.

19. OSS, U.S. State Department, "Japanese Administration in Malaya", marked "Restricted", 8 June 1944, in BMA/ADM 9/1, p. 6. I have drawn

heavily from this intelligence report as well as from a British document from the Far Eastern Bureau, Ministry of Information, entitled "Malaya under the Japanese", n.d. (c. 1944), in BMA PS/404, marked "Secret".

20. Akira Oki, "Social Change in the West Sumatra Village, 1908–1945" (Ph.D. diss., Australian National University, 1977), p. 208.

21. See Yap Hong Kuan, "Perak under the Japanese, 1942–45" (B.A. hons. thesis, University of Singapore, 1957), Chart D.

22. OSS, "Japanese Administration in Malaya", p. 4.

23. Ibid.; see also the British Far Eastern Bureau document, "Malaya under the Japanese", pp. 2–3.

24. Political Affairs Section, Ministry of Foreign Affairs, Tokyo, "Marai dokuritsu mondai" [On the problems of the independence of Malaya], 20 Feb. 1945, microfilm no. 50 in Wason Collection, Cornell University.

25. Ibid., pp. 95–6.

26. "Marai dokuritsu mondai" [On the problems of the independence of Malaya].

27. Yoji Akashi, "Education and Indoctrination Policy in Malaya and Singapore under the Japanese Rule, 1942–45", *Malaysian Journal of Education* 13, 1 and 2 (Dec. 1976): 18–20.

28. Akashi, "Education and Indoctrination Policy in Malaya", p. 4; Yap, "Perak under the Japanese", p. 17.

29. Ibid.

30. Goh Kok Leong, "A Legal History of the Japanese Occupation in Singapore", p. xxi.

31. Halinah Bamadhaj, "The Impact of the Japanese Occupation of Malaya on Malay Society and Politics, 1941–45" (M.A. thesis, University of Auckland, 1975), p. 152.

32. Ibid., pp. 11–3. Bamadhaj is the main source on the "rice police".

33. Ibid., p. 14.

34. I am indebted to Datuk (Dr) Awang Hassan, the Malaysian High Commissioner to Australia, for throwing light on the difficult job of the DO during the Japanese occupation. Interview, Canberra, 15 June 1978. Dr Awang was a medical officer in Kluang (Johor) during the occupation.

35. See the novels *Amrun*, by Muhammad Haji Kidin (Penang, 1965), and *Embun dan Tanah*, by Ibrahim Omar (Kuala Lumpur, 1965). Both deal with class conflict between the *penghulu* and the Malay *raayat* in different parts of Johor during the Japanese occupation.

36. OSS, "Japanese Military Administration in Malaya", pp. 13–4.

37. Information on the Japanese police is drawn mainly from Yap, "Perak under the Japanese", p. 12. A former officer in the British police, Yap was granted permission to consult police files and refer to statements of former officers who had served in the Japanese police force.

38. OSS, "Japanese Military Administration in Malaya", p. 13.

39. Ibid., p. 14; Joyce C. Lebra, *Japanese-Trained Armies in Southeast Asia* (Hong Kong, 1977), pp. 118–9; Yap, "Perak under the Japanese", p. 17. Information on the Women's Auxiliary Corps is given by A. Samad Ismail, editor of *Berita Harian* (Kuala Lumpur), Interview, April 1973.

40. Yap, "Perak under the Japanese", p. 15.

41. *Syonan Shimbun*, 13 Jan. 1944.

42. *Syonan Shimbun*, 23 May 1944.

43. For the most detailed study of Malaya's wartime economy, currency, banking, rationing and food production see Paul H. Kratoska, *The Japanese Occupation of Malaya, 1941–1945: A Social and Economic History* (London, 1998).

44. Kratoska, *The Japanese Occupation of Malaya*, pp. 214–5.

45. OSS, "Japanese Administration in Malaya", p. 20.

46. Kratoska, *The Japanese Occupation of Malaya*, p. 221.

47. Ibid, p. 22.

48. Chin, *Malaya Upside Down*, p. 82.

49. Ibid., p. 63.

50. OSS, "Japanese Administration in Malaya", p. 23. See also the British Far Eastern Bureau Ministry of Information report, "Malaya under the Japanese", p. 6, in BMA PS/404.

51. OSS, "Japanese Administration in Malaya", p. 24. See also Bamadhaj, "The Impact of the Japanese", pp. 2–23.

52. Chin, *Malaya Upside Down*, pp. 136–44.

53. Akashi, "Education and Indoctrination Policy in Malaya", pp. 6–8. See also Victor Purcell, *The Chinese in Southeast Asia* (London, 1951), p. 372.

54. Purcell, *Malaya: Communist or Free?*, pp. 371–2; Chin, *Malaya Upside Down*, p. 139. OSS, "Japanese Administration in Malaya", p. 28.

55. Chin, *Malaya Upside Down*, p. 139; Akashi, "Education and Indoctrination Policy in Malaya", pp. 21–2.

56. See the account of MPAJA executions given by the Englishwoman Nona Baker in Dorothy Thatcher and Robert Cross, *Pai Naa* (*The Story of Nona Baker*) (London, 1959). Nona Baker joined the MPAJA regiment in east Pahang during the war.

57. OSS, "Japanese Administration in Malaya", p. 28.

58. Yoichi Itagaki, "Some Aspects of the Japanese Policy for Malaya under the Occupation, with Special Reference to Nationalism", in *Papers on Malayan History*, ed. K.G. Tregonning (Singapore, 1962), p. 257.

59. Ibid.

60. A.J. Stockwell, "The Development of Malay Politics During the Course of the Malayan Union Experiment, 1942–1948" (Ph.D. diss., University of London, 1973), pp. 15–7.

61. Abu Talib Ahmad, *The Malay Muslims, Islam and the Rising Sun: 1941–45* (Kuala Lumpur, 2003), pp. 177–81.

62. Immediately after the British reoccupied Malaya in September 1945 the Sultans of Johor, Terengganu, and Pahang complained to BMA officials about the activities of the MPAJA during the war. See Brig. H.C. Willan's reports, "Interview with the Malay Rulers between 14 and 28 September 1945", in WO 203/5642.

63. Shinozaki, in *Syonan: My Story*, pp. 83–4, cites two instances of MPAJA assassination of OCA officials at the Japanese-sponsored settlement at Endau (Johor). Chin, in *Malaya Upside Down*, pp. 106–7, reveals how some local OCA officials were caught in a conflict of loyalties between the MPAJA and the Japanese authorities.

64. Y.S. Tan, "History of the Formation of the OCA", pp. 7–8.

65. Akashi, "Japanese Policy towards the Malayan Chinese", pp. 87–8.

66. Joyce Lebra, *Jungle Alliance: Japan and the Indian National Army* (Singapore, 1971), pp. 40–2.

67. Nedyam Raghavan, *India and Malaya* (Bombay, 1954), pp. 75–8. Raghavan was president of the Malaya IIL.

68. P. Ramasamy, "Indian War Memory in Malaya", in *War and Memory in Malaysia and Singapore*, ed. P. Lim Pui Huen and Diana Wong (Singapore, 2000), pp. 96–7.

69. Usha Mahajani, *Role of Indian Minorities in Burma and Malaya* (Bombay, 1960), p. 148.

70. See telegram from BMA (Malaya), Singapore to War Office, London, 6 Sept. 1945: "Sikhs have earned very bad reputation during Japanese occupation…. Sikh police confined to barracks". See also Sultan of Johor's memorandum to Sir Harold MacMichael, 15 Oct. 1945, in which he complained about the behaviour of the Sikh policemen during the Japanese occupation. See file 50823/7/3, Pt. II, in CO 273/675. An escaped Indian POW in Singapore witnessed two Sikhs being attacked by Chinese in the city's Serangoon Road after the Japanese surrender, one of whom was beaten to death. See Lt.-Col. Mahood Khan Durrani, *The Sixth Column* (London, 1955), p. 285.

71. "Marai dokuritsu mondai" [On the problems of the independence of Malaya], 20 Feb. 1945.

72. Ibid.

73. Political Affairs Section, Ministry of Foreign Affairs, Tokyo, "Marai dokuritsu no kanosei ni tsuite" [On the possibility of granting independence to Malaya], 20 Feb. 1945, in *Senryochi gyosei kankei* [Documents relating to the administration of Occupied Areas], File *Daitoa senso kankei* [Greater East Asian War]. This document, cited only in Akashi, "Education and Indoctrination Policy in Malaya", pp. 1–2, appears to contain the actual decisions of the Ministry, while the other document "Marai dokuritsu mondai" [On the problems of the independence of Malaya] outlines the main problems.

74. See Maj.-Gen. S. Woodburn Kirby, *The War against Japan*, Vol. 5, United Kingdom military series, History of the Second World War (London, 1969), pp. 396–7, 408.
75. Mitsuo Nakamura, "General Imamura and the Early Period of Japanese Occupation", *Indonesia* 10 (Oct. 1970): 3; see also Okuma Memorial Social Sciences Institute, *Japanese Military Administration in Indonesia*, pp. 122–3.
76. Ibid., pp. 371–87.
77. Tojo's speech and the Japanese government drafts discussing Independence of Indonesia are in Benda *et al.*, *Japanese Military Administration*, pp. 49–52, 253–9. For a detailed discussion of the major implications of Tojo's speech for Indonesia, see Okuma Social Sciences Institute, *Japanese Military Administration*, pp. 271–87.
78. Itagaki, "Some Aspects of the Japanese Policy for Malaya", pp. 259–60.
79. Willard H. Elsbree, *Japan's Role in Southeast Asian National Movements, 1940–45* (Cambridge, 1953), p. 149.

Chapter 3

1. For a detailed account of the CCP's role and influence in the MCP, see C.F. Yong, *The Origins of Malayan Communism* (Singapore, 1997).
2. For detailed studies of MCP policies during this period, see Gene Z. Hanrahan, *The Communist Struggle in Malaya*, first published in New York in 1954 (reprinted Kuala Lumpur, 1971), pp. 19–60; Charles B. McLane, *Soviet Strategies in Southeast Asia* (New Jersey, 1966), and J.H. Brimmell, *Communism in Southeast Asia* (London, 1959).
3. The Malayan Communist Party, *Nan Tao Chih Ch'un* [Spring in the southern islands] (Singapore, 1946), p. 8. This booklet contains both theories of communism as well as the party's history up to 1940, and its programmes and strategies up to the end of the Second World War. It was intended as an introduction to new party recruits. I am indebted to Dr Louis Siegel of the Department of Far Eastern History, Australian National University, for obtaining a copy of this rare document. Apparently, an English translation of some of its contents is to be found in the Malayan government records. Professor McLane is the only writer to have drawn heavily on a document entitled "History of the Malayan Communist Party" in the records. The details, which he cites from this history in his *Soviet Strategies in the Far East*, are in most respects identical to the MCP's history given in *Nan Tao Chih Ch'un*, though there are a few discrepancies in facts. One discrepancy is that McLane refers to the date of the document as "1945" (p. 132), while *Nan Tao Chih Ch'un* is dated 1946. Elsewhere in his book, especially on p. 241, McLane calls it the "1940 party history".

4. Stephen Leong, "The Kuomintang-Communist United Front in Malaya during the National Salvation Period, 1937–1941", *Journal of Southeast Asian Studies* 8, 1 (Mar. 1977): 31–47.

5. *Nan Tao Chih Ch'un*, p. 22.

6. Ibid.

7. Hanrahan (*The Communist Struggle in Malaya*, p. 61), identifies him by his name Ch'en Chia-keng.

8. Yap, "Perak under the Japanese", p. 26. Yap's thesis is based on confidential and secret files of the Singapore Police, Special Branch, which he was allowed to consult as a former member of the Police Force. Because some of the information he used was classified, the Special Branch initially requested the university to embargo the thesis. The ban was lifted later. The Special Branch subsequently agreed to release information of its pre-war role and operations to another Singapore scholar. See Ban Kah Choon's *Absent History: The Untold Story of Special Branch Operations in Singapore, 1915–1942* (Singapore, 2001).

9. Ibid.

10. Lai T'e (Lai Tek), *Wei-min-tsu t'uan-chieh min-chu tzu-yu min-sheng kai shan erh t'ou-cheng* [Struggle for national unity, democracy and liberty, and improvement of people's livelihood], a Report to the Eighth Central Committee Conference, 22–27 Jan. 1946, Singapore, 4 (mimeo.). This report devotes a section to the MCP's activities during the Japanese occupation.

11. See the biography of John Davis by Margaret Shennan, *Our Man in Malaya* (London, 2008), p. 16. Davis is reported to have said in a recorded interview: "I personally find a character like that — a person who has spent the whole of his life as an informer or traitor, or whatever word you like to use, for one side or another, then doubly, develops a strange sort of character. You can't dislike a man intensely just because of that — you've just got to look behind and understand a certain amount about him. And I don't think Lai Tek let us down: we couldn't have got anywhere without him." Shennan, ibid., p. 121.

12. Yap, "Perak under the Japanese", p. 26. While fleeing after the fall of Singapore, Dalley was captured by the Japanese Army in Sumatra with his colleagues and brought back to Singapore where he was interned for the rest of the war. After the war, he became Director of the Malayan Security Service (MSS). For more details on Dalley, see Leon Comber, *Malaya's Secret Police 1945–60: The Role of the Special Branch in the Malayan Emergency* (Singapore, 2008), pp. 30–3.

13. Ibid.

14. Hai Shang-ou, *Ma-lai-ya jen-min k'ang-jih chun* [The Malayan People's Anti-Japanese Army] (Singapore, 1945), pp. 34–9, 40–1, 58. This is an independent account by a newspaperman, based on interviews with

several MPAJA leaders including the chairman of the Central Military Committee, Liu Yau.

15. A fairly detailed background of the MPAJA is found in Hanrahan, *The Communist Struggle in Malaya*; Edgar O'Ballance, *Malaya: The Communist Insurgent War, 1948–60* (London, 1966); and Richard Clutterbuck, *The Long Long War* (London, 1967).

16. The MPAJA Ex-Servicemen's Association, *Ma-lai-ya jen min k'ang-jih chun chan-chi* [The war diary of the MPAJA], in *Ta-chan yu Nan Ch'iao (Ma-lai-ya chih pu)* [The World War and the Overseas Chinese in Southeast Asia (The Malaya section)], Li Tieh Min *et al.*, *Ta-chan yu Nan-ch'iao*, pp. 28–9; see also Hai Shang Ou, *Ma-lai-ya jen-min k'ang-jih chun*, p. 14.

17. *The War Diary of the MPAJA*, p. 28.

18. Hanrahan, *The Communist Struggle in Malaya*, p. 72; Yap, "Perak under the Japanese", pp. 40, 47.

19. Yap, "Perak under the Japanese".

20. Interview, John Davis (Force 136), Kent, Apr. 1976. See Chapman, *The Jungle Is Neutral*, p. 158.

21. The figures 3,000–4,000 are given in Mountbatten of Burma, *Post-Surrender Tasks: Section E of the Report to the Combined Chiefs of Staff* (London, 1969), p. 301; the figures 6,000–7,000 are in Victor Purcell, *The Chinese in Malaya* (London, 1949), p. 262.

22. Yap, "Perak under the Japanese", pp. 45, 52–3; Harry Miller, *Prince and Premier* (London, 1959), p. 48.

23. Ibid.

24. McLane, *Soviet Strategies in Southeast Asia*, p. 307.

25. Chin Peng, *My Side of History* (Singapore, 2003), p. 118.

26. Yap, "Perak under the Japanese", pp. 43–4.

27. Chapman, *The Jungle Is Neutral*, p. 129; see also Dorothy Thatcher and Robert Cross, *Pai Naa* [The story of Nona Baker, an Englishwoman who lived with the MPAJA in Pahang] (London, 1959), p. 164.

28. *The War Diary of the MPAJA*, p. 30.

29. Ibid.

30. See Appendices B and C.

31. Yap, "Perak under the Japanese", p. 49fn.

32. Mamoru Shinozaki, *Syonan: My Story* (Singapore, 1975), pp. 83–4.

33. Chapman, *The Jungle Is Neutral*, p. 158.

34. *The War Diary of the MPAJA*, pp. 27–30.

35. See "Decision of Central for a Working Plan, 22.8.46", *Political Intelligence Journal*, Malayan Security Service, Singapore, 30 Sept. 1946.

36. Ibid.

37. Chapman, *The Jungle Is Neutral*, pp. 163–74.

38. As an example, see the article "Lenggong: An Account of a Catastrophe" (in Chinese), in *Ta-chan yu Nan Ch'iao (Ma-lai-ya-chih pu)* [The

World War and the Overseas Chinese in Southeast Asia (the Malaya section)], Li Tieh Min *et al.*, *Ta-chan yu Nan-ch'iao*, pp. 169–70, 211.

39. Chapman, *The Jungle Is Neutral*, pp. 105, 118, 127–8, 164, 213.

40. R. Balan, interview, Kuala Lumpur, Apr. 1975. Chinese-speaking Balan was in the MPAJA's propaganda bureau in Perak and claims that Abdullah C.D. and other Malays were then members of the MCP.

41. *The War Diary of the MPAJA*, p. 28; the MPAJA Fourth Independent Regiment, *Kang-Jih ying hsiung zai Jou-nan* [The anti-Japanese heroes in Southern Johor] (Singapore, 1946), p. 45.

42. See Ibrahim Yaacob, *Sekitar Malaya Merdeka*, p. 32; and also I.K. Agastja (adopted Indonesian name of Ibrahim Yaacob), *Sedjarah dan Perjuangan di Malaya* [History and struggle in Malaya] (Jogjakarta, 1951), p. 106.

43. Agastja, *Sedjarah dan Perjuangan di Malaya*, p. 106.

44. Abdul Malek Haji Md. Hanafiah, "Sejarah Perjuangan Kesatuan Melayu Muda [History of the struggle of the Young Malay Union], 1937–1945" (B.A. Hons. thesis, Universiti Kebangsaan Malaysia, Kuala Lumpur, 1975), pp. 299–300.

45. Interviews with Mohd. Shahid and Zakaria Tais, former members of the Malay Giyu Gun, 28 May and 24 Aug. 1974 respectively, by Abdul Malek, "Sejarah Perjuangan Kesatuan Melayu Muda", p. 300. Both individuals claimed to have obtained the information regarding Ibrahim's agreement with the MCP/MPAJA from their Malay officer, Col. Osman Daim.

46. Chin Peng, *My Side of History*, pp. 126–7.

47. Chapman, *The Jungle Is Neutral*, pp. 232–40.

48. Ibid., p. 241.

49. See the detailed Memorandum by Head of the Malayan Country Section, Force 136 on Resistance Forces on the Eve of the Japanese Capitulation, Top Secret, 15 Aug. 1945, in WO 203/5642/X/LO1782. See also F.S.V. Donnison, *British Military Administration in the Far East, 1943–46* (London, 1956), pp. 380–1.

50. Chapman, *The Jungle Is Neutral*, pp. 254–8; Donnison, *British Military Administration in the Far East*, p. 381.

51. Memorandum by Head of the Malayan Country Section, Force 136, in WO 203/5642/X/LO1782.

52. Ibid., par. 12.

53. See the report, "The Chinese Resistance Forces", *Secret Weekly Intelligence Review*, no. 11, 25 Indian Division, H.Q. Malaya Command Papers, Kuala Lumpur, 28 Nov. 1945, pp. 4–5.

54. Ibid.

55. See his *Malaya Upside Down* (Singapore, 1946), p. 109.

56. See N.I. Low and H.M. Cheng, *This Singapore*, p. 67.

57. See para. 37–9 in Memorandum by Head of Malayan Country Section, Force 136, in WO 203/5642.

58. Ibid.
59. Ibid. For other accounts of the MPAJA/KMT clashes, see Victor Purcell, *The Chinese in Malaya* (London, 1949), pp. 258–62; W.L. Blythe, *The Impact of Chinese Secret Societies in Malaya* (London, 1968), pp. 332–3.
60. Tok Muda Raja Razman bin Raja Abdul Hamid *et al.*, *Hulu Perak Dalam Sejarah* [Upper Perak in history] (Ipoh, 1963), pp. 80–2.
61. For an interesting Malay account of the Askar Melayu Setia, see Abdul Aziz bin Zakaria, *Lt. Nor. Pahlawan Gerila* (Kuala Lumpur, 1963).
62. Aziz and Silcock, "Nationalism in Malaya", in *Asian Nationalism and the West*, ed. William Holland (New York, 1953), p. 292.
63. Chapman, *The Jungle Is Neutral*, p. 412.
64. O'Ballance, *Malaya: The Communist Insurgent War*, p. 62; see also Abdul Aziz bin Zakaria, *Lt. Nor. Pahlawan Gerila*.
65. See Memorandum by Head of Malaya Country Section, Force 136, on Resistance Forces in Malaya, in WO 203/5642.
66. See Gurchan Singh, *Singa: The Lion of Malaya* (Kuala Lumpur, 1969) and Sybil Karthigasu, *No Dream of Mercy* (London, 1954).
67. The Special Branch document "Basic Paper on the Malayan Communist Party", cited in McLane, *Soviet Strategies in Southeast Asia*, p. 241. McLane notes that sources differ on the date of his arrival. Lai Tek himself claims to have joined the MCP in 1934 (this was stated in an interrogation with the Malayan Police, 16 Mar. 1947). An official MCP document entitled "Statement of the Incident of Wright (alias Lai Tek)", issued following Lai Tek's removal in 1947, dates his entry in the party in "late 1934 or 1935". MCP official Wu Tien Wang, as cited in Hanrahan, *The Communist Struggle in Malaya*, p. 55, writes that the Comintern dispatched Lai Tek to Singapore in 1936 specifically to resolve the party crisis of that year. It is most probable that the date of his arrival was some time in 1934, soon after the first internal crisis. *Nan Tao Chih Ch'un*, written at the time of his leadership, makes no reference to his date of arrival or to him at all.
68. According to Chin Peng, the findings from the MCP's investigations "support none of these conjectures". See his *My Side of History*, p. 58. Chin Peng said Lai Tek spoke "heavily accented Cantonese and Mandarin".
69. Anthony Short, *The Communist Insurrection in Malaya*, pp. 38–43.
70. Chihiro Tsutsui, *Nampo gunsei-ron* [Military administration in the southern regions] (Tokyo, 1944), p. 152. Tsutsui's account is based on MCP documents as well as former British police records taken over by the Kempeitai. See also Hanrahan, *The Communist Struggle in Malaya*, p. 55.
71. Wu Tien Wang, p. 3, cited in Hanrahan, *The Communist Struggle in Malaya*, p. 55.

72. Ibid., p. 53. See also Yeo Kim Wah, "The Communist Involvement in Malayan Labour Strikes, 1936", *JMBRAS* 49 (1976): 36–79.

73. Mamoru Shinozaki, *My Wartime Experiences in Singapore* (Singapore, 1973), p. 111. Shinozaki obtained details about Lai Tek from Maj. Sartoru Onishi of the Kempeitai.

74. Special Branch, Singapore, file Ref. OF/A/1/81 (Y) No. 31 (n.d.), cited in Yap, "Perak under the Japanese", p. 30.

75. See Isaacs' report entitled "Wright helps Japs to trap Reds at Batu Caves" in *Malay Mail* (Kuala Lumpur), 31 Aug. 1953.

76. Ibid.

77. Ibid.

78. Shinozaki, *My Wartime Experiences in Singapore*, p. 113.

79. Personal communication from Sartoru Onishi, Tokyo, to Prof. Yoji Akashi of Nanzan University, 29 Oct. 1976. I am grateful to Prof. Akashi for putting several questions to Mr Onishi on my behalf. For a more detailed account of Lai Tek's war-time activities, based on Japanese sources, see Yoji Akashi, "Lai Teck (sic) secretary-general of the Malayan Communist Party, 1939–1947", *Journal of the South Seas Society* 49 (1994): 57–103.

80. Shinozaki, *My Wartime Experiences in Singapore*, p. 113.

81. Ng Yeh Lu, "How MCP Central's Secretary General Lai Tek slaughtered KMT, MCP and Allied Forces cadres", p. 23.

82. Ibid.

83. Ibid.

84. Commenting on these early acts of treachery, Chin, in *My Side of History*, p. 84, says, "...his collaboration with the Kempeitai saw the Party's Central Committee methodically eliminated to the point that it became a virtual one-man show — Lai Tek himself."

85. Based on personal communication from Sartoru Onishi, Tokyo, to Prof. Yoji Akashi of Nanzan University, 29 Oct. 1976. See also Maj. Isaacs' report in *Malay Mail*, 31 Aug. 1953.

86. *Nan Tao Chih Ch'un*, p. 24. Yap Hong Kuan quotes from a secret MCP document dated January 1945 containing identical points as in *Nan Tao Chih Ch'un* which, however, dates the resolution as 30 May 1942. Yap's source is the Special Branch file OF/A/1/81 (Y) No. 31 based on information obtained during interrogation of Kempeitai officials.

87. See Isaacs' report in *Malay Mail*, 31 Aug. 1953.

88. Hai Shang Ou, *Ma-lai-ya-jen-min k'ang jih chun*, p. 35, claims that there were more than 1,000 Japanese troops involved in the operation.

89. Sartoru Onishi, "Malai Kyosanto chuo taikai no tobatsu" [Raids on the Central Committee of the Malayan Communist Party], in the National Association of Military Police, *Nippon Kempei Seishi* [Official history of the Japanese military police] (Tokyo, 1976), p. 984. Hai Shang Ou, *Ma-lai-ya-jen-min k'ang jih chun*, p. 35, claims that more than 100 MCP

officials and members were killed. Among those reported killed were Hsiao Chung, CEC member, and Chu Wei, political commissar of the Fourth Independent Regiment, MPAJA (South Johor). The Kempeitai figures appear to be more reliable.

90. Chapman, *The Jungle Is Neutral*, pp. 159–60.
91. Sartoru Onishi, "Raids on the Central Committee of the Malayan Communist Party", p. 984.
92. Isaacs report in *Malay Mail*, 31 Aug. 1953. Chin Peng in his autobiography, *My Side of History*, p. 81, admits to the party's failure to detect Lai Tek's treachery: "When one analyses the chain of raids, arrests, tortures, and executions carried out against the CPM [Communist Party of Malaya] by the Kempeitai during this early occupation period, it seems quite extraordinary that the finger of suspicion failed to fall on Lai Te much earlier than it finally did. Our natural reaction was to look to other possible betrayers."
93. Ibid.
94. Shinozaki, *My Wartime Experiences in Singapore*, p. 113.
95. Major Isaacs puts out this theory in *Malay Mail*, 31 Aug. 1953.
96. The Japanese Malayan Military Administration, Police Department, "Malai ni okeru chianjo ichiko satsu" [Observations on the security situation in Malaya], Dec. 1942, p. 14, in the Tokugawa Papers, Self-Defence Agency archives, Tokyo. See also Sartoru Onishi, "Malai kyosanto chuo taikai no tobatsu" [Raids on the Malayan Communist Party], in *Nippon Kempei Seishi*, p. 984.
97. Chin Peng, *My Side of History*, pp. 85–6.
98. *Nan Tao Chih Ch'un*, p. 25.
99. Anthony Short, *The Communist Insurrection in Malaya*, p. 22.
100. See Police Department, "Observations on the Security Situation in Malaya", p. 15; see also Sartoru Onishi, "Raids on the Malayan Communist Party", p. 984.
101. Sartoru Onishi, pers. comm. to Prof. Yoji Akashi.
102. Quoted by Major Isaacs in his report in *Malay Mail*, 31 Aug. 1953.
103. Special Branch File OF/A/l/81 (Y) No. 31, cited in Yap, "Perak under the Japanese", p. 50.
104. Yap, "Perak under the Japanese", p. 50.
105. Ibid., p. 33.
106. McLane, *Soviet Strategies in Southeast Asia*, p. 310.
107. Yap, "Perak under the Japanese", p. 141.
108. John Cross, *Red Jungle*, p. 95.
109. Sartoru Onishi, "Teki sensuikan no senyu chosha" [Espionage agents smuggled by submarine], in *Nippon Kempei Seishi*, p. 987. See also Ng Yeh Lu, "How MCP Central's Secretary General Lai Tek slaughtered KMT, MCP and Allied Forces cadres", p. 28.
110. Ibid.

111. Pers. comm. from Richard Broome, Dorset, England, 18 Jan. 1978.
112. Chapman, *The Jungle Is Neutral*, p. 249.
113. See Lai T'e's report, op. cit., p. 5.
114. Sartoru Onishi, "Espionage agents smuggled by submarine", in *Nippon Kempei Seishi*, pp. 987–8. Some details of Lim Bo Seng's arrest are given in Chapman, *The Jungle Is Neutral*, p. 375. See also Chin Peng, *My Side of History*, p. 106.
115. John Davis, interview at his home, Kent, Apr. 1976.
116. Chapman, *The Jungle Is Neutral*, p. 375.
117. Short, *The Communist Insurrection in Malaya*, p. 34.
118. See Chin Peng, *My Side of History*, pp. 87–8.
119. O'Ballance, *Malaya: The Communist Insurgent War*, pp. 62–3.
120. Ibid.
121. See Ibrahim Yaacob, *Sekitar Malaya Merdeka*, p. 35. See also Chin Peng, *My Side of History*, p. 126, who reveals that due to Lai Tek's directive, "the union of Chinese, Malay and Japanese forces against Britain" came to naught.
122. McLane, *Soviet Strategies in Southeast Asia* , p. 313.
123. See Appendix A for full text of the statement found in BMA Sel. C.A. 162/45.
124. Ibid.
125. Ibid.
126. Ibid.
127. Ibid.
128. See Statement by the Central Committee of the Communist Party of Malaya commemorating the 40th anniversary of its birth, dated 25 Apr. 1970 (mimeo.), University of London Library.

Chapter 4

1. Ibrahim Yaacob, *Sekitar Malaya Merdeka* [Concerning Independent Malaya] (Jakarta, 1957), p. 33.
2. Iskander Kamel Agastya (adopted Indonesian name of Ibrahim Yaacob), *Sedjarah dan Perdjuangan di Malaya* [History and struggle in Malaya] (Jogjakarta, 1951), pp. 87–8. See also Abdul Malek Haji Md. Hanafiah, "Sejarah Perjuangan Kesatuan Melayu Muda, 1937–45" [History of the Struggle of the KMM, 1937–45] (B.A. Hons. thesis, Universiti Kebang-saan Malaysia, 1975), p. 205.
3. Interview with Maj. Fujiwara Iwaichi, head of the espionage agency, which directed Fifth Column activities in Malaya during the war (Tokyo, Sept. 1976). See also Nagai Shinichi, "The Malay Nationalist Movement during the Pacific War: From the Perspective of the Leftist Nationalist Leadership – Part I] (in Japanese), in *Azia Keizai*, Institute of Developing Economies, Tokyo, 15 Oct. 1975, pp. 40–50; and Fujiwara

Iwaichi, *F Kikan* (F Agency) (Tokyo, 1966), pp. 168–9. For a war-time British Special Branch account confirming the Japanese transaction, see Eric Robertson, *The Japanese File: Pre-war Japanese Penetration in Southeast Asia* (Kuala Lumpur, 1979), pp. 116–22.

4. For a more detailed discussion of Mustapha Hussein's assistance, see Abdul Malek, "Sejarah Perjuangan", pp. 212–3, 225–30; Agastya, *Sedjarah*, p. 97; and Cheah Boon Kheng, "The Japanese Occupation of Malaya, 1941–45: Ibrahim Yaacob and the Struggle for Indonesia Raya", *Indonesia* 28 (Oct. 1979): 85–120.

5. Agastya, *Sedjarah*, p. 96.

6. Ibid., p. 68.

7. Ibrahim Yaacob, *Nusa dan Bangsa Melayu* [The Malays and their islands] (Jakarta, 1951), p. 61.

8. Interviews with Fujiwara and Prof. Itagaki Yoichi, who was chief adviser on Malay affairs to the Japanese military administration in Malaya; both in Tokyo, Sept. 1976. See also Document No. 1, "Principles governing the administration of Occupied Southern Areas", in *Japanese Military Administration in Indonesia: Selected Documents*, ed. Harry J. Benda *et al.* (New Haven, 1965), p. 2.

9. Bamadhaj, "Impact of the Japanese Occupation", pp. 93–4.

10. Interview, Tokyo, Sept. 1976.

11. "Director-General of the Japanese Military Administration (Malaya) in Singapore".

12. Agastya, *Sedjarah*, p. 101.

13. Ibid.

14. Interview with Prof. Itagaki, Tokyo, Sept. 1976.

15. Abdul Malek, "Kesatuan Melayu Muda", pp. 132–48, 210–1, 266–9.

16. Ibid.

17. For the full text of Tojo's speech, see Document No. 9, in *Japanese Military Administration*, ed. Benda *et al.*, p. 51.

18. *Syonan Shimbun*, 30 July 1943. See also FIR Nos. 7, 10, 12, and 13 (covering the period July to September 1943), which contain announcements and reports of Ibrahim's visit to Japan, in CO 273/669/5074417.

19. Domei carried biographical details of Ibrahim and his contribution to Japanese intelligence during the campaign leading to the fall of Singapore. See FIR No. 13, 11 Sept. 1943, ibid.

20. FIR No. 12, 12 Aug. 1943.

21. Ibrahim Yaacob, "Sejarah Perintis Kemerdekaan Malaysia" [The history of pioneers of Malaysian independence], Part I, Aug. 1973, prepared for delivery to the History Department, Universiti Kebangsaan Malaysia, Kuala Lumpur, under its oral history project, but not delivered as the Malaysian government refused him permission to speak. It is cited here with permission of the History Department, Universiti Kebangsaan Malaysia.

22. *Fajar Asia* (Singapore), Dec. 1943.
23. See the article entitled "Bangunkanlah Tentera Sukarela!" [Raise the volunteer army!], *Fajar Asia* (Singapore), Oct. 1943.
24. See Yoji Akashi, "Japanese Policy towards the Malayan Chinese, 1941– 1945", *Journal of Southeast Asian Studies* 1, 2 (Sept. 1970): 66, 78.
25. The composition of the various sangi kai is discussed in Yoichi Itagaki, "Outlines of Japanese Policy in Indonesia and Malaya during the War, with Special Reference to Nationalism of Respective Countries", *The Annals of the Hitotsubashi Academy* [Tokyo] 11, 2 (Apr. 1952): 188.
26. *Syonan Shimbun*, 1 Jan. 1944.
27. Abdul Malek, "Kesatuan Melayu Muda", pp. 297–302.
28. Agastya, *Sedjarah*, p. 106.
29. Samad Ismail, *Patah Sayap Terbang Jua*, p. 201.
30. See Koiso's statement, and the draft statements of the Army Ministry (1944) in *Japanese Military Administration*, ed. Benda *et al.*, p. 120.
31. See the issues of *Fajar Asia* from Dec. 1944 to Feb. 1945, which carried articles on Sukarno, such Indonesian historical heroes as Diponegoro, and the Indonesian national anthem "Indonesia Raya".
32. Prof. Itagaki, interview, Tokyo, Sept. 1976.
33. See the account in his memoirs, *Azia tono Taiwa* [Dialogue with Asia] (Tokyo, 1968), pp. 158–61.
34. Ibid., pp. 161–2.
35. Ibid.
36. Ibid.
37. Ibrahim Yaacob, *Sekitar Malaya Merdeka*, p. 28. According to Prof. Itagaki, this was not the name originally agreed to at the May 1945 meeting but had been invented by Ibrahim subsequently to fit in with his exile in Indonesia.
38. Arena Wati, *Cherpen Zaman Jepun* [Short stories of the Japanese occupation] (Kuala Lumpur, 1968), p. 26n.
39. Itagaki, *Azia tono Taiwa*, pp. 162–3.
40. Ibid.
41. See Muhammad Yamin, *Naskah Persiapan Undang-Undang Dasar* 1945 [Documents on the Preparation of the 1945 Constitution] (Jakarta, 1959), vol. 1, pp. 205–6. See also G.S. Kanahele, "The Japanese Occupation of Indonesia: Prelude to Independence" (Ph.D. thesis, Cornell University, 1967), pp. 210–1, 319.
42. Yamin, *Naskah Persiapan Undang-Undang Dasar* 1945, vol. 1, p. 206.
43. Ibid., p. 212.
44. Itagaki, *Azia tono Taiwa*, pp. 167–9.
45. For the names in the cabinet, see Abdul Malek, "Kesatuan Melayu Muda", pp. 302–7, who is the only source for this information.
46. Ibrahim Yaacob, *Sekitar Malaya Merdeka*, p. 30.
47. Abdul Malek, "Kesatuan Melayu Muda", pp. 302–7.
48. Itagaki, *Azia tono Taiwa*, pp. 203–5.

49. Ibrahim Yaacob, *Sekitar Malaya Merdeka*, p. 29, and Agastya, *Sedjarah*, pp. 136–7.

50. Interview, Tokyo, Sept. 1976.

51. Arena Wati, *Cherpen Zaman Jepun*, p. 26n.

52. Information from Sardon Haji Zubir is given in Bamadhaj, "Impact of the Japanese Occupation", p. 120. Information from Samad Ismail, interview, Kuala Lumpur, June 1973.

53. Itagaki, *Azia tono Taiwa*, pp. 169–74.

54. Abdul Malek, "Kesatuan Melayu Muda", pp. 313 and 316, claims that the KRIS meeting was held on 15 August 1945, and Ibrahim Yaacob, *Sekitar Malaya Merdeka*, p. 33, says that it was on 16 August.

55. Hassan Manan, KMM secretary-general, in an interview on 30 April 1970 with journalist Zubaidah binte Abdul Rahman of the daily *Berita Harian* (Kuala Lumpur). Hassan Manan, resident in Yogyakarta, was on a short visit to Kuala Lumpur when Zubaidah interviewed him. I am grateful to Zubaidah for her notes, which contain details of the KRIS meeting not found in her published reports on Hassan Manan.

56. Abdul Malek, "Kesatuan Melayu Muda", pp. 313–24, gives the most detailed account of the KRIS meeting, based on interviews with several of the participants.

57. Ibid.

58. Ibid., p. 315.

59. Itagaki, *Azia tona Taiwa*, p. 169.

60. Ibid.

61. Ibrahim Yaacob, *Sekitar Malaya Merdeka*, pp. 33–4. However, there is no corroboration of this story in available MCP documents.

62. Ibid.

63. See Ibrahim Yaacob, *Sekitar Malaya Merdeka*, p. 36, for the secret help given by the MPAJA to KMM/KRIS and Giyu Gun members after the British return.

64. Abdul Malek, "Kesatuan Melayu Muda", pp. 323–4.

65. Ibid., p. 326.

66. Nagai, "Malay Nationalist Movement", pp. 40–50.

67. Agastya, *Sedjarah*, p. 139. Ibrahim Yaacob dedicates his book *Nusa dan Bangsa* to Giyu Gun leader Major Manaf and also to Capt. Abdul Karim Rashid, Capt. Ramli bin Hj. Tahir, and others who were arrested by the British and subsequently released. Nasution, *Sekitar Perang Kemerdekaan*, p. 275, also pays tribute to Manaf's sacrifice.

68. Ibid., p. 276.

Chapter 5

1. Ibrahim himself blames his departure for Jakarta as a factor for the loss of morale among the KRIS rank and file. See Agastya, *Sedjarah*, p. 186.

2. *Syonan Shimbun*, 15 Aug. 1945.

3. N.I. Low and H.M. Cheng, *This Singapore* (Singapore, 1946), pp. 162–3. Their work, based partly on the papers in the Singapore Chinese Affairs Secretariat where Cheng worked, is generally regarded as a pro-Kuomintang account because of the authors' sympathies for the Malayan KMT official, the late Lim Bo Seng who died in a Japanese prison camp at Batu Gajah in 1944. In 1973 Low brought out a revised version of the book called *When Singapore Was Syonan-to*.

4. Samad Ismail, editor of *Berita Harian*, Kuala Lumpur, interview, Apr. 1973.

5. Pers. comm. of Chin Kee Onn, 26 July 1977. Chin is the well-known author of *Malaya Upside Down* and *Ma-Rai-Ee*, both books dealing with the Japanese occupation.

6. See O'Ballance, *Malaya: The Communist Insurgent War, 1948–60*, p. 63. See also Chapter 3.

7. Kin'ichiro Nakazawa, "Shusen – Marakka no hyojo" [The end of the war and the expressions of Malacca], in Takizo Sato (ed.), *Sekidohyo* [Equator monuments] (Tokyo, 1975), pp. 116–7. *Sekidohyo* is a collection of reminiscences published by the Japanese Veterans of the Equator Association whose members had served in civilian sections of the Japanese wartime administration in Southeast Asia.

8. Ibid.

9. Allied Land Forces, South East Asia, Weekly Intelligence Review [hereafter referred to as ALFSEA, WIR], No. 49 for week ending 7 Sept. 1945, in WO 172/1782. See also the news report, "General Itagaki's First Refusal", *Straits Times* (Singapore), 7 Sept. 1945.

10. Revealed during Dutch interrogation of Generals Tanaba and Shimura, both of the Twenty-fifth Army in Sumatra in June 1946 at Singapore. See the reports of the Consulate-General of the Netherlands, Singapore, I.C. 009402. Notes of Dr Anthony Reid.

11. Mamoru Shinozaki, *Syonan – My Story* (Singapore, 1975), pp. 94–5.

12. Dutch interrogation of General Shimura.

13. Shinozaki, *Syonan*, pp. 94–5.

14. ALFSEA, WIR No. 49 for week ending 7 Sept. 1945, in WO 172/1782.

15. See Chin Peng, *My Side of History*, pp. 124–5, 146–8.

16. Pers. comm. of Dr Anthony Reid who interviewed Adachi in Tokyo, 1973. See also the British Psychological Warfare Information Review No. 19 for an intelligence report dated July 1945 on Japanese attempts at establishing friendly contacts with MPAJA in WO 172/1776.

17. British army intelligence reports in Malaya between September and December 1945 indicate that the number of Japanese deserters attempting to join the communists was at least about 50 or more. Most were captured, however. Following are some reports. Intelligence Summary [hereafter ISUM] Hqs. Malaya Command, 28 Nov. 1945 reads: "Klang area [Selangor]. Three Japanese war criminals found in hiding.

Two captured, one escaped. Suspected they were associating with local Chinese leftists." ISUM, 29 Nov. 1945: "Third Japanese in Kuala Langat forests [Selangor) captured by local Malays." ISUM, 5 Dec. 1945: "Much activity by Chinese leftwing elements Sungei Buloh area [Selangor]." Two Japanese officers reported to be in this area.... Enclosures in BMA ADM9/16.

18. *Far Eastern Economic Review* (Hong Kong), 2 Sept. 1977, p. 42.

19. See Psychological Warfare Information Review No. 19 (for reports up to August 1945), in WO 172/1776.

20. Japanese Self-Defence Agency, War History Library, *Nansei homen rikugun sakusen* (*Malai ran in no bogi*) [Army operations in Southwest areas (Defence of Malaya and the Netherlands East Indies) (Tokyo, 1966), p. 454.

21. ALFSEA, WIR No. 49, 7 Sept. 1945, in WO 172/1782.

22. Ibid.

23. Ibid.; see also Shinozaki, *Syonan – My Story*, pp. 96–7.

24. Shinozaki, *Syonan*, p. 97.

25. Datuk (Dr) Awang Hassan, Malaysian High Commissioner to Australia, interview, Canberra, 15 June 1978. See also Chapter 2.

26. Mountbatten of Burma, *Post- Surrender Tasks: Section E of the Report to the Combined Chiefs of Staff, 1943–45*, 1969, p. 301.

27. Interview, Kuala Lumpur, Nov. 1976. Informant's identity withheld at his request.

28. Shigeru Saito, "Taiping-no yuutsu" [The melancholy of Taiping], in Sato (ed.), *Sekidohyo*, pp. 116– 7.

29. Kin'ichiro Nakazawa, "Shusen – Marakka no Hyojo" [The end of the war and the expressions of Malacca], in Sato, *Sekidohyo*, pp. 135–6.

30. Ibid.

31. See ALFSEA, WIR No. 51 for week ending 21 Sept. 1945, in WO 172/1784. The extensive breakdown of Japanese authority is best conveyed in a lengthy report entitled "Bandits attempt to disturb peace of Malai: Series of serious incidents reported from all parts of the country", in *Malai Sinpo* (Kuala Lumpur), 3 Sept. 1945. See Appendix E.

32. ALFSEA WIR No. 51 for week ending 21 Sept. 1945, in WO 172/1784.

33. See report "The Japanese and Malayan Resistance Forces" by a senior Force 136 officer (name not given) in 25 Indian Division, Hqs. Malaya Command, WIR No. 13 for week ending 12 Dec. 1945, 5–6, in MU Secret 335/46, vol. I.

34. John Davis, interview, Kent, 14 Apr. 1976; see also F.S.V. Donnison, *British Military Administration in the Far East, 1943–46* (London, 1956), pp. 384–5.

35. See the Force 136 report, "Chinese resistance forces", 28 Nov. 1945, in BMA PSDI29.

36. Ibid.

37. See the Japanese statistics of guerrilla attacks from the surrender to 31 August 1945 in Appendices B and C, as found in ibid.

38. Ibid.; see also Donnison, *British Military Administration*, p. 384.

39. See Hannah's report in Yap, "Perak under the Japanese", pp. 79–82.

40. John Davis, interview.

41. *Syonan Shimbun*, 27 Aug. 1945. Capt. Alastair Morrison of Force 136 who was in the MPAJA camp at Ulu Yam (Selangor) heard the Japanese broadcast calling for Force 136 help on 25 Aug. 1945. He recorded it in his diary. Interview, Canberra, 13 June 1978.

42. Shinozaki, *Syonan*, pp. 94–5.

43. Ibid., p. 97.

44. Ibid.

45. *Syonan Shimbun*, 22 Aug. 1945.

46. See the editorial, "Respect the law", *Syonan Shimbun*, 25 Aug. 1945.

47. Ibid.

48. *Syonan Shimbun*, 3 Sept. 1945.

49. *Syonan Shimbun*, 4 Sept. 1945.

50. Khor Cheang Kee, former Penang bureau news editor of *New Straits Times*, interview, Penang, 11 Jan. 1977.

51. See Hilken's diary, "Report of the Proceedings at Penang", 25 Sept. 1945, in WO 172/1784.

52. Ibid.

53. See Minutes of Naval and Civil Affairs Officers conference at Penang, 6–10 Sept. 1945, in Appendix to Hilken's Diary, in WO 172/1784.

54. See their story in *Straits Times* (Singapore), 8 Sept. 1945.

55. Ibid.

56. Maj.-Gen. S. Woodburn-Kirby, *The War against Japan*, vol. 5 (London, 1969), p. 266.

57. See signal from Haywood to McKelvie on the surrender ceremony aboard the Sussex, 6 Sept. 1945, in WO 172/1781. The signal reads in part: "His [Itagaki's] eyes were red with sorrow. He signed Singapore away to Britain. Tears trickled down his face near the end. Later he left the ship, a sad beaten man who was once Chief of Staff of the famed Kwangtung Army in China but whose hardness could not stand surrender."

58. Donnison, *British Military Administration*, pp. 154–5.

59. Ibid.

60. Maj.-Gen. S. Woodburn-Kirby, *The War against Japan*, pp. 271–2.

61. From the memoirs of Gen. Shibata Tai'chiro of the Twenty-fifth Army in Sumatra, being translated into English.

62. Alwee bin Jantan, "Terengganu, 1945–47: A Study in Political Development" (B.A. Hons. thesis, University of Malaya in Singapore, 1958), pp. 19–20.

Chapter 6

1. Memorandum on the Force 136 Organization in Malaya, by Lt.-Col. D.G. Gill-Davies, 13 Sept. 1945, p. 3, in BMA PSD/39.
2. Ibid.
3. Victor Purcell, *The Chinese in Malaya*, p. 262.
4. Anthony Short, *The Communist Insurrection in Malaya*, pp. 34–5.
5. Chin Peng, *My Side of History*, pp. 119–25; 128–9.
6. See extract of joint statement of 4th Independent Regiment, MPAJA, and South Johor MPAJU, entitled "Announcement in Felicitation of Victory in Far Eastern Anti-Japanese Campaign", dated 1 Sept. 1945, in WO 203/5642.
7. Ibid.
8. R. Balan, former MCP/MPAJA member. Interview, Kuala Lumpur, 2 Apr. 1973.
9. See Draft Telegram to All Allied Liaison Officers in Malaya, n.d., in WO 203/5642. F.S.V. Donnison, *British Military Administration in the Far East*, 1943–6, p. 384, quotes an almost identical message dated 11 August.
10. Draft Telegram to All Allied Liaison Officers in Malaya. Emphasis added.
11. Donnison, *British Military Administration*, p. 384.
12. Ibid.
13. Commander Force 136 to H.P.D., Reports on MPAJA from Malaya, 21 Aug. 1945, in WO 203/5642.
14. Hqs. MPAJA Ex-Servicemen's Association, "Ma-lai-ya ren ming kang jih chun chan ji" [The war diary of the MPAJA, in Li Tieh Min (ed.), *The Overseas Chinese and the Second World War* (The Malaya Section) (in Chinese), p. 29.
15. Ibid.
16. Memorandum on the Force 136 Organization in Malaya, by Lt.-Col. D.G. Gill-Davies, 13 Sept. 1945, in BMA PSD/39. See also another Force 136 report in 25 Indian Division, Hqs. Malaya Command WIR, 12 Dec. 1945, in ibid.
17. For statistics of guerrilla attacks and casualties, see Appendices B and C.
18. Memorandum on the Force 136 Organization in Malaya, by Lt.-Col. D.G. Gill-Davies.
19. See Memorandum by Secretary of State for the Colonies on Constitutional Policy in Malaya, 9 Dec. 1944, in CAB 98/41.
20. Ibid.
21. Telegram from Mountbatten to British Chiefs of Staff, "Malayan Resistance Movement — Chinese in Malaya", 11 May 1945, in WO 172/1763. Copies of this enclosure are also found in WO 20312967 and FO 371/46339/01382.

22. Ibid.
23. Mountbatten to Oliver Stanley, Secretary of State for the Colonies, 11 May 1945, in WO 172/1763.
24. Ibid. Emphasis added.
25. Top Secret Telegram of Chiefs of Staff to Mountbatten, 7 June 1945, in WO 172/1767. Copy also available in WO 203/56.
26. Ibid.
27. Donnison, *British Military Administration*, p. 383.
28. Ibid.
29. Conference Secretariat Minute 5/235, "Action to be taken by clandestine organisations and indigenous resistance movements in the event of Japanese capitulation", 15 Aug. 1945, for discussion at Supreme Allied Commander's staff meeting on 15 Aug. 1945, in WO 172/1777.
30. Hqs. Force 136 to H.P.D., "Directive to AJUF on conclusion of Armistice", 13 Aug. 1945, in WO 203/5642.
31. Ibid.
32. Ibid.
33. Hqs. Force 136 to H.P.D., "Directive to AJUF on conclusion of Armistice", 13 Aug. 1945, in WO 203/5642. Emphasis in original text.
34. Ibid.
35. Minutes of SAC's 78th staff meeting on 15 August 1945, in WO 172/1727.
36. Minutes of SAC's meeting on clandestine organisations, 16 Aug. 1945, in WO 172/1776.
37. Top secret telegram from War Office to SACSEA, TOO 181100, 18 Aug. 1945, in WO 172/1777.
38. Draft Telegram to All Allied Liaison Officers in Malaya, n.d., in WO 203/5642.
39. Message of Col. John Davis, attached to Memorandum of Commander, Force 136 to H.P.D., "Force 136 policy – Malaya", 19 Aug. 1945, in WO 203/5642.
40. Commander Force 136 to H.P.D., "Reports on MPAJA from Malaya", 21 Aug. 1945, in WO 203/5642.
41. Minutes of SAC's Meeting at Hq. SACSEA, Kandy, 21 Aug. 1945, on "Guerrilla activities in Malaya", in WO 172/1778.
42. Ibid.
43. Mountbatten to chiefs of staff on delay in surrender procedure, 20 Aug. 1945, in WO 172/1778.
44. Telegrams 220327Z and 220329Z to Mountbatten, 22 Aug. 1945, in WO 172/1778.
45. Chapman, *The Jungle Is Neutral*, pp. 414–8.
46. Ibid.
47. Sir Ralph Hone, in reply to questionnaire from Hull University student George Sweeney, 21 May 1971, in "Papers of General Hone", MSS Brit. Empire S. 407/3, Rhodes House Library, Oxford.

48. Director of Intelligence to SACSEA, "An estimate of likelihood of disturbances which would require military forces in various areas of the Far East", 22 Aug. 1945, in WO 172/1778.
49. Top Secret Memorandum of Commander, Force 136 to H.P.D., C.P.A., etc., 24 Aug. 1945, in WO 203/5642/X/102339. The C.P.A. (or Chief Political Adviser to Mountbatten) M.E. Dening was one of the most influential officials at SEAC headquarters. He was shortly to urge Mountbatten to act on this Force 136 request.
50. Ibid.
51. Ibid.
52. SACSEA to Psychological Warfare, Broadcasting Unit, "Official directive for output to Malaya", 18 Aug. 1945, in WO 172/1777.
53. Dominions Office to Australian government, 22 Aug. 1945, "Broadcasts to Malaya", in FO 317/46340.
54. Ibid.
55. Ibid.
56. SACSEA to Rear SACSEA, "Special talk for resistance movements in Malaya to be used in Malay, Chinese and English", 25 Aug. 1945, in WO 172/1778.
57. Ibid.
58. Ibid.
59. Alastair Morrison, Interview, Canberra, 13 June 1978.
60. See copies of the *Victory Herald*, 25 Aug. 1945, in WO 203/4015. They contain the item "Future of the Resistance Movement in Malaya".
61. Donnison, *British Military Administration*, p. 384.
62. Telegram from Lt.-Gen. Numata to Field-Marshal Terauchi, 10 Sept. 1945, in WO 172/1782.
63. Chin Kee Onn, *Malaya Upside Down* (Singapore, 1946), p. 202.
64. Hanrahan, *The Communist Struggle in Malaya*, p. 49.
65. ISUM No. 50, Hqs. 14th Army, 6 Oct. 1945, in BMA PSDI27.
66. Ibid.
67. H.C. Cheah, Interview, Klang, Dec. 1976.
68. Ibid.
69. Chapman, *The Jungle Is Neutral*, pp. 419–20.
70. R. Balan, former MCP/MPAJA member. Interview, Kuala Lumpur, 23 Apr. 1973.
71. See Appendices B and C.

Chapter 7

1. Edgar O'Ballance, *Malaya: The Communist Insurgent War*, p. 62.
2. William Shaw, *Tun Razak: His Life and Times* (Kuala Lumpur, 1976), p. 53. See also Haji Buyong Adil, *Sejarah Pahang* (Kuala Lumpur,

1972), p. 365, and Harry Miller, "The Ruler Who Was Kidnapped", *The Straits Times* (Singapore), 29 May 1957. The Americans were members of an O.S.S. force in Pahang.

3. Ibid.
4. See Harry Miller, *Menace in Malaya* (London, 1954), p. 51.
5. See Harry Miller, *Prince and Premier* (London, 1959), pp. 70–1. See also Baharuddin Abdul Majir, "Saberkas: Pergerakan dan Perjuangannya [Saberkas: the movement and its struggle], 1944–1946" (B.A. Hons. thesis, University of Malaya, 1975/76), pp. 178–80.
6. Baharuddin, "Saberkas", p. 178.
7. Miller, *Menace in Malaya*, pp. 72–3.
8. Ibid.
9. W.L. Blythe, *The Impact of Chinese Secret Societies in Malaya* (London, 1968), pp. 229–32.
10. Ibid.
11. Ibid., pp. 229–32.
12. Ibid., p. 232.
13. Ibid.
14. Ibid.
15. ALFSEA, Weekly Intelligence Summary No. 99, 10 Oct. 1945, in WQ 172/1787.
16. Miller, *Menace in Malaya*, p. 51.
17. The story is told by Tan Tai Tee, deputy commander of the First Regiment, MPAJA, in *Sin Min Chu* [New Democracy] (Singapore), 17 Oct. 1945.
18. Albert Lim Shee Ping, a lawyer. Interview, London, Apr. 1976.
19. See Hamzah bin Mohamed, "The Fourteen Days of Terror: Before, During and After" (B.A. Hons. thesis, University of Malaya, 1969/70).
20. Chin Kee Onn, *Malaya Upside Down* (Singapore, 1976), pp. 203–4.
21. Thatcher and Cross, *Pai Naa*, pp. 158–9; Chapman, op. cit., pp. 316–30.
22. Lawrence Siaw, "A Local History of the Chinese Community in Titi, Malaysia, 1870–1960" (Ph.D. thesis, Monash University, 1975), pp. 158–59. This work has since been published under the title, *Chinese Society in Rural Malaysia: A Local History of the Chinese in Titi, Jelebu* (Kuala Lumpur, 1983).
23. Ibid.
24. H.C. Cheah, interview.
25. Soong Mun Wai, a librarian in University of Malaya. Interview, Kuala Lumpur, Jan. 1977.
26. See Osman China's story in J.B. Perry Robinson, *Transformation in Malaya* (London, 1956), p. 158.
27. M.G. Swift, *Malay Peasant Society in Jelebu* (London, 1965), p. 85.
28. See article "Kenangan Hidup Pak Sako" [Memories of Ishak Haji

Mohamed], No. 33, in the weekly *Mingguan Malaysia* (Kuala Lumpur), 15 Aug. 1976.

29. Ibid.
30. Haji Buyong Adil, *Sejarah Johor* [History of Johor] (Kuala Lumpur, 1971), pp. 323-24.
31. Musak Mantrak, "Ancaman Komunis [The communist threat], 1945–46" in the monthly *Dian* (Kota Bharu), No. 96, Jan. 1977, p. 20.
32. Lawrence Siaw, "A Local History of the Chinese Community", pp. 203–4.
33. R. Balan, interview.
34. Chin Kee Onn, *Malaya Upside Down*, pp. 203–4.
35. R. Balan, interview.
36. Chin Kee Onn, *Malaya Upside Down*, pp. 203–4.
37. Lawrence Siaw, "A Local History of the Chinese Community", pp. 311–2.
38. J.M. Tsang, KMT agent and wireless operator with Force 136 group under Hislop. Interview, Penang, Nov. 1976.
39. Ibid.
40. Lawrence Siaw, "A Local History of the Chinese Community", p. 311.
41. Ibid., p. 313.
42. H.C. Cheah, interview.
43. H.C. Cheah, interview. Force 136 officer Maj. Hislop had done the same thing when he saw a Communist Party flag flying atop the flagpole at the forestry office at Kampong Weng in Kedah.
44. H.C. Cheah, interview.
45. Chapman, *The Jungle is Neutral*, pp. 419–20.
46. Ibid.
47. Ibid.
48. Lawrence Siaw, "A Local History of the Chinese Community", pp. 315–36.
49. G.A. Garnon-Williams to CPA and Director of Intelligence, 29 Aug. 1945, in WO 203/5642/X/L02339.
50. Dening to Foreign Office, with a request that the message be passed to the Colonial Office, 3 Sept. 1945, in ibid.
51. Ibid.
52. Ibid.
53. See the chapter "Nationalism in Burma", in Donnison, *British Military Administration*, pp. 343–74.
54. 34 Indian Corps, SEAC, to Force 136 Hdqrs., Memorandum on Discipline: The MPAJA, 23 Oct. 1945, in BMA PSD/39 and related matters in MU Secretariat 1763/46.
55. See Political Intelligence Journal, Malayan Security Service, Singapore, issues of 30 Apr. and 15 Aug. 1946 respectively.

Chapter 8

1. See M.A. Rauf, *A Brief History of Islam*, with special reference to Malaya (Kuala Lumpur, 1965); and Naguib al-'Attas, *Preliminary Statement on a General Theory of the Islamization of the Malay–Indonesian Archipelago* (Kuala Lumpur, 1969); and *The Cambridge History of Islam*, vol. 2: The Indian Sub-Continent, Southeast Asia, Africa and the Muslim West, 1977.

2. The best account on this uprising is Sartono Kartodirdjo, *The Peasants' Revolt of Banten in 1888* (The Hague, 1966).

3. B.O. Martin, *Muslim Brotherhoods in Nineteenth-Century Africa* (Cambridge, 1976), pp. 1–12.

4. Rudolph Peters, *Jihad in Mediaeval and Modern Islam* (Leiden, 1977), pp. 3–4.

5. I have used the translation of *jihad fi Sabilillah* in H.A.R. Gibb and J.H. Kramers (eds.), *A Shorter Encyclopaedia of Islam* (London, 1961), p. 89.

6. See Hamzah bin Mohamed, "The 14 Days of Terror: Before, During and After" (B.A. Hons. thesis, University of Malaya, 1969/70), p. 29.

7. This refers to the early period of the Japanese occupation. See Kamaruddin bin Mohd. Piah, "Kampung Bekur sejak 1900: satu kajian tempatan dengan rujukan khas kepada trajedi 6hb. Mac 1946" (B.A. Hons. thesis, University of Malaya, 1974/5), pp. 22–4.

8. See Halinah Bamadhaj, "The Impact of the Japanese Occupation of Malaya on Malay Society and Politics, 1941–45" (M.A. thesis, University of Auckland, 1975), pp. 206–7.

9. Kenelm O.L. Burridge, "Racial Relations in Johore", *Australian Politics and History Journal* 2, 2 (1957): 162–3.

10. Muhammad Haji Kidin, *Kerana Si Kuntum* (Penang, 1965), p. 67.

11. Ibid.

12. Naguib, *Some Aspects of Sufism*, pp. 49–50.

13. Ibid., p. 34.

14. Gibb and Kramers, *A Shorter Encyclopaedia of Islam*, p. 236.

15. Kenelm O.L. Burridge, "Managerial Influences in a Johore Village", *JMBRAS* 30 (May 1957): 94.

16. Musak Mantrak, "Sejarah Masyarakat Majemuk di Mukim VII, Batu Pahat [History of the plural society in Mukim VII, Batu Pahat], Johor, 1900–1945" (B.A. Hons. history thesis, University of Malaya, 1974/5), p. 2.

17. A.B. Ramsay, "Indonesians in Malaya", *JMBRAS* 29 (May 1956): 120.

18. Halinah Bamadhaj, "The Impact of the Japanese Occupation of Malaya", p. 210. See also Hqs. Malaya Command WIR No. 14, "Malay Religious Activity", in WO 172/9773 and Salmah Sheikh Brix, "Panglima Salleh" (B.A. Hons. thesis, University of Malaya), 1976/7, p. 11.

19. M.V. del Tufo, *Malaya: A Report on the 1947 Census of Population* (London, 1947), p. 150.

20. Halinah Bamadhaj, "The Impact of the Japanese Occupation of Malaya", pp. 205–14. Musak Mantrak uses the expression *berjihad fi sabilillah* to describe the Malay religious movement in Batu Pahat in his article, "Ancaman Komunis [The communist threat], 1945–46", in the magazine *Dian Diges* (Kota Bharu), Jan. 1977, p. 21, and in his more detailed thesis, op. cit., pp. 66, 70. Hairi Abdullah also uses the term *Sabil* frequently in his article, "Kebangkitan dan Gerakan Tentera Selendang Merah dalam sejarah daerah Muar dan Batu Pahat" [The emergence and development of the army of the Red Bands in the local history of Muar and Batu Pahat], in *Jebat* (*Journal of the Historical Society*, Universiti Kebangsaan Malaysia), 1973/5, pp. 9–10. Another source that clearly calls it the "Sabilillah" is the British military intelligence report entitled "Malay religious activity", in WIR No. 14, Hq. Malaya Command, 2 Feb. 1946, in WO 172/9773.

21. See WIR No. 14, Hq. Malaya Command, "Malay religious activity", in WO 172/9773.

22. Hairi Abdullah, "Kebangkitan dan Gerakan Tentera Selendang Merah dalam sejarah…", p. 11, gives an elaborate description of the ritual. See also WIR No. 14, Hq. Malaya Command, "Malay religious activity".

23. The use of the stone *delima* was told to me by Ahmad Jais, First Secretary (Information), Malaysian High Commission, Canberra. Interview, 15 Oct. 1977.

24. WIR No. 14, "Malay religious activity", in WO 172/9773.

25. Hairi Abdullah, "Kebangkitan dan Gerakan Tentera Selendang Merah dalam sejarah…", p. 11.

26. These two stories are cited in Naguib, *Some Aspects of Sufism*, p. 48.

27. See WIR No. 31, "Che Salleh and his Red Bands", up to 11 June 1946, in WO 172/9773.

28. Ibid.

29. Halinah Bamadhaj, "The Impact of the Japanese Occupation of Malaya", pp. 210–1; see also Salmah Sheikh Brix, "Panglima Salleh", pp. 11–3.

30. Naguib, *Some Aspects of Sufism*, p. 47.

31. Ibid., p. 48.

32. The full title is given in Hairi Abdullah, "Kebangkitan dan Gerakan Tentera Selendang Merah dalam sejarah…", p. 9.

33. Ibid.

34. Hairi Abdullah, "Kebangkitan dan Gerakan Tentera Selendang Merah dalam sejarah…", p. 10.

35. Musak Mantrak, "Sejarah Masyarakat Majemuk di Mukim VII, Batu Pahat", p. 70.

36. Ibid., p. 74.

37. Halinah Bamadhaj, "The Impact of the Japanese Occupation of Malaya", pp. 209–11.

38. Anwar Abdullah, *Dato Onn* (Petaling Jaya, 1971), pp. 96–7.

39. Two sources which give 10 June as the date of the killing are Musak Mantrak, "Sejarah Masyarakat Majemuk di Mukim VII, Batu Pahat", pp. 60, 72; and Zabha, *Tan Sri Haji Mohamed Noah, a biography* (Kuala Lumpur, 1976).

40. See Anwar Abdullah, *Dato Onn*, pp. 95–100.

41. Tan Sri S. Chelvasingam-MacIntyre, a former Malaysian High Court judge, in his memoirs, *Through Memory Lane* (Singapore, 1973), pp. 116–7. Of Ceylon-Tamil origin, MacIntyre was a lawyer who practised in Batu Pahat during the war.

42. *Penang Shimbun*, 22 June 1945.

43. Ibid.

44. *Penang Shimbun*, 22 June 1945.

45. Ibid.

46. Ibid.

47. *Malai Sinpo* (Kuala Lumpur), 6 July 1945.

48. Ibid.

49. Ibid.

50. See Su-ssu (ed.) *K'ang Jih ying hsiung tsai Jou-nan* [The anti-Japanese heroes in southern Johor] (Singapore, 1945), pp. 25–6.

51. Ibid., p. 25.

52. Ibid., p. 26.

53. Hqs. Ex-MPAJA Servicemen's Association, *Ma-lai-ya ren min K'ang Jih zi chun chan ji* [The diary of the MPAJA's battles], in Li Tieh Min *et al.*, *Ta-chan yu Nan-ch'iao* [Ma-lai-ya chih pu], p. 20.

54. Chin Peng, *My Side of History*, p. 127.

55. Chinese Ministry of Foreign Affairs to the British Embassy in Nanking, 7 Feb. 1946, in MU Secret 346/46, Kuala Lumpur. Regarding the Batu Pahat incident, the Selangor branch of the Malayan Kuomintang in a statement issued after the war described it as a "massacre". Their statement, dated September 1945, said: "In May 1945 at Batu Pahat, Johor the Malays, instigated and variously armed by the Japanese, started an attack on the Chinese residents of the place. As a result, the Chinese being taken unawares, between 15,000 and 20,000 Chinese inhabitants, including women and children were killed and rendered destitute and homeless. The Japanese authorities treated the incident as a mere disturbance of peace, and punished [the people] indiscriminately." See memorandum entitled "Treatment of People in Malaya during the Japanese Military Occupation" compiled by the "Extraordinary General Affairs" Section of the Kuomintang, Selangor Branch, Kuala Lumpur, Sept. 1945, in BMA ADM 8/1.

56. Shih Ming, "Jih kuo chai Jou-fou shou shan Ton bu ren chi hua zhi shi shih" [Japanese instigation behind the anti-Chinese activities of the Malays in Johor], in Li Tieh Min *et al.*, *Ta-chan yu Nan-ch'iao*, p. 169.

57. Chin Kee Onn, pers. comm., 26 July 1977.

58. Shih Ming, "Japanese instigation behind the anti-Chinese activities of the Malays in Johore", in Li Tieh Min *et al.*, *Ta-chan yu Nan-ch'iao*, p. 169.

59. Ibid.

60. Ibid., p. 170.

61. Leaflet P.W. SMA/40 in file "Malaya-Psychological Warfare leaflets, 1945 June-July", in WO 203/4015.

62. See P.W. leaflet SMA/41, in WO 203/4015.

63. Chin Kee Onn, *Malaya Upside Down* (Singapore, 1977 reprint), p. 183.

64. A Malay journalist of Javanese extraction. Name withheld. Interview, Kuala Lumpur, Sept. 1977.

65. See Hamzah bin Mohamed, "The Fourteen Days of Terror: Before, During and After", pp. 11–22; and Musak Mantrak, who also uses the expression "regime of terror" in "Sejarah Masyarakat Majemuk di Mukim VII, Batu Pahat", p. 87.

66. Ibid., pp. 16–7.

67. See "A Note on the Invulnerability Cult", *Journal of Political Intelligence*, Malayan Security Service, Singapore, 15 July 1946, in J.W. Dalley Papers, Rhodes House Library, Oxford.

68. Halinah Bamadhaj, "The Impact of the Japanese Occupation of Malaya", p. 230.

69. Anwar Abdullah, *Dato Onn*, p. 95.

70. Hairi Abdullah, "Kebangkitan dan Gerakan Tentera Selendang Merah dalam sejarah ...", pp. 12–4.

71. There are conflicting accounts of where the meeting took place. Anwar Abdullah, *Dato Onn*, pp. 110–1, says Kampong Bagan; Hairi Abdullah, "Kebangkitan dan Gerakan Tentera Selendang Merah dalam sejarah ...", p. 14, mentions Peserai. Halinah Bamadhaj, "The Impact of the Japanese Occupation of Malaya", p. 213, does not disclose where the meeting took place, but says that Datuk Onn brought two Chinese who were prominent businessmen and leaders of the Overseas Chinese Association during the occupation. Peserai seems the most likely place as it lies between Kampong Bagan and Bandar Penggaram.

72. Chin Peng, *My Side of History*, p. 127.

73. Anwar Abdullah, *Dato Onn*, pp. 100–1.

74. Musak Mantrak, "Sejarak Masyarkat Majemuk di Mukim VII, Batu Pahat", p. 86. He quotes as his source, "Batu Pahat Bergolak" [Batu Pahat in Crisis], from *Kebudayaan 1972 Kenangan 75 Tahun Bandar Penggaram* [The 1972 Cultural Souvenir Commemorating the 75th Anniversary of Batu Pahat], p. 52.

75. Anwar Abdullah, *Dato Onn*, pp. 109–10. Hairi Abdullah, "Kebangkitan dan Gerakan Tentera Selendang Merah dalam sejarah …", p. 14, claims it was several Chinese who had begged Datuk Onn to use his good offices to stop Kiyai Salleh from carrying out his proposed attack. Musak Mantrak, "Sejarah Masyarakat Majemuk di Mukim VII, Batu Pahat", p. 87, says it was a Chinese community leader who asked Datuk Onn to intervene and stop the attack.

76. Anwar Abdullah, *Dato Onn*, p. 111.

77. Ibid. In an interview with Goh Kim Guat, in Johor Bahru, October 1959, Datuk Onn spoke of his efforts to bring about a peaceful solution in that incident. He had accosted Panglima Salleh and his followers who were advancing to a nearby Chinese village to carry out their "massacre campaign". Stopping them on the bank of the Batu Pahat river, he told them to go back to their respective homes, for "only over his dead body would they be allowed to proceed any further". Goh Kim Guat, "Sino-Malay Relations in Malaya, 1945–55" (Unpublished B.A. Honours thesis, History Department, University of Malaya, Singapore, 1960), pp. 14–5. A police officer who was an eyewitness to the Batu Pahat incidents, also interviewed by Goh, stated "The Batu Pahat river was red with blood". He confirmed Datuk Onn's role in the peace efforts. Goh does not mention the story that Datuk Onn was arrested by communists and told to stop the fighting, as claimed by Chin Peng in his autobiography, *My Side of History*, p. 127.

78. Ibid.

79. Halinah Bamadhaj, "The Impact of the Japanese Occupation of Malaya", pp. 213, 232.

80. Hairi Abdullah, "Kebangkitan dan Gerakan Tentera Selendang Merah dalam sejarah …", p. 14.

81. Halinah Bamadhaj, "The Impact of the Japanese Occupation of Malaya", p. 213.

82. Maj.-Gen. Ralph Hone, *Report on the British Military Administration of Malaya, September 1945 to March 1946* (Kuala Lumpur, 1946), p. 40. The report does not state whether the refugees were Malays or Chinese, but it would seem likely that the majority were Chinese.

83. Anthony Stockwell, "The Development of Malay Politics During the Course of the Malayan Union Experiment, 1942–1948" (Ph.D. thesis, University of London, 1973), p. 274, quoting the Johor Resident Commissioner's file, RCJ No. 549/46.

84. Information on the Sungai Manik incidents is drawn mainly from Ghazali Basri, "Hilir Perak: Sejarah Hubungan Ras Zaman Pendudukan Jepun Sehingga Pemerintahan Inggeris, 1942–46" [Lower Perak: the history of race relations from the Japanese occupation until the BMA, 1942–45] (B.A. thesis, University of Malaya, 1974/5).

85. Ibid., p. 46.

86. Ibid., pp. 46–8.
87. Force 136 field intelligence report, 11 Sept. 1945, in BMA PSD/39.
88.. Force 136 report, 15 and 16 Sept. 1945, in BMA PSD/39.
89. Force 136 report, 26 Sept. 1945, in BMA PSD/39.
90. Victor Purcell's "Malaya's Political Climate III, 19 October–9 November 1945", in WO 203/5302; see also Purcell, *The Chinese in Malaya* (London, 1948), p. 268.
91. Hamzah bin Mohamad, "The Fourteen Days of Terror: Before, During and After" (B.A. thesis, University of Malaya, 1969/70), pp. 17–20. See also ISUM, Hqs. Malaya Command, 2 Feb. 1946, in WO 172/9773.
92. Purcell, "Malaya's Political Climate III".
93. Ibid.
94. Ibid.
95. Ibid.
96. Report, "Situation in Malaya", 14 Nov. 1945, in WO 172/1791.
97. SACSEA to War Office on Malaya, 17 Nov. 1945, in WO 172/1792.
98. *Nanyang Siang Pau*, 17 Nov. 1945.
99. Telegram from Johor Bharu to SACSEA, 20 Nov. 1945, in WO 172/1792.
100. BMA (Malaya) Monthly Report No. 3 for Nov. 1945, p. 3, in Confidential BMA PSD/39/45.
101. BMA Monthly Report for Nov. 1945, Confidential SCA9/45, p. 3.
102. WIR, No. 61 Hqs. SACSEA, 10 Dec. 1945,307, in WO 172/1794.
103. WIR, 25 Indian Division, 12 Dec. 1945, p. 4, in MU Secret 335/46.
104. *Min Sheng Pau*, 20 Dec. 1945.
105. ISUM Hqs. Malaya Command No. 10, up to 5 Jan. 1946, in WO 172/9773.
106. Ibid.
107. H.R. Hone, *Report on the British Military Administration in Malaya, September 1945–March 1946*, p. 41.
108. William Shaw, *Tun Razak: His Life and Times* (Kuala Lumpur, 1976), p. 58. The account is believed to be based on interviews with the late Malaysian prime minister.
109. Ibid.
110. *Nanyang Siang Pau*, 12 Mar. 1946.

Chapter 9

1. See H.R. Hone, *Report on the British Military Administration of Malaya, September 1945 to March* 1946 (Kuala Lumpur, 1946), p. 38.
2. See for instance typescript of broadcast by Victor Purcell, entitled "Malaya in Crisis", over Radio Singapore, 12 Nov. 1945, in which he states: "We came back to Malaya with the policy of free association and free speech", in Sel. CA 238/45.

3. Resume of BMA policies in Memorandum, "Control of Societies: Proposed Introduction of Legislation", by W.L. Blythe, Acting Secretary for Chinese Affairs, Malayan Union, n.d. (1946?), in MU 266/46 Vol. I Secret.

4. Minutes of meeting held at BMA (Malaya), Hqs. Singapore, on 29 Sept. 1945, BMA/PSD/39.

5. *Sin Min Chu* (Singapore), 8 Nov. 1945.

6. Anthony Short, *The Communist Insurrection in Malaya*, p. 39. Harry Miller, in *Menace in Malaya* (London, 1954), p. 62, mentions that the denunciation by Ng Yeh Lu gave Lai Tek a fright. The story of how Yeh Lu tried to get his story to expose Lai Tek published in 1945 is told in Chuan Hui Tsuan, "Wo shou zhi dao de Lai Te/Yeh Lu" in the weekly *Kuo Ji Shi Pau* [International Times], Singapore, July 1968, pp. 19–20.

7. Short, *The Communist Insurrection in Malaya*, p. 39, mentions Yeung Kuo as the main investigator of Lai Tek's past and present activities. However, McLane credits it to Chin Peng, who subsequently became the MCP's secretary-general. See C.B. McLane, *Soviet Strategies in Southeast Asia* (Princeton, 1966), p. 311. Both Short and McLane had access to government reports and Special Branch files.

8. *Min Sheng Pau* (Kuala Lumpur), 28 Nov. 1945.

9. *Kin Kwok Daily News* (Ipoh), 27 Nov. 1945.

10. Ibid.

11. Chin Peng in *My Side of History*, pp. 181–3 confirms their collaboration to oust Li Tek. Yap, "Perak under the Japanese", Appendices X and XI.

12. McLane, *Soviet Strategies in Southeast Asia*, p. 310. It is believed that Lai Tek went into hiding in Singapore. In late 1947 he made his way to Hong Kong and then to Bangkok where a communist killer squad tracked him down and eliminated him. His death, however, has never been officially confirmed.

13. ISUM No. 50, Hqs. 14th Army, 6 Oct. 1945, p. 8, in BMA PSD/39. In none of these reports is Lai Tek mentioned. I have identified Chang Hong as Lai Tek mainly on the strength of the information given by John Davis, formerly of Force 136, in an interview at his home in Kent, June 1976.

14. Force 136 field intelligence report, 24 Sept. 1945, in BMA PSD/39.

15. Top Secret telegram from SACSEA to Hqs. Malaya Command (SAC 2180), 22 Dec. 1945, in WO 172/1795. He appears to be Maj. R.J. Isaacs who revealed the identity of Lai Tek in 1953. See *Malay Mail* (Kuala Lumpur), 31 Aug. 1953.

16. Ibid.

17. This is disclosed in the biography of John Davis by Margaret Shennan, *Our Man in Malaya*, (London, 2008), pp. 118–20.

18. Short, *The Communist Insurrection in Malaya*, p. 40.
19. Gene Z. Hanrahan, *The Communist Struggle in Malaya* (New York, 1954), p. 51.
20. Lai-T'e, *Wei-min-tsu t'uan chieh min-chu tzu-yu min-sheng kai-shan erh tou-cheng* [Struggle for national unity, democracy and liberty and improvement of people's livelihood], report to the 8th Enlarged Plenum, 22–27 Jan., p. 15; see also Hanrahan, *The Communist Struggle in Malaya*, p. 51.
21. See Cheah Boon Kheng, "The Malayan Democratic Union, 1945–48" (M.A. thesis, University of Malaya, 1975), pp. 34–5, 41.
22. Lai-T'e, *Wei-min-tsu …*, p. 15.
23. Lai-T'e, *Wei-min-tsu*, pp. 15–6.
24. Ibid.
25. See "Proclamation for convening the Selangor Peoples' Representatives Conference and forming the Selangor Peoples' State Committee", n.d. (Aug. 1945?), in Sel. CA162/45.
26. *Sin Min Chu*, 2 Nov. 1945.
27. See the BMA's Report of the Military Administration of Region Four (Selangor) for October 1945, p. 14, in MU C/1/1/4, which dismisses MPAJA attempts at government as follows: "Whatever was their success in this militant and adventurous project it has not qualified them [MCP/MPAJU/MPAJA] for participation in the more involved sphere of government."
28. ISUM, No. 50, Hqs. 14th Army, 6 Oct. 1945, in BMA PSD/29.
29. Victor Purcell's "Malaya's Political Climate II", 1–19 Oct. 1945, p. 5, in WO 203/5302.
30. "The Soong Kwong Case", in MU Secret 1763/46; also Donnison, *British Military Administration in the Far East* , p. 394.
31. Purcell, *The Chinese in Malaya*, p. 267.
32. *Sin Min Chu*, 12 Dec. 1945.
33. Director of Intelligence, Report, "Strikes and Disturbances in Malaya", 8 Nov. 1945, in WO 203/4381, and "Review of Internal Situation", 1 Dec. 1945, in WO 203/5642. What follows is based mainly on these two reports, unless otherwise stated.
34. Victor Purcell's "Malaya's Political Climate III", 19 Oct.–9 Nov. 1945, in WO 203/5302.
35. Ibid.
36. Ibid.
37. Director of Intelligence, "Strikes and Disturbances in Malaya", 8 Nov. 1945, in WO 203/4381.
38. Ibid., p. 3.
39. Ibid.
40. Victor Purcell's "Malaya's Political Climate V", 1–20 Dec. 1945, pp. 5–7, in WO 203/5302.

41. One field security report is dated 28 Nov. 1945: "Loi Tik or Loi Te. Believed Russian trained ex-FIC [French Indochina) now in Johore. Penang reports leader MCP an Armenian rumoured moving north from Singapore." See signal from Hqs. Malaya Command to SACSEA, in WO 172/1793.
42. McLane, *Soviet Strategies in Southeast Asia*, pp. 307, 310.
43. Director of Intelligence, "Strikes and Disturbances", 8 Nov. 1945, in WO 293/4381.
44. Victor Purcell, "Malaya's Political Climate IV", 10–30 Nov. 1945, in WO 203/5302.
45. Ibid.
46. Short, *The Communist Insurrection in Malaya*, p. 43; Hanrahan, *The Communist Struggle in Malaya*, pp. 50–1.
47. Telegram giving the terms of agreement from Rear SACSEA to War Office, 6 Nov. 1945, in WO 172/1790.
48. Short, *The Communist Insurrection in Malaya*, pp. 35–6; Miller, *Menace in Malaya*, pp. 60–1.
49. See "The Bekor Raid", p. 7 in WIR 25 Indian Division, 28 Nov. 1945, in MU 335/46 Vol. 1.
50. See "The KMT in Kota Bharu", in WIR, 25 Indian Division, 12 Dec./ 1945, in MU 335/46 Vol. 1.
51. Hai Shang Ou, *Ma-lai-ya jen-ming k'ang jih jin* [The MPAJA] (Singapore, 1945), pp. 56–7.
52. See report, "Campaign ribbons for guerrillas", 7 Dec. 1945, in WO 172/1794; see also Miller, *Menace in Malaya*, p. 60.
53. Purcell, *The Chinese in Malaya*, p. 270.
54. Among the newspapers prohibited were the *Min Sheng Pau* of Kuala Lumpur and the *Min Pao* of Seremban. See the list in MU 395/46.
55. Mountbatten of Burma, Earl, *Post-Surrender Tasks: Section E of the Report to the Combined Chiefs of Staff, 1943–45* (London, 1969), p. 304.
56. Letter from Assistant Chief of Staff to Chief of Staff entitled "Disturbances in Malaya", 26 Oct. 1945, which read: "SAC feels that Hone is not handling Malaya as successfully as Rance [CCAO] handled Burma, and considers that it is a grave reflection on the administration in Malaya that it should be necessary to inflict casualties on local demonstrators when no such action was ever considered necessary in Burma."
57. Mountbatten, *Post-Surrender Tasks*, p. 304.
58. Ibid.
59. Lai-T'e, *Wei-min-tsu...*, p. 15.
60. Donnison, *British Military Administration in the Far East*, p. 391.
61. Ibid., pp. 392–3; Mountbatten, *Post-Surrender Task*, pp. 304–5.
62. Donnison, *British Military Administration in the Far East*, p. 345.
63. See Appendix C, "Malayan Communist Party Policy and Organisation", WIR, Hqs. Malaya Command, 2 Apr. 1946, in WO 172/9773.

64. Victor Purcell, "The Issues Before Us", a report on Chinese affairs, 18 Feb. 1946, in SCA/FM/A/7/1.
65. Victor Purcell, "Memorandum on Advisory Councils", 21 Feb. 1946, in MU Secret 158/46.

Chapter 10

1. See Extracts of SAC's policy for Military Administration in Malaya, n.d., Appendix K, p. 320, in Mountbatten of Burma, Earl, *Post-Surrender Tasks: Section E of the Report to the Combined Chiefs of Staff, 1943–1945* (London, 1969).
2. See Classification of Suspects, Appendix C, 6 Aug. 1945, in Principal Civil Affairs Directives for BMA of Malaya, in WO 203/5406.
3. Information on the Japanese-appointed Sultans is based mainly on Willan's reports of his interviews with the Sultans, between 12 and 30 Sept. 1945, in WO 203/5642, and Sir Harold MacMichael's Report on a Mission to Malaya (Oct. 1945–Jan. 1946), Kuala Lumpur, 1946, which appears as Appendix C, J. de V. Allen, *The Malayan Union* (Yale University, 1967), p. 154. Most scholars have regarded MacMichael's mission as more important than Willan's, and consequently have neglected Willan's reports. In fact. Willan did the preliminary work for Mac-Michael's mission.
4. For an account of how Tengku Musa-Eddin was passed over, see Yeo Kim Wah, "The Selangor Succession Dispute, 1933–38", *Journal of Southeast Asian Studies* 2, 2 (Sept. 1971): 169–84.
5. SAC's memorandum, "Initial Relations with Malay Sultans", 3–6 Sept. 1945, in WO 172/1781.
6. Willan's report of his interview with Sultan Ibrahim, 8 Sept. 1945, in WO 203/564.
7. Ibid.
8. Willan's confidential telegram to CCAO (Malaya) and SAC, II, Sept. 1945, in WO 203/5642.
9. Confidential telegram from Willan to ALFSEA, 10 Oct. 1945, in WO 172/1787.
10. See Willan's report of interview with Sultan of Selangor, 18 Sept. 1945, in WO 203/5642.
11. Willan's report of his interview with the Regent of Perlis, 17 Sept. 1945, in WO 203/5642.
12. Ibid.
13. The State Council statement, dated 13 January 1948, gives 5 Nov. 1945 as the date of its meeting which deposed Sultan Ali, but the Malay historian Haji Buyong Adil claims that the Council's first meeting was held some time in Sept. 1945 and that it was widely believed by the Malay public that the move had been sponsored by the British. See

Haji Buyong Adil, *Sejarah Terengganu* [History of Terengganu] (Kuala Lumpur, 1974), pp. 203-4, for the full text of the Council's statement, which first appeared in *Cermin Malaya* [Malayan Mirror], Information Services Department, Federation of Malaya. No reason is given as to why the council issued its statement so late. It is probable that the matter had become controversial in 1948. Tengku Ismail was not crowned Sultan of Terengganu until 6 June 1949.

14. See Willan's report of his interview with Sultan of Johor, 8 Sept. 1945, in WO 203/5642.
15. Ibid.
16. MU Secret 64/46, "Situation Reports, Kelantan", 3 May 1946.
17. Willan's report of his interview with Sultan of Johor, 8 Sept. 1945, in WO 203/5642.
18. Donnison, *British Military Administration in the Far East*, p. 156.
19. DCCAO's Report on the Military Government of the Malay Peninsula for the period 12–30 Sept. 1945, in MU Secret C/1/4.
20. Report by Major J.M. MacLean, Officer-in-Charge of Police, Johor Bharu, 21 Sept. 1945, in BMA PSD 13.
21. See letter from Maj. A.J.A. Blake, Senior Officer, Batu Pahat, to Major MacLean, Johor Bharu, 20 Sept. 1945, in BMA PSD 1/3.
22. Donnison, *British Military Administration in the Far East*, pp. 303-4.
23. ISUM No. 32, Hqs. Malaya Command, Kuala Lumpur, 20 Oct. 1945; and also Arena Wati, *Cherpen Zaman Jepun* [Short stories of the Japanese occupation period] (Kuala Lumpur), p. 25n.
24. ISUM No. 32.
25. Ishak Haji Mohamed. Interview, Kuala Lumpur, Jan. 1977. See also his article, "Kenangan Pak Sako" [Memories of Pak Sako, his Japanese wartime pen name], in the weekly *Mingguan Malaysia*, 4 July 1976.
26. ISUM No. 6, 8 Dec. 1945, Hqs. Malaya Command in MU Secret 335/46 Vol. 1, gives a lengthy background of the KMM's wartime activities.
27. *Straits Times* (Singapore), 11 Oct. 1945.
28. Ibid.
29. See Annex I, "Draft of memorandum which Sir Harold MacMichael will hand to the Malay rulers in explaining to them His Majesty's Government's intentions as regards the future of Malaya", attached to "Policy in regard to Malaya", CP (45) Oct. 1945, in CO 273/675/50823 Pt. I.
30. Ibid.
31. Ibid.
32. See telegram from MacMichael to Secretary of State for Colonies, 20 Oct. 1945, in CO 273/675/50823/Pt. I.
33. See Memorandum by Secretary of State for the Colonies, "Policy in regard to Malaya", to Cabinet, Oct. 1945, in CO 273/675/50823.
34. James V. Allen, *The Malayan Union* (Yale University, 1967), pp. 31-3.

35. MacMichael to War Office, 25 Oct. 1945, in WO 203/5293.
36. Allen, *The Malayan Union*, p. 32, also noted that the appellation "Your Excellency" was used instead of "Your Highness" to mean that the Regent had not been formally recognized, and also that the reference to Siam meant that he could be replaced and exiled.
37. Ahmad Boestamam, *Merintis Jalan Kepunchak* (Petaling Jaya, 1973), pp. 23–30.
38. Victor Purcell's "Malaya's Political Climate V", 1–20 Dec. 1945, in WO 203/5302.
39. WIR, 25 Indian Division, 27 Nov. 1945, in MU 335/46 Vol. I. This intelligence report claims Moktaruddin was not present, while subsequent reports say he was. Local newspaper reports of the meeting did not mention his presence or his speech at all.
40. Ibid., see also ISUM No. 6, Hq. Malaya Command, 8 Dec. 1945.
41. ISUM No. 6, Hqs. Malaya Command, 8 Dec. 1945.
42. ISUM No. 7, Hqs. Malaya Command, 15 Dec. 1945, in MU Secret 335/46 Vol. I.
43. Ibid.
44. Dahari Ali, former MNP secretary-general, interview Kuala Lumpur, Jan. 1974.
45. ISUM No. 6, Hqs. Malaya Command, 8 Dec. 1945.
46. Political Intelligence Journal, Malayan Security Service, Singapore, 31 July 1946, p. 2.
47. Ibid.
48. Benedict Anderson, *Java in a Time of Revolution* (New York, 1972), pp. 278–80.
49. See the White Paper, *Malayan Union and Singapore: Statement of Policy on Future Constitution*, Cmd. 6724, Jan. 1946, London.
50. Allen, *The Malayan Union*, p. 33.
51. *Malay Mail* (Kuala Lumpur), 26 Jan. 1946.
52. Ishak Tadin, "Dato Onn and Malay Nationalism, 1946–1951", *Journal of Southeast Asian History* 1, 1 (Mar. 1960): 59.
53. Anwar Abdullah, *Dato Onn* (Petaling Jaya, 1971), pp. 118–23; see also Zabha, *Tan Sri Haji Mohamed Noah* (Kuala Lumpur, 1976), pp. 71–4.
54. Ishak Tadin, "Dato Onn and Malay Nationalism", p. 59.
55. ISUM No. 12, Hqs. Malaya Command, 19.Jan. 1946, in WO 172/9772.
56. ISUM No. 14, Hqs. Malaya Command, 2 Feb. 1946, in WO 172/9773.
57. Ibid.
58. Ibid.
59. Ibid.
60. Ibid.
61. Zabha, *Tan Sri Haji Mohamed Noah*, p. 73.
62. See Allen, *The Malayan Union*, pp. 34, 35 for other details of this episode.

63. See the full list of participating associations, in Mohamad Yunus Hamidi, *Sejarah Pergerakan Politik Melayu Semenanjung* [The history of the Peninsular Malay Political Movement] (Kuala Lumpur, 1961), pp. 17–24.

64. M.V. Del Tufo, *Malaya: A Report on the 1947 Census of Population* (London, 1949), p. 84.

65. *Chung Hua*, 24 Jan. 1946.

66. Report, "Malayan Press Comment on the White Paper on Malayan Union", in SCA 26/46 CC/1/2.

67. M.N. Sopiee, *From Malayan Union to Singapore Separation 1945–1965* (Kuala Lumpur, 1974), pp. 37–8; Allen, *The Malayan Union*, pp. 66–71.

68. *Sin Min Chu* (Singapore), 15 Oct. 1945.

69. Ibid.

70. *Sin Min Chu* (Singapore), 25 Feb. 1946.

71. *The Democrat* (Kuala Lumpur), 9 Mar. 1946.

72. Miller, *Menace in Malaya*, p. 69, quotes the MCP Document, "Statement on Wright", dated 28 May 1948.

73. Allen, *The Malayan Union*, pp. 50–1.

74. See A.J. Stockwell, ed., *British Documents on the End of Empire Series B*; especially *Malaya. Part I: The Malayan Union Experiment 1942–1948* and *Malaya. Part II: The Communist Insurrection*, London 1995; and Albert Lau, *The Malayan Union Controversy* (Singapore, 1991).

75. Ibid., pp. 65–6.

76. See Report of the Working Committee, *Constitutional Proposals for Malaya* (Kuala Lumpur, 1946), p. 6.

77. Ibid. Emphasis added.

BIBLIOGRAPHY

UNPUBLISHED SOURCES

A general listing of the items in the British Cabinet, Colonial Office, Foreign Office, and War Office records is available in the official registers at the Public Record Office, London. A checklist of the manuscript collections at Rhodes House can be found in Louis B. Frewer, *Manuscript Collections (Excluding Africana) in Rhodes House Library*, Bodleian Library, Oxford, 1970. At the National Archives, Malaysia, too, registers for the BMA (Malaya) and Malayan Union records are available. For the Japanese military records, a catalogue of the Tokugawa Papers is available at the Library of the University of Singapore. I have given below a listing of only some of the principal items which I have used in these archives.

GREAT BRITAIN

A. The Public Record Office, London

COLONIAL OFFICE RECORDS

Malay States, 1944–6, CO 717/141 – CO 717/149.
Straits Settlements. 1944–6, CO 273/662 – CO 273/680.
Far Eastern Construction, 1943–6, CO 865/18 – CO 865/50.

(i) *CO 717 (Malay States)*
CO 717/147/File 52035. 1941–5. "Reconstruction. Postwar positions. Rulers and governments".

(ii) *CO 273 (Straits Settlements)*
CO 273/669/File 50744/7. 1942–3. "War with Japan. Conditions in enemy-occupied Malayan territory".
CO 273/671/File 50790. 1943. "Malayan campaign. Attitude of local population (Fifth Column allegations)".
CO 273/673/File 50744/7. 1944. "Conditions in enemy-occupied territory".
CO 273/675/File 50823/15. 1945. "Future policy in Malaya. Creation of Malayan Union citizenship".

CO 273/675/File 50823/7/3. 1945. "Future policy. Memoranda submitted by Malay rulers to Sir Harold MacMichael".

(iii) *CO 865 (Far Eastern Construction)*
CO 865/18. Nov. 1943–Nov. 1945. "Long-term policy directives".
CO 865/47. June 1943. "Chinese affairs".
CO 825/50/File 55360 T3. Feb. 1946. "Chinese affairs".

FOREIGN OFFICE

FO 371 (Malaya)
FO 371/46244. 1945. "Overseas Chinese: Position in Malaya and other territories".
FO 371/46340. "Malay native rulers".
FO 371/46340. "Fortnightly intelligence reports on Malaya".
FO 371/46388. "Expansion of communism in Asia".
FO 371/46394. "Situation after defeat of Japan: Reports from War Office".
FO 371/46432. 1945. "Problems arising Out of liberation of Burma and Malaya".
FO 371/46458. "Situation: Reports after surrender of Japan".
FO 379/37/61. "Fortnightly intelligence reports on Malaya".

WAR OFFICE

(i) *WO 172 (Mountbatten's Diary)*
WO 172/1754 (13–18 Mar. 1945) to WO 172/1790 (11 Jan. 1946).
WO 172/1767. 5–10 June 1945. "Resistance movements, Malaya".
WO 172/1781. 3–6 Sept. 1945. "Initial Relations with Sultans".
WO 172/1774. 25–31 July 1945. "Force 136 operations in Malaya".
WO 172/1776. 13 Aug. 1945. "Minutes of 142nd staff meeting at SEAC Headquarters on action to be taken by indigenous resistance movements".
WO 172/1786. 4 Oct. 1945. "Report, Force 136 operations in Malaya".

(ii) *WO 203 (Civil Affairs, SEAC Headquarters)*
WO 203/366 (June–Sept. 1944) to WO 203/5650 (Aug.–Nov. 1945).
WO 203/1235. May 1944–May 1945. "SAC's reports to Prime Minister and Chiefs of Staff".
WO 20312190. Sept. 1943–Jan. 1946. "Psychological and political warfare".
WO 20312321. Sept. 1945–Mar. 1946. "BMA of Malaya: Report".
WO 20312967. May–June 1945. "Malaya: Resistance movements".

(iii) *WO 220 (Civil Affairs)*
WO 220/554. Feb.–May 1944, "Committee on future constitutional policy (Malaya)".
W0 220/565. 1945. "BMA principal directives".

WAR CABINET

CAB 98/41/303.9 Dec. 1944. "Memorandum by Secretary of State for Colonies on constitutional policy in Malaya".

CAB 98/41/01637. 14 Jan. 1944. "Memorandum by Secretary of State for Colonies on future constitutional policy for British colonial territories in Southeast Asia".

CAB 98/41/10637. 18 May 1944. "Report of Committee –Policy in regard to Malaya and Borneo".

B. Rhodes House, Oxford

MSS. Ind. Ocn. S. 116. W.L. Blythe, "Papers as Colonial Secretary, Singapore, including reports on Chinese Affairs, 1946, by Victor Purcell".

MSS. Br. Emp. S. 407/3. "Papers of Maj.-Gen. Hone."

MSS. Ind. Ocn. S. 182. L.A. Laffan, "Diary, 9–29 Sept. 1945. Liberation of Malaya".

MSS. Ind. Ocn. S. 25. J.D. Dalley, "Political Intelligence Journal, Malayan Security Service, 1946–47".

MALAYSIA

Arkib Negara Malaysia

(i) BMA Confidential and Secret Correspondence. Sept. 1945–Mar. 1946 (Listed under Prime Minister's Department).

SCA C/l/1/4. 11 Oct. 1945. "BMA Reports".

SCA 9/45. Jan. 1946. "BMA Monthly and Fortnightly Reports".

SCA 162/45. Sept.–Nov. 1945. "The Selangor Peoples' Committee".

Confidential and Secret Correspondence of the Governor and Chief Secretary, Malayan Union. 1946–8.

MU 103.45. 25 Sept. 1945–15 Jan. 1946. "DCCAO Circulars and Instructions".

MU 79/45. 9 Dec. 1945. "Inter-racial clashes between Malays and Chinese in Kelantan" (now reclassified).

MU 335/46. Oct. 1945–Jan. 1946. "Intelligence Reports. Malaya Command".

(ii) Despatches, Savingrams and Correspondence from Secretary of State to the Colonies to Malayan Union, 1946 and 1947.

(iii) Secretariat of Chinese Affairs files, 1945–7.

JAPAN

Boeicho Boei Kenshujo Senshishitsu (Defence Agency, Defence Training Institute, War History Library), Tokyo.

Boeicho Boei Kenshujo Senshishitsu, *Mare shinko sakusen* (Malay offensive operation), Tokyo, 1966.

Tokugawa shiyo (Tokugawa Materials), especially no. 28. "Reference materials on nationality policy", marked Somubo somuka (General Affairs Division), 25th Army.

UNITED STATES

National Archives of America

Office of Strategic Services (OSS), Research and Analysis (R and A) Branch, State Department.

R and A No. 2072. 8 June 1944. "Japanese administration in Malaya". Also available in *BMA PSD 29/6*.

R and A, Assemblage no. 60. to Oct. 1945 (Broadcasts from Radio Tokyo). "Programs of Japan in Malaya" (Feb. 1942–June 1945), Honolulu.

R and A, Office of Intelligence Research (OIR) no. 3780/47.16 Mar. 1947. "The role of the communists in Malaya."

NEWSPAPERS

Collections of several newspapers consulted at the various centres of holdings in Malaysia and Singapore are incomplete. See P. Lim Pui Huen, *Newspapers Published in the Malaysian Area, With a Union List of Local Holdings* (Singapore, April 1970).

MALAY

Fajar Asia, Singapore, 1943–5.
Majlis, Kuala Lumpur, Oct. 1945–Jan. 1946.
Seruan Ra'ayat, Kuala Lumpur, Sept. 1945–Mar. 1946.
Utusan Melayu, Singapore, Sept. 1945–Mar. 1946.

CHINESE

Cham Yew Pau, Kuala Lumpur, organ of the Ex-MPAJA Comrades' Association, Mar. 1946, May 1947.
Chung Hua, Penang, 15–24 Nov. 1945.
Hua Ch'iao, Singapore, Jan.–Mar. 1946.
Min Sheng Pau, Kuala Lumpur, Sept.–Nov. 1945, Jan.–Mar. 1946.
Nanyang Siang Pau, Sept. 1945–Mar. 1946.
Sin Chew Jit Pau, Singapore, Sept. 1945–Mar. 1946.

ENGLISH

Indian Daily Mail, Singapore, Mar. 1946.
Malai Sinpo, Kuala Lumpur, 1943–5.
Malay Mail, Kuala Lumpur, Sept. 1945–Mar. 1946.

Perak Shimbun, 1944.

Penang Shimbun, 1945.

SEAC, 9 Sept. 1945–May 1946. "The Services Newspaper of South East Asia Command".

Straits Times, Singapore, Sept. 1945–Mar. 1946.

Syonan Shimbun, Singapore, May 1942–Sept. 1945.

PUBLISHED OFFICIAL RECORDS

British Malaya: A report on the 1931 Census and on certain problems of vital statistics, by C.A. Vlieland. London: Crown Agents for the Colonies, 1932.

British Military Administration Gazette. Kuala Lumpur, 1945–6.

Constitutional Proposals for Malaya: Report of the Working Committee appointed by a Conference of His Excellency the Governor of the Malayan Union, Their Highnesses the Rulers of the Malay States and the Representatives of the United Malays National Organization. Revised up to 19 Dec. 1946. Kuala Lumpur: Malayan Union Government, 1946.

Federation of Malaya. Summary of Revised Constitutional Proposals Accepted by His Majesty's Government, 21 July 1947. Kuala Lumpur, 1947.

del Tufo, M.V. *Malaya: A Report on the 1947 Census of Population*. London, 1949.

Malayan Union and Singapore: Statement of Policy on Future Constitution. London: Cmd. 6724, 1946.

Malayan Union and Singapore: Summary of Proposed Constitutional Arrangements. London: Cmd. 6749, 1946.

Malayan Union Advisory Council Proceedings. Kuala Lumpur, 1946.

Malayan Union Annual Report, 1946.

Malayan Union Government Gazette, 1946.

Report on a Mission to Malaya, October 1945–January 1946, by Sir H. MacMichael. London: H.M.S.O., 1946.

Report on the British Military Administration of Malaya, September 1945 to March 1946, by Maj.-Gen. H.R. Hone. Kuala Lumpur, 1946.

Report on Social Science Research in Malaya, by Raymond Firth. Singapore, 1948.

Singapore Advisory Council Proceedings, 1946.

Singapore Annual Report, 1946. Summary of Constitutional Proposals for Malaya. Revised up to 19 Dec. 1946. Kuala Lumpur, 1946.

White Paper, Communism in Malaya and Singapore. Kuala Lumpur, Mar. 1971.

SELECTED LIST OF BOOKS AND ARTICLES

Entries are listed in four categories: (A) Chinese-language sources, (B) English-language sources, (C) Japanese-language sources, and (D) Malay-language sources.

A. Chinese-Language Sources

Cheng Wei-fang. "Ling Kung Kuo–hou chi". In Li Tieh Min *et al.*, *Ta-chan yu Nan-ch'iao (Ma-lai-ya chih pu)*. Singapore: Sin Nan Yang chu ban she, 1947, p. 211.

Chuan Hui-tsuan. "Wo-sou-chih tao-ti Lai T'e yu Yeh Lu – Yu Kuan Makung-Ii shih-ti yu-tsung-mi–wen". In *Kuo ji shi pao*. Singapore, July 1968, pp. 19–20.

Hai Shang-ou. *Ma-lai-ya jen-min k'ang Jih chun*. Singapore: Hua Ch'iao chu ban she, 1945.

Lai T'e. *Wei-min-tsu t'uan-chieh min-chu tzu-yu min-sheng kai shan erh cheng t'ou*. Singapore: Ma-lai-ya chu ban she, 1946.

Ma-lai-ya kung chang tang. *Nan tao chih ch'un*. Singapore: Ma-lai-ya chu ban she, 1946.

Ng Yeh Lu. "Ma-kung chung-yang tsung-shu-chi Lai T'i ju-ho sh-hai kuokung liang-tang chi lien-chun kan-pu kei yi-ch'ieh ai-hu Ma-kung yuanyi ch-t'ai kung-tao-ti", in *Kuoji shi pao* (International Times). Singapore, July 1968, pp. 20–4.

Shih Ming. "Chih guo tsai Jou-fou shou shan tou bu jen chi shi-shih." In Li Tieh Min *et al.*, *Ta-chan yu Nan-ch'iao (Ma-lai-ya chih pu)*. Singapore: Sin Nan Yang chu ban she, 1947, pp. 169–70.

Ssu-ssu, ed. *K'ang-Jih ying-hsiung tsai Jou-nan*. Singapore: Sin min chu ban she, 1946.

B. English-Language Sources

Abu Talib Ahmad. *The Malay Muslims, Islam and the Rising Sun: 1941–45*. Kuala Lumpur, 2003.

Akashi, Yoji. "Japanese Military Administration in Malaya: Its Formation and Evolution in Reference to Sultans, the Islamic Religion and the Muslim Malays, 1941–45", *Asian Studies* 7, 1 (Apr. 1969).

————. *The Nanyang Chinese National Salvation Movement, 1937–41*. Lawrence, Kansas, 1970.

————. "Japanese Policy towards the Malayan Chinese, 1941–45", *Journal of Southeast Asian Studies* 1, 2 (Sept. 1970): 66–8.

————. "Education and Indoctrination Policy in Malaya and Singapore under the Japanese Rule, 1942–45", *Malaysian Journal of Education* 13, 1 and 2 (Dec. 1976).

————. "Lai Teck, Secretary General of the Malayan Communist Party, 1939–1947", *Journal of South Seas Society* 49 (1994).

Allen, J. de V. "The Kelantan Rising of 1915: Some Thoughts on the Concept of Resistance in British Malayan History", *Journal of Southeast Asian History* 9, 2 (Sept. 1968).

————. "The Malayan Civil Service, 1874–1941: Colonial Bureaucracy/Malayan Elite", *Comparative Studies in Society and History* 12 (1970).

————. *The Malayan Union*. New Haven, Conn., 1970.

Allen, Louis; *The End of the War*. London, 1976.

Alwee bin Jantan. "Trengganu, 1945–1957: A Study in Political Development". B.A. Hons. thesis, University of Malaya, Singapore, 1958.

Alwi bin Sheikh Alhady. *Malay Customs and Traditions*. Singapore, 1962.

Anderson, B.R.O'G. *Java in a Time of Revolution*. Cornell Modern Indonesia Project. Ithaca, N.Y., 1972.

————. "Japan: 'The Light of Asia'", in Josef Silverstein, ed., *Southeast Asia in World War II: Four Essays*. New Haven, Conn., 1966.

Arasaratnam, S. *Indians in Malaya and Singapore*. Kuala Lumpur, 1969.

Archer, R. Le R. "Muhammedan Mysticism in Sumatra", *Journal of the Malayan Branch, Royal Asiatic Society* 15, 2 (Sept. 1937).

Ardizzone, M. *A Nation is Born*. London, 1946.

Bamadhaj, Halinah. "The Impact of the Japanese Occupation of Malaya on Malay Society and Politics, 1941–45", M.A. thesis, Auckland University, 1975.

Ban Kah Choon, *Absent History: The Untold Story of Special Branch Operations in Singapore, 1915–1942*. Singapore, 2001.

Barker, Ralph. *One Man's Jungle: A Biography of F. Spencer Chapman*. London, 1975.

Benda, H.J. "Political Elites in Colonial Southeast Asia: A Historical Analysis", *Comparative Study of Society and History* (Apr. 1965).

————. "The Japanese Interregnum in S.E. Asia". In Grant K. Goodman, *Imperial Japan and Asia. A Reassessment*. Occasional Papers of the East Asia Institute, Columbia University. New York, 1967.

Benda, H.J., James K. Irikura and Koichi Kishi, eds., *Japanese Military Administration in Indonesia: Selected Documents*. Southeast Asia Studies, Translation Series no. 6. New Haven, 1965.

Blythe, W.L. *The Impact of Chinese Secret Societies in Malaya*. London: [publisher?], 1969.

Brand, Mona, and Richardson, Lesley. *Two Plays about Malaya*. London, 1954.

Brett, C.C. "Japanese Rule in Malaya." M.A. thesis, University of Washington, 1950.

Brimmell, J.H. *A Short History of the Malayan Communist Party*. Singapore, 1956.

————. *Communism in Southeast Asia*. London, 1959.

Burridge, Kenelm O.L. "Managerial Influences in a Johore Village", *JMBRAS* 30, 1 (May 1957).

————. "Race Relations in Johore", *Australian Journal of Politics and History* 2, 2 (1957).

Chapman, Spencer. *The Jungle Is Neutral*. London, 1952.

Cheah Boon Kheng. "The Malayan Democratic Union, 1945–1948", M.A. thesis, University of Malaya, 1974.

_____. "Some Aspects of the Interregnum in Malaya, 15 Aug.–2 Sept. 1945", *JSEAS* 8, 1 (Mar. 1977).

_____. "The Japanese Occupation of Malaya, 1941–45: Ibrahim Yaacob and the Struggle for Indonesia Raya", *Indonesia* 28 (Oct. 1979).

_____. *The Masked Comrades*. Singapore, 1979.

Chin Kee Onn. *Malaya Upside Down*. Singapore, 1946.

_____. *Ma-Rai-Ee* (a novel). London, 1952. (Also issued as a paperback under the title *The Silent Army*.)

Chin, C.C. and Hack, Karl. *Dialogues with Chin Peng: New Light on the Malayan Communist Party*. Singapore, 2004.

Chin Peng. *My Side of History*. Singapore, 2003.

Choy Su-Mei, Mrs Elizabeth. "Autobiography", *Intisari* 4, 1 (n.d.).

Clutterbuck, Richard. *Riot and Revolution in Singapore and Malaya, 1945–63*. London, 1974.

Comber, Leon. *Malaya's Secret Police, 1945–60: The Role of the Special Branch in the Malayan Emergency*. Singapore, 2008.

Cross, John. *Red Jungle*. London, 1957.

Dawson, Thomas. *Amusing Sidelights of the Japanese Occupation: Malaya, Jan. 1942–Aug. 1945*. Seremban, 1946.

Dimitroff, Georgi. *The United Front*. London, 1938.

Donnison, F.S.V. *British Military Administration in the Far East, 1943–46*. London, 1956.

Draeger, Donn F. *Weapons and Fighting Arts of the Indonesian Archipelago*. Tokyo, 1972.

Durrani, Lt.-Gen. Mahmood Khan. *The Sixth Column*. London, 1955.

Elsbree, W.H. *Japan's Role in Southeast Asian National Movements, 1940–45*. Cambridge, 1953.

Emerson, R. *Malaysia: A Study in Direct and Indirect Rule*. Reprint. Kuala Lumpur, 1964.

Furnivall, J.S. *Netherlands India: A Study of Plural Economy*. Cambridge, 1939.

_____. *Colonial Policy and Practice*. Cambridge, 1948.

Garrit, Michael. "Malaya Reoccupied", *Labour Monthly*, London, May 1946.

Ginsburg, N. and Roberts, C.F. Jr. *Malaya*. Seattle, 1958.

Goh Kok Leong, "Legal History of the Japanese Occupation in Singapore", *Malayan Law Journal* 1 (Jan. 1981): xx–xxiv.

Goh Kim Guat, "Sino-Malay Relations in Malaya, 1945–1955," Unpublished B.A. thesis, History Department, University of Malaya in Singapore, 1960.

Gullick, J.M. *Indigenous Political Systems of Western Malaya*. London, 1965.

Hake, H.B. *The New Malaya and You*. London, 1945.

Hamzah bin Mohamed. "Fourteen Days of Terror, Before, During and After", B.A. Hons. thesis, University of Malaya, 1970.

Hanrahan, G.Z. *The Communist Struggle in Malaya*. New York, 1954. Reprinted in Kuala Lumpur, 1971.

Harper, T.N. *The End of Empire and the Making of Malaya*. Cambridge, 1999.

Hopper, Rex D. "The Revolutionary Process: A Frame of Reference for the Study of Revolutionary Movements", *Social Forces* 28, 3 (Mar. 1950).

Homer, F. "Japanese Military Administration in Malaya and the Philippines", Ph.D. thesis, University of Arizona, 1973.

Husin, Ali S. "Social Stratification in Kampong Bagan: A Study of Class, Status, Conflict and Mobility in a Rural Malay Community", M.A. thesis, University of Malaya, 1962.

Ishak Tadin. "Dato Onn, 1946–1951", *Journal of Southeast Asian History* 1, 1 (Mar. 1960).

Itagaki, Yoichi. "Outlines of Japanese Policy in Indonesia and Malaya during the War", *Annals of the Hitotsubashi Academy* 2, 2 (Apr. 1952).

———— and Kishi, K. "Japanese Islamic Policy: Sumatra and Malaya", *Intisari* (Journal of Malaysian Sociological Institute, Singapore) 2, 3 (n.d.).

Jansen, G.H. *Militant Islam*. London, 1979.

Jones, Alun. "Internal Security in British Malaya, 1895–1942", Ph.D. thesis, Yale University, 1970.

Jones, F.C. *Japan's New Order in East Asia: Its Rise and Fall, 1937–45*. London, 1954.

Jones, S.W. *Public Administration in Malaya*. London, 1953.

Kahin, G. MeT. *Nationalism and Revolution in Indonesia*. Ithaca, N.Y., 1952.

Kanahele, George Sanford. "The Japanese Occupation of Indonesia: Prelude to Independence", Ph.D. thesis, Cornell University, 1967.

Karthigasu, S. *No Dram of Mercy*. London, 1954.

Kartodirdjo, Sartono. *The Peasants' Revolt of Banten*. The Hague, 1966.

Kautsky, John H., ed., *Political Change in Underdeveloped Countries*. New York, 1967.

Kee Yeh Siew. "The Japanese in Malaya before 1942", *Journal of South Seas Society* 20, 1/2 (1965).

Khoo Kay Kim. *The Western Malay States*. Kuala Lumpur, 1972.

————. "The Beginnings of Political Extremism in Malaya, 1915–35", Ph.D. thesis, University of Malaya, 1973.

Kratoska, Paul H. *The Japanese Occupation of Malaya, 1941–1945: A Social and Economic History*. London, 1998.

Lau, Albert. *The Malayan Union Controversy*. Singapore, 1991.

Lebra, Joyce. "Japanese and Western Models for the Indian National Army", *The Japan Interpreter* 7, 3/4.

————. *Jungle Alliance: Japan and the Indian National Army*. Singapore, 1971.

————. *Japan's Greater East Asia Co-Prosperity Sphere in World War II*. Kuala Lumpur, 1975.

————. "The Significance of the Japanese Military Model for Southeast Asia", *Pacific Affairs* 48, 2 (Summer 1975).

Lee, Karen. "The Japanese Occupation of Selangor", B.A. Hons. Thesis, University of Malaya, 1974.

Lee Ting Hui. "Singapore under the Japanese, 1942–1945", *Journal of South Seas Society* 17.

Leong, S. "Sources, Agencies and Manifestations of Overseas Chinese Nationalism in Malaya, 1937–1941", Ph.D. thesis, University of California, Los Angeles, 1976.

Lim Beng Kooi. "The Japanese Occupation in Penang, 1941–1945", B.A. Hons. thesis, University of Singapore, 1973/4.

Lim Teck Ghee. "Peasant Agriculture in Colonial Malaya, 1874–1974", Ph.D. thesis, Australian National University, 1971.

_____. *Peasants and Their Agricultural Economy in Colonial Malaya, 1874–1941*. Kuala Lumpur, 1977.

Lim Thean Soo. *Southward Lies the Fortress*. Singapore, 1971.

Linehan, W. "A History of Pahang", *JMBRAS* 17, 2 (1936).

Low, N.I. *When Singapore Was Syonan-to*. Singapore, 1973.

_____ and Cheng, H.M. *This Singapore*. Singapore, 1946.

McHugh, Dato J.N. "Psychological Warfare in Malaya", *Journal of Historical Society* (University of Malaya) 4 (1965/6).

McLane, C.B. *Soviet Strategies in Southeast Asia*. Princeton, 1966.

MacIntyre, S. Chelvasingam. *Through Memory Lane*. Singapore, 1973.

Mahajani, U. *The Role of Indian Minorities in Burma and Malaya*. Bombay, 1960.

Mallal, Bashir, ed. *The Double Tenth Trial*. Singapore, 1947.

Mao Tse-tung. *Selected Works*. 4 vols. London, 1954.

Martin, B.G. *Muslim Brotherhoods in Nineteenth-Century Africa*. Cambridge, 1976.

Maxwell, Sir George. *The Civil Defence of Malaya*. London, 1944.

McCoy, Alfred W., ed. *Southeast Asia under Japanese Occupation*. Yale University Southeast Asia Studies Monograph no. 22 (1980).

Means, Gordon, P. *Malaysian Politics*. London, 1970.

Miller, Harry. *Menace in Malaya*. London, 1954.

_____. "The Ruler Who Was Kidnapped", *Straits Times*, 29 May 1957.

_____. *Prince and Premier*. London, 1959.

_____. *Jungle War in Malaya: The Campaign against Communism, 1948–60*. London, 1972.

Milne, R.S. *Government and Politics in Malaysia*. Boston, 1967.

Mohamed Amin and Caldwell, Malcolm. *Malaya: The Making of a Neo-Colony*. London, 1977.

Mohamed Noordin Sopiee. *From Malayan Union to Singapore Separation 1945–1965*. Kuala Lumpur, 1974.

Mountbatten of Burma, Earl. *Report to the Combined Chiefs of Staff 1943–1945*. London, 1951.

_____. *Post-Surrender Tasks: Section E of the Report to the Combined Chiefs of Staff, 1943–45*. London, 1969.

Morrison, Ian. *Malayan Postscript*. London, 1942.

Naguib, AI-Attas Syed. *Some Aspects of Sufism as Understood and Practised among the Malays*. Singapore, 1963.

Nakamura, Mitsuo. "General Imamura and the Early Period of Japanese Occupation", *Indonesia* 10 (Oct. 1970).

Ness, Gayl D. *Bureaucracy and Rural Development in Malaysia*. Berkeley, 1967.

Nevill-Dupuy, T. *Asian and Axis Resistance Movement's*. London, 1965.

O'Ballance, Edgar. *Malaya: The Communist Insurgent War, 1948–1960*. London, 1966.

Okuma Memorial Social Sciences Research Institute. *Japanese Military Administration in Indonesia*. U.S. Department of Commerce, 23 Mar. 1965, Washington, D.C.

Onraet, H.R. *Singapore – A Police Background*. London, 1946.

_____. "Crime and Communism in Malaya", *British Malaya* 23, 5 (Sept. 1948).

Parmer, Norman. *Colonial Labor Policy and Administration: A History of Labor in the Rubber Plantation Industry in Malaya, 1910–1940*. New York, 1960.

Peters, Rudolph. *Jihad in Medieval and Modern Islam*. Leiden, 1977.

Png Poh-seng. "The Kuomintang in Malaya, 1912–1941", *Journal of Southeast Asian History* 2, 1 (Mar. 1961).

Purcell, Victor. *The Chinese in Malaya*. London, 1948.

_____. *Malaya: Communist or Free?* London, 1954.

_____. *The Chinese in Southeast Asia*. London, 1951.

_____. *The Memoirs of a Malayan Official*. London, 1965.

PUTERA-AMCJA. *People's Constitutional Proposals*. Kuala Lumpur, 1947.

Pye, L.W. *Guerrilla Communism in Malaya: Its Social and Political Meaning*. Princeton, N.J., 1956.

Ratnam, K.J. *Communalism and the Political Process in the Federation of Malaya*. Kuala Lumpur, 1965.

Rauf, M.A. *A Brief History of Islam (with Special Reference to Malaya)*. Kuala Lumpur, 1965.

Reid, A.J.S. *The Indonesian National Revolution, 1945–50*. Melbourne, 1974.

_____. "The Japanese Occupation and Rival Indonesian Elites: Northern Sumatra in 1942", *Journal of Asian Studies* 35, 1 (Nov. 1975).

Richards, Warwick. "The MPAJA and the Revolutionary Struggle in Malaya 1939–45", M.A. thesis, University of Sydney, 1975.

Robertson, Eric. *The Japanese File*. Kuala Lumpur, 1979.

Robinson, J.B.P. *Transformation in Malaya*. London, 1956.

Roff, William R. "Indonesian and Malay Students in Cairo in the 1920s", *Indonesia* 9, Cornell Modern Indonesia Project (Apr. 1970).

————, *The Origins of Malay Nationalism*. Kuala Lumpur, 1967.

Rudner, Martin. "The Organization of the British Military Administration in Malaya, 1945–46", *Journal of Southeast Asian History* 9, 1 (1968).

————. "Financial Policies in Postwar Malaya: The Fiscal and Monetary Measures of Liberation and Reconstruction", *Journal of Imperial and Commonwealth History* 3, 3 (May 1975).

Sandhu, Kernial Singh. "The Saga of the Malayan Squatter", *Journal of Southeast Asian History* 5 (1964).

Scott, James C. "Patron–client Politics and Political Change in Southeast Asia", *American Political Science Review* 66, 1 (Mar. 1972).

————. "The Erosion of Patron-Client Bonds and Social Change in Rural Southeast Asia", *Journal of Asian Studies* 32, 1 (1972).

Shaw, William. *Tun Razak: His Life and Times*. Kuala Lumpur, 1976.

Shennan, Margaret. *Our Man in Malaya*. London, 2008.

Sheppard, M.C. "A Short History of Trengganu", *JMBRAS* 22, 3 (1949).

Shinozaki, Mamoru. *Syonan: My Story*. Singapore, 1975.

Short, Anthony. "Communism and the Emergency", in *Malaysia*, ed. Wang Gungwu. Melbourne, 1964.

————. 'The Communist Party of Malaya: In Search of Revolutionary Situations", *The World Today*, Dec. 1970.

————. "Communism, Race and Politics in Malaya", *Asian Survey 10*, 12 (Dec. 1970).

————. "Nationalism. and the Emergency in Malaya", in *Nationalism, Revolution and Evolution in Southeast Asia*, ed. Michael Leifer. Hull Monograph on Southeast Asia no. 2 (1970).

Siaw, Lawrence. "A Local History of the Ethnic Chinese Community in Titi Malaysia – circa A.D. 1870 to 1960", Ph.D. thesis, Monash University, 1975.

————. *Chinese Society in Rural Malaysia: A Local History of the Chinese in Titi, Jelebu*. Kuala Lumpur, 1983.

Silcock, T.H. and Ungku Abdul Aziz. "Nationalism in Malaya", in *Asian Nationalism and the West*, ed. William Holland. New York, 1953.

Silverstein, Josef, ed. *Southeast Asia in World War II: Four Essays*. New Haven, 1966.

Singh, Gurchan. *Singa: The Lion of Malaya*. London, 1949.

Singh, Rajendra. *Post-War Occupation Forces: Japan and South-East Asia*. In the series Official History of the Indian Armed Forces in the Second World War, 1939–1945. New Delhi – Combined Indian Services Historical Section, India and Pakistan. New Delhi, 1958.

Smail, John R.W. *Bandung in the Early Revolution, 1945–1946: A Study in the Social History of the Indonesian Revolution*. Cornell Modern Indonesia Project, Monograph Series. Ithaca, N.Y., 1964.

Soenarno, Raden. "Malay Nationalism, 1900–45", *Journal of South Asian History* 1, 1 (Mar. 1960).

Soh Eng Lim. "Tan Cheng Lock: His Leadership of the Malayan Chinese", *JSEAH* 1, 1 (Mar. 1960).

Stenson, M.R. *Repression and Revolt*. Ohio University Centre for International Studies, Southeast Asia Program. Athens, Ohio, 1969.

_____. *Industrial Conflict in Malaya*. Kuala Lumpur, 1970.

Stockwell, Anthony. "The Development of Malay Politics During the Course of the Malayan Union Experiment, 1942–1948", Ph.D. thesis, University of London, 1973.

_____. "The Formation and First Years of the United Malays National Organisation (UMNO), 1946–1948", *Modern Asian Studies* 2, 4 (1977).

_____. *British Policy and Malay Politics during the Malayan Union Experiment*, 1942–1948, Malaysian Branch of the Royal Asiatic Society Monograph no. 8 (1979).

_____ (ed.). *British Documents on the End of Empire Series B: Malaya*, 3 Vols. London, 1995.

Swift, M.F. *Malay Peasant Society in Jelebu*. London, 1965.

Tan, Y.S. "History of the Extortion of S50,000,000 Military Contribution from the Chinese in Malaya by the Japanese Army", *Journal of South Seas Society* 3, 1 (Sept. 1946).

Tan Cheng Lock. *Malayan Problems from a Chinese Point of View*. Singapore, 1947.

Thatcher, Dorothy and Robert Cross. *Pai Naa (The Story of Nona Baker)*. London, 1959.

Thompson, V. and Adloff, R. *The Left Wing in Southeast Asia*. New York, 1950.

_____. *Minority Problems in Southeast Asia*. Stanford, 1955.

Tilman, R.O, "Bureaucratic Development in Malaya", in *Asian Bureaucratic Systems Emergent from the British Imperial Tradition*, ed. Ralf Braibanti. Durham, N.C., 1966.

Togo Shigenori. *The Cause of Japan*. New York, 1956.

Tsuji, Col. Masanobu. *Singapore: The Japanese Version*. Sydney, 1960.

Uchida, Naosaku. *The Overseas Chinese*. Hoover Institution on War. Washington, D.C., 1960.

Wang Gung-wu, ed. *Malaysia*. Melbourne, 1964.

Wang Gungwu. "Sun Yat-sen and Singapore", *Journal of South Seas Society* 15, 2 (Dec. 1959): 55–68.

Windstedt, R.O., and Wilkinson, J. "A History of Perak", *JMBRAS 12* (1934).

Wong Lin Ken. *The Malayan Tin Industry to 1914*. Tucson, 1965.

Woodburn-Kirby, Maj.-Gen. S. *The War against Japan*, Vol. 5, United Kingdom military series, History of the Second World War. London, 1969.

Woodhouse, C.M. *The Struggle for Greece, 1941–1949*. London, 1976.

Yap Hong Kuan. "Perak under the Japanese, 1942–1945", B.A. Hons. thesis, University of Singapore, 1957.

Yen Ching Hwang. *The Overseas Chinese and the 1911 Revolution, with Special Reference to Singapore and Malaya*. Kuala Lumpur, 1976.

Yeo Kim Wah. *Political Development of Singapore, 1945–1955*. Singapore, 1973.

Yong, C.F. *The Origins of Malayan Communism*. Singapore, 1997.

Yuen Choy Leng. "Japanese Rubber and Iron Investments in Malaya, 1900–1941", *Journal of Southeast Asian Studies* 5, 1 (Mar. 1974).

C. Japanese-Language Sources

Itagaki, Yoichi. *Ajia-to No Taiwa* (Dialogue with Asia). Tokyo: Shinkeigen Sha, 1968.

Keimubu Genseikan Malaya [The Japanese Malayan Military Administration, Police Department]. "Malai ni okeru chianjo no ichikosatsu [Observations on the security situation in Malaya]". Tokugawa Papers, Boeicho. Tokyo, 1942.

Kishi, Hoichi, Shigetada Nishijima *et al*. *Indoneshia ni okeru Nihon gunsei no Kenyu* [Study of the effect of the Japanese military occupation of Indonesia]. Okuma Foundation for Studies in the Social Sciences, Tokyo, Waseda University, 1959.

Ministry of Foreign Affairs, Tokyo. Memorandum. "Marai Dokuritsu Mondai", 20 Feb. 1945. In Microfilm no. 50, Wason Collection, Cornell University. Also in the Nishijima Collection, Waseda University.

Nagai, Shinichi. "Taiheyo-senso-ki no Marei Minzoku Undo, (I and II) – Sayoku minzoku Undo Shidosha no Zahyo Kora". In *Azia Keizai*, Oct. and Dec. 1975.

Nakazawa, Kin'ichiro. "Shusen-Morakka no Nyojo". In Sato, Takizo, ed., *Sekidohyo*, Sekidokai, Jimusho. Tokyo, 1975.

Onishi, Maj. Sartoru. "Malai-Singaporu Kempeitai." In *Nippon Kempei Seishi*, Kenyukai (National Association of former Military Police). Tokyo, 1976.

─────. "Malai Kyosanto chuo taikai no tobatsu [Raids on the Central Committee of the Malayan Communist Party]", in *Nippon Kempei Seishi*. Tokyo: Kenyukai (National Association of former Military Police), 1976.

─────. "Teki sensuikan no senyu chosha [Espionage agents smuggled by submarine]", in *Nippon Kempei Seishi*. Tokyo: Kenyukai (National Association of former Military Police), 1976.

Shigeru, Saito. "Taiping-no yuutsu". In Sato, ed., *Sekidohyo*. Tokyo, 1975.

Tsutsui, Chihiro. *Nampo gunsei-ron*. Tokyo, 1944.

D. Malay-Language Sources

Anon. *Peringatan Sewindu Hilangnya Tan Malaka*. Jakarta, 1957.

A. Hasjmy. *Dimana Letaknya Negara Islam*. Singapore: Pustaka Negara Nasional, 1970.

A. Rashid bin Ngah. *Di-bawah Alunan Ombak*. Kuala Lumpur: Dewan Bahasa dan Pustaka, 1970.

A. Samad Ismail. *Patah Sayap Terbang Jua*. Kuala Lumpur: Setia Murni, 1966.

A. Talib Haji Ahmad. *Darah Mengalir di-Pasir Salak*. Kuala Lumpur: Pustaka Antara, 1961.

Abdul Aziz bin Zakaria. *Leftenan Noor, Pahlawan Gerila*. Kuala Lumpur: Dewan Pustaka dan Bahasa, 1959.

Abdul Malek Hj. Md. Hanafiah. "Sejarah Perjuangan Kesatuan Melayu Muda [History of the struggle of the Young Malay Union], 1937–1945", B.A. Hons. thesis, Universiti Kebangsaan Malaysia, 1975.

Abdullah Hussein. *Terjebak*. Kuala Lumpur: Pustaka Antara, 1965.

Ahmad Boestamam. *Testament Politik A.P.I.* 21 Dec. 1946. A.P.I. Malaya – Lembaga Tetap, Kuala Lumpur.

_____. *Dr Burhanuddin: Putera Setia Melayu Raya*. Kuala Lumpur: Pustaka Kejora, 1972.

_____. *Merintis Jalan Kepunchak*. Kuala Lumpur: Pustaka Kejora, 1972.

_____. *Tujuh Tahun Malam Memanjang*. Kuala Lumpur: Amir Enterprise, 1976.

Ahmad Murad. *Nyawa di-Hujong Pedang*. Kuala Lumpur: Khu Meng Press, 1963.

Anwar Abdullah. *Data Onn*. Petaling Jaya: Pustaka Nusantara, 1971.

Arena Wati. *Cherpen Zaman Jepun*. Kuala Lumpur: Pustaka Antara, 1968.

Baharuddin Abd. Majid. "Saberkas: Pergerakan dan perjuangannya 1944–1956", B.A. thesis, University of Malaya, 1975/76.

Burhanuddin Elhulaimy. *Asas Falsafah Kebangsaan Melayu*. Jakarta: Penerbitan FA 'Tekad', 1963.

_____. *Perjuangan Kita*. Malay Nationalist Party. Singapore, October 1946.

Ghazali Basri. "Hilir Perak: Sejarah hubungan ras zaman Pendudukan Jepun sehingga Pemerintahan Tentera Inggeris (BMA), 1942–1946", B.A. thesis, Universiti Malaya, 1974/5.

Ghazali bin Mayudin. *Johor Semasa Pendudukan Jepun 1942–1945*. History Department, Universiti Kebangsaan Malaysia. Kuala Lumpur, 1978.

Haji Buyong Adil. *Sejarah Johor*. Kuala Lumpur: Dewan Bahasa dan Pustaka, 1971.

_____. *Sejarah Kelantan*. Kuala Lumpur: Dewan Bahasa dan Pustaka, 1973.

_____. *Sejarah Perak*. Kuala Lumpur: Dewan Bahasa dan Pustaka, 1971.

Hairi Abdullah. "Kebangkitan dan Gerakan Tentera Selendang Merah Dalam Sejarah Daerah Muar dan Batu Pahat", *JEBAT* (Journal of Historical Society, Universiti Kebangsaan Malaysia), nos. 3/4 (1973/5).

Ibrahim Omar. *Embun dan Tanah*. Kuala Lumpur: Pustaka Melayu Baru, 1965.

Ibrahim Yaacob. *Melihat Tanah Ayer*. Kota Bharu: Penggal Satu, 1941.

_____. *Nusa dan Bangsa Melayu*. Jakarta: N.V. Alma'arief, 1951.

_____. *Sekitar Malaya Merdeka* [Concerning Malayan independence]. Jakarta: Kesatuan Malaya Merdeka, 1957.

_____. "Sejarah Perintis Kemerdekaan Malaysia (bahagian pertama)". Working Paper, History Department, Universiti Kebangsaan Malaysia, Kuala Lumpur, 28 Aug. 1973.

_____. "Sejarah Perintis Kemerdekaan Malaysia (bahagian kedua)". Working Paper, History Department, Universiti Kebangsaan Malaysia, Kuala Lumpur. 29 Aug. 1973.

I.K. Agastya (alias Ibrahim Jaacob). *Sedjarah dan Perdjuangan di Malaya* [History and struggle in Malaya]. Jogjakarta: Penerbit Nusantara, 1951.

Kamaruddin bin Mohd. Piah. "Kampong Bekur Sejak 1900: satu kajian sejarah tempatan dengan rujukan khas kepada tragedi 6 Mar. 1946", B.A. thesis, University of Malaya, 1974/5.

Mohamed Yamin. *Naskah-Persiapan Undang undang Dasar 1945*. Vol. 1. Jakarta, 1954.

Mohamed Yunus Hamidi. *Sejarah Pergerakan Polilik Melayu Semenanjang*. Kuala Lumpur: Pustaka Antara, 1961.

Mohammad Hatta. *Sekitar Proklamasi, 17 Agustus 1945*. Jakarta: Penerbit Tintomos, 1970.

Muhammad Haji Kidin. *Kerana si kuntum*. Penang: Saudara Sinaran, 1959.

_____. *Amrun*. Penang: Saudara Sinaran, 1965.

Musak Mantrak. "Sejarah masyarakat majemuk di Mukim VII, Batu Pahat, Johor 1900–1945", B.A. Hons. thesis, University of Malaya, 1974/5.

_____, "Ancaman Komunis, 1945–1946". In *Dian Diges*, Kota Bharu (Kelantan), Jan. 1977.

Nasution, Abdul Haris. *Sekitar Perang Kemerdekaan*, vol. 1, Bandung: Penerbit Angkasa, 1977.

Pringgodigdo, A.K. *Sedjarah Pergerakan Rakjat Indonesia*. Jakarta: Penerbitan dan Rakyat, 1970.

Rauf, M.A. *Ikhtisar Sejarah Islam dan hubongan-nya yang khusus dengan Malaya*. Kuala Lumpur, 1967. Sa'ad Shukri bin Haji Muda. *Detik-detik Sejarah Kelantan*. Kota Bharu: Pustaka Aman Press, 1971.

Tajul Ariffin bin Darus. *Manja*. Penang: Saudara Sinaran, 1964.

Tok Muda Raja Razman bin Raja Abdul Hamid *et al. Hulu Perak dalam Sejarah* [Upper Perak in history]. Ipoh: Regina Press, 1963.

Zabha. *Tan Sri Haji Mohamed Noah*. Kuala Lumpur: Utusan Melayu Press, 1976.

Zalfan Mohd. Rashid. "Pendudukan Jepun di Malaka, 1942–1945: Politik dan Pentadbiran", B.A. Hons. thesis, Universiti Kebangsaan Malaysia, 1973.

INDEX